EDUCATIONAL TESTING AND MEASUREMENT

Classroom Application and Practice

Second Edition

TOM KUBISZYN
The University of Texas at Austin

GARY BORICH
The University of Texas at Austin

SCOTT, FORESMAN AND COMPANY
GLENVIEW, ILLINOIS
LONDON, ENGLAND

Library of Congress Cataloging-in-Publication Data

Kubiszyn, Tom.
    Educational testing and measurement.

    Bibliography: p.
    Includes index.
    1. Educational tests and measurements—United States.
I. Borich, Gary D. II. Title.
LB3051.K8 1987   371.2′6   86-26122
ISBN 0-673-16683-X

PREFACE

|A|s anyone familiar with educational measurement knows, there is certainly no shortage of introductory measurement texts. Sheer weight of numbers would seem to make yet another introductory measurement text redundant. Yet while the content of this text has been presented before, our intention is to present this content in a different and unique manner.

We have written *Educational Testing and Measurement,* Second Edition, with an emphasis on application. Rather than overwhelm students with jargon and theory, we have attempted to focus on the classroom application of theory with a friendly, conversational style. At the same time, we believe we have provided sufficient theory to ensure that students will understand the foundations of testing and measurement and to minimize the likelihood that students will practice an oversimplified "cookbook" approach to measurement.

We have tried to avoid turning students off with topics and language that are too far removed from the everyday lives and practical needs of teachers. Both authors, having taught in the public schools, thought it was of utmost importance to write in a way that would help everyday decision making in the classroom. As we see it, there is a need for a text for both the preservice and the beginning teacher that covers relevant measurement content in sufficient depth and plain language. We have been encouraged by student responses to our text and welcome your comments and suggestions.

We have divided our text into 22 chapters according to measurement concepts that are of immediate practical value for the classroom teacher. We have tried to select topics and organize our writing to help the teacher, especially the beginning teacher, deal with the prevailing problems of testing students and measuring their behavior.

This practical orientation led us to provide at the conclusion of each chapter a step-by-step summary in which all important concepts in the chapter are identified for review. Additionally, we have prepared discussion questions or exercises, or both, for each chapter. These discussion questions and exercises should particularly help students learn how to apply the concepts presented and help instructors identify organized activities and assignments that can be integrated into their class presentations. Discussion questions and exercises marked with an asterisk have answers listed in Appendix D.

Also of special interest to many instructors and students will be specially prepared chapters on the role of the regular classroom teacher in testing and measuring the handicapped child (Chapter 20) and the role of microcomputers in testing and measurement (Chapter 21).

The topics we have chosen, their natural sequencing according to the real-life tasks of teachers, the step-by-step summaries of major concepts, and our discussion questions and exercises all work, we believe, to make this text a valuable tool and an important resource for observing, measuring, and understanding life in classrooms.

New in the Second Edition. In preparing this new edition, we have included a chapter on evaluating student products, procedures, and performances and added new material on combining and weighting the components of a mark. We have also updated the chapter on the use of microcomputers in testing and measurement, including a section on software packages for the teacher.

Acknowledgments

The authors would like to express their appreciation to Jason Millman, Cornell University; David Payne, University of Georgia; Victor Dupuis, Pennsylvania State University; Ben Layne, Georgia State University; Glen Nicholson, University of Arizona; Carol Mardell-Czudnowski, Northern Illinois University; and James Collins, University of Wyoming, for their constructive comments on earlier versions of the manuscript. The authors would also like to thank Marty Tombari, our colleague at The University of Texas, for his many contributions to the examples, illustrations, and test items in this volume. Finally, we would like to thank Phil Herbst, our editor at Scott, Foresman, for his helpful editorial comments and Jana Schultz and Lorraine Sheffield for their excellent typing of many drafts of this volume.

CONTENTS

8

CHAPTER

9

CHAPTER

10

CHAPTER

CHAPTER 22

1

CHAPTER

AN INTRODUCTION TO EDUCATIONAL TESTING AND MEASUREMENT

|C| hances are that some of your strongest, if not fondest, childhood and adolescent memories include test taking in school. More recently, you probably remember taking a great number of tests in college. If your experiences are like those of most who come through our educational system, you probably have very strong or mixed feelings about tests and testing. Indeed, some of you may swear that you will never test your students when you become teachers. If so, you may feel that test results add little to the educational process, fail to reflect learning, or that testing may turn off students.

Others may feel that tests are necessary and vital to the educational process. For you, they may represent irrefutable evidence as to whether learning has occurred. Rather than view tests as deterrents that turn off students, you may see them as motivators that stimulate students to study and provide them with feedback about their achievement.

Between these extremes may lie a third group, those who see tests as necessary to the educational process but who question the status and power often afforded tests and test scores. It is within this group that the authors of this text may best be classified. We see tests as tools that can effectively enhance the educational process, but only if they are well designed and properly used. Tools can be used and abused, and we are acutely aware that both poorly designed tools and well-designed tools in the hands of ill-trained or inexperienced users can be dangerous. It was in hopes of minimizing abuse of tests that we decided to write this text. We will discuss test use and test abuse more thoroughly later in the text, but for now let us restate our position:

1. Tests are necessary in order for teachers to teach and for students to learn.
2. To be potentially useful, tests must be well designed.
3. Even well-designed tests can be abused.

Thus, our goals for this text are to:

1. Sensitize you to current and future trends in education, which strongly suggest that test use is unlikely to decrease and may actually increase,
2. Teach you how to construct well-designed tests that yield valid and reliable measures of how well you teach and how well your students learn, and
3. Help you learn to use test results appropriately and effectively and to know the advantages and limitations of tests and test scores.

Let's now turn to some recent, current, and future trends in testing and measurement in the classroom so you will see why we chose these goals for our text.

RECENT TRENDS IN CLASSROOM MEASUREMENT

Beginning in the late 1960s, a fairly strong anti-test sentiment began to develop in our country. Over the next several years many scholarly papers and popular articles questioned or denounced testing for a variety of reasons. Some decried tests as weapons willfully used to suppress minorities. To others, tests represented simplistic attempts to measure complex traits or attributes. Still others questioned whether the traits or attributes tested could be measured, or whether these traits or attributes even existed! From the classroom to the Supreme Court, testing and measurement practice came under close scrutiny. It seemed that tests were largely responsible for many of our society's ills.

Initially it looked as though the anti-test movement might succeed in abolishing testing in education—and there was professional and lay support for such a move. Today, it appears that this movement was part of a swinging pendulum. Advocates and critics of testing now seem to have taken more moderate stances. Advocates, rather than stubbornly trying to convince critics that test scores represent scientific evidence that should be challenged only by those thoroughly steeped in test theory and construction, have begun instead to respond to the concerns voiced by the general public. The result has been that test advocates have come to be much more tempered and realistic in their attempts to convince others of the utility of test scores. Indeed, it is now common practice for measurement experts and instructors to emphasize that *all* test scores are at best *estimates* that are subject to greater or lesser margins of error. Nevertheless, advocates will argue strongly that, in spite of their shortcomings, test data, when not abused, often represent the most objective, valid, and reliable information that can be gathered about individuals.

On the other hand, while critics continue to raise important issues related to testing, they have come to realize that abolishing testing will not be a panacea for the problems of education and contemporary society. Even the most outspoken critics of testing would have to agree that in our everyday world decisions must be made. Test data are often used to help make such decisions. If tests were eliminated, these decisions would still be made, but would be based on nontest data that might be subjective, opinionated, and biased. For example, you may have dreaded taking the Scholastic Aptitude Test (SAT) during your junior or senior year in high school. You may have had some preconceived, stereotyped notions about the test. However, the SAT had no preconceived, stereotyped, or biased notions about you! Advocates and many critics of testing would now agree that it is not the tests themselves that discriminate or are otherwise destructive, but the people who abuse them. We hope you will be a much wiser and more careful user of test data after reading this text.

CURRENT AND FUTURE TRENDS IN EDUCATIONAL MEASUREMENT

With the passage of Public Law 94–142, all handicapped persons were guaranteed the right to a free and appropriate public education. The notion of "mainstreaming," or incorporating handicapped children into the regular classroom, is one alternative suggested by this legislation. The implications of PL 94–142 and mainstreaming on the testing and measurement skills of teachers will be discussed more thoroughly in Chapter 20. For now, suffice it to say that full implementation of the law will require more rather than less testing. Some of this may be required within the regular classroom in order to help determine whether a student is in need of special education, to adhere to each student's Individual Educational Plan (IEP), and to meet the law's accountability requirements.

The public's demand for accountability also suggests an increase in test use in the future. Since education is supported by taxpayers, educators must be responsive to the demands of taxpayers. With declining SAT scores, grade inflation, and decreasing confidence in public education, school boards and the general public are becoming more and more concerned that they "get what they pay for." Yearly achievement test scores are one way that these accountability demands are currently being met. Many larger school districts already have begun yearly standardized achievement testing to ascertain their district's position compared with other districts. It is only a matter of time until smaller districts follow suit.

The trend toward competency testing for high-school graduates is another indication of the increasing role of testing in education today. The competency testing movement developed in response to the public pressure that was put on educators to demonstrate that our schools were actually teaching the skills and competencies necessary to survive in contemporary society. This trend is closely tied to specific measurement practices that will be discussed in more detail later in the text.

Another current trend in our educational system is the notion of competency testing for teachers. Pilot projects in several areas of the country have been undertaken to determine whether such test data can effectively identify "good" and "poor" teachers. These efforts have been fairly simplistic and rather unsuccessful to date. This movement has grown out of the same public demand for accountability that spawned the now widespread yearly standardized achievement test program and the rapidly growing student competency testing movement. In spite of strong resistance from teachers, the testing of teachers has a great deal of popular and legislative support. Soon, prospective teachers may have to demonstrate minimum levels of competency in a variety of areas related to successful classroom teaching. Some teacher training programs already require it.

In summary, the wave of anti-test sentiment that once seemed to pervade education has passed, in part because educators understand that test data, fallible as they may be, are more objective when used properly than any of the alternatives. Educators realize that they must make decisions and that properly used test data can enhance their ability to make sound decisions. Increasing demands for accountability are also being made by the general public. By and large, the public tends to respect and accept test data to judge accountability. Remember, the taxpaying public, through school boards and voting behavior, controls educational programs and the purse strings of these programs. The accountability movement grew in reaction to the public's increasing disenchantment with education. As long as the public continues to be disenchanted with education, calls for accountability and testing will be heard. Since the public's disenchantment with current education is not likely to subside quickly, we are likely to see strong demands for accountability and testing in the future.

EFFECTS ON THE CLASSROOM TEACHER

The likelihood that test use will increase in the foreseeable future implies that the average teacher ought to have a good working knowledge of testing and measurement practice. However, teachers traditionally have not been well trained in test construction and use. Many teachers see no need for training in testing and measurement practice because they feel testing is supplemental to the instructional process. Indeed, many prospective teachers have been heard to say things like, "If I need to know about tests I'll go to the counselor!" Perhaps the trend toward seemingly ever-increasing "specialists" in education has fostered or reinforced such beliefs. Nevertheless, regardless of how a teacher feels about the relationship of tests to instruction, regardless of whether a counselor—who is often scarce in elementary schools—is available, and regardless of whether test data were collected by "specialists," one fact stands out: *It is frequently the classroom teacher who must organize and interpret standardized and teacher-constructed test data to curious and sometimes hostile parents and other concerned parties.* Figure 1.1 illustrates many sources of pressure influencing a teacher's use of tests. It is intended to convince you of the seriousness with which you should consider your knowledge or lack of knowledge of testing and measurement.

After years of consulting and teaching experience in the public schools we have concluded that discussing test results with parents is frequently an anxiety-provoking experience for teachers. Lacking appropriate training, some teachers are tempted to try to avoid interpretation entirely by dismissing test data as "unimportant" or "inaccurate," not realizing that such data are often very important and thought to be quite accurate by parents. The following dialogue occurred when one of the authors had a conference with his son's second-grade teacher in September.

TEACHER: Hi, I'm Jeff's second-grade teacher. What can I do for you so early in the year?

AUTHOR: Jeff says he's in the low reading group, and I am curious about why he is. Could you explain that to me?

TEACHER: Oh, don't worry—we don't label kids at this school. I think that would be a terrible injustice.

AUTHOR: I see, but could you explain why Jeff is in the "Walkers" instead of the "Runners"?

TEACHER: Oh, those are just names, that's all.

AUTHOR: Are both groups at the same level in reading?

TEACHER: They're both at the first-grade level, yes.

AUTHOR: I'm beginning to catch on. Are they reading in the same level books in the same reading series?

TEACHER: Of course not! Some children are further along than others—that's all—but the kids don't know.

AUTHOR: Let me guess, the "Runners" are further ahead?

TEACHER: Yes, they're in book 9.

AUTHOR: And the "Walkers" are in . . .

TEACHER: Book 5. But they are grouped for instructional purposes—I have twenty-five students you know!

AUTHOR: I'm confused. Jeff's reading scores on the California Achievement Test (CAT) last May were above the ninetieth percentile.

TEACHER: (*chuckles to herself*) I can understand your confusion. Those test scores are so hard to understand. Why even we professionals can't understand them.

FIGURE 1.1 | Some of the Many Forces Influencing the Teacher's Use of Tests

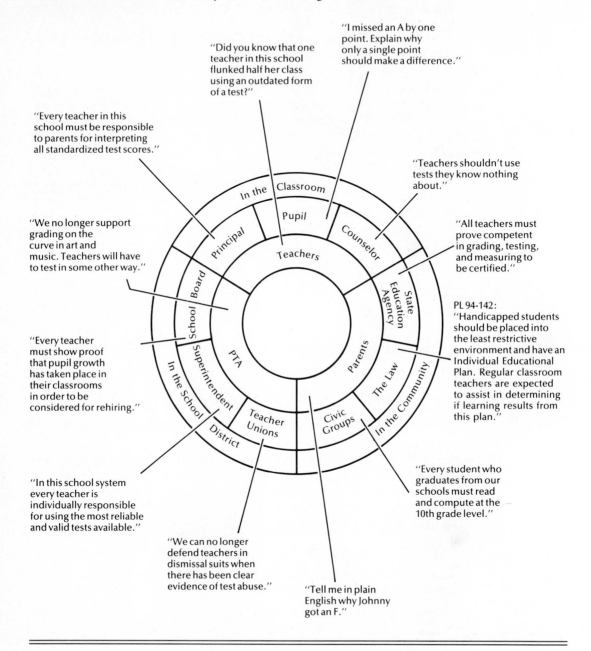

AUTHOR: A score at the ninetieth percentile means the score was higher than the scores of 90 percent of the students who took the test all across the country.

TEACHER: Oh, really? It is very complicated. As I said, even professional educators don't understand testing.

AUTHOR: Some do, Mrs. B.

Had the teacher understood the data she was dealing with, an obviously embarrassing situation may have been avoided. Similar experiences are unfortunately experienced by many classroom teachers.

Another often overheard statement is "I don't even have time to teach, how can I learn about test construction and interpretation?" We are well aware that teachers and most other professionals have become increasingly burdened by paperwork and bureaucratic requirements. However, the trends discussed earlier point toward comparable or increased levels of test use in the future. And the public will be keeping an increasingly watchful eye on the users of these data! Thus, it appears that teachers of the future will now more than ever need adequate training in testing and measurement practice. Ignoring or denying the need for proper training in this area will make neither this need nor the watchful eye of the public go away. Given the time constraints under which the average teacher must operate, it appears wiser to seek such training now, before you begin teaching. The alternative may be to attend what might seem like an endless series of workshops later on, while you also have your class of students and all the attendant responsibilities as well.

In short, it looks like tomorrow's teachers will be increasingly exposed to testing and test data. With increasing public pressure for accountability, it does not appear likely that the average teacher will be able to get ahead or even get by without a good working knowledge of tests and measurement practice. With practicing teachers getting more and more involved with paperwork, prospective teachers should acquire this working knowledge before beginning to teach. We sincerely hope that this text will help you acquire such knowledge and the skills necessary to construct good tests and to use test data knowledgeably and professionally.

ABOUT THE TEXT

When you talk to teachers who have completed courses in testing and measurement you often find that they are somewhat less than inspired by their courses. In fact, talking with such veterans may have made you a little reluctant to register for this course. Nevertheless, here you are! The authors have taught testing and measurement courses for many years and, quite frankly, are accustomed to hearing the course content described as "dry, but necessary." Too many times, however, we have heard "The course is dry, but necessary—I think!" Since there is a fair amount of straightforward, technical information presented, we could understand calling a course in testing and measurement "dry." Indeed, this is almost how we feel about the content when we teach it! Thus, hearing "dry, but necessary" from students did little more than confirm our own feelings. But, to hear "dry, but necessary—*I think!*" made us think and led us to evaluate our courses to determine the cause for this uncertainty. Remember, we stated earlier that we feel knowledge of tests and measurement practice is vital to today's teacher—yet somehow this was not coming across to some of our students.

We considered many different potential problems and each of us came to the same conclusion: Although each of us had used several different textbooks, we were never really satisfied with them. There are several introductory testing and measurement texts available, but each seemed to be lacking in one major respect. They all did a fine job of relating information and explaining concepts, but seemed to fall short in *applying these facts and concepts to real-world situations.* We found that we were supplementing the texts with anecdotes and suggestions based on our own experiences in the public schools. However, it still appeared that many prospective teachers had difficulty relating the real-world examples to the facts and concepts detailed in the text. Our conclusion was that what is needed is a text that emphasizes the relationship of the necessary facts and concepts to real-world situations. With this aim in mind we wrote this text. Only you can tell whether we have succeeded. We invite your comments and criticisms.

WHAT IF YOU'RE "NO GOOD IN MATH"?

Since tests yield numerical scores and test theory is based on statistical principles, it is no surprise that many who feel weak in math have great reservations about being able to succeed in a course in tests and measurements. If you fall into this category, rest assured that many of your fears are groundless or exaggerated. In our experience, fewer than 1 percent of the students who have completed the tests and measurements courses we have taught have done poorly solely because of a "weak" math background.

Naturally, knowledge of the basic mathematical functions—addition, subtraction, multiplication, and division—is a necessity. Mix these with fractions, decimals, and a sprinkling of algebra and you are all set! If you are still doubtful, work your way through the review of math skills provided in Appendix A. This review and accompanying self-check test should also prove useful to you if you feel a little "rusty" in math—a fairly common experience in this age of electronic calculators and computers. All operations necessary to complete the calculations in this text are covered in this review. We think you will agree that our review of math skills in Appendix A will be all that's needed.

SUMMARY

In this chapter we have introduced you to issues related to educational testing and measurement and have described the orientation of the text. Its major points are:

1. Test use is more likely to increase than decrease in the foreseeable future.
2. The public has begun clamoring for evidence that schools and teachers are in fact educating children and relies on test scores for such evidence.
3. Since test use is likely to increase, the burden of interpreting test results likely will fall more and more on the classroom teacher.
4. The classroom teacher who is trained in educational testing procedures will be able to use test results more efficiently and effectively and will be less likely to abuse test results.
5. This text is oriented toward the application of measurement principles to real-world situations.

For Discussion

1. Thinking back to your own high-school days, what were some of the factors that "turned you off" about tests?
2. Were these factors connected with the tests themselves, or were they the result of how the tests were used?
3. Point out some societal trends (for example, industrialization, increased population, or increasing adult literacy) occurring in your city, state, or region that will likely make testing and measurement in our schools more important in the future.
4. Imagine the modern American high school twenty years from now. Identify several ways in which testing and measurement will have changed since the time you were attending high school.
5. You notice that one student is "different" from the rest of the class. The student is a behavior problem, and you feel he or she needs special attention. You say so to your principal, expecting the principal to transfer the student to a special class. However, the principal says, "We have to collect the data first—get started." What kind of data do you believe the principal would want you to collect?

THE PURPOSE OF TESTING

I|n the classroom, decisions are constantly being made. As a teacher you may decide:

> John, Don, Marie, and Jeri, but not Chris and Linda, are ready to advance to level seven in reading.
> Mark receives an A; Mary receives a C.
> Ed has difficulty discriminating between long and short vowel sounds.
> My teaching method is not effective for this group of students.
> Arthur is a social isolate.
> Mike's attitude toward school has improved.
> Mary should be moved to a higher reading group.
> Mrs. Morrison's class is better at math concepts than my class.
> Donna is a "slow learner."

On what basis do teachers make decisions such as these? In some cases the teacher relies solely on personal judgment. In other cases the teacher relies solely on measurement data. In still other cases the teacher combines measurement data with judgment or subjective data. Which approach is best?

Anti-test advocates suggest that testing should be done away with. Unfortunately, decisions will still have to be made. Teachers, as human beings, are subject to "good and bad days," biases, student and parent pressures, faulty perceptions, and a variety of other influences. In other words, relying solely on a teacher's judgment means relying on a subjective decision-making process. Naturally, no teacher would intentionally make a "wrong" decision about a student. However, all of us make mistakes.

Tests represent an attempt to provide objective data that can be used with subjective impressions to make better, more defensible decisions. This is the purpose of testing, or *why* we test. Tests are not subject to the ups and downs or other influences that affect teachers. And subjective impressions can often place in perspective important aspects of a decision-making problem for which no objective data exist. Thus, it seems likely that a combination of subjective judgments and objective data will result in more appropriate rather than less appropriate decisions. Reliance on measurement data alone can even prove to be detrimental to decision making. Although such data are objective, we must remember that they are only *estimates* of a student's behavior. Test data are never 100 percent accurate!

In summary, we test to provide objective information, which we combine with our subjective, commonsense impressions to make better educational decisions. However, suggesting that better educational decisions are made by combining objective measurement data and subjective impressions assumes that the:

> measurement data are valid
> teacher or individual interpreting such data understands the uses and limitations of such data.

Unfortunately, too often one or both of these assumptions are violated in the decision-making process. Obviously, when this happens, the resultant educational decisions may be invalid.

TESTING, ACCOUNTABILITY, AND THE CLASSROOM TEACHER

It is no longer surprising to say that the American public has become disenchanted with education. Reduced school budgets, defeated bond issues, and the elimination of special programs are all too common occurrences on today's educational scene. The reasons for this disenchantment are many and complex, but at least some can be traced to poor decision making in our schools—decision making not just at the classroom level, but at the grade, school, district, and national levels as well. Nevertheless, the most frequently made decisions are the everyday decisions of the classroom teacher, which also form the cornerstone for other decisions at higher levels of the educational structure. If the cornerstone is weak, the structure itself cannot be sound.

At the classroom level, the extent to which unsound educational decision making occurs is not yet known. However, the everyday decisions of classroom teachers are coming under closer and closer scrutiny. Classroom teachers are increasingly being asked such questions as the following:

PARENT: On what grounds was Jane moved to the slower reading group?

PRINCIPAL: What method are you using to measure student achievement in Social Studies?

COUNSELOR: How is it that you've determined Tom is a behavior problem?

Individuals asking such questions are asking teachers for the data on which these decisions were based. With mounting accountability pressures it is no longer sufficient to rely solely on judgment to make such decisions. Indeed, such decisions should never be made based on judgments alone.

What does the teacher do? Give up? Complain? Yearn for the "good old days"? We hope not! Yet, the answers to these and many other questions need to be provided if education is to improve. In many cases, it will be classroom teachers who will be asked to answer these questions. It seems likely that those who can understand and respond to such questions will swim in the educational sea, while those who cannot will sink. In other words, a good working knowledge and understanding of testing and measurement is no longer just a useful skill in education, but one that is necessary for survival. The successful teacher of tomorrow not only will have to report test data to parents, principals, counselors, academic review committees, and even the courts, but will have to interpret test data and be fully aware of the uses and limitations of such data. One of the first steps toward acquiring the ability to interpret test data is to understand the different types of educational decisions that are made from measurement data.

Types of Educational Decisions

Measurement data enter into decisions at all levels of education, from those made by the individual classroom teacher to those made by the State Commissioner of Education. There are several ways of categorizing these decisions. We have found the following classification approach, suggested by Thorndike and Hagen (1977), useful for understanding the various types of decisions that can be made in schools. The categories range from specific everyday in-class decision making to much less frequent administrative decisions. The categories of decisions discussed below are instructional, grading, diagnostic, selection, placement, counseling and guidance, program or curriculum, and administrative policy.

Instructional Decisions.   Instructional decisions are the nuts-and-bolts types of decisions made by all classroom teachers. In fact, these are the most frequently made decisions in education. Examples of such decisions include deciding to:

spend more time in math class on addition with regrouping
skip the review you planned before the test
stick to your instructional plan

Since educational decisions at lower levels have a way of affecting decisions at higher levels, it is important that these types of decisions be sound ones. Deciding more time should be spent on addition with regrouping when it doesn't need to be wastes valuable instructional time and may have very noticeable effects on classroom management. Students may get turned off, tune you out, or act up. And such problems may not be confined to the classroom. A student's home life, interactions with peers, and even lifelong ambitions can be affected by these seemingly small misjudgments at the classroom level.

You may expect similar detrimental effects when you present material too quickly. Moving too quickly almost invariably results in skill deficiencies in some students. You can be sure that many of the Johnnys and Janes who can't read were unable to master various reading skills in school because their teachers moved through the curricula too quickly for them to acquire the needed skills.

It seems reasonable to suggest that instructional decisions will become part of the accountability picture in the near future. If so, classroom teachers will have to do more than say they "felt" it was time to move ahead in the curriculum or that they had "always kept the same schedule." Remember, your judgments or impressions are fallible and the students you teach may not be aware of your "schedule."

Grading Decisions.

Educational decisions based on grades are also made by the classroom teacher, but much less frequently than instructional decisions. Grades are usually assigned about every six weeks, and the teacher often considers test scores and other data in making decisions about who gets A's, B's, and so on. If test data are used, naturally it is important that such data be acquired from appropriate tests. As with instructional decisions, teacher-made tests are usually the most appropriate for grading decisions.

Other factors, such as attendance, ability, attitude, behavior, and effort are sometimes graded also. A common mistake is to combine one or more of these with achievement data to decide on grades. Although each of these factors represents an area of legitimate concern to classroom teachers, and although assigning grades for one or more of these factors is perfectly acceptable, these grades should be kept separate from grades for achievement. These issues will be discussed at length in Chapter 9. Methods used to measure nonachievement factors will be presented in Chapter 10 and Chapter 11.

Grade inflation—or the tendency for teachers to assign higher grades today than in the past for the same level of performance—has become a matter of considerable public concern. Consequently, it will be no surprise if grading decisions and policies come under increasing public scrutiny and become subject to accountability procedures as well. For most students, grading decisions are probably the most influential decisions made about them during their school years. All students are familiar with the effects grades have on them, their peers, and their parents. The teacher who adheres to an acceptable grading policy, who uses data obtained through appropriate measurement instruments, and who knows the uses and limitations of such data will be the teacher who makes sound grading decisions, most likely will be fair in assigning grades, and most likely will be able to defend the grades that are assigned.

Diagnostic Decisions.   Diagnostic decisions are those made about a student's strengths and weaknesses and the reason or reasons for them. For example, you may know Martha is having trouble in reading. When you determine *why* she is having trouble you are making a diagnostic decision. Such decisions should be based on test data. In schools, formal diagnostic decisions are often made by specialists. These may include the resource teacher, school psychologist, or educational diagnostician. In making diagnostic decisions, these specialists normally rely primarily on standardized tests and, secondarily, on tests of their own construction.

However, the regular classroom teacher also makes diagnostic decisions, which are usually based on a teacher-made test. For example, a teacher may notice in test results that Dick can successfully subtract four-digit numbers from four-digit numbers, but not if carrying is involved. Given this information, the teacher decides that Dick does not fully understand the carrying process. The teacher has made a diagnostic decision based on information yielded by an informal, teacher-made test.

For the most part, though, diagnostic decisions have been delegated to specialists. However, with the passage of PL 94–142 requiring the placement of handicapped pupils in the least restrictive environment, the regular classroom teacher can increasingly be expected to make diagnostic decisions. We will discuss the role of the regular classroom teacher in providing test data and in making decisions for the handicapped child in Chapter 20, but for now it should be obvious that the teacher who uses appropriate tests and properly interprets the data they yield will make better diagnostic decisions.

The three types of decisions listed above—instructional, grading, and diagnostic—are types of educational decisions every classroom teacher must make. The five remaining types of decisions are made by specialists, administrators, or committees composed of teachers, specialists, and administrators. Their decisions are typically based on standardized rather than teacher-made tests. Although teachers are not directly involved in the decisions based on standardized test data, it is a fact that teachers are often called upon to interpret the results of standardized tests for parents and students since the tests are part of a student's cumulative work record. Standardized testing will be discussed in Chapters 18 and 19. For now, let's get familiar with the types of decisions in which standardized tests play a role.

Selection Decisions.   Selection decisions involve test data used in part for accepting or rejecting applicants for admission into a group, program, or institution. The Scholastic Aptitude Test (SAT) that you probably took before being admitted to college and the Graduate Record Examination (GRE) that you will be required to take if you intend to go to graduate school are examples of standardized tests that are used to help make selection decisions. At the elementary- and secondary-school level, teachers are often asked to assist with the testing of pupils for selection into Title I or other remedial programs that are designed to improve educational opportunities for economically disadvantaged pupils.

Placement Decisions.

Placement decisions are made after an individual has been accepted into a program. They involve determining where in a program someone is best suited to begin work. For example, you may have had to take an English test prior to freshman college registration to determine whether you were ready for freshman college English courses, needed remedial work, or were ready for intermediate or advanced courses. Standardized achievement test data are often used in elementary and secondary schools for placing students in courses that are at their current level of functioning.

Counseling and Guidance Decisions.

Counseling and guidance decisions involve the use of test data to help recommend programs of study that are likely to be appropriate for a student. For example, in your junior or senior year in high school you probably took the Differential Aptitude Test (DAT) or some similar aptitude test battery. Partly based on your scores, your guidance counselor may have recommended that you apply to a particular set of colleges.

Program or Curriculum Decisions.

Program or curriculum decisions are usually made at the school-district level after an evaluation study comparing two or more programs has been completed. Your district's decision to abandon a traditional math program in favor of a "new math" program is an example of a program or curriculum decision. Teachers are often required to participate in these studies and even to help collect test data for them.

Administrative Policy Decisions

Administrative policy decisions may be made at the school-district, state, or national level. Based at least in part on measurement data, these decisions may determine the amount of money to be channeled into a school or district, whether a school or district is entitled to special funding, or what needs to be done to improve a school, district, or the nation's achievement scores.

Thus far we have considered the purposes of testing, or why we test. Next, let's consider two other aspects of educational measurement: how we measure and what we measure.

A PINCH OF SALT

Jean-Pierre, the master French chef, was watching Marcel, who was Jean-Pierre's best student, do a flawless job of preparing the master's Hollandaise sauce. Suddenly, Jean-Pierre began pummeling Marcel with his fists. "Fool!" he shouted. "I said a pinch of salt, not a pound!" Jean-Pierre was furious. He threatened to pour the sauce over Marcel's head, but before he could, Marcel indignantly emptied the whole salt container into the pot.

"There, you old goat, I only added a pinch to begin with, but now there *is* a pound of salt in the sauce—and I'm going to make you eat it!"

Startled by his student's response, Jean-Pierre regained his composure. "All right, all right. So you didn't add a pound, but you certainly added more than a pinch!"

Still upset, Marcel shouted, "Are you senile? You were watching me all the time and you saw me add only one pinch!" Marcel pressed his right thumb and index finger together an inch from the master's nose to emphasize his point.

"Ah-hah! You see! There you have it!" Jean-Pierre said elatedly. "That is not the way to measure a pinch. Only the *tips* of the thumb and index finger make contact when you measure a pinch!"

Marcel looked at the difference between his idea of a "pinch" of salt and the master's. Indeed, there was quite a difference. Marcel's finger and thumb made contact not just at the fingertips, but all the way down to the knuckle. At Jean-Pierre's request, they both deposited a "pinch" of salt on the table. Marcel's pinch contained four or five times as much salt as Jean-Pierre's.

Who is correct? Is Marcel's pinch too much? Is Jean-Pierre's pinch too little? Whose method would you use to measure a pinch of salt? Perhaps relying on an established standard will help. *Webster's New Collegiate Dictionary* defines a pinch this way: "As much as may be taken between the finger and the thumb." If *Webster's* is our standard of comparison, we may conclude that both Jean-Pierre and Marcel are correct. Yet, we see that Marcel's pinch contains a lot more salt than Jean-Pierre's. It seems we have a problem. Until Marcel and Jean-Pierre decide on who is correct and adopt a more specific or standard definition of a "pinch," they may never resolve their argument. Furthermore, if we were to try to match the recipes they develop for their culinary masterpieces, we might never succeed unless we know which measuring method to use.

This measurement problem resulted from the lack of a clear, unambiguous method of measurement. Who is to say Jean-Pierre's method is better than Marcel's or vice versa? In Jean-Pierre's eyes, his method is correct and Marcel's is not. In Marcel's eyes, his method is correct and Jean-Pierre's is not. According to *Webster's,* both are correct. A clear and unambiguous method of measuring a "pinch" would resolve the problem. It seems reasonable to suggest that any time measurement procedures—that is, *how* we measure—are somewhat subjective and lack specificity, similar interpretative problems may arise.

"Pinching" in the Classroom

Mr. Walsh assigns his history grades based entirely on his monthly tests and a comprehensive final examination. He takes attendance, comments on homework assignments, encourages classroom participation, and tries to help his students develop positive attitudes toward history, but none of these is considered in assigning grades. Mr. Carter, another history teacher, assigns grades in the following manner:

monthly tests	20%
comprehensive final	20%
homework	10%
attendance	20%
class participation	15%
attitude	15%

Both teachers assign roughly the same numbers of A's, B's, C's, D's, and F's each semester. Does an A in Mr. Walsh's class mean the same thing as an A in Mr. Carter's class? Obviously, Mr. Walsh "pinches" more heavily when it comes to test data than does Mr. Carter (100% versus 40%). On the other hand, Mr. Carter "pinches" more heavily on attendance and participation in assigning grades than does Mr. Walsh (35% versus 0%).

Which method is correct? In interpreting grades earned in each class, would you say that students who earn A's in either class are likely to do equally well on history tests constructed by a third teacher? Should Mr. Walsh "pinch," that is, assign grades, more like Mr. Carter, or should Mr. Carter assign grades more like Mr. Walsh? Obviously, there are no easy answers to these questions. The differences in how Jean-Pierre and Marcel measure a "pinch" of salt is the result of the lack of a clear, unambiguous definition of a "pinch." Similarly, the differences in how Mr. Walsh and Mr. Carter measure learning in history is the result of the lack of a clear, unambiguous definition of what constitutes a grade. As a result, their grades represent somewhat different aspects of their student's performance. The way they "pinch" or how they measure differs.

For Jean-Pierre and Marcel, there is a relatively easy way out of the disagreement. Only their method of measurement or how they measure is in question, not what they are measuring. It would be easy to develop a small container, a common standard, that could then be used to uniformly measure "pinches" of salt. In the classroom, the task is more difficult for Mr. Walsh and Mr. Carter. What is in question is not only their measurement method, or *how* they weigh components of a grade, but *what* they are measuring.

Much of what we measure or attempt to measure in the classroom is not clearly defined. For example, think of how many different ways you have heard *learning, intelligence,* or *adjustment* defined. Yet, we constantly attempt to assess or measure these traits. Furthermore, the methods we use to measure these often ill-defined traits are not very precise. But even good methods cannot accurately measure ill-defined or undefined traits.

Only when both what to measure and how to measure have been considered, specified, and clearly defined can we hope to eliminate the problems involved in measuring and interpreting classroom information. The task is formidable. We cannot hope to entirely solve it, but we can minimize the subjectivity, inaccuracy and the more common interpretive errors often inherent in classroom measurement. Achieving these goals will go far toward helping us "pinch" properly. Sound measurement practice will benefit you professionally. Moreover, it will benefit most those unwitting and captive receptors of measurement practice, your students.

The examples presented are intended to alert you to two general problems encountered in classroom measurement:

1. Defining what it is that you want to measure, and
2. Determining how to measure whatever it is that you are measuring.

WHAT TO MEASURE

Defining what to measure may, at first glance, not appear like much of a problem, but consider the following example:

> Mrs. Norton was a freshman math teacher in a small private high school comprised of high-achieving students. She prided herself on her tests, which stressed the ability to apply math concepts to real-life situations. She did this by constructing fairly elaborate word problems. When she moved to another part of the state she went to work in an inner-city high school teaching an introductory math skills course. Realizing that her new students were not nearly as "sharp" as her private-school students, she "toned-down" her tests by substituting simpler computations in her word problems. Even with this substitution, 29 of her 31 students failed this "easier" test. Dejected, she substituted even simpler computations into her next test, only to have 30 out of 31 fail. She concluded that her students "totally lack even basic math skills," and applied for a transfer.

Think about these questions:

> Do you agree with Mrs. Norton's conclusion? If so, why? If not, why not?
> Are there any possible alternative conclusions?
> What might she have done differently?

We disagree with Mrs. Norton. While it may be that some of her students lack or are weak in basic math skills, there seems to be little conclusive evidence that all, or even most, lack these skills. There may be another explanation for her students' poor performance.

Her tests were originally designed to measure the ability of her high-achieving private-school students to *apply* their skills to real-life situations. This is what she wanted to measure.

In her public school skills class, *what* Mrs. Norton wanted to measure was a bit different. What she wanted to measure was not the ability to *apply* skills (at least not at first) but whether the skills were ever acquired. How she measured must also be considered. Her tests consisted of fairly elaborate word problems. They may have been tests of reading ability as much as tests of math applications. Their reading level may have been appropriate for her "bright" students but too advanced for her new students. Since her tests measured skill application and reading ability rather than skill acquisition, how Mrs. Norton measured also was not appropriate. Assuming you are convinced it is important to define *what* you are measuring, let's look in more detail at what we mean by determining *how* to measure.

HOW TO MEASURE

Mrs. Norton got into trouble mainly because she wasn't sure what she was measuring. At least by giving a written test she had the right idea about one aspect of how to measure basic math skills . . . or did she? How else could basic math skills be measured? An oral test, you say? But in a class of 31 students? Any other ideas? What about a questionnaire without any math problems, just questions about math skills to which students respond yes or no to indicate whether they *believe* they have acquired a certain skill? Or how about simply observing your students?

The techniques mentioned above are all possible measurement methods, not for measuring basic math skills, of course, but quite useful in the proper situation. Questionnaires and observation are common methods used when what we want to measure is an individual's attitude, for example. These and a variety of other measurement techniques and situations for which they are appropriate will be treated in Chapter 10. For now, simply be aware that there are alternatives to written tests and that how we measure is often determined by what we measure. Let's return to Mrs. Norton and the most commonly used form of measurement, the written test.

Written Tests

The test Mrs. Norton used was heavily verbal, which suggests that it relied almost exclusively on words to ask questions. Although the answers to her questions may have been numerical, the questions themselves were word problems. While there is probably no better way to measure basic math skills than through a written test, was the written test that Mrs. Norton used the best type of written test? We would say no and suggest that her test should have looked more like the following instead of consisting of only word problems:

$$(1) \quad \begin{array}{r} 1431 \\ +\ \ 467 \\ \hline \end{array} \qquad (2) \quad \begin{array}{r} 798 \\ -\ 581 \\ \hline \end{array} \qquad (3) \quad \begin{array}{r} 125 \\ \times \quad 7 \\ \hline \end{array} \qquad (4)\ 121 \div 11 =$$

The advantages of a basic math skills test with items similar in format to those above include the following:

They do not rely on reading ability
Basic skills are measured directly
More items can be included in the same amount of test time

All these points are important. The first two help ensure that the test measures what it is supposed to measure. The last improves the test's reliability or the consistency of the scores it yields over time. Furthermore, inspecting a student's written work on such a test can help you diagnose errors in the process used by students to arrive at an answer.

So, you see, there can be different types of written tests. The point of our discussion about Mrs. Norton is simply that *how* you measure must always match *what* you measure. Whether you give word problems, use number formats, or provide real-world examples depends on whether you are measuring problem-solving ability, knowledge of facts or processes, application, and so on. Table 2.1 defines some common types of written tests.

In this section we have considered the importance of knowing what we want to measure and how we want to measure. We also saw that determining what and how may not be as simple as it appears. However, both considerations are vitally important in classroom measurement, since failing to be clear about them is likely to result in invalid measurement.

SUMMARY

This chapter has introduced you to *why* we test, *what* we test, and *how* we test. Its major points are:

1. The purpose of testing is to collect objective information that may be used in conjunction with subjective information to make better educational decisions.
2. In our age of increasing demands for accountability, it has become imperative that teachers be able to understand and demonstrate the role that objective test data can play in educational decision making.
3. Classroom teachers are responsible for the bulk of educational decision making, such as everyday instructional decisions, grading decisions, and diagnostic decisions. Such decisions are often based, or ought to be based, on information obtained from teacher-made tests.
4. Other less frequent kinds of educational decisions are usually made by administrators or specialists other than the classroom teacher. These include decisions about selection, placement, counseling and guidance, programs and curriculum, and administration. Such decisions are usually based on information obtained from standardized tests.

TABLE 2.1	Types of Written Tests

Type of Written Test	*Description*
Verbal	Emphasizes reading, writing, or speaking. Most tests in education are verbal tests.
Nonverbal	Does *not* require reading, writing, or speaking ability. Tests composed of numerals or drawings are examples.
Objective	Refers to the scoring of tests. When two or more scorers can easily agree on whether an answer is correct or incorrect, the test is an objective one. True-false, multiple-choice, and matching tests are the best examples.
Subjective	Also refers to scoring. When it is difficult for two scorers to agree on whether an item is correct or incorrect the test is a subjective one. Essay tests are examples.
Teacher-made	Tests constructed entirely by teachers for use in the teacher's classroom.
Standardized	Tests constructed by measurement experts over a period of years. They are designed to measure broad, national objectives, and have a uniform set of instructions that are adhered to during each administration. Most also have tables of norms, to which a student's performance may be compared to determine where a student stands in relation to a national sample of students at his or her grade or age level.
Power	Tests with liberal time limits that allow each student to attempt each item. Items tend to be difficult.
Speed	Tests with time limits so strict that no one is expected to complete all items. Items tend to be easy.

5. Measurement problems may be expected any time testing procedures lack definition or specificity, or when we fail to specify clearly the trait we are measuring.
6. Specifying or defining *what* we want to measure often determines *how* the trait should be measured.

For Discussion

1. Identify some of the ways we measure "pinches" of achievement, intelligence, and classroom conduct.
2. Make a list of all the different kinds of behaviors you will need to measure, formally or informally, during your first month of teaching. Identify two different ways of measuring each of these behaviors.
3. List some of the instructional, grading, and diagnostic decisions you will be expected to make during your first month of teaching. Identify which category each decision represents.
4. Using Mrs. Norton's problem as a guide, make up some examples in your own subject area that illustrate mismatches between what is being tested and how it is being tested.

3

CHAPTER

NORM-REFERENCED AND CRITERION-REFERENCED TESTS

I n Chapter 2 we stated that the purpose of testing is to provide objective data that can be used along with subjective impressions to make better educational decisions. In this chapter we will discuss the two main types of tests used to make educational decisions and the different types of information that each test yields.

DEFINING NORM-REFERENCED AND CRITERION-REFERENCED TESTS

One type of information tells us where a student stands compared to other students. In other words, certain kinds of test data help us determine a student's "place" or "rank." This is accomplished by comparing the student's performance to a norm or average of performances by other, similar students. A test that yields this kind of information is called a *norm-referenced test* (NRT) because the information it conveys refers to the performance of a large sample of pupils representative of those we are testing. Such information is useful *only* for certain types of decisions, which we will discuss later in this chapter.

A second type of information provided by tests tells us about a student's level of proficiency in or mastery of some skill or set of skills. This is accomplished by comparing a student's performance to a standard of mastery called a *criterion.* A test that yields this kind of information is called a ***criterion-referenced test*** (CRT) because the information it conveys refers to a comparison with a criterion or absolute standard. Such information helps us decide whether a student needs more or less work on some skill or set of skills. It says nothing about the student's place or rank compared to other students and, hence, it too is useful *only* for certain types of decisions. Figure 3.1 illustrates the relationship of NRT's and CRT's to the purpose of testing.

As you may have guessed, it is important to identify the type of information you need *before* you administer a test. If you fail to do so, you may have test data, but be unable to use the data to make necessary decisions. Unfortunately, teachers often know little more about a student after testing than they did before testing. In our technically oriented society, test scores have sometimes become ends in themselves while the meaning of the test scores has tended to be ignored. With methods of measurement sometimes comes the illusion that the scores themselves are what is important, not the judgment criteria by which the scores must be interpreted and made meaningful for decision making. In such cases teachers,

FIGURE 3.1 | Relationships Among the Purpose of Testing, Information Desired, and the Type of Test Required

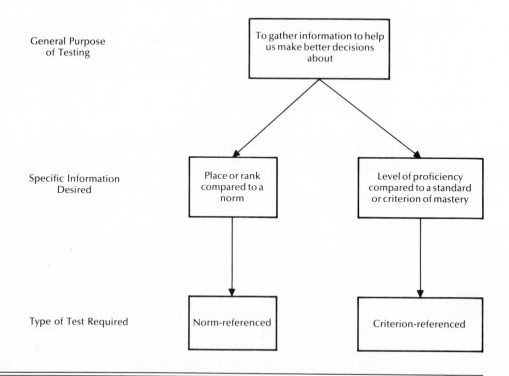

parents, and others may be quick to denounce or blame the test, often suggesting that such test abuse "proves" that test data are useless. In reality, all it indicates is that the teacher selecting the test either failed to identify the specific information desired *before* administering the test or failed to carefully match the test to this purpose. A similar situation can occur when existing test data are used or interpreted inappropriately. Consider the following:

John, the counselor, was checking his records when he heard a knock at the door. It was Mary, the sixth-grade teacher.

JOHN: Come in. What can I do for you?

MARY: I just stopped by to get the latest test information you have on Danny. As you know, he's going to be in my class this year after being in remedial classes for the last five years. Mrs. French, his teacher last year, said you have all the test information on him.

JOHN: Well, I'd be glad to help out. In fact, I was just reviewing his folder.

MARY: Great! Can I see it?

JOHN: Well, his Math Cluster score on the Woodcock-Johnson is at the sixth percentile, and his Reading Cluster is at the first percentile. Good luck with him.

MARY: Boy, he sure is low. I guess that's why he's been in the remedial classroom for so long.

JOHN: You've got it!

MARY: Okay. Well, really that's about what I was expecting. Now what about his skill levels?

JOHN: What do you mean?

MARY: You know, his academic skill levels.

JOHN: Oh, his grade levels! Now let's see, his math grade equivalent is 2.6, and his reading grade equivalent is even lower, 1.7.

MARY: Well . . . that's not really what I need to know. I know he's way below grade level, but I'm wondering about his skills—specific skills, that is. You know, like what words he can read, what phonetic skills he has, if he can subtract two-digit numbers with regrouping . . . things like that.

JOHN: *(becoming a bit irritated)* Mary, what more do you need than what I've given you? Don't you know how to interpret these scores? Perhaps you should have taken a tests and measurements course in college.

MARY: *(beginning to get frustrated)* John, I *have* taken a tests and measurements course and I *do* know what those scores mean, but they only compare

Danny to other students. I'm not interested in that, I want to know what he *can* and *can't* do, so I can begin teaching him at the proper skill level.

JOHN: *(shaking his head)* Look, he's at a first-grade level in reading and second-grade level in math. Isn't that enough?

MARY: But, what level of mastery has he demonstrated?

JOHN: Mastery? He's years behind! He has mastered very little of anything.

MARY: This has been a very enlightening conversation. Thank you for your time.

It appears there is a communication gap between Mary and John. John has provided a lot of test data to Mary, and yet Mary doesn't seem to get much out of it. John is frustrated, Mary is frustrated, and little that may be of help to Danny has been accomplished. Why? Just what is the problem? Is it John or is it Mary? Or is it something else?

Take another look at the situation. Do you think Mary was being unreasonable? Would a course in tests and measurements have helped her "understand" the test data better? What if Danny's mother were asking the questions instead of Mary? Would the outcome have been different? Finding answers to these questions may help us. Let's consider each of these in turn.

Was Mary being unreasonable? Mary's questions were specific: Does he have phonetic skills? Can he subtract two-digit numbers with regrouping? Certainly these are not unreasonable questions. She was probably expecting answers that were fairly specific. Maybe something like "yes" or "no" or maybe something like "about 80 percent of the time" or "about 20 percent of the time." Responses like these would have helped her plan instruction for Danny. She would know which skills he had mastered, which he was a little deficient in, and which would require a lot of work. However, the grade-equivalent and percentile scores that John reported provided her with none of this information. No wonder she was frustrated.

Then why was John reporting these scores? Obviously, they were close at hand, and he probably thought he was conveying useful information. Actually, he *was* conveying useful information; it just wasn't very useful in this particular case. In relaying this information to Mary, he may have thought he was answering her questions.

Does Mary need another course in tests and measurements? Maybe, but we don't really know. Mary seems to have a perfectly adequate understanding of the information that grade-equivalent scores convey. If we agree that her questions were reasonable, is it necessarily a lack of understanding of test scores that prevented her from making use of the data John provided? Or could it be that the information provided failed to answer her questions? The latter explanation appears most satisfactory. Indeed, as you will discover shortly, it seems that it is John, not Mary, who would benefit most from a tests and measurements course.

Would things be different if a parent questioned? Maybe. Teachers may respond differently to other teachers than to parents. In some cases inquisitive parents can be intimidated by authoritative-sounding test scores and jargon. But is a parent-teacher conference supposed to cloud or sidestep issues, rather than deal with them directly? We think not. If a parent were as concerned as Mary was about certain skills, that parent would probably end up feeling as frustrated as Mary. While Mary might go home and complain to a friend or husband, a parent might complain to a principal or a superintendent!

Mary's questions, whether raised by her or a parent, are legitimate. John probably could answer these questions if he thought about them, However, he seems to think that the test scores he reported are acceptable substitutes for direct answers to questions about specific skills.

Then what is the problem? The problem appears to be John's, not Mary's. Her questions refer to competencies or mastery of skills. Referring back to Figure 3.1, we can conclude that she was interested in information about Danny's *level of proficiency.* John's answers refer to test performance compared to other students, which, according to Figure 3.1, means information about Danny's *place or rank compared to others.* Answers to Mary's questions can come only from a test designed to indicate whether John exceeded some standard of performance taken to indicate mastery of some skill. If a test indicated that Danny could subtract two-digit numbers with regrouping, he would probably be considered to have "mastered" this skill, at least if, say, 80 percent or more correct was the standard for having attained mastery. In other words, he would have exceeded the standard or criterion of "80 percent mastery of subtraction of two-digit numbers with regrouping." Recall that a criterion-referenced test is a test designed to measure whether a student has mastered a skill, where the definition of mastery depends on the level or criterion of performance set.

The information John was providing was normative or comparative rather than mastery information. Grade-equivalent scores only allow you to make decisions involving comparisons between a child's performance and that of the typical or average performance of a child in a "norm" group. Danny's grade-equivalent score of 1.7 in reading indicates that Danny's reading ability is equivalent to that of the average first-grader after seven months in the first grade. It says nothing about which words he knows, nor does it give any information about the process he uses to read new words, nor does it indicate how long it takes Danny to comprehend what he reads or learn the meaning of new words. All this score indicates is that his ability to read is below that of the average fifth-grader and equivalent to that of an average first-grader after seven months of school. In short, grade-equivalent scores, and a variety of other scores obtained from standardized, norm-referenced tests, allow one to make only general, comparative decisions, not decisions about mastery of specific skills. Unfortunately, situations like the one described above occur every day. Only by becoming knowledgeable about the information yielded by CRT's and NRT's can we avoid these situations.

Recall that in the previous chapter we talked about eight types of decisions for which test data are used. Of these eight we decided that for instructional and grading decisions a teacher-made test was most appropriate. We said that both teacher-made and standardized tests are useful in diagnostic decisions and that standardized tests are most appropriate for selection, placement, counseling and guidance, program or curriculum evaluation, and administrative policy decisions. Most teacher-made tests should be of the mastery type, since these are most useful for instructional decisions—the type of decision most frequently made.

Mary's questions were related to instructional decisions. She was interested in Danny's skill levels. The information John was providing came from a norm-referenced, standardized test. If Mary was interested in where Danny stands compared to national norms, then John's information would have been perfectly appropriate. However, she was apparently not all that interested in his position relative to others; she was interested in what he knew or what he had mastered. Most often in the classroom we are concerned with mastery information. Although we are constantly reminded of where our class, school, or district stands in comparison to national norms, these reminders are usually of secondary importance to the classroom teacher. Of prime importance in the classroom is whether our students are mastering what we teach—whether they are reaching the goals and objectives set for them. Daily decisions to reteach, review, or push ahead depend on whether mastery is occurring. What better way to measure whether our students have mastered an objective than to test them to see if they can perform the learning outcome specified, under the conditions or with the materials specified, and at or above the standard of performance specified for them.

COMPARING NORM-REFERENCED AND CRITERION-REFERENCED TESTS

As you may have guessed, criterion-referenced tests must be very specific if they are to yield information about individual skills. This is both an advantage and a disadvantage. Using a very specific test enables you to be relatively certain that your students have mastered or failed to master the skill in question. The major disadvantage of criterion-referenced tests is that many such tests would be necessary to make decisions about the multitude of skills typically taught in the average classroom.

The norm-referenced test, on the other hand, tends to be general. It measures a variety of specific and general skills at once, but fails to measure them thoroughly. Thus, you are not as sure as you would be with a criterion-referenced test that your students have mastered the individual skills in question. On the other hand, you get an estimate of ability in a variety of skills in much shorter time than you could through a battery of criterion-referenced tests. Since there is a trade-off in the uses of criterion- and norm-referenced measures, there are situations in which each is appropriate. Determining the appropriateness of a given type of test depends on the purpose of testing.

Finally, the difficulty of items in NRT's and CRT's also differs. In the NRT, items vary in level of difficulty from those that almost no one answers correctly to those that almost everyone answers correctly. In the CRT, the items tend to be equivalent to each other in difficulty. Following a period of instruction students tend to find CRT items easy and answer most correctly. In a CRT, about 80 percent of the students completing a unit of instruction are expected to answer each item correctly, while in an NRT about 50 percent are expected to do so. Table 3.1 illustrates differences between NRT's and CRT's.

TABLE 3.1 ❙ Comparing NRT's and CRT's

Dimension	NRT	CRT
Average number of students who get an item right	50%	80%
Compares a student's performance to	The performance of other students	Standards indicative of mastery
Breadth of content sampled	Broad, covers many objectives	Narrow, covers a few objectives
Comprehensiveness of content sampled	Shallow, usually one or two items per objective	Comprehensive, usually three or more items per objective
Variability	Since the meaningfulness of a norm-referenced score basically depends on the relative position of the score in comparison with other scores, the more variability or spread of scores the better.	The meaning of the score does not depend on comparison with other scores: It flows directly from the connection between the items and the criterion. Thus, variability may be minimal.
Item construction	Items are chosen to promote variance or spread. Items that are "too easy" or "too hard" are avoided. One aim is to produce good "distractor options."	Items are chosen to reflect the criterion behavior. Emphasis is placed upon identifying the domain of relevant responses.
Reporting and interpreting considerations	Percentile rank and standard scores used (relative rankings).*	Number succeeding or failing or range of acceptable performance used (e.g., 90% proficiency achieved, or 80% of class reached 90% proficiency).

---

*For a further discussion of percentile rank and standard scores, see Chapter 19.

SUMMARY

In this chapter we have introduced the norm-referenced and criterion-referenced tests. The major points covered were:

1. A norm-referenced test (NRT) indicates how a pupil's performance compares to that of other pupils.
2. A criterion-referenced test (CRT) indicates how a pupil's performance compares to an established standard or criterion thought to indicate mastery of a skill.
3. What type of test you use depends on the purpose of the testing, which should be determined before you administer the test.
4. Information from NRT's is usually not as useful for classroom decision making as information from CRT's.
5. In addition to differing in regard to what a pupil's performance is compared to, NRT's and CRT's differ in the following dimensions:
   a. item difficulty
   b. content sampling (breadth and depth)
   c. variability of scores
   d. item construction
   e. reporting and interpreting considerations

[handwritten margin notes: NRT — very easy to very broad hard / shallow / wide variability of scores / to promote spread / % : standard scores   CRT — same difficulty / narrow / comprehensive / may be minimal / constructed to degree of obj mastery 80%]

For Discussion

1. Identify five characteristics that distinguish a norm-referenced from a criterion-referenced test.
2. Describe several testing decisions for which you would want to use a norm-referenced test and several situations in which you would want to use a criterion-referenced test.
3. A parent calls you and wants to set up a conference to discuss Johnny's potential for getting into the college of his choice. Which type of test score, NRT or CRT, should you be prepared to discuss first? Why?
4. Another parent calls and wants to discuss why Sally received a D in math this grading period. Which type of test score, NRT or CRT, should you be prepared to discuss first? Why?
5. Imagine that you have been randomly chosen to be evaluated by your school district's Office of Evaluation. They ask you for your students' scores on an achievement test. What type of test scores, NRT or CRT, would be most indicative of your success as a teacher?

[handwritten margin note: parent interested in own child's performance]

[handwritten note at bottom: CRT would indicate your success at the local level; hopefully teaching to obj. and having success on CRT would also result in higher NRT.]

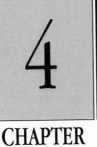

CHAPTER

INSTRUCTIONAL GOALS AND OBJECTIVES

I n Chapter 2 we discussed what, how, and especially why we measure. Chapter 3 elaborated on how we measure. In this chapter and the several that follow we will look more closely at what and how we measure. We have discussed the importance of defining what we want to measure and now will learn how to determine if what we actually measure is what we want to measure. A model for classroom measurement will be presented that can help you determine when students have attained the instructional objectives you set for them.

We will not be concerned with the differences between educational goals and objectives, or even the differences among different kinds of objectives. What we will be concerned with is the fact that all teachers have some objectives in mind when they teach. Usually these are both long- and short-term objectives. An example of a long-term objective would be:

The student will master all phases of addition.

With this long-term objective are several short-term objectives, which might include such objectives as:

The student will add correctly one-, two-, three-, and four-digit numbers without regrouping.

The student will add correctly two-digit numbers with regrouping.

The student will add correctly three-digit numbers with regrouping.

Regardless of whether we are talking about long- or short-term objectives, it is important to know when your students have mastered your objectives. Remember Mrs. Norton? One of her objectives was probably "The student will master basic math skills." Like any good teacher, she tried to determine through a test whether her students mastered this objective. The problem was that her test did not measure mastery of basic math skills. It measured the ability to *apply* math skills and to *read* and to *comprehend* word problems. In short, she knew what she wanted to measure, but her test did not actually measure it. This is another way of saying that her test lacked *validity*. More specifically, it lacked *content validity*. She knew what she wanted to measure, but how she did so was inappropriate. In the classroom, content validity is of utmost importance. Simply stated, content validity describes the extent to which a test actually measures the teacher's instructional objectives. Later in this chapter we will introduce procedures for examining a test to determine whether it has content validity. Since most educational decisions are based on classroom achievement tests, we cannot overemphasize the importance of constructing tests that have content validity. If you construct content-valid tests, you will be likely to make sound instructional decisions and will have valid evidence to support your decisions should they ever be questioned.

A THREE-STAGE MODEL OF CLASSROOM MEASUREMENT

Most classroom instruction takes place with some objective in mind. One way to determine whether the objective has been reached is through a test. The three-stage classroom measurement model in Figure 4.1 depicts these relationships. We will illustrate this model by describing how a criterion-referenced test is constructed.

The first stage in the model is the first step in constructing a criterion-referenced test. It is also the first step in sound instructional planning. For our purposes we will use as examples only a few of the many possible objectives in a unit on writing instructional objectives. Some of these objectives might be:

> The student will discriminate learning activities from learning outcomes.
> The student will discriminate observable learning outcomes from unobservable learning outcomes.
> The student will construct well-written instructional objectives.

Each of these objectives would fit in stage 1 of the model.

In stage 2, instructional activities designed to develop student mastery of these objectives would be implemented. For example:

FIGURE 4.1 | The Three-Stage Classroom Measurement Model

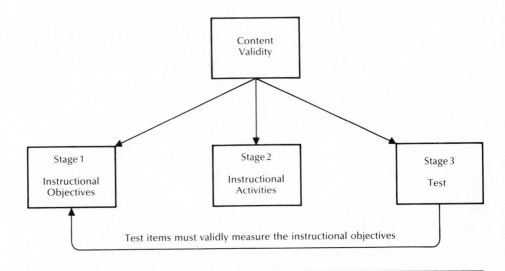

OBJECTIVE:
The student will discriminate learning activities from learning outcomes.

INSTRUCTIONAL ACTIVITY:
Define and provide examples of learning activities and learning outcomes.
Point out similarities and differences between the two.

Naturally, the instructional procedures will vary depending on the content and type of learning outcomes desired. Courses in teaching methods are most concerned with the structure of the procedures in stage 2 of this model. For our purposes, however, we are more concerned with determining the effectiveness of the procedures, not necessarily the nature of the procedures themselves. Thus, it is stages 1 and 3 that will be of most interest.

In constructing a criterion-referenced test, our task is made easier if we develop clear and measurable instructional objectives. In Chapter 5 we will learn how to do this. Once we have measurable instructional objectives, our task is to construct several items to validly measure each objective. Typically, this means about three to ten items per objective. Furthermore, we normally define mastery not as perfect performance but as 70, 80, or 90 percent correct performance. A student who answers four out of five or eight out of ten items that validly measure an objective generally is considered to have mastered the objective. The following is an example of a five-item test to measure the first objective.

OBJECTIVE:
The student will discriminate learning activities from learning outcomes.

TEST ITEM: Indicate which terms in the following list are learning activities by placing an A in the space to the left of the term, and indicate which are learning outcomes by placing an O in the space.

_____ 1. Practice multiplication tables
_____ 2. List the parts of a carburetor
_____ 3. Recall the main events in a story
_____ 4. Listen to a foreign language tape
_____ 5. Memorize the names of the first five United States presidents

Answers: **1.** A; **2.** O; **3.** O; **4.** A; **5.** A.

These response alternatives are content-valid measures of the objective. They ask the student to do exactly what the objective requires. There are certainly other equally valid ways of measuring this objective, but the response alternatives listed above are appropriate. If a student answers four out of five or five out of five correctly on this criterion-referenced test, the teacher could feel reasonably secure in concluding that the student has mastered the objective. These types of tests are called criterion-referenced because a specific level of acceptable performance called the criterion is established directly from the instructional objectives. As we shall see, we are less confident of the mastery of specific objectives when a norm-referenced test is employed.

Regardless of the type of achievement test you select, the issue of content-validity is of paramount concern. Keep the three-stage model in mind when you select or develop an achievement test and you are likely to be aware of the issue of content validity.

Well, now that we have an overall framework for thinking about classroom measurement, let's get into test construction itself. Keep in mind that any good classroom test begins with your objectives, Stage 1 of our three-stage measurement model. Much of the remainder of this chapter and the next will be devoted to considering instructional objectives and ways of ensuring the content validity of items intended to measure instructional objectives.

WHY OBJECTIVES?
WHY NOT JUST WRITE TEST ITEMS?

What if you don't believe that instructional objectives are necessary? What if you feel that they are a waste of time? What if you don't feel you will need to use or construct instructional objectives in your teaching careers? Many believe that objectives for classroom instruction are unnecessary, limiting, too time-consuming, and mechanistic. If you agree, then learning to write instructional objectives may be a frustrating, difficult task. If we told you they're necessary and you're better off learning to write them, you probably would not believe us. We *do* feel it is important for teachers to be able to write measurable instructional objectives, but we also understand and respect your right to hold another opinion. You should, however, take the time to consider the place of instructional objectives in the overall instructional process. Consider the situation described below and then decide whether it's worthwhile to take the time to learn to write instructional objectives.

TWO SCHOOLS: THEIR OBJECTIVES

Getting off the bus at her destination, Maude was immediately taken by the name of the first of the two schools she was about to visit: The Center for Self-Actualization and Humanistic Experiences. Maude was awestruck. At last she would see what education really should be about—free from dry, mechanical methods and curricula, and characterized by the teachers' loving acceptance and excitement and the students' sense of freedom. To her surprise, the door was open, so Maude walked in and was greeted with a warm smile and hug from the "facilitator."

"Is that another name for teacher?" Maude asked.

"Heavens no!" said the facilitator. "I only facilitate learning, I don't teach. For your information, use of the words *teacher* and *educator* are forbidden here at the Center; we are all facilitators." Maude was confused, but decided not to press the issue.

The students were engaged in a variety of activities or lack of activities. One was reading a book, another worked with an abacus, a third was asleep on a couch, others were talking, playing, and generally having what appeared to Maude to be a pretty good time. Maude was encouraged by the facilitator to "experience" the students. Almost unanimously the students felt the Center was "fun." One said, "You never have to do nuthin' around here."

Concerned, Maude questioned the facilitator about this comment. The facilitator's reply was that freedom of choice is strongly encouraged at the Center. All students are free to choose what to do or not to do.

"But are they learning anything?" Maude asked.

"They are learning that they are free and independent human beings," said the facilitator. "When they are ready, they will choose to learn on their own. Now, if you'll excuse me, I have an appointment with my therapist." At a loss for words and feeling troubled, Maude said goodbye and left the Center for Self-Actualization and Humanistic Experiences.

The Center for Accelerated Education was Maude's next stop. After knocking on the door she was greeted by a rather stern-faced middle-aged man who was wearing a "Better Living Through Behaviorism" button on his lapel. A "behavioral engineer" he called himself. He said hello and handed

Maude a list of "behaviors" that the students would be engaging in for the next thirty minutes or so and told her to feel free to "collect data." He then picked up a box of plastic strips, "tokens" he called them, muttered something about a "reinforcement schedule" and "consequating appropriate behaviors," and walked off toward his "subjects."

The students at the Center for Accelerated Education sat in individual cubicles or carrels. Each student had a contract specifying what was expected of him or her. Privileges, such as free time, and rewards from the "reinforcer menu" were earned by performing on-task behavior (like sitting quietly in your cubicle, working on your worksheet, or reading). The behavioral engineer circulated around the room, periodically "reinforcing" on-task behavior with tokens and also providing tokens for each completed worksheet. Students demonstrating off-task and disruptive behavior relinquished tokens or, in extreme cases, were required to spend several minutes in the time-out room. The time-out room was "devoid of all potential reinforces," according to the behavioral engineer. In other words it was a barren room—no windows, tables, or anything interesting.

When Maude asked whether the pupils were learning, the behavioral engineer pointed to the stacks of completed worksheets almost filling a large storeroom.

"Let's see you get that much learning from the kids at the Center for Self-Actualization and Humanistic Experiences," chuckled the behavioral engineer.

More confused and concerned than she had been before she entered, Maude decided not to press the issue and to engage in some exiting behaviors.

As you probably guessed, both the Center for Self-Actualization and Humanistic Experiences and the Center for Accelerated Education are, we hope, exaggerations. They represent extremes in educational theory. On the one hand, the "hands-off" approach is characteristic of nondirective, discovery approaches to learning. On the other hand, the regimented approach is characteristic of a directive, guided approach to learning. Which approach is better? We don't know, and probably no one knows. Fortunately, most educational institutions operate with some combination of directive and nondirective approaches.

Instruction is not a rigid, easily defined procedure. It tends to be different things to different people. No one will ever be completely happy with any one approach to instruction since no *one* approach is really a single method but a combination of methods. As a result, specific educational goals and objectives are unlikely to be approved or supported by everyone. So where do the goals and objectives come from, and who decides on the goals and objectives of education? The answer is that society, government, school boards, school administration, teachers, students, and parents all, to some extent, set educational goals and objectives.

Where Do Goals Come From?

Educators must be responsive to societal needs and pressures. This is especially true for public-school educators, since the purse strings that made public education a reality are controlled by all who make up our society. If a superintendent or school board implements educational policies or procedures that are too far removed from what the community wants and needs, the superintendent may find himself or herself looking for work elsewhere, and board members may not be reelected.

We frequently make the mistake of thinking that it is the administration that is completely responsible for the curriculum implemented in a given school or district. This is only partially true. Ultimately, the general public, or society, sets the goals for education. Figure 4.2 illustrates with a specific example the flow from goals to objectives in education. This illustration shows how public pressure for a back-to-basics movement can reach the classroom.

We may also view this process as a funneling or narrowing of focus, with the often ambiguous wants and needs of society gradually translated into manageable "bits" called instructional objectives, as shown in Figure 4.3.

Are There Different Kinds of Goals and Objectives?

What do you think are the instructional goals and objectives of the schools Maude visited? Well, you probably can't say precisely, but you could probably look at a list of objectives and decide which would be accepted by the Center for Self-

---

FIGURE 4.2 | Back to Basics: The Flow of Goals to Objective

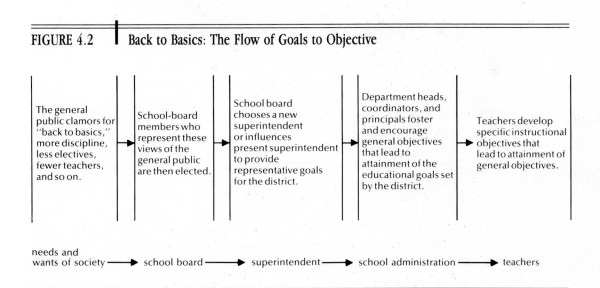

| The general public clamors for "back to basics," more discipline, less electives, fewer teachers, and so on. | School-board members who represent these views of the general public are then elected. | School board chooses a new superintendent or influences present superintendent to provide representative goals for the district. | Department heads, coordinators, and principals foster and encourage general objectives that lead to attainment of the educational goals set by the district. | Teachers develop specific instructional objectives that lead to attainment of general objectives. |

needs and wants of society ⟶ school board ⟶ superintendent ⟶ school administration ⟶ teachers

FIGURE 4.3 ▌ The Funneling of Societal Wants into Objectives

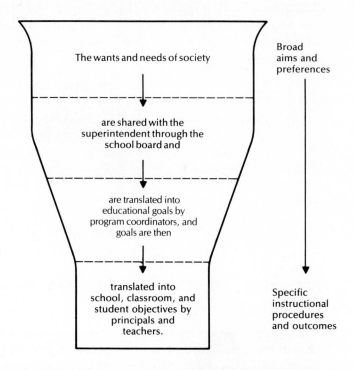

The wants and needs of society

Broad aims and preferences

are shared with the superintendent through the school board and

are translated into educational goals by program coordinators, and goals are then

translated into school, classroom, and student objectives by principals and teachers.

Specific instructional procedures and outcomes

Actualization and Humanistic Experiences or by the behaviorist Center for Accelerated Education. Look at the objectives in the following exercise and indicate the school with which they would most likely be associated.

EXERCISE: Write H for Humanistic or B for Behavioristic in the blank to the left of each objective to indicate which school they would probably go with.

_____B____ 1. With 80 percent accuracy, subtract two-digit numbers from three-digit numbers without borrowing.

_____B____ 2. Identify initial consonant sounds correctly 90 percent of the time when listening to an audiocassette.

✗ _____H____ 3. Enjoy the beauty of nature.

_____B____ 4. Interpret "The Lion, the Witch, and the Wardrobe."

_____B____ 5. Type at least twenty-five words per minute with no more than two errors, using a manual typewriter.

_____H____ 6. Visit the zoo and discuss what was of interest.

✗ _____H____ 7. Be creative.

_____ 8. Be spontaneous.

_____ 9. List the days of the week in proper order, from memory with 100 percent accuracy.

This exercise points out the difference between two types of educational objectives: behavioral (specific) and expressive (general). A behavioral objective is a precise statement of behavior to be exhibited, the criterion by which mastery of the objective will be judged, and, at times, a statement of the conditions under which the behavior must be demonstrated. Objectives 1, 2, 5, and 9 are examples. As you can see, they are specific statements or "bits" of *observable* behavior with specific conditions under which the behavior is to be observed and the level of performance attained. Using these objectives, two or more observers would likely agree about whether a student was, for example, able to list the days of the week in proper order, from memory, with 100 percent accuracy.

An expressive objective is somewhat different. Behaviors are *not* usually specified, *nor* is a criterion performance level generally stated. What is stated in an expressive objective is the experience or educational activity to be undertaken. The outcome of the activity is not detailed in specific terms, but in general terms such as *interpret* or *analyze*. Examples of expressive objectives would include items 4 and 6 from the above list. They specify an activity or experience and a broad educational outcome.

Now you might ask, "What about items 3, 7, and 8?" They do *not* describe a specific, observable behavior, conditions, and criterion level of performance, and they do *not* describe an educational activity or experience. What do they describe? They describe broad, hard-to-define entities. We would have little agreement among individuals trying to define enjoyment, creativity, and spontaneity. These may be best classified as broad goals, rather than objectives, because they are the end result of perhaps a complete educational program.

Educational goals reflect the general needs of society. As a result, most goals, if stated in general terms, tend to be accepted or adopted by most educators and educational institutions. Regardless of whether a program is directive or non-directive, behavioral or humanistic, rigid or flexible, various general goals will be held in common. When we get more specific, often at the local school level, disagreements over methods used to reach these goals arise. For example, the two schools described above would probably agree that creativity is an important goal for education but disagree as to how creativity should be fostered or developed. One school may feel creativity is best developed through structured experiences. Another school may feel creativity is best developed in an open, unstructured environment.

As a result, sometimes different methods are employed to reach the same goal. But it is important to realize that, in addition to having a goal, any method must also have some implicit or explicit steps thought necessary to achieve the goal. Such steps may vary in specificity but are present in any logically constructed instructional program. For example, in the Center for Self-Actualization and

Humanistic Experiences the facilitators most certainly had some steps in mind in trying to foster creativity. It is unlikely that they expected creativity to develop without any guidance. If they did, why would they see a need for their Center? The expressive objectives mentioned might be one of the steps they would use. Others might include:

> Making all students feel welcome.
> Encouraging students to try out new activities and methods of expression.
> Encouraging students to express all ideas, regardless of how inappropriate they may seem.

Statements such as these help define the atmosphere or philosophy of the Center, but are they instructional objectives? Some would say yes, and some would say no. We would say no, since they do not meet our criteria for instructional objectives. That is, they do not (1) specify student behaviors and do not (2) specify observable, measurable behaviors. This is not to say that they are unimportant, but for our purposes instructional objectives must specify observable, overt student behavior. The test of this is whether two independent observers would agree as to the presence or absence of the student behavior in question. Would two or more observers agree that "expression of student ideas is always encouraged, regardless of how inappropriate they may seem"? Some probably would agree and some would not. Thus, this statement would not qualify as an instructional objective according to our criteria, but consider this statement: "During each period the students will write an alternative ending to each assigned short story." Here is seems more likely that observers would agree as to whether students displayed this behavior. It is student-oriented, and it is easily observed.

   Thus far, we have discussed the difference between specific instructional objectives and general expressive objectives. These tend to reflect a school's educational philosophy. We have also mentioned general goals that tend to reflect the overall needs of society. From this point on, we will focus on specific instructional objectives, but we will also consider another type of objective called a *general* or *program objective*. Although these are usually formulated at the school-district level, they are sometimes confused with classroom instructional objectives. Table 4.1 illustrates the difference among educational goals, program objectives, and instructional objectives.

   Since the average classroom teacher will have little input into the formulation of either educational goals or general educational program objectives, we will not concern ourselves further with these. For the remainder of this chapter we will focus on those objectives that classroom teachers must formulate themselves. In other words, we will concentrate on instructional objectives. Instructional objectives can make a teacher's day-to-day job easier, save time, and result in more effective instruction.

TABLE 4.1	Goals, Program Objectives and Instructional Objectives	
Category	*Description*	*Examples*
Goals:	Broad statements of very general educational outcomes that: Do *not* include specific levels of performance Tend to change infrequently and in response to societal pressure	Become a good citizen Be competent in the basic skills areas Be creative Learn problem solving Appreciate art Develop high-level thinking skills
General Educational Program Objectives:	More narrowly defined statements of educational outcomes that: Apply to specific educational programs May be formulated on an annual basis Are developed by program coordinators, principals, and other school administrators	By the end of the academic year, students receiving Title I reading program services will realize achievement gains of at least .8 grade levels, as measured by the Iowa Test of Basic Skills.
Instructional Objectives:	Specific statements of learner behavior or outcomes that are expected to be exhibited by students after completing a unit of instruction. A unit of instruction may, for example, mean: A six-week lesson on "Foreign Culture" A one-week lesson on "Deciduous Trees" A class period on "Subtracting with Borrowing" A five-minute lesson on "Cursive Letters: Lower Case b." These objectives are often included in teacher manuals, and more and more frequently instructional objectives are also being included for specific lessons. Unfortunately, they are *not* always well written and do *not* always "fit" a particular class or teacher style. Thus, instructional objectives often have to be formulated by classroom teachers to "fit" their individual classrooms.	By Friday, the students will be able to recite the names of the months in order. The student will be able to take apart and reassemble correctly within forty-five minutes a one-barrel carburetor with the tools provided.

HOW CAN INSTRUCTIONAL OBJECTIVES MAKE A TEACHER'S JOB EASIER?

When we were first learning about goals and objectives we also wondered how instructional objectives can make a teacher's job easier. How can something that takes time to prepare actually save time, and how does that make a teacher's job easier?

You've probably heard the old saying that it takes money to make money. It's true. An equally relevant, but far less popular expression is that it takes time to save time. In other words, taking time to plan and to organize will save you time in the long run. Planning your lessons, getting organized, and being efficient all take time but can save time later.

Research has identified several factors that are associated with effective, successful teaching. Among these are organization and clarity, which typically go hand-in-hand. While it is possible to be clear without being organized, and vice versa, it is unlikely. Unfortunately, we spend a lot of time "spinning our wheels" because we do not have clear objectives for ourselves, or for our students. In other words, we often don't know where we're going so we don't know when we get where we're going. Using instructional objectives helps minimize this floundering by clearing the way. Thus, we know where we're going and when we get there. The result is increased efficiency and effectiveness in teaching and learning.

SUMMARY

This chapter introduced you to educational goals and objectives. Its major points were:

1. *Content validity* describes the extent to which a test measures or matches the teacher's instructional objectives.
2. There are three stages involved in classroom measurement:
   a. constructing instructional objectives,
   b. implementing instructional activities, and
   c. testing to measure the attainment of the instructional objectives.
   Each of these must match with each other for measurement to be valid.
3. Instructional activities tend to vary across educational institutions, ranging from flexible to rigid.
4. These instructional activities tend to be determined by instructional objectives, which tend to be derived from educational goals, which tend to reflect societal attitudes and values.
5. One type of instructional objective is the behavioral objective. It specifies an observable, measurable behavior to be exhibited, the conditions under which it is to be exhibited, and the criterion for mastery.

6. Another type of instructional objective is the expressive objective. It specifies an educational activity but does not specify the specific outcome of the activity.
7. Instructional objectives help the teacher clarify and organize instruction, enabling the teacher to save time in the long run.

For Discussion

1. Compare and contrast the following:
   a. behavioral and expressive objectives
   b. program objectives and instructional objectives
   c. educational goals and instructional objectives.
2. A teacher is complaining about having to write instructional objectives. He just cannot see any benefit they may have and feels they are too time-consuming. Role-play with another student and describe how well-written objectives can make teaching more effective.
*3. Identify which of the following are expressive (E) and which are behavioral (B) objectives.
   _____ a. properly use and adjust a microscope
   _____ b. understand the nature of plant growth
   _____ c. know how to drive a car
   _____ d. appreciate the role of physics in everyday life
   _____ e. be able to divide fractions
   _____ f. be able to dissect a starfish
   _____ g. understand the importance of eating the right foods
   _____ h. list the parts of the abdomen
*4. Convert the following goals to general objectives:
   a. become a good citizen
   b. be creative
   c. appreciate art
   d. know math
   e. develop musical ability
*5. Match the following general objectives to the most content-valid method of testing.

Objectives	*Testing Method*
_____ 1. From memory, describe the main figures in classical music.	a. Copy by hand at least two classical compositions.
_____ 2. Match the classical composers with their compositions.	b. Associate the composers listed with their compositions.
	c. Chronicle the lives of three European composers who lived between 1500 and 1875.

Objectives	*Testing Method*
———— 3. Identify the titles and composers of the classical pieces discussed in class, after listening to no more than two minutes of each piece.	d. After listening to this tape, identify the composer.
———— 4. Play two classical compositions on the piano by the end of the semester.	e. Play flawlessly the 1815 Overture.
	f. Using a microcomputer, create a variation of one of Mozart's works.
	g. Play two classical selections of your choice.

*Answers to questions 3, 4, and 5 appear in Appendix D.

5
CHAPTER

MEASURING LEARNING OUTCOMES

In Chapter 4 we considered the differences between goals and objectives and some reasons instructional objectives are helpful to the teacher. Next we will consider a method for actually writing instructional objectives.

WRITING INSTRUCTIONAL OBJECTIVES

An instructional objective should be a clear and concise statement of the skill or skills that your students will be expected to perform after a unit of instruction. It should include the level of proficiency to be demonstrated and the special conditions under which the skill must be demonstrated. Furthermore, an instructional objective should be stated in observable, behavioral terms, in order for two or more individuals to agree that a student has or has not displayed the learning outcome in question. In short, a complete instructional objective includes:

> an observable behavior (action verb specifying the learning outcome)
> any special conditions under which the behavior must be displayed, and a
> performance level considered sufficient to demonstrate mastery.

The following series of exercises should help you become familiar with each of these components. With practice, they should lead to your mastery in writing instructional objectives.

Identifying Learning Outcomes

An instructional objective must include an action verb that specifies a learning outcome. However, not all action verbs specify learning outcomes. Learning outcomes are often confused with learning activities. Try to determine which of the following examples represent learning outcomes and which represent learning activities:

1. The child will identify pictures of words that sound alike.
2. The child will demonstrate an appreciation of poetry.
3. The student will subtract one-digit numbers.
4. The student will show a knowledge of punctuation.
5. The student will practice the multiplication tables.
6. The student will sing the "Star-Spangled Banner."

In the first four objectives the action words *identify, demonstrate, subtract,* and *show* all point to outcomes, or end products of units of instruction. However, *practice,* the action word in 5, only implies an activity that will *lead* to a learning outcome. Thus, 5 has no learning outcome; it is a learning activity. The means rather than the end is identified. Objective 6 is a little troublesome, too. Is *sing* an outcome or an activity? It's hard to say without more information. If your goal is to have a stage-frightened pupil sing in public, this may be a learning outcome. However, if singing is only practice for a later performance, it is a learning activity. The following exercise should help you discriminate between learning outcomes and learning activities. Look at the examples of outcomes and activities, then work through the exercise and check your answers.

Learning Outcomes (Ends)	*Learning Activities (Means)*
identify	study
recall	watch
list	listen
write	read

EXERCISE: Distinguish learning outcomes from learning activities by marking an O next to outcomes and an A next to activities.

_____ 1. Fixing a car radio
_____ 2. Reciting the four components of a good essay
_____ 3. Adding signed numbers correctly
_____ 4. Practicing the violin
_____ 5. Recalling the parts of speech
_____ 6. Outlining the main theme in *House of the Seven Gables*
_____ 7. Reciting the alphabet
_____ 8. Punctuating an essay correctly

Answers: **1.** O;   **2.** O;   **3.** O;   **4.** A;   **5.** O;   **6.** O;   **7.** A;   **8.** O.

By now you should be catching on. What we want our instructional objective to include is the *end* product of the instructional procedure. It is on this end product that we will base our test item. If you find your objective includes a learning activity (means) and not an outcome (end), rewrite it so that the product of the intended study is stated. Next, let's consider two types of learning outcomes: those that are observable and directly measurable, and those that are not.

Identifying Observable and Directly Measurable Learning Outcomes

At this stage, your task is to determine whether the outcome is stated as a measurable, observable behavior or an unmeasurable, unobservable behavior. That is, would two or more individuals observing a student agree that the student had demonstrated the learning outcome? Sometimes we need to replace the unobservable behavior with an observable indicator of the learning outcome. For example, if our objective is:

The student will show a knowledge of punctuation.

then the learning outcome, "show a knowledge of punctuation," is unmeasurable. How would we know whether knowledge was shown? Ask the student? Would we assume that if a student was present for a lecture or read the appropriate section of a text, knowledge followed? Probably not. Instead we would need some indication that would serve to demonstrate evidence of knowledge. For example, to indicate knowledge of punctuation, a student would have to "insert commas where appropriate" in sentences, "list the rules governing the use of colons or semicolons," and so on. Thus, there are actually *two* kinds of instructional objectives commonly found in method textbooks, teachers manuals, and in school memos and directives. The first is more correctly called *instructional goals* because they are broad, often difficult to measure statements of instructional intent (know math and reading, appreciate music, and so forth). Only the second deserves the title "instructional objectives" because they are specific, measurable statements of the *outcomes* of instruction that indicate whether instructional intents have been achieved (add two-digit numbers with regrouping, independently pick up a musical instrument and play it, and so on).

For the purpose of classroom instruction, we are most concerned with instructional objectives, as these are the "meat and potatoes" of a teacher's everyday life. When a teacher writes or comes across an instructional goal, the task, for instructional purposes, is to select an indicator of the goal and write an appropriate objective around the indicator. There is an added bonus to such practice: Constructing the test is then much easier. Imagine how difficult it would be to evaluate objectively whether a student "shows a knowledge of punctuation." On the other hand, it is fairly easy to determine whether a student is able to "insert commas where appropriate in sentences."

Let's practice identifying observable learning outcomes. Study the following examples of observable and unobservable outcomes, work through the exercise, then check your answers.

Observables	*Unobservables*
list	value
recite	appreciate
build	know
draw	understand

EXERCISE: Distinguish observable learning outcomes from unobservable outcomes by marking O next to observables and U next to unobservables.

_____ 1. Circle the initial sound of words.
_____ 2. Be familiar with the law.
_____ 3. Add two-digit numbers on paper.
_____ 4. Understand the process of osmosis.
_____ 5. Enjoy speaking French.
_____ 6. Change the spark plugs on an engine.
_____ 7. Recite the names of the characters in *Tom Sawyer*.
_____ 8. Really understand set theory.
_____ 9. Appreciate art deco.
_____ 10. Recite a short poem from memory.

Answers: **1.** O; **2.** U; **3.** O; **4.** U; **5.** U; **6.** O; **7.** O;
8. U; **9.** U; **10.** O.

Stating Conditions

An instructional objective describes any special conditions in which the learning will take place. If the observable learning outcome is to take place at a particular time, in a particular place, with particular materials, equipment, tools, or other resources, then the conditions must be stated explicitly in the objective, as the following examples show:

> Given a calculator, multiply two-digit numbers, correct to the nearest whole number.
> Given a typed list, correct any typographical errors.
> Given a list of six scrambled words, arrange the words to form a sentence.

EXERCISE: Write conditions for the following learning outcomes:

1. Given _____, change the oil and oil filter.
2. Given _____, identify the correct temperature.
3. Given _____, add three-digit numbers.

Possible Answers: **1.** a foreign automobile; **2.** a thermometer; **3.** an electronic calculator.

Stating Criterion Levels

An instructional objective indicates how well the behavior is to be performed. For any given objective a number of test items will be written. The criterion level of acceptable performance specifies how many of these items the student must get correct for him or her to have passed the objective.

The following are examples of objectives with criterion stated:

> Given twenty two-digit addition problems, the student will compute all answers correctly.
>
> Given twenty two-digit addition problems, the student will compute 90 percent correctly.

EXERCISE: Write criterion levels of acceptable performance for the following objectives.

1. Given ten goal statements, write an instructional objective for _____ .
2. The student will swim freestyle for one-hundred yards in _____ .
3. The good student must be able to leap tall buildings _____ .

Possible Answers: **1.** each goal statement;   **2.** sixty seconds;   **3.** in a single bound.

Remember, criterion levels need not always be specified in terms of percentages of items answered correctly. They may also be stated as:

> number of items correct
> number of consecutive items correct (or consecutive errorless performances)
> essential features included (as in an essay question or paper)
> completion within a prescribed time limit (where speed of performance is important)
> completion with a certain degree of accuracy

Now that you have worked through these exercises, you have some idea of what is necessary for a complete instructional objective. The following are examples of complete instructional objectives:

With a ball-point pen, write your name, address, birthdate, telephone number, and grade with 100 percent accuracy.

Without reference to class notes, describe correctly four out of five alternative sources of energy discussed in class.

The student will reply in grammatically correct French to 95 percent of the French questions spoken orally during an examination.

Given a human skeleton, the student will identify at least forty of the bones correctly.

To this point we have shown you how to:

discriminate learning outcomes from learning activities
discriminate observable/measurable learning outcomes from unobserv-
able/unmeasurable learning outcomes
state conditions
state criterion levels

Before moving on to our next topic, let's consider one more issue related to the construction of instructional objectives.

Keeping It Simple and Straightforward

We often make the mistake of being too "sophisticated" in measuring learning outcomes. As a result, we often resort to indirect or unnecessarily complex methods to measure learning outcomes. If you want to know whether students can write their name, ask them to write their name—but not blindfolded! Resist the temptation to be tricky. Consider the following examples:

The student will show his or her ability to recall characters of the book *Tom Sawyer* by painting a picture of each.

Discriminate between a telephone and a television by drawing an electrical diagram of each.

Demonstrate that you understand how to use an encyclopedia index by listing the page a given subject can be found on in the *Encyclopedia Britannica*.

In the first example, painting a picture would likely allow us to determine whether the pupils could recall the characters in *Tom Sawyer,* but isn't there an easier (and less time-consuming) way to measure recall? How about asking the students to simply list the characters? If your objective is to determine recall, listing is sufficient.

For the second example, another unnecessarily complex task is suggested. Instead, how about presenting students with two illustrations, one of a telephone, the other of a television, and simply ask them to tell you (orally or in writing) which is which?

Finally, the third example is on target. The task required is a simple and efficient way of measuring whether someone can use an encyclopedia index.

The next step is to practice writing objectives on your own. Return to the exercises when you have trouble and be sure you include the three components in each objective. Remember, the three components are:

observable learning outcome,
conditions, and
criterion level.

Once you have written an instructional objective, it is always a good idea to analyze it to make sure that the necessary components are included. Determining whether an observable learning outcome has been stated is usually the initial step. The Checklist for Written Objectives in Figure 5.1 addresses this point and provides you with a step-by-step method to analyze and improve written objectives.

We are now ready to consider the third stage of the classroom measurement model introduced in Chapter 4—matching a test item to the instructional objective.

MATCHING TEST ITEMS TO INSTRUCTIONAL OBJECTIVES

In matching test items to instructional objectives, there is one basic rule to keep in mind: *The learning outcome and conditions specified in the test question must match the learning outcome and conditions described in the objective.*

Figure 5.1   Checklist for Written Objectives

	Yes	No
1. Are the objectives composed of only learning outcomes and *not* learning activities?	_____	_____
a. If yes, go to step 2.		
b. If no, eliminate the learning activities or replace them with the learning outcomes.		
2. Are the learning outcomes stated in overt observable terms?	_____	_____
a. If yes, go to step 3.		
b. If no, replace the covert outcomes with indicators of the outcomes. Remember, because this almost always results in more specific objectives, you may have to write several overt objectives to adequately "sample" the covert learning outcome.		
3. Now that you have all overt learning outcomes listed, are they the simplest and most direct ways to measure the learning outcomes?	_____	_____
a. If yes, you now have a useful list of instructional objectives that will serve as a basis for a content-valid test.		
b. If no, rewrite the indirect or complicated means of measurement so that they are as simple and direct as possible. Once you have done so, you have the basis for a content-valid test.		

This rule will ensure that the test you are developing will have content validity. Because content validity is so important, let's go through some exercises to be sure we actually can match correctly. The following exercises illustrate the two steps involved in matching items to objectives.

STEP 1: Identify the learning outcome called for by the objective. Check to determine if your item requires the same learning outcome.

EXERCISE: For the following, employ Step 1 and decide whether the learning outcomes match.

	Match?	
	Yes	No
1. *Objectives:* Recall the names of the capital of all fifty states. *Test Item:* List the capitals of Texas, New York, California, and Rhode Island.	_____	_____
2. *Objective:* Discriminate fact from opinion in the president's most recent state of the union address. *Test Item:* Given a text of the state of the union address, list three examples of facts and three examples of opinion.	_____	_____
3. *Objective:* The student will write complete instructional objectives, including behavior, conditions, and criteria. *Test Item:* Describe why instructional objectives must contain an observable behavior, conditions, and criteria.	_____	_____
4. *Objective:* Using your text as a reference, recognize the names of the various components of the central nervous system. *Test Item:* From memory, list the various components of the central nervous system.	_____	_____
5. *Objective:* Given a written story, list the main events in chronological order. *Test Item:* From the story provided, list the main events in chronological order.	_____	_____

Answers: Items 1, 2, and 5 have learning outcomes that match; items 3 and 4 do not have learning outcomes that match.

STEP 2: Identify the learning conditions that are called for by the objective. Check to determine if your item requires the same learning conditions.

EXERCISE: For the following, assume Step 1 has been performed. Employ Step 2.

	Match?	
	Yes	No

1. *Objective:* Using your map as a guide, make a freehand drawing of Australia.
   Item: Without using your map, draw the continent of Australia. _____ _____
2. *Objective:* Given a complete instructional objective, write a test item that matches the objective's learning outcome and conditions.
   Item: Write an item that matches the learning outcome and conditions of the following objective: "The student will add on paper ten two-digit numbers without regrouping within one minute with 80 percent accuracy." _____ _____
3. *Objective:* Given a list of words, the student will circle the nouns with 90 percent accuracy.
   Item: Give ten examples of nouns and ten examples of verbs. _____ _____
4. *Objective:* Using their own nondigital watches, the students will tell time to the quarter hour with 90 percent accuracy.
   Item: Look at the digital clock on my desk and write down the correct time when I ask. _____ _____
5. *Objective:* The student will sing the "Star-Spangled Banner" in front of the class with the aid of a record.
   Item: Sing the "Star-Spangled Banner" in front of the class. _____ _____

Answers: Item 2 has matching conditions; items 1, 3, 4, and 5 do not have matching conditions.

In summary, ensuring content validity is as simple as making sure that both the learning outcomes and conditions called for by your test items match the learning outcomes and conditions called for by your instructional objectives. Remember, your goal is to measure achievement, not to trick your students or to have them guess what kind of answer you are looking for. The best way to measure achievement is to ask your students to demonstrate mastery of a skill under the conditions you specify in your instructional objectives. With time, Steps 1 and 2 will become second nature. Until then, subject your items to these steps to ensure their content validity.

TAXONOMY OF EDUCATIONAL OBJECTIVES

We've now considered methods not only to analyze objectives already written, but to write instructional objectives and to match test items to instructional objectives. In the rest of this chapter we will consider different levels at which objectives and test items may be written and a method for test construction that will help us write items at these levels.

Cognitive Domain

The *level* of an objective refers to the cognitive, mental, or thought complexity called for by the objective. For example, the objective "The student will list from memory the names of at least three of the last four United States presidents" is a relatively straightforward cognitive task. It involves only recall of the information. Such an objective would be considered lower-level. On the other hand, an objective such as "Given an eyewitness account of an event, separate fact from opinion with at least 75 percent accuracy" is a relatively complex cognitive task. It requires the ability to analyze an eyewitness account and apply some criteria in determining whether statements are observable and objective or subjective and based on inference. Such an objective would be considered higher-level.

One method of categorizing objectives according to cognitive complexity was devised by Bloom, Englehart, Hill, Furst, and Krathwohl (1956). It is a taxonomy of educational objectives for the cognitive domain and delineates six levels of cognitive complexity ranging from the knowledge level (simplest) to the evaluation level (most complex). As illustrated in Figure 5.2, the levels are presumed to be hierarchi-

FIGURE 5.2   Taxonomy of Educational Objectives: Cognitive Domain

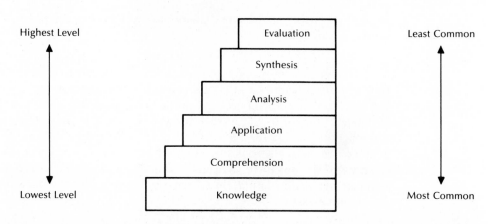

cal. That is, higher-level objectives are assumed to include, and be dependent on, lower-level cognitive skills. Each level of the taxonomy has different characteristics. Each of these is described next with examples of action verbs usually indicative of the different levels.

Knowledge.

Objectives at the knowledge level require the students to remember. Test items ask the student to recall or recognize facts, terminology, problem-solving strategies, or rules. Some action verbs that describe learning outcomes at the knowledge level are:

define	list	recall
describe	match	recite
identify	name	select
label	outline	state

Some example objectives are:

The student will recall the four major food groups without error, by Friday.

From memory, the student will match each United States General with his most famous battle, with 80 percent accuracy.

Comprehension.

Objectives at this level require some level of understanding. Test items require the student to change the form of a communication (translate), to restate what has been read, to see connections or relationships among parts of a communication (interpretation), or to draw conclusions or consequences from information (inference). Some action verbs that describe learning outcomes at the comprehension level are:

convert	estimate	summarize
defend	explain	infer
distinguish	extend	paraphrase
discriminate	generalize	predict

Some example objectives are:

By the end of the semester, the student will summarize the main events of a story in grammatically correct English.

The student will discriminate between the "realists" and the "naturalists," citing examples from the readings.

Application.

Objectives written at this level require the student to use previously acquired information in a setting other than that in which it was learned. Application differs from comprehension in that questions requiring application present the problem in a different and often applied context. Thus, the student can rely on neither the question nor the context to decide what prior learning information must be used to solve the problem. Some action verbs that describe learning outcomes at the application level are:

change	modify	relate
compute	operate	solve
demonstrate	organize	transfer
develop	prepare	use
employ	produce	

Some example objectives are:

On Monday, the student will tell the class what he or she did over the holiday.

Given fractions not covered in class, the student will multiply them on paper with 85 percent accuracy.

Analysis.

Objectives written at the analysis level require the student to identify logical errors (for example, point out a contradiction or an erroneous inference) or to differentiate among facts, opinions, assumptions, hypotheses, or conclusions. Questions at the analysis level often require the student to draw relationships among ideas or to compare and contrast. Some action verbs that describe learning outcomes at the analysis level are:

break down	distinguish	point out
deduce	illustrate	relate
diagram	infer	separate out
differentiate	outline	subdivide

Some example objectives are:

Given a presidential speech, the student will be able to point out the positions that attack an individual rather than his or her program.

Given absurd statements (for example: A man had flu twice. The first time it killed him. The second time he got well quickly.), the student will be able to point out the contradiction.

Synthesis.

Objectives written at the synthesis level require the student to produce something unique or original. Questions at the synthesis level require students to solve some unfamiliar problem in a unique way, or combine parts to form a unique or novel whole. Some action verbs that describe learning outcomes at the synthesis level are:

categorize	create	formulate
compile	design	rewrite
compose	devise	summarize

Some example objectives at the synthesis level are:

Given a short story, the student will write a different but plausible ending.

Given a problem to be solved, the student will design on paper a scientific experiment to address the problem.

Evaluation.   Instructional objectives written at this level require the student to form judgments about the value or worth of methods, ideas, people, or products that have a specific purpose. Questions require the student to state the bases for his or her judgments (for example, what external criteria or principles were drawn upon to reach a conclusion). Some action verbs that describe learning outcomes at the evaluation level are:

appraise	criticize	support
compare	defend	validate
contrast	justify	
conclude	interpret	

Some example objectives at the evaluation level are:

Given a previously unread paragraph, the student will judge its value according to the five criteria discussed in class.

Given a description of a country's economic system, the student will defend it, basing arguments on principles of socialism.

Affective Domain

A taxonomy to describe objectives that reflect underlying *emotions, feelings,* or *values* rather than cognitive or thought complexity and called the Affective Taxonomy has been developed by Krathwohl, Bloom, and Masia (1964). This taxonomy describes a process by which another person's, group's, or society's ideas, beliefs, customs, philosophies, attitudes, etc., are gradually accepted and internalized by a different person, group, or society. This process usually begins with a minimal, partial, or incomplete acceptance of an alternative point of view and culminates with the complete integration of this point of view into an individual's personal belief system.

For example, an individual who naively believed in early 1985 that the return of Halley's Comet in 1986 would cause the end of life on earth may at first have found it difficult even to listen to, *receive,* or *attend* to information that indicated that the comet's return would have no significant or lasting effect on life on earth. Instead, the individual may have ignored such information, attempting instead to convince others of the earth's impending doom. However, with the passage of time throughout the year, and with increased media and educational reports about the event, the individual may have come increasingly to listen to such information and even to consider, discuss, or *respond* to explanations regarding the earth's safety due to the comet's distance from earth, its lack of mass, the protection afforded by the earth's atmosphere, etc. Eventually, the individual likely began to *value* the argument that the comet would have little or no effect on life on earth and ceased preaching the earth's demise. Finally, after trying unsuccessfully even to see the comet on numerous occasions during its closest approach to earth, the individual may have accepted and *organized* the arguments against the total destruction of the human race to the extent that these have come to be internalized and now *characterize* the individual's *value complex*. This would be evident by the individual's calm acceptance of near approaches by celestial bodies in the future and efforts to reassure others of their safety in the face of such events.

The preceding italicized words indicate the five categories or levels of the Affective Domain. Each of these is described further under the following heads, and sublevels within each of these levels are italicized also. As with the cognitive taxonomy, the levels and sublevels are generally considered to be hierarchical.

Receiving (Attending).

Progressing through this level requires that a student have at least an *awareness* of some stimulus. Once this has occurred, a *willingness* at least to listen or attend to the stimulus must be present (i.e., tolerance). A student will next be able to *attend selectively* to various aspects of the context within which the stimulus exists, differentiating those which are relevant to the stimulus from those which are not.

Responding.

Student responses at this level indicate more than passive listening/attending; they require active participation. In the most basic form of responding, a student will at least *acquiesce* to a teacher's or other's request, although given a choice the student might choose some other activity. More complete responding would be indicated by a student's *willingness* to engage in an activity, even when allowed a choice. The highest level within this category is indicated by *satisfaction* after engaging in a response. The student not only participates, but it is evident that the student enjoys the activity.

Valuing.

At this level students judge an activity as to its worthiness and tend to do so consistently enough that the pattern is recognizable to others. The most basic sublevel involves the *acceptance* of a belief, idea, attitude, etc. The individual may not be willing to defend publicly the idea, but has internalized it. When a student actively pursues an idea, the student is demonstrating a *preference* for it, the next sublevel of valuing. Finally, after becoming convinced of the validity of an idea, a student expresses *commitment* to the idea. At this point the student demonstrates conviction, pursuing the goal or idea diligently.

Organization.

As ideas are internalized they become increasingly interrelated and prioritized. That is, they become organized into a value system. This requires first that a student *conceptualize* a value by analyzing interrelationships and drawing generalizations that reflect the valued idea. It may be noted that such an activity is cognitive. However, it is classified here because such conceptualizing would only be undertaken after an idea or philosophy was valued. Next, values that have been conceptualized are subject to the *organization of a value system*. That is, the valued ideas are arranged to foster their consistency and compatibility with each other.

Characterization by a Value or Value Complex.

Students operating at this level behave in a way that is consistent with their value system, avoiding hypocrisy and behaving consistently with underlying philosophy "automatically." The first sublevel is characterized by a *generalized set*. This means the individual is predisposed to perceive, process, and react to a situation in accordance with an internalized value system. The next level, *characterization,* is evident in the consistency between an individual's thoughts and behaviors. Such individuals would never say "Do as I say, not as I do."

Now that you are familiar with the Affective Taxonomy you may ask, "What do I do with it in the classroom?" First of all, it is probably unrealistic to expect a classroom teacher to structure experiences over a one-year period that would lead a student through all five levels. Indeed, there are many who would argue that few human beings ever reach a point in their lives where they function at the fifth, or even the fourth, level. Nonetheless, this taxonomy has important implications for instructional activities and for methods to evaluate instructional activities.

Let's look at an example. Suppose most of the children in your class say they "hate" history and avoid all stimuli related to history. Asking those students to write a paper describing the importance of history courses in the public school curriculum would likely be a frustrating experience for them and for you, since those students are not even at the *receiving/attending* level when it comes to history. You might spend a good deal of time developing a reliable scoring scheme for such a paper and grading the papers only to find that the students failed to see any *value* in history courses in general or the topic of the paper. Thus, it would be more appropriate, given this example, to develop activities and ways to evaluate these activities that are aimed initially at the *receiving/attending* level; progressing to the *responding* level only after the students have demonstrated their willingness to consider history as an important part of the curriculum and after they have demonstrated the ability to attend selectively to history when distracting stimuli are present; and progressing to the *valuing* level only after the students have demonstrated their willingness to deal objectively with history and/or their satisfaction with history as a subject. While individualizing instruction in this way may not always be completely practical, the Affective Taxonomy will at least provide you with a framework to allow you to better assess "where they're at" regarding various topics. This should help you keep your expectations for the class realistic and keep you from pushing for "too much too soon," perhaps frustrating yourself and the class in the process. Practically speaking, it is probably unrealistic to expect students to progress much beyond the *valuing* level as a result of their elementary and secondary school experiences.

The Psychomotor Domain

In addition to the cognitive and affective taxonomies, a taxonomy to describe psychomotor behaviors has been developed by Harrow (1972). This domain includes virtually all behaviors: speaking, writing, eating, jumping, throwing, catching, running, walking, driving a car, opening a door, dancing, flying an airplane, etc. The psychomotor domain has proven most difficult to classify into taxonomic levels since all but the simplest reflex actions involve cognitive, and often affective, components. Nonetheless, Harrow's taxonomy is presented because it does again provide a framework within which to consider the design of instructional activities and methods to evaluate the activities. This taxonomy may prove especially useful to teachers in the lower elementary grades and teachers of physical education, dance, theater, and other courses that require considerable movement. The Psychomotor Taxonomy listed under the following heads ranges from the lowest level of observable reflexive behavior to the highest level, representing the most complex forms of nonverbal communication.

Reflex Movements. Reflex movements are involuntary movements that either are evident at birth or develop with maturation. Sublevels include *segmental reflexes, intersegmental reflexes,* and *suprasegmental reflexes.*

Basic-Fundamental Movements. Basic-fundamental movements are inherent in more complex or skilled motor movements. Sublevels include *locomotor movements, nonlocomotor movements,* and *manipulative movements.*

Perceptual Abilities. Perceptual abilities refer to all the abilities of an individual that send input to the brain for interpretation, which in turn affects motor movements. Sublevels include *kinesthetic, visual, auditory* and *tactile discrimination,* and *coordinated abilities.*

Physical Abilities. Physical abilities are the characteristics of an individual's physical self which, when developed properly, enable smooth and efficient movement. Sublevels include *endurance, strength, flexibility,* and *agility.*

Skilled Movements. Skilled movements are the result of learning, often complex learning. They result in efficiency in carrying out a complex movement task. Sublevels include *simple, compound,* and *complex adaptive skills.*

Nondiscursive Communication. Nondiscursive communication is a form of communication through movement. Such nonverbal communication as facial expressions, postures, and expressive dance routines are examples. Sublevels include *expressive movement* and *interpretive movement.*

THE TEST BLUEPRINT

Thus far we've devoted a good deal of time to writing and analyzing objectives and showing you how to match test items to objectives. We also need to spend some time discussing a technique to help you remember to write objectives and test items at different levels. This technique is referred to as a *test blueprint*. Much like a blueprint used by a builder to guide building construction, the test blueprint used by a teacher guides test construction. The test blueprint is also called a table of specifications.

The blueprint for a building ensures that the builder will not overlook details considered essential. Similarly, the test blueprint ensures that the teacher will not overlook details considered essential to a good test. More specifically, it ensures that a test will sample whether learning has taken place across the range of (1) content areas covered in class and readings and (2) cognitive processes considered important. It ensures that your test will include a variety of items that tap different levels of cognitive complexity. To get an idea of what a test blueprint helps you avoid, consider the following:

Joan was nervous. She knew she had to do very well on the comprehensive final in order to pass American History: 1945–1975. To make matters worse, her teacher was new and no one knew what his final exams were like.

"Well," she told herself. "There's really no point in worrying. Even if I don't do well on this test, I have learned to analyze information and think critically—the discussions were great. I've studied the text and lessons very hard and managed to cover every topic very thoroughly beginning with the end of World War II in 1945 through the Vietnam War. I realize I missed the last class, dealing with the 1970s, but that stuff wasn't in the text anyway, and we only spent one class on it!"

Feeling more relaxed and confident, Joan felt even better when she saw that the entire final was only one page long. After receiving her copy, Joan began shaking. Her test is reproduced here.

American History: 1945–1975

Name:_____ Date:_____

It has been a long year and you have been good students. This test is your reward.

1. On what date did American soldiers first begin to fight in Vietnam?
   _____

2. How many years did Americans fight in Vietnam? _____

3. What was the capital of South Vietnam? _____

4. On what date did Richard Nixon become president? _____

5. Who was Richard Nixon's vice president during his second administration?
   _____

6. What is Vietnam's largest seaport? _____

7. Who was the president of South Vietnam? _____

8. On what date did Americans begin to leave Vietnam? _____

Have a good summer!

We wish we could safely say that things like this never happen, but they do! Chances are you have had a similar experience, perhaps not as extreme, but similar. This test is not a comprehensive assessment of American History: 1945–1975. It is not comprehensive; it focuses on events that occurred during the Vietnam War. It fails to sample content presented in the text and omits content presented in class, except for the last class of the year. Finally, it fails to tap any higher-level thinking processes. Each question requires rote memorization at the knowledge level. A test blueprint, as shown in Table 5.1, helps us avoid falling into this or similar traps in test construction.

A test blueprint is essential to good test construction. It not only ensures that your test will sample all important content areas and processes (levels of cognitive complexity), but is also useful in planning and organizing instruction. The blueprint should be assembled *before* you actually begin a unit. Table 5.1 illustrates a test blueprint appropriate for a unit on instructional objectives being taught in an education course.

Let's consider each component of the blueprint. Once we understand how the components are interrelated, the significance of a test blueprint will become more clear.

Content Outline

The content outline lists the topic and the important objectives included under the topic. It is for these objectives that you will write test items. Try to keep the total number of objectives to a manageable number, certainly no more than about fifteen for any one unit. Otherwise, you will end up with too many test items.

Categories

The categories serve as a reminder or a check on the "cognitive complexity" of the test. Obviously many units over which you want to test will contain objectives that do not go beyond the comprehension level. However, the outline can suggest that you try to incorporate higher levels of learning into your instruction and evaluations. In the cells under these categories report the number of items in your tests that are included in that level for a particular objective. For example, five items are to be constructed to measure comprehension level objective 2b in Table 5.1.

Number of Items

Fill in the cells in Table 5.1 using the following procedure:

1. Determine the classification of each instructional objective.
2. Record the number of items that are to be constructed for the objective in the cell corresponding to the category for that objective.
3. Repeat steps 1 and 2 for every objective in the outline.
4. Total the number of items for the instructional objective, and record the number in the *Total* column.

Shown in class.

TABLE 5.1 | Test Blueprint for a Unit on Instructional Objectives

Content Outline	knowledge	comprehension	application	analysis	total	percent
	Categories					
	Number of Items					
1. Role of Objectives						
a. The student can state purposes for objectives in education.	4				4	12%
b. The student can describe a classroom system model and the role of objectives in it.		1			1	3%
2. Writing Objectives						
a. Given a general educational goal, the student will write an instructional objective that specifies that goal.			5		5	14%
b. The student can match instructional objectives with their appropriate level in the cognitive domain.		5			5	14%
c. The student can identify the three parts of an objective: behavior, conditions, criteria.		5			5	14%
d. The student can distinguish learning activities from learning outcomes when given examples of each.		10			10	29%
3. Decoding Ready-Made Objectives						
a. Given instructional objectives in need of modification, the student will rewrite the objective so that it is a suitable instructional objective.				5	5	14%
Total	4	21	5	5	35	
Percent	12%	60%	14%	14%	100%	

5. Repeat steps 1 through 4 for each topic.
6. Total the number of items falling into each category and record the number at the bottom of the table.
7. Compute the column and row percentages by dividing each total by the number of items in the test.

Functions

The information in Table 5.1 is intended to convey to the teacher the following:

how many items are to be constructed for which objectives and content topics, whether the test will reflect a balanced picture of what was taught, and whether all topics and objectives will be assessed.

Seldom can such "balance" be so easily attained. The little extra time required to construct such a blueprint for your test (and your instruction!) will quickly repay itself. You will not only avoid constructing a bad test, but will have to make fewer and less extensive revisions of your test. You'll also have a sense of satisfaction from realizing you've constructed a representative test.

Since test blueprints are so important to test construction (not to mention instructional planning!) we have included a second example of a test blueprint in Table 5.2. This table illustrates a test blueprint appropriate for an elementary unit on subtraction without borrowing.

This concludes our introduction to test planning and instructional objectives. In the next two chapters we'll consider the actual process by which objective and essay test items are constructed. Soon you'll be able to construct not just a representative test, but a *good* representative test!

|SUMMARY

Chapter 5 introduced you to the first two steps in test construction, writing instructional objectives and preparing a test blueprint. Its main points were:

1. A complete instructional objective includes:

   a. An observable behavior or learning outcome,

   b. Any special conditions under which the behavior must be displayed, and

   c. A performance level considered to be indicative of mastery.

2. Learning outcomes are ends (products); learning activities are the means (practices) to the ends.

3. Objectives may be analyzed to determine their adequacy by:

   a. Determining whether a learning outcome or learning activity is stated in the objective,

   b. Rewriting the objective if a learning outcome is not stated,

TABLE 5.2 | Test Blueprint for a Unit on Subtraction Without Borrowing *Shown in class*

Content Outline	knowledge	comprehension	application	total	percent
1. The student will discriminate the subtraction sign from the addition sign.	1			1	4%
2. The student will discriminate addition problems from subtraction problems.	2			2	8%
3. The student will discriminate correctly solved subtraction problems from incorrectly solved subtraction problems.		4		4	16%
4. The student will solve correctly single-digit subtraction problems.			6	6	24%
5. The student will solve correctly subtraction problems with double-digit numerators and single-digit denominators.			6	6	24%
6. The student will solve correctly double-digit subtraction problems.			6	6	24%
Total	3	4	18	25	
Percent	12%	16%	72%		100%

    c. Determining whether the learning outcomes are stated in measurable or unmeasurable terms, and

    d. Determining whether the objective states the simplest and most direct way of measuring the learning outcome.

4. Learning outcomes and conditions stated in a test item must match the outcomes and conditions stated in the objective if the item is to be considered a valid measure of or match for the objective.

5. The taxonomy of educational objectives for the cognitive domain helps categorize objectives at different levels of cognitive complexity. There are six levels: knowledge, comprehension, application, analysis, synthesis, and evaluation.

6. A test blueprint, including instructional objectives covering the content areas to be covered and the relevant cognitive processes, should be constructed to guide item writing and test construction.
7. The test blueprint conveys to the teacher the number of items to be constructed per objective and their level in the taxonomy and whether the test represents a balanced picture based on what was taught.

For Practice

1. For the same content area, make up two objectives each at the knowledge, comprehension, application, analysis, synthesis, and evaluation levels of the taxonomy of cognitive objectives. Select verbs for each level from the lists provided. Try to make your objectives cover the same subject.
2. Exchange the objectives you have just written with a classmate. Have him or her check each objective for (1) an observable behavior, (2) any special conditions under which the behavior must be displayed, and (3) a performance level considered sufficient to demonstrate mastery. Revise your objectives, if necessary.
3. Now take your list of objectives and arrange them into the format of a test blueprint (see Table 5.1). To construct a test blueprint determine some general content headings under which your specific objectives can be placed. List these with your objectives vertically down the left side of the page. Next, across the top of the page, indicate the levels of behavior at which you have written your objectives. In the cells of the table, place the number of items you would write for each objective if you were to prepare a one hundred-item test over this content. Total the items and compute percentages, as indicated in Table 5.1.
*4. Column A contains instructional objectives. Column B contains levels of cognitive learning outcomes. Match the levels in Column B with the most appropriate objective in Column A. Write in the space next to the numbers in Column A the letter that indicates the highest level of cognitive outcome implied. Column B levels *can* be used more than once.

Column A

_____ 1. Given a two-page essay, the student can distinguish the assumptions basic to the author's position.

_____ 2. The student will correctly spell the word *mountain*.

_____ 3. The student will convert the following English passage into Spanish.

Column B

a. knowledge
b. comprehension
c. application
d. analysis
e. synthesis
f. evaluation

_____ 4. The student will compose new pieces of prose and poetry according to the classification system emphasized in lecture.

_____ 5. Given a sinking passenger ship with nineteen of its twenty lifeboats destroyed, the captain will decide who is to be placed on the last lifeboat based on perceptions of their potential worth to society.

*5. Using this test blueprint or table of specifications for a unit on mathematics, answer the following questions:

a. How many questions will deal with long division at the comprehension, application, and analysis levels?

b. What percentage of the test questions will deal with multiplication and division?

Major areas	Minor areas	Knowledge	Comprehension	Application	Analysis	Synthesis	Evaluation	Total	Percentage
Addition	whole numbers	2	1	2				5	
	fractions	1	1	2	1			5	20%
Subtraction	whole numbers	1	1	2	1			5	
	fractions	1	1	2	1			5	20%
Multiplication	tables	2	2					4	
	whole numbers			2	2	1		5	
	fractions	1	1	2	1	1		6	30%
Division	long division	1	2	1				4	
	whole numbers	1	1	2	1			5	
	fractions	1	2	2	1			6	30%

*Answers to questions 4 and 5 appear in Appendix D.

CHAPTER

WRITING OBJECTIVE TEST ITEMS

T hus far, we have discussed how to establish general goals for instruction and how to develop instructional objectives derived from these goals. We have also discussed using the test blueprint to ensure an adequate sampling of the content area and accurate matching of test items to instructional objectives. We are now ready to put some "meat" on this test "skeleton." In this chapter we will discuss objective test items and how to construct them. Objective test items include items with the following formats: true-false, matching, multiple-choice, and completion or short-answer. The essay item, because of its special characteristics and scoring considerations, will be treated in Chapter 7.

WHICH FORMAT?

Once you have reached the item-writing stage of test construction you will have to choose a format or combination of formats to use for your test. Although your choice can be somewhat arbitrary at times, this is not always the case. Often your decision has already been made for you, or more correctly, you may have at least partially made the decision when you wrote the objective or objectives. In many instances, however, you will have a choice among several item formats. For example, consider the following objectives and item formats:

OBJECTIVE 1: Given a story, the student can recognize the meaning of all new words.

TEST ITEM: Circle the letter that represents the correct meaning of the following words.

1. intention
   a. desire
   b. need
   c. direction
   d. command
2. crisis
   a. feeling
   b. message
   c. pending
   d. critical

OBJECTIVE 2: The student can associate the characteristics of leading characters with their names.

TEST ITEM: The first column below is a list of the names of the main characters in *Huckleberry Finn*. Descriptions of the main characters are listed in the second column. In the space provided, write the letter of the description that matches each character.

Characters

_____ 1. Tom
_____ 2. Becky
_____ 3. Jim
_____ 4. Huck
_____ 5. Mrs. Watson

Descriptions

a. Cruel
b. Always by himself, a loner
c. Popular, outgoing, fun-loving
d. Always critical
e. Sneaky, lying, scheming
f. Kind, gentle, loving
g. Dull, slow-moving

OBJECTIVE 3: The student can write a plausible alternative ending to a story.

TEST ITEM: You have just read the story *Huckleberry Finn*. In forty words, write a different ending to the story that would be believable.

OBJECTIVE 4: The student will recognize whether certain events occurred.

TEST ITEM: Below is a list of incidents in *Huckleberry Finn*. Circle T if it happened in the story and F if it did not.

1. The thieves were killed in the storm on the river.   T   F
2. Jim gained his freedom.   T   F
3. Tom broke his leg.   T   F

Objective 1 was measured using a multiple-choice format. We might also have tested this objective using a true-false or matching format. Similarly, objective 2 lends itself to a multiple-choice as well as a matching format. Since in many circumstances alternative item formats may be appropriate, the choice between them will be made on the basis of other considerations. For example, time constraints or your preference for, or skill in, writing different types of items will undoubtedly influence your choice of item format. However, objective 3 requires an essay item. There is no way this objective can be measured with an objective item. Similarly, objective 4 lends itself almost exclusively to a single format. Perhaps other formats would work, but the true-false format certainly does the job. In short, there are times our objectives tell us which format to use. At other times we must consider other factors. Now let's look more closely at the different item formats.

True-False Items

True-false items are popular probably because they are quick and easy to write, or at least they seem to be. Actually, true-false items do take less time to write than good objective items of any other format, but *good* true-false items are not all that easy to write. Consider the following true-false items. Use your common sense to help you determine which are good items and which are poor.

EXERCISE: Put a G in the space next to the items you believe are good true-false items and a P next to the items you feel are poor.

_____ 1. High-IQ children always get high grades in school.
_____ 2. Will Rogers said, "I never met a man I didn't like."
_____ 3. If a plane crashes on the Mexican-American border, half the survivors would be buried in Mexico and half in the United States.
_____ 4. The use of double negatives is not an altogether undesirable characteristic of diplomats and academicians.
_____ 5. Prayer should *not* be outlawed in the schools.
_____ 6. Of the objective items, true-false items are the least time-consuming to construct.
_____ 7. The trend toward competency testing of high-school graduates began in the late 1970s and represents a big step forward for slow learners.

Answers: **1.** P;   **2.** G;   **3.** P;   **4.** P;   **5.** P;   **6.** G;   **7.** P.

In item 1, the word *always* is an absolute. To some extent, true-false items depend on absolute judgments. However, statements or facts are seldom *completely* true or *completely* false. Thus, an alert student will usually answer "false" to items that include *always, all, never,* or *only.*

To avoid this problem, avoid using terms like *all, always, never,* or *only.* Item 1 could be improved by replacing *always* with a less absolute term, perhaps *tend.* Thus, item 1 might read:

High IQ children tend to get high grades in school.

Item 2 is a good one. To answer the item correctly, the student would have to know whether Will Rogers made the statement. Or does he? Consider the following situation:

Mrs. Allen, a history teacher and crusader against grade inflation, couldn't wait to spring her latest creation on her students. She had spent weeks inserting trick words, phrases, and complicated grammatical constructions into her hundred-item true-false test. In order to ensure low grades on the test, she allowed only thirty minutes for the test. Although her harried students worked as quickly as they could, no one completed more than half the items, and no one answered more than forty items correctly. No one, that is, except Tina. When Tina handed her test back to Mrs. Allen after two minutes, Mrs. Allen announced, "Class, Tina has handed in her test! Obviously, she hasn't read the questions and will earn a zero!" However, when she scored the test, Mrs. Allen was shocked to see that in fact Tina had answered fifty items correctly. She earned the highest score on the test without even reading Mrs. Allen's tricky questions. Confused and embarrassed, Mrs. Allen told the class they would have no more true-false tests and would have essay tests in the future.

This points to the most serious shortcoming of true-false items: With every true-false item, regardless of how well or poorly written, the student has a 50 percent chance of guessing correctly even without reading the item! In other words, on a fifty-item true-false test, we would expect individuals who were totally unfamiliar with the content being tested to answer about twenty-five items correctly. However, this doesn't mean you should avoid true-false items entirely, since they are appropriate at times. Fortunately, there are ways of reducing the effects of guessing. Some of these are described next and another will be presented in Chapter 8.

1. Encourage *all* students to guess when they do not know the correct answer. Since it is virtually impossible to prevent certain students from guessing, encouraging all students to guess should equalize the effects of guessing. The test scores will then reflect a more or less equal "guessing factor" *plus* the actual level of each student's knowledge. This will also prevent testwise students from having an unfair advantage over nontestwise students.
2. Require revision of statements that are false. With this approach, space is provided for students to alter false items to make them true. Usually the student also underlines or circles the false part of the item. Item 1 is revised below along with other examples.

T ⓕ   High-IQ children <u>always</u> get high grades in school. *tend to*
T ⓕ   Panama is <u>north</u> of Cuba. *south*
T ⓕ   <u>September</u> has an extra day during leap year. *February*

With such a strategy full credit is awarded only if the revision is correct. The disadvantage of such an approach is that more test time is required for the same number of items and scoring time is increased.

Item 3 is a poor item, but Mrs. Allen would probably like it because it is a trick question. "Survivors" of a plane crash are *not* buried! Chances are that you never even noticed the word *survivors* and probably assumed the item referred to fatalities. Trick items may have a place in tests of critical reading or visual discrimination (in which case they would no longer be trick questions), but seldom are they appropriate in the average classroom test. Rewritten, item 3 might read:

If a plane crashes on the Mexican-American border, half the fatalities would be buried in Mexico and half in the United States.

Item 4 is also poor. First of all, it includes a double negative—*not* and *undesirable*. Items with a single negative are confusing enough. Negating the first negative with a second wastes space and test-taking time and also confuses most students. If you want to say something, say it positively. The following revision makes this item slightly more palatable.

The use of double negatives is an altogether desirable trait of diplomats and academicians.

We said slightly more palatable because the item is still troublesome. The world *altogether* is an absolute, and we now know we should avoid absolutes, since there usually are exceptions to the rules they imply. Thus, when we eliminate *altogether* the item reads:

The use of double negatives is a desirable trait of diplomats and academicians.

However, the item is still flawed because it states an opinion, not a fact. Is the item true or false? The answer depends on whom you ask. To most of us, the use of double negatives is probably undesirable, for the reasons already stated. To some diplomats, the use of double negatives may seem highly desirable. In short, true-false statements should normally be used to measure knowledge of factual information. If you must use a true-false item to measure knowledge of an opinionated position or statement, state the referent (the person or group that made the statement or took the position) as illustrated in the following revision:

According to the National Institute of Diplomacy, the use of double negatives is a desirable trait of diplomats and academicians.

Item 5 further illustrates this point. It is deficient because it states an opinion. It is neither obviously true nor obviously false. The revision below includes a referent which makes it acceptable.

The American Civil Liberties Union (ACLU) has taken the position that prayer should *not* be outlawed in the schools.

Notice the word *not* in item 5. When you include a negative in a test item, highlight it in italics, underlining, or uppercase letters so the reader will not overlook it. Remember that, unlike Mrs. Allen, you intend to determine whether your students have mastered your objective, not to ensure low test scores.

Item 6 represents a good item. It measures factual information, and the phrase "Of the objective items" qualifies the item and limits it to a specific frame of reference.

The last item is deficient because it is double-barreled. It is actually two items in one. When do you mark *true* for a double-barreled item? When both parts of the item are true? When one part is true? Or only when the most important part is true? The point is that items should measure a single idea. Double-barreled items take too much time to read and comprehend. To avoid this problem, simply construct two items, as we have done here:

The trend toward competency testing of high-school graduates began in the late 1970s.

The trend toward competency testing represents a big step forward for slow learners.

Better? Yes. Acceptable? Not quite. The second item is opinionated. According to whom is this statement true or false? Let's include a referent.

According to the Office of Education, the trend toward competency testing of high-school graduates is a big step forward for slow learners.

Whose position is being represented is now clear, and the item is straightforward.

Suggestions for Writing True-False Items

1. The desired method of marking *true* or *false* should be clearly explained before students begin the test.
2. Construct statements that are definitely true or definitely false, without additional qualifications. If opinion is used, attribute it to some source.
3. Use relatively short statements and eliminate extraneous material.
4. Keep true and false statements at approximately the same length, and be sure that there are approximately equal numbers of true and false items.
5. Avoid using double-negative statements. They take extra time to decipher and are difficult to interpret.
6. Avoid the following:
   a. verbal clues, absolutes, and complex sentences
   b. broad general statements that are usually not true or false without further qualifications.
   c. terms denoting indefinite degree (for example, *large, long time, regularly*), or absolutes (for example, *never, only, always*)
   d. placing items in a systematic order (for example, TTFF, TFTF, and so on)
   e. taking statements directly from the text and presenting them out of context.

Matching Items

Like true-false items, matching items represent a popular and convenient testing format. Just like good true-false items, though, good matching items are not as easy to write as you might think. Imagine you are back in your tenth-grade American History class and the following matching item shows up on your test. Is it a good matching exercise or not? If not, what is wrong with it?

DIRECTIONS: Match A and B.

A	*B*
1. Lincoln	a. president during the twentieth century
2. Nixon	b. invented the telephone
3. Whitney	c. delivered the Emancipation Proclamation
4. Ford	d. only president to resign from office
5. Bell	e. black civil-rights leader
6. King	f. invented the cotton gin
7. Washington	g. our first president
8. Roosevelt	h. only president elected for more than two terms

See any problems? Compare those you have identified with the list of faults and explanations below.

Homogeneity.   The lists are *not* homogeneous. Column A contains names of presidents, inventors, and a civil-rights leader. Unless specifically taught as a set of related men or ideas, this represents too wide a variety for a matching exercise. To prevent this from happening you might title your lists (for example, "United States Presidents"). This will help keep irrelevant or filler items from creeping in. If you really want to measure student knowledge of presidents, inventors, and civil-rights leaders, then build *three separate* matching exercises. Doing so will prevent implausible options from being eliminated by the student. When students can eliminate implausible options they are more likely to guess correctly. For example, the student may not know who a black civil-rights leader was, but he may know that Washington, Lincoln, Ford, and Nixon were all presidents, and that none was black. Thus, he or she could eliminate these four as options, increasing the chance of guessing correctly from one out of eight to only one out of four.

Order of Lists.   The lists should be reversed, that is, column A should be column B, and column B should be column A. This is a consideration to save time for the test taker. We are trained to read from left to right. By placing the longer descriptions in the left column the student only reads the description once and glances down the list of names to find the answer. As the exercise is now written, the student reads a name and then has to read through all or many of the more lengthy descriptions to find the answer, a much more time-consuming process.

Easy Guessing.   There are equal numbers of options and descriptions in each column. Again, this increases the chances of guessing correctly through elimination. In the preceding exercise, if a student did not know who invented the cotton gin but knew which of the names went with the other seven descriptions, the student would arrive at the correct answer through elimination. If there are at least three more options than descriptions, the chances of guessing correctly in such a situation are reduced to one chance in four. Alternatively, the instructions for the exercise may be written to indicate that each option *may* be used more than once.

Poor Directions.

Speaking of directions, those included above are much too brief. Matching directions should specify the basis for matching, for example,

Column A contains brief descriptions of historical events. Column B contains the names of presidents. Indicate which man was president when the historical event took place by placing the appropriate letter to the left of the number in column A.

The directions also do not indicate *how* the matches should be shown. Should lines be drawn? Should letters be written next to numbers, or numbers next to letters? Failure to indicate how matches should be marked can greatly increase your scoring time.

Too Many Correct Responses.

The description "president during the twentieth century" has three defensible answers: Nixon, Ford, and Roosevelt. You say you meant Henry Ford, inventor of the Model T, not Gerald Ford! Well, that brings us to our final criticism of this matching exercise.

Ambiguous Lists.

The list of names is ambiguous. Franklin Roosevelt or Teddy Roosevelt? Henry Ford or Gerald Ford? When using names, always include first and last names to avoid such ambiguities.

Now that we have completed our analysis of this test item, we can easily conclude that it needs revision. Let's revise it, starting by breaking the exercise into homogeneous groupings.

DIRECTIONS: Column A describes events associated with United States presidents. Indicate which name in Column B matches each event by placing the appropriate letter to the left of the number of Column A. Each name may be used only once.

Column A

_____ **1.** Only president not elected to office.

_____ **2.** Delivered the Emancipation Proclamation.

_____ **3.** Only president to resign from office.

_____ **4.** Only president elected for more than two terms.

_____ **5.** Our first president.

Column B

a. Abraham Lincoln
b. Richard Nixon
c. Gerald Ford
d. George Washington
e. Franklin Roosevelt
f. Theodore Roosevelt
g. Thomas Jefferson
h. Woodrow Wilson

We can make one more clarification. It is a good idea to introduce some sort of order, chronological, numerical, or alphabetical, to your list of options. This saves the reader time. Students usually go through the list several times in answering a matching exercise, and it is easier to remember a name's or date's location in a list if it is in some sort of order. Thus, we can arrange the list of names in alphabetical order to look like this:

Column A

_____ 1. Only president not elected to office.

_____ 2. Delivered the Emancipation Proclamation.

_____ 3. Only president to resign from office.

_____ 4. Only president elected for more than two terms.

_____ 5. Our first president.

Column B

a. Gerald Ford
b. Thomas Jefferson
c. Abraham Lincoln
d. Richard Nixon
e. Franklin Roosevelt
f. Theodore Roosevelt
g. George Washington
h. Woodrow Wilson

Our original exercise contained two items relating to invention. If we were determined to measure only knowledge of inventors through a matching exercise, we would want to add at least one more item. Normally, at least three items are used for matching exercises. Such an exercise might look like the following:

DIRECTIONS: Column A lists famous inventions and Column B famous inventors. Match the inventor with the invention by placing the appropriate letter in the space to the left of the number in Column A. Each name may be used only once.

Column A

_____ 1. Invented the cotton gin.

_____ 2. One of his inventions was the telephone.

_____ 3. Famous for inventing the wireless.

Column B

a. Alexander Graham Bell
b. Henry Bessemer
c. Thomas Edison
d. Guglielmo Marconi
e. Eli Whitney
f. Orville Wright

Notice we have complete directions, there are three more options than descriptions, the lists are homogeneous, and the list of names is alphabetically ordered. But what about the final item remaining from our original exercise? Let's say we still want to determine whether our students know that Martin Luther King, Jr., was a black civil-rights leader. Obviously, we would construct another matching exercise with one column listing the names of black civil-rights leaders and another listing civil-rights accomplishments. However, an alternative would be simply to switch item formats. Usually, single items that are removed from matching exercises because of nonhomogeneity are easily converted into true-false, completion, or, with a little more difficulty, multiple-choice items. For example:

True-False
T   F   Martin Luther King, Jr., was a black civil-rights leader.

Completion
The name of the black civil-rights leader assassinated in 1968 was _____ .

Multiple-Choice
Which of the following was a black civil-rights leader?
a. George Washington Carver
b. Martin Luther King, Jr.
c. John Quincy Adams
d. John Wilkes Booth

Suggestions for Writing Matching Items

1. Keep both the list of descriptions and the list of options fairly short and homogeneous—they should both fit on the same page. Title the lists to ensure homogeneity, and arrange the descriptions and options in some logical order. If this is impossible you're probably including too wide a variety in the exercise. Try two or more exercises.
2. Make sure that all the options are plausible distractors for each description to ensure homogeneity of lists.
3. The list of descriptions should contain the longer phrases or statements, while the options should consist of short phrases, words or symbols.
4. Each description in the list should be numbered (each is an item), and the list of options should be identified by letter.
5. Include more options than descriptions. If the option list is longer than the description list, it is harder for students to eliminate options. If the option list is shorter, some options must be used more than once. Always include some options that do not match any of the descriptions, or some that match more than one, or both.
6. In the directions, specify the basis for matching and whether options can be used more than once.

Multiple-Choice Items

Another popular item format is the multiple-choice question. Practically everyone has taken multiple-choice tests at one time or another, but probably more often in high school and college than elementary school. This doesn't mean that multiple-choice items are not appropriate in the elementary years; it suggests only that one needs to be cautious about using them with younger children.

Multiple-choice items are unique among objective test items because they enable you to measure at the higher levels of the Taxonomy of Educational Objectives. Our discussion of multiple-choice items will be in two parts. The first part will consider the mechanics of multiple-choice item construction applied to knowledge-level questions. The second part will deal with the construction of higher-level multiple-choice items. As before, let's start by using common sense to identify good and poor multiple-choice items in the following exercise:

EXERCISE: Place a G next to a good item and a P next to a poor item.

_____ 1. U.S. Grant was an
   a. president
   b. man
   c. alcoholic
   d. general

_____ 2. In what year did man first set foot on the moon?
   a. 1975
   b. 1957
   c. 1969
   d. 1963

_____ 3. The free-floating structures within the cell that synthesize protein are called
   a. chromosomes.
   b. lysosomes.
   c. mitochondria.
   d. free ribosomes.

_____ 4. The principal value of a balanced diet is that it
   a. increases your intelligence.
   b. gives you something to talk about with friends.
   c. promotes mental health.
   d. promotes physical health.
   e. improves self-discipline.

_____ 5. Some test items
   a. are too difficult.
   b. are objective.
   c. are poorly constructed.
   d. have multiple defensible answers.

_____ 6. Which of the following are not associated with pneumonia?
   a. quiet breathing
   b. fever
   c. clear chest X ray
   d. a and c
   e. b and c

_____ 7. When fifty-three Americans were held hostage in Iran,
    a. the United States did nothing to try to free them.
    b. the United States declared war on Iran.
    c. the United States first attempted to free them by diplomatic means and later attempted a rescue.
    d. the United States expelled all Iranian students.

_____ 8. The square root of 256 is
    a. 14.
    b. 16.
    c. 4×4.
    d. both a and c
    e. both b and c
    f. all of the above
    g. none of the above

_____ 9. When a test item and the objective it is intended to measure match in learning outcome and conditions, the item
    a. is called an objective item.
    b. has content validity.
    c. is too easy.
    d. should be discarded.

Go over the exercise again. Chances are you'll find a few more problems the second time. Here's the answer key and a breakdown of the faults found in each item.

Answers: **1.**P; **2.**G; **3.**P; **4.**P; **5.**P; **6.**P; **7.**P; **8.**P; **9.**G.

Most students would probably pick up on the "grammatical clue" in the first item. The article "an" eliminates options a, b, and d immediately, since "U.S. Grant was an man," "an president," or "an general" are not grammatically correct statements. Thus, option c is the only option that forms a grammatically correct sentence. Inadvertently providing students with grammatical clues to the correct answer is very common in multiple-choice items. The result is decreased test validity. Students can answer items correctly because of knowledge of grammar, not content.

Replacing "an" with "a/an" would be one way to eliminate grammatical clues in your own writing. Other examples would be "is/are," "was/were," "his/her," and so on. As an alternative, the article, verb, or pronoun may be included in the list of options, as the following example illustrates:

Poor: Christopher Columbus came to America in a
a. car.
b. boat.
c. airplane.
d. balloon.

Better: Christopher Columbus came to America in
a. a car.
b. a boat.
c. an airplane.
d. a balloon.

Let's return to the first item again and replace "an" with "a/an":

U. S. Grant was a/an
a. president.
b. man.
c. alcoholic.
d. general.

There! We've removed the grammatical clue, and we now have an acceptable item, right? Not quite. We now have an item free of grammatical clues, but it is
still seriously deficient. What is the correct answer?

This item still has a serious flaw: multiple defensible answers. In fact, all
four options are defensible answers! U. S. Grant was a president, a man, a general,
and, as historians tell us, an alcoholic. Including such an item on a test would contribute nothing to your understanding of student knowledge. But what can you do
when you have an item with more than one defensible answer? The answer, of
course, is to eliminate the incorrect but defensible option or options.

Let's assume item 1 was written to measure the following objective:

The student will discriminate among the United States presidents immediately before, during, and immediately after the United States Civil War.

We could modify item 1 to look like this:

U. S. Grant was a
a. general.
b. slave.
c. pirate.
d. trader.

This item is fine, from a technical standpoint. The grammatical clue has
been eliminated and there is but one defensible answer. However, it does *not*
match the instructional objective; it is not very valuable as a measure of student
achievement of the objective. We could also modify the item to look like this:

Of the following, who was elected president after the Civil War?
a. U. S. Grant.
b. Andrew Johnson.
c. Abraham Lincoln.
d. Andrew Jackson.

This item is technically sound, and all response alternatives are relevant to the instructional objective. It meets the two main criteria for inclusion in a test: The item is technically well-constructed, and it matches the instructional objectives.

We said item 2 was good, but it can still stand some improvement. Remember when we recommended arranging lists for matching items in alphabetical or chronological order? The same holds true for multiple-choice items. To make a good item even better, arrange the options in chronological order. Revised, the item should look like this:

In what year did man first set foot on the moon?
a. 1957
b. 1963
c. 1969
d. 1975

The major deficiency in item 3 is referred to as a "stem clue." The statement portion of a multiple-choice item is called the *stem,* and the correct answer and incorrect choices are called *options* or *response alternatives.* A stem clue occurs when the same word or a close derivative occurs in both the stem and options, thereby clueing the test taker to the correct answer. In item 3 the word *free* in the option is identical to *free* in the stem. Thus, the wise test taker has a good chance of answering the item correctly without mastery of the content being measured. This fault can be eliminated by simply rewording the item without the word *free.*

The structures within the cell that synthesize protein are called
a. chromosomes.
b. lysosomes.
c. mitochondria.
d. ribosomes.

Item 4 is related to the "opinionated" items we considered when we discussed true-false items. Depending on the source, or referent, different answers may be the "right" answer. To person X, the principal value may be to promote physical health; to person Y, the principal value may be to improve self-discipline. As stated earlier, when you are measuring a viewpoint or opinion, be sure to state the referent or source. To be acceptable the item should be rewritten to include the name of an authority:

Dr. Ima Health feels the principal value of a balanced diet is that it
a. increases your intelligence.
b. gives you something to talk about.
c. promotes mental health.
d. promotes physical health.
e. improves self-discipline.

Item 5 is, of course, meaningless. It has at least two serious faults. To begin with, the stem fails to present a problem, and it fails to focus the item. What is the item getting at? The test taker has no idea what to look for in trying to discriminate among the options. The only way to approach such an item is to look at each option as an individual true-false item. This is very time-consuming and frustrating for the test taker. Be sure to focus your multiple-choice items by presenting a problem or situation in the stem.

Like item 1, item 5 also has more than one defensible answer. However, option d seems to control this problem. But if more than a single option is defensible, then how can you mark as incorrect someone who chooses a, b, or c and not d? Sometimes, however, you may wish to construct items that have two defensible answers. Is there any way to avoid the problem just mentioned? Fortunately, there is a way to avoid the problem, as illustrated in item 6:

Which of the following are not associated with pneumonia?
a. quiet breathing
b. fever
c. clear chest X ray
d. a and c
e. b and c

Where the possibility of more than one answer is desirable, use an option format like that just shown. This approach avoids the wording problems we ran into in the previous item. We would caution, however, that "a and b," "b and c," and so on should be used sparingly.

Now, how about the rest of item 6; is it okay? No, again a grammatical clue is present. The word *are* indicates a plural response is appropriate. Thus, options a, b, and c can automatically be eliminated, leaving the test taker with a 50 percent chance of guessing correctly. This fault can be corrected by using the same approach we used with item 1, where we substituted "a/an" for "an." Of course, in this instance we would substitute "is/are" for "are." Rewritten the item looks like this:

Which of the following is/are not associated with pneumonia?
a. quiet breathing
b. fever
c. clear chest X ray
d. a and c
e. b and c

All set? Not yet! Remember what we said about negatives? Let's highlight the "not" with uppercase letters, italics, or underlining to minimize the likelihood of someone misreading the item. After this revision we have an acceptable multiple-choice item.

Two very common faults in multiple-choice construction are illustrated by item 7. First, the phrase "the United States" is included in each option. To save space and time, add it to the stem. Second, the length of options could be a give-away. Multiple-choice item writers have a tendency to include more information in the correct option than in the incorrect options. Test-wise students take advantage of this tendency, since past experience tells them that longer options are more often than not the correct answer. Naturally, it is impossible to make all options exactly the same length, but try to avoid situations where correct answers are more than one and a half times the length of incorrect options. Eliminating the redundancies in the options and condensing the correct option, we have:

> When fifty-three Americans were held hostage in Iran, the United States
> a. did nothing to try to free them.
> b. declared war on Iran.
> c. undertook diplomatic and military efforts to free them.
> d. expelled all Iranian students.

Item 8 has some problems, too. First, let's consider the use of "all of the above" and "none of the above." In general, "none of the above" should be used sparingly. Some item writers tend to use "none of the above" only when there is no clearly correct option presented. However, students can quickly catch on to such a practice and guess that "none of the above" is the correct answer without knowledge of the content being measured.

As far as "all of the above" goes, we cannot think of *any* circumstances in which its use may be justified. Thus, our recommendation is to avoid this option entirely.

The use of "both a and c" and "both b and c" was already discussed in the relation to item 6. In that item, their use was appropriate and justifiable, but here it is questionable.

Again, let us see just what it takes to arrive at the correct choice, option e. Presumably, the item is intended to measure knowledge of square roots. However, the correct answer can be arrived at without considering square roots at all! A logical approach to this item, which would pay off with the right answer for someone who doesn't know the answer, might go something like this:

> Sure wish I'd studied the square-root table. Oh, well, there's more than one way to get to the root of the problem. Let's see, 14 might be right, 16 might be right, and 4×4 might be right. Hmmm, both a and c? No, that can't be it because I know that $4 \times 4 = 16$ and not 14. Well, both b and c have to be it! I know it's not "none of the above" because the teacher never uses "none of the above" as the right answer when she uses "both a and c" and "both b and c" as options.

Thus, when using "both a and c" and "both b and c," be on the alert for logical inconsistencies that can be used to eliminate options. Naturally, this problem can be minimized by using such options sparingly. Also try to monitor your item-construction patterns to make sure you're not overusing certain types of options.

Finally, we come to a good item. Item 9 is free of the flaws and faults we've pointed out in this section. There are a lot of things to consider when you write items, and keeping them all in mind will help you write better items. But it's virtually impossible for anyone to write good items *all* the time. So, when you've written a poor item, don't be too critical of yourself. Analyze it, revise or replace it, and learn from your mistakes.

Higher-Level Multiple-Choice Questions

Good multiple-choice items are the most time-consuming kind of objective test items to write. Unfortunately, most multiple-choice items are also written at the knowledge level of the taxonomy of educational objectives. As a new item writer (and, if you're not careful, as an experienced item writer) you will have a tendency to write items at this level. In this section we will provide you with suggestions for writing multiple-choice items to measure higher-level thinking.

The first step is to write at least some objectives that measure comprehension, application, analysis, synthesis, or evaluation to ensure that your items will be at the higher-than-knowledge level—*if your items match your objectives!* The following objectives measure at the knowledge level:

The student will name, from memory, the first three presidents of the United States by next Friday.

Given a color chart, the students will identify each of the primary colors.

Objectives such as these will generate multiple-choice items that will measure only memorization. We are not saying you should not measure at this level—only that you may have a tendency to do so too often. By contrast, the following objectives measure at higher than the knowledge level:

Given a copy of the president's state of the union address, the student will be able to identify one example of a simile and one of a metaphor.

The student will be able to solve correctly three-digit addition problems without regrouping.

With objectives such as these, higher-level multiple-choice items would have to be constructed to match the objectives. Some suggestions for other approaches to measuring at higher than the knowledge level follow.

Use Pictorial, Graphical, or Tabular Stimuli.   Pictures, drawings, graphs, tables, and so on minimally require the student to think at the application level of the taxonomy of educational objectives and may involve even higher levels of cognitive processes. Also, the use of such stimuli can often generate several higher-level multiple-choice items rather than a single higher-level multiple-choice item, as Figure 6.1 illustrates.

Other items based on the map in Figure 6.1 could be:

FIGURE 6.1 | Use of Pictorial Stimulus to Measure High-Level Cognitive Processes

In the following questions you are asked to make inferences from the data which are given you on the map of the imaginary country, Serendip. The answers in most instances must be probabilities rather than certainties. The relative size of towns and cities is not shown. To assist you in the location of the places mentioned in the questions, the map is divided into squares lettered vertically from A to E and numbered horizontally from 1 to 5.

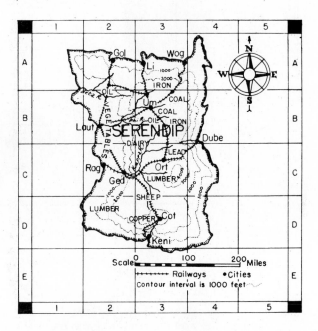

Which of the following cities would be the best location for a steel mill?

(A) Li	(3A)
(B) Um	(3B)
(C) Cot	(3D)
(D) Dube	(4B)

1. Approximately how many miles is it from Dube to Rag?
   a. 100 miles
   b. 150 miles
   c. 200 miles
   d. 250 miles

2. In what direction would someone have to travel to get from Wog to Um?
   a. northwest
   b. northeast
   c. southwest
   d. southeast

A variation on this same theme is to include several pictorial stimuli to represent options and build several stems around them. The following items would be appropriate for a plane geometry class:

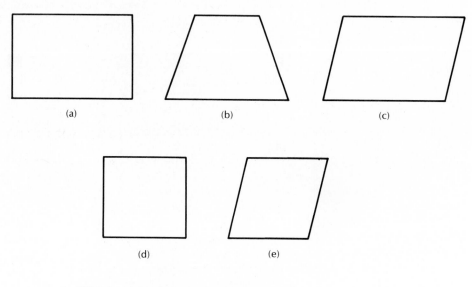

_____ 1. Which of the figures is a rhombus?
_____ 2. Which of the figures is a parallelogram?
_____ 3. Which of the figures is a trapezoid?

Naturally, it would be important to include several more stimulus pictures than items to minimize guessing.

Use Analogies That Demonstrate Relationships among Terms.

To answer analogies correctly students must not only be familiar with the terms, but be able to *understand* how the terms relate to each other, as the following examples show:

1. Man is to woman as boy is to
   a. father
   b. mother
   c. girl
   d. boy
2. Physician is to humans as veterinarian is to
   a. fruits
   b. animals
   c. minerals
   d. vegetables

Require the Application of Previously Learned Principles or Procedures to Novel Situations. To test whether students really comprehend the implications of a procedure or principle, have the students use the principle or procedure with new information or in a novel way. This requires that the student do more than simply "follow the steps" in solving a problem. It asks the student to demonstrate an ability to go beyond the confines within which a principle or procedure was originally learned.

1. In class we discussed at length Darwin's notion of the "survival of the fittest" within the animal world. Which of the following best describes how this principle applies to the current competitive, residential construction industry?
   a. Those builders in existence today are those who have formed alliances with powerful financial institutions.
   b. Only those builders that emphasize matching their homes to the changing structure of the family will survive in the future.
   c. The intense competition for a limited number of qualified home buyers will eventually "weed out" poorly managed construction firms.
   d. Only those home builders who construct the strongest and most durable homes will survive in the long term.

2. (Follows a lesson on division which relied on computation of grade-point averages as examples.)
   After filling up his tank with 18 gallons of gasoline, Mr. Watts said to his son "We've come 450 miles since the last fill-up, what kind of gas mileage are we getting?" Which of the following is the best answer?
   a. 4 miles per gallon
   b. 25 miles per gallon
   c. between 30 and 35 miles per gallon
   d. It can't be determined from the information given.

These examples are intended to stimulate your creativity—they are by no means exhaustive of the many approaches to measuring higher-level cognitive skills with multiple-choice items. Rather than limit yourself to pictorial items and analogies, use them where appropriate and also develop your own approaches. Remember the main point: be sure your items match your objectives. Do not write higher-level items if your objectives are at the knowledge level. Doing so will impair your test's content validity.

Suggestions for Writing Multiple-Choice Items

1. The stem of the item should clearly formulate a problem. Include as much of the item as possible, keeping the response options as short as possible. However, include only the material needed to make the problem clear and specific. Be concise—don't add extraneous information.

2. Be sure that there is one and only one correct or clearly best answer.

3. Be sure wrong answer choices (distractors) are plausible. Eliminate unintentional grammatical clues, and keep the length and form of all the answer choices equal. Rotate the position of the correct answer from item to item randomly.

4. Use negative questions or statements only if the knowledge being tested requires it. In most cases it is more important for the student to know what a specific item of information *is* rather than what it is not.

5. Include from three to five options (two to four distractors plus one correct answer) to optimize testing for knowledge rather than encouraging guessing. It is not necessary to provide additional distractors for an item simply to maintain the same number of distractors for each item. This usually leads to poorly constructed distractors that add nothing to test validity and reliability.

6. To increase the difficulty of a multiple-choice item, increase the similarity of content among the options.

7. Use the option "none of the above" sparingly and only when the keyed answer can be classified unequivocally as right or wrong. Don't use this option when asking for a best answer.

8. Avoid using "all of the above." It is usually the correct answer and makes the item too easy for students with partial information.

Thus far, we have considered true-false, matching, and multiple-choice items. We have called these items *objective* items, but they are also referred to as *recognition* items. They are recognition items because the test taker needs only to "recognize" the correct answer. Contrast this with "recall" or "supply" formats such as essays and completion items. With essays and completion items it is much more difficult to guess the right answer than with true-false, matching, or multiple-choice items.

Nevertheless, we will classify completion items with true-false, matching, and multiple-choice items. We call items written in these formats *objective items* because of the way they are scored, which tends to be fairly straightforward and reliable. This is in contrast to essays, which we will call *subjective,* because of their somewhat less reliable scoring, which is considerably more prone to bias.

Completion Items

Like true-false items, completion items are relatively easy to write. Perhaps the first tests classroom teachers construct and students take are completion tests. Like items of all other formats, though, there are good and poor completion items. Work through the following exercise, again relying on your common sense to identify good and poor items. After having worked through the three previous exercises, you are probably now adept at recognizing common item-writing flaws.

EXERCISE: Put a G in the space next to the items you feel are good, and a P next to the items you feel are poor.

_____ 1. The evolutionary theory of [Darwin] is based on the principle of [survival of the fittest].

_____ 2. Columbus discovered America in [1492].

_____ 3. The capital of Mexico is [Mexico City].

_____ 4. In what year did Gerald Ford become president of the United States? [1973]

_____ 5. [Too many] blanks cause much frustration in [both test takers and test scorers].

_____ 6. [Armstrong] was the first American to [walk on the moon].

Answers: **1.** P;   **2.** P;   **3.** P;   **4.** G;   **5.** P;   **6.** P.

The first item probably reminds you of many you have seen. It is a good rule of thumb to avoid using more than one blank per item. The item writer had a specific evolutionary theorist in mind when writing this item, but the final form of the item is not at all focused toward one, single theorist. Thus, there are a variety of possible *correct* answers to this item. Not only are such items disturbing and confusing to test takers, they are very time-consuming and frustrating to score. An acceptable revision might look like this:

The evolutionary theory of Darwin is based on the principle of [survival of the fittest].

If you marked item 2 with a G, you were probably in the majority. This is a standard type of completion item that is frequently used. It is also the kind of item that can generate student-teacher conflict. Granted, "1492" is probably the answer most students who studied their lesson would write. But how would you score a response like "a boat," or, "the fifteenth century," or "a search for India?" These may not be the answers you wanted, but they are correct answers.

This illustrates the major disadvantage of completion items and gives you some idea on a much smaller scale of the kinds of difficulties encountered in scoring essay items as well. Unless you take pains to be *very* specific when you word completion items, you will come across similar situations frequently. In general, it's better to be very specific in writing completion items. Item 2 could be made specific by adding the words "the year," as illustrated here:

Columbus discovered America in the year [1492].

In this form the item leaves little to be interpreted subjectively by the student. The test taker doesn't spend time thinking about what the question is "really" asking, and the test-scorer doesn't spend time trying to decide how to score a variety of different, but correct, answers. For once everybody's happy.

Item 3 is a similar case. Consider the following dialogue as heard by one of the authors in a teachers' lounge at an elementary school:

MISS RIGIDITY: (*to no one in particular*) Smart-aleck kids nowadays! Ask them a simple question and you get a smart-aleck answer. Kids today don't give you any respect.

MISS FEELINGS: I hear some frustration in what you're saying. Anything I can do?

MISS RIGIDITY: No, there's nothing you can do but listen to this. On the last test one of the questions was "The largest city in Puerto Rico is _____." Simple enough, right? Well, not for Sally! Instead of answering "San Juan," she answered "the capital city." Smart-aleck kid. We'll see how smart she feels when she gets no credit for that ridiculous answer.

MISS FEELINGS: What I hear you saying is that you feel Sally may not have known that San Juan is the largest city in Puerto Rico.

MISS RIGIDITY: Of course she doesn't know, otherwise she would have given the correct answer. That's the whole point!

AUTHOR: (*never known for his tactfulness*) She *did* give a correct answer. Your question wasn't specific enough.

MISS RIGIDITY: I've been using this same test for years and there are always one or two kids who give me the same answer Sally did! And, they are always kids who lack respect!

AUTHOR: How do you know they lack respect?

MISS RIGIDITY: Because they always argue with me when they get their tests back. In fact, they say the same thing you did! You're as bad as they are!

MISS FEELINGS: I'm hearing some frustration from both of you. . . .

How could this have been avoided? Let's look at Miss Rigidity's item again.

The largest city in Puerto Rico is _____.

Since San Juan *is* the largest city in Puerto Rico and *is* the capital city of Puerto Rico as well, then "the largest city in Puerto Rico is the capital city." There are at least two defensible answers. Just as in true-false, matching, and multiple-choice items, we should strive to avoid multiple defensible answers in completion items. But how can this be avoided? Again, be specific. Made more specific, Miss Rigidity's item looks like this:

The name of the largest city in Puerto Rico is [San Juan].

Of course, you could have students who carry things to an extreme. For example, some might claim the following is a defensible answer:

The name of the largest city in Puerto Rico is [familiar to many people].

Thus, only you, as the classroom teacher, can determine which answers are defensible and which are not. Your job will be to determine which responses are logical derivations of your test item and which responses are creative attempts to cover up for lack of mastery of content. Keep an open mind and good luck! Don't be like Miss Rigidity!

We can clean up item 3 in much the same fashion as we did Miss Rigidity's item. Revised in this way, item 3 looks like this:

The name of the capital city of Mexico is [Mexico City].

Adding "name of the" to the original item minimizes your chances of students responding that the capital of Mexico is "a city," "very pretty," "huge," "near central Mexico," and so forth.

Item 4 is an example of a well-written completion item. It is specific, and it would be difficult to think of defensible answers other than "1973."

Both the fifth and sixth items illustrate a case of having too many blanks, which prevent the item from taking on any single theme. Blanks are contagious—avoid using more than one.

Suggestions for Writing Completion or Supply Items

1. If at all possible, items should require a single-word answer, or a brief and definite statement. Avoid statements that are so indefinite that they may be logically answered by several terms.
   Poor item: World War II ended in _____ .
   Better item: World War II ended in the year _____ .
2. Be sure the question or statement poses a problem to the examinee. A direct question is often more desirable than an incomplete statement (it provides more structure).
3. Be sure the answer that the student is required to produce is factually correct. Be sure the language used in the question is precise and accurate in relation to the subject matter area being tested.
4. Omit only key words; don't eliminate so many elements that the sense of the content is impaired.
   Poor item: The _____ type of test item is usually more _____ than the _____ type.
   Better item: The supply type of test item is usually graded more objectively than the _____ type.
5. Word the statement such that the blank is near the end of the sentence rather than near the beginning. This will prevent awkward sentences.
6. If the problem requires a numerical answer, indicate the units in which it is to be expressed.

You've now used common sense and an increased level of "test-wiseness" to analyze and think about different types of objective test items. In Chapter 7 we will extend our discussion to essay items. Before we move on to essays, however, let's consider one more topic related to item-writing, one that applies equally to objective and essay items. This topic is sexual and racial bias in test items.

SEXUAL AND RACIAL BIAS IN TEST ITEMS

An important but often overlooked aspect of item writing involves sexual or racial bias. Over the last several years many have become increasingly aware of, and sensitive to, such issues. Professional item writers take great care to eliminate or minimize the extent to which such biases are present in their test items. The classroom teacher would be wise to follow their lead.

One example of sexual bias is the exclusive use of the male pronoun *he* in test items. Since the item writer may use it unconsciously, it does not necessarily follow that the item writer has a sexist attitude. However, this does not prevent the practice from offending a proportion of the population. Similarly, referring exclusively in our items only to members of a single ethnic group will likely be offensive to individuals of different ethnicity. Again, such a practice may be almost unconscious and not reflect a racist attitude, but this will not prevent others from taking offense to it.

To avoid such bias, you should carefully balance your references in items. That is, always check your items to be sure that fairly equal numbers of references to males and females are made. Obviously, equal care and time should be devoted to ensure that ethnic groups are appropriately represented in your items. Such considerations are especially relevant when items are being written at higher than the knowledge level. Since such items often are word problems involving people, sexual and racial bias can easily creep in. The checklist in Chapter 8 will help remind you to be on the watch for such bias.

Remember, our goal is to measure learning in as valid and reliable a fashion as possible. When emotions are stimulated by sexually or racially biased items, these emotions can interfere with valid measurement, leaving us with results that are less useful than they would be otherwise. Given all the care and time we have taken to learn to develop good tests, it makes good sense to take just a bit more to avoid racial and sexual bias in our items.

In this chapter we have provided you with a good deal of information related to item-writing. Much of this information is condensed in the summary and some general guidelines for item-writing are also included. Following these guidelines you will find a summary of the advantages and disadvantages of various item formats. This section should help you make decisions about the type of format to use for your test items. Remember, you will write poor items until the recommendations we have provided become second nature, which comes only with practice.

GUIDELINES FOR WRITING TEST ITEMS

1. Begin writing items far enough in advance that you will have time to revise them.
2. Match items to intended outcomes at the proper difficulty level to provide a valid measure of instructional objectives. Limit the question to the skill being assessed.
3. Be sure each item deals with an important aspect of the content area and not with trivia.
4. Be sure that the problem posed is clear and unambiguous.
5. Be sure that each item is independent of all other items. The answer to one item should not be required as a condition for answering the next item, nor should a hint to one answer be unintentionally embedded in another item.
6. Be sure the item has one correct or best answer on which experts would agree.
7. Prevent unintended clues to the answer in the statement or question. Grammatical inconsistencies such as "a," or "an" give clues to the correct answer to those students who are not well prepared for the test.
8. Avoid replication of the textbook in writing test items; don't quote directly from textual materials. You're usually not interested in how well the student memorized the text. Besides, taken out of context, direct quotes from the text are often ambiguous.
9. Avoid trick or catch questions in an achievement test. Don't waste time testing how well the students can interpret your intentions.
10. Try to write items that require higher-level thinking.

ADVANTAGES AND DISADVANTAGES OF DIFFERENT OBJECTIVE-ITEM FORMATS

True-False Tests

Advantages

Because T-F questions tend to be short, more material can be covered than with any other item format. Thus, T-F items tend to be used when a great deal of content has been covered.

T-F questions take less time to construct. But avoid taking statements directly from the text and modifying them slightly to create an item.

Scoring is easier with T-F questions. But avoid having students write "true" or "false" or "T" or "F." Instead have them circle "T" or "F" provided for each item.

Disadvantages

T-F questions tend to emphasize rote memorization of knowledge, although sometimes complex questions *can* be asked using T-F items.

T-F questions presume that the answer to the question or issue is unequivocally true or false. It would be unfair to ask the student to guess at the teacher's criteria for evaluating the truth of a statement.

T-F questions allow for and sometimes encourage a high degree of guessing. Generally longer examinations are needed to compensate for this.

Matching Tests

Advantages

Matching questions are usually simple to construct and to score.

Matching items are ideally suited to measure associations between facts.

Matching questions can be more efficient than multiple-choice questions because they avoid repetition of options in measuring associations.

Matching questions reduce the effects of guessing.

Disadvantages

Matching questions sometimes tend to ask students *trivial* information.

They emphasize memorization.

Most commercial answer sheets can accommodate no more than five options, thus limiting the size of any particular matching item.

Multiple-Choice Tests

Advantages

Multiple-choice questions have considerable versatility in measuring objectives from the knowledge to the evaluation level.

Since writing is minimized, a substantial amount of course material can be sampled in a relatively short time.

Scoring is highly objective, requiring only a count of the number of correct responses.

Multiple-choice items can be written so that students must discriminate among options that vary in degree of correctness. This allows students to select the best alternative and avoids the absolute judgments found in T-F tests.

Since there are multiple options, effects of guessing are reduced.

Multiple-choice items are amenable to item analysis (see Chapter 8), which permits a determination of which items are ambiguous or too difficult.

Disadvantages

Multiple-choice questions can be time consuming to write.

If not carefully written, multiple-choice questions can sometimes have more than one defensible correct answer.

Completion Tests

Advantages

Construction of a completion question is relatively easy.

Guessing is eliminated since the question requires recall.

Completion questions take less time to complete than multiple-choice items, so greater amounts of content can be covered.

Disadvantages

Completion questions usually encourage a relatively low level of response complexity.

The responses can be difficult to score since the stem must be general enough so as to not communicate the correct answer. This can lead unintentionally to more than one defensible answer.

The restriction of an answer to a few words tends to measure the recall of specific facts, names, places, and events as opposed to more complex behaviors.

｜SUMMARY

This chapter introduced you to four types of objective test items: true-false, matching, multiple-choice, and completion. The major points were:

1. Choice of item format is sometimes determined by your instructional objectives. At other times the advantages and disadvantages of the different formats should influence your choice.
2. True-false items require less time to construct than other objective items, but they are most prone to guessing, as well as a variety of other faults. These include absolutes in wording, double negatives, opinionated and double-barreled statements, excessive wordiness, and a tendency to reflect statements taken verbatim from readings.
3. Matching items are fairly easy to construct but tend to be subject to the following faults: lack of clarity and specificity in directions, dissimilar and non-ordered lists, and reversal of options and descriptions.
4. Multiple-choice items are the most difficult of the objective items to construct. However, higher-order multiple-choice items lend themselves well to measuring higher-level thinking skills. They are subject to several faults including grammatical cues or specific determiners, multiple defensible answers, unordered option lists, stem clues, opinionated statements, failure to state a problem in the stem, redundant wording, wordiness in the correct option, use of "all of the above," and indiscriminate use of "none of the above."
5. Completion items rival true-false items in ease of construction. Since answers must be supplied, they are least subject to guessing. On the other hand, they require more scoring time than other objective formats. Common faults include too many blanks, lack of specificity (too many responses), and failure to state a problem.
6. To avoid sexual and/or racial biases in test items, avoid using stereotypes and be sure to make equal reference to both males and females and to various ethnic groups.

For Practice

1. Write a behavioral objective in some area with which you are familiar. Using this objective as your guide, write a test item using each of the four test item formats (true-false, matching, multiple choice, and completion) discussed in this chapter.

2. Exchange your test items with a classmate. Have him or her check the appropriateness of each of your items for a match with the appropriate objective and against the criteria and guidelines given in this chapter for each test item format. List and correct any deficiencies.

*3. Each of the following items is defective in some way(s). Identify the principal fault or faults in each item and rewrite the item so that it is fault-free.

   a. "The Time Machine" is considered to be a
      a. adventure story
      b. science fiction story
      c. historical novel
      d. autobiography

   b. Thaddeus Kosciusko and Casimer Pulaski were heroes in the Revolutionary War. What was their country of origin?
      a. Great Britain
      b. Poland
      c. France
      d. Italy

   c. The use of force to attain political goals is never justifiable. (true or false)

   d. The microcomputer was invented in _____.

   e. _____ spent his life trying to demonstrate that _____ .

   f. _____ 1. discovered Zambezi River   a. Webb
      _____ 2. first female governor   b. Armstrong
      _____ 3. invented the cotton gin   c. Minuit
      _____ 4. first to swim the English   d. Livingstone
                      Channel   e. Whitney
      _____ 5. purchased Manhattan   f. Edison
                      Island   g. Cortez
      _____ 6. first to walk on the moon   h. Keller
                                                   i. Rhodes

*Answers for question 3 appear in Appendix D.

7

WRITING ESSAY TEST ITEMS

9:00 A.M., Tuesday, October 20

"I can't believe it! I just *can't* believe it!" Donna thought to herself. "How can he do this to us?" Donna was becoming more and more upset by the second, as were many of the other students in Mr. Smith's government class. They were taking the midterm exam, on which 50 percent of their grade would be based. Before the exam, the students spent two classes discussing this issue. All other classes that semester dealt with a rather mechanical review of the federal government. The exam consisted of a single essay item: Why should presidents be limited or not be limited to two consecutive terms in office? (100 points).

|D| oes this ring a bell? Test questions that do not reflect classroom emphases can frustrate test takers. "How could he do it?" Well, there are probably several answers to this question, and we could only speculate about the reasons for Mr. Smith's question. Just as we could generate a variety of explanations for Mr. Smith's test item, students could generate a variety of answers to his question! Let's look at his question again.

Why should presidents be limited or not be limited to two consecutive terms in office? (100 points)

What answer is he looking for? Again, only Mr. Smith knows for sure. "Come on," some of you may say. "He's not looking for any specific answer—he wants you to take a position and defend it, to test your knowledge and writing ability, that's all!" Well, if that's the case, why didn't he phrase the test item something like this:

In class and in your assigned readings, arguments both for and against giving presidents the opportunity to complete more than two consecutive terms in office were presented. Take a stand either for or against two consecutive terms in office. Use at least three points made in class or in your readings to support your position. Both the content and organization of your argument will be considered in assigning your final grade. Use no more than one page for your answer. (28 points)

This item *focuses* the task for the student—he or she has a clearer idea of what is expected, and, therefore, how he or she will be evaluated. Remember, your goal is not to see whether students can guess correctly what you are expecting as an answer. Your goal is to assess learning—to determine whether your instructional objectives have been met.

In the remainder of this chapter we will discuss various aspects of essay-item construction. While this will go far in helping you avoid writing deficient essay items, we will also discuss several other equally important issues related to essay items. We will begin with a general discussion of what an essay item is, describe the two major types of essay items and their relationships to instructional objectives, identify the major advantages and disadvantages of essay items, provide you with suggestions for writing essay items, and discuss various approaches to scoring essays. With this comprehensive treatment, we hope to increase your awareness of the complexities of essay items and thereby minimize the likelihood of poorly constructed, ambiguous essay items.

WHAT IS AN ESSAY ITEM?

An essay item is one for which the student supplies, rather than selects, the correct answer. It demands that the student compose a response, often extensive, to a question for which no *single* response or pattern of responses can be cited as correct to the exclusion of all other answers. The accuracy and quality of such a response can often be judged only by a person skilled and informed in the subject area being tested.

Like objective test items, essay items may be well constructed or poorly constructed. The well-constructed essay item aims to test complex cognitive skills by requiring the student to organize, integrate, and synthesize knowledge, to use information to solve novel problems, or to be original and innovative in problem solving. The poorly constructed essay item may require the student to do no more than recall information as it was presented in the textbook or lecture. Worse, the poorly constructed essay may not even let the student know what is required for a satisfactory response.

The potential of the essay item as an evaluation device depends not only upon writing appropriate questions that elicit complex cognitive skills, but also upon being able to structure the situation so that other factors do not obscure the intent of the item. Differences in knowledge of factual material are often hidden by differences in ability to use and organize those facts. The time pressures of a test situation can cause students to demonstrate less than optimum communication skills. The way the item is constructed determines to a large extent the types of learning outcomes being tested. Consider the following two essay items:

Question 1. What methods have been used in the United States to prevent industrial accidents?

What learning outcomes are being tested? To provide an acceptable answer, a student need only recall information. The item is at the knowledge level; no higher level mental processes are tapped. It would be easy and much less time-consuming to score a series of objective items covering this same topic. This is *not* abuse of the essay item, but it is a misuse. Now consider the question.

Question 2. Examine the data provided in the table on causes of accidents. Explain how the introduction of occupational health and safety standards in the United States account for changes in the number of industrial accidents shown in the table.

Causes of Accidents and Rate for Each in 1960 and 1980

Cause of Accident	Accident Rate per 100,000 Employees 1960	1980
1. Defective equipment	135.1	16.7
2. Failure to use safety-related equipment	222.8	36.1
3. Failure to heed instructions	422.1	128.6
4. Improperly trained for job	598.7	26.4
5. Medical or health-related impairment	41.0	13.5

This question requires that the student recall something about the occupational health and safety standards. Then, the student must relate these standards to such things as occupational training programs, plant safety inspections, the display of warning or danger signs, equipment manufacturing, codes related to safety, and so forth, which may have been incorporated in industrial settings between 1960 and 1980.

In short, the student must use higher-level mental processes to answer this question successfully. The student must be able to analyze, infer, organize, apply, and so on. No objective item or series of items would suffice. This is an *appropriate* use of the essay item. However, not all essays are alike. We will consider two types of essay items: extended-response and restricted-response items.

Extended Response Items

An essay item that allows the student to determine the length and complexity of response is called an *extended-response essay item.* This type of essay is most useful at the synthesis or evaluation levels of the cognitive taxonomy. Because of the length of this type of item and the time required in organizing and expressing the response, the extended response item is sometimes better as a term paper assignment or a take-home test. The extended response item is often of value more in assessing communication ability than in assessing achievement.

Example: Compare and contrast the presidential administrations of Carter and Reagan. Consider economic, social, and military policies. Avoid taking a position in support of either president. Your response will be graded on objectivity, accuracy, organization, and clarity.

Restricted-Response Items

An essay item that poses a specific problem for which the student must recall proper information, organize it in a suitable manner, derive a defensible conclusion, and express it within the limits of the posed problem is called a *restricted-response essay item.* The statement of the problem specifies response limitations that guide the student in responding and provide evaluation criteria for scoring.

Example: List the major similarities and differences between U.S. participation in the Korean War and World War II, being sure to consider political, military, economic and social factors. Limit your answer to one page. Your score will depend on accuracy, organization, and brevity.

ESSAY ITEMS AND INSTRUCTIONAL OBJECTIVES

Essays may be used to measure general or specific outcomes of instruction. The restricted-response item is most likely to be used to assess knowledge, comprehension, and application types of learning outcomes.

EXAMPLE: The Learning to Like It Company is proposing a profit-sharing plan for its employees. For each 1-percent increase in production compared to the average production figures over the last ten years, workers will get a 1-percent increase in pay.

1. List the advantages and disadvantages to the workers of such a profit-sharing plan.
2. List the advantages and disadvantages to the corporation of such a profit-sharing plan.

Multiple-choice items may also be effectively used for these learning outcomes, except when recall of information rather than recognition is desired. Restricted-response items may also be used for instructional objectives requiring students to be able to apply data to hypothesizing, to stating testable hypotheses, or to formulating conclusions.

To assess the ability to evaluate, to organize, and to select viewpoints, an extended response essay is more appropriate.

EXAMPLE: Describe the two views of the creation of the universe that your text describes. Select the view you think is most probable and defend your selection. Be sure to discriminate between fact and opinion in your defense. *Evaluation*

The following are some of the learning outcomes for which essay items may be put to use:

Analyze relationships
Arrange items in sequence
Compare positions
State necessary assumptions
Identify appropriate conclusions
Explain cause-and-effect relations
Formulate hypotheses
Organize data to support a viewpoint
Point out strengths and weaknesses
Produce a solution for a problem
Integrate data from several sources
Evaluate the quality or worth of an item, product, or action
Create an original solution, arrangement, or procedure

Thus far we've discussed essay items in terms of appropriateness, specificity, range of response, and relationship to instructional objectives. These are all important to the appropriate use of essay tests, but now we must also consider specifics—the nuts and bolts of essay-item construction.

The next section provides generally accepted suggestions for essay-item construction and use, followed by examples of poorly written and well-written essay items. If it seems as though we are spending a lot of time dealing with what you may have thought was a simple topic, you're right. Our reasons for doing so are two-fold. First, essay item writing is not simple or easy. It is a higher-level cognitive skill. As with all higher-level skills, it requires awareness of issues and knowledge of specifics, as well as lots of practice for mastery. Second, there is probably no other item type that is misused or abused as often as the essay item.

SUGGESTIONS FOR WRITING AND USING ESSAY ITEMS

1. Have clearly in mind what mental processes you want the student to use before starting to write the question. Refer to the processes described in Chapter 5 about the taxonomy of educational objectives for the cognitive domain. If you want students to analyze, judge, or think critically, what mental processes involve analysis, judgment, or critical thinking? Once you've determined this, use the appropriate verbs in your question.
   Poor Item: Criticize the following speech by our president.
   Better Item: Consider the following presidential speech. Focus on the section dealing with economic policy and discriminate between factual statements and opinions. List these statements separately, label them, and indicate whether each statement is or is not consistent with the president's overall economic policy.

2. Write the question in such a way that the task is clearly and unambiguously defined for the student. Tasks should be explained (1) in the overall instructions preceding the test items and/or (2) in the test items themselves. Include instructions for the type of writing style desired (for example, scientific vs. prose), whether spelling and grammar will be counted, and whether organization of the response will be an important scoring element. Also, indicate the level of detail and supporting data required.
   Poor Item: Discuss the value of behavioral objectives.
   Better Item: Behavioral objectives have enjoyed increased popularity in education over the past several years. In your text and in class the advantages and disadvantages of behavioral objectives have been discussed. Take a position for or against the use of behavioral objectives in education and support your position with at least three of the arguments covered in class or in the text.
   Poor Item: What were the forces that led to the outbreak of the Civil War?
   Better Item: Compare and contrast the positions of the North and South at the outbreak of the Civil War. Include in your discussion economic conditions, foreign policies, political sentiments, and social conditions.

3. Start essay questions with such words or phrases as *compare, contrast, give reasons for, give original examples of, predict what would happen if,* and so on. Don't begin with such words as *what, who, when,* and *list,* since these words generally lead to tasks that require only recall of information.
   Poor Item: List three reasons behind America's withdrawal from Vietnam.
   Better Item: After more than ten years of involvement, the United States withdrew from Vietnam in 1975. Predict what would have happened if America had *not* withdrawn at that time and had *not* increased significantly its military presence above 1972 levels.

4. A question dealing with a controversial issue should ask for and be evaluated in terms of the presentation of evidence for a position, rather than the posi-

tion taken. It is not defensible to demand that a student accept a specific conclusion or solution, but it is reasonable to appraise how well he or she has learned to utilize the evidence upon which a specific conclusion is based.

Poor Item: What laws should Congress pass to improve the medical care of all citizens in the United States?

Better Item: Some feel that the cost of all medical care should be borne by the federal government. Do you agree or disagree? Support your position with at least three logical arguments.

5. Avoid using optional items. That is, require all students to complete the same items. Allowing students to select 3 of 5, 4 of 7, and so forth decreases test validity, as well as decreases your basis for comparison among students.

6. Establish reasonable time and/or page limits for each essay item to help the student complete the entire test and to give indications of the level of detail you have in mind for each item. Indicate such time limits either within the statement of the problem or close to the number of the question.

7. Restrict the use of essays to those learning outcomes that cannot be satisfactorily measured by objective items.

8. Be sure each question relates to an instructional objective.

Not all of the above suggestions may be relevant for each item you write. However, the suggestions are worth going over even *after* you've written items, as a means of checking and, when necessary, modifying your items. With time you will get better and more efficient at writing essay items.

WHY USE ESSAY ITEMS?

We've already mentioned some of the benefits of using essay items, and the following list summarizes the advantages of essay over objective items.

Advantages of the Essay Item

Most Effective in Assessing Complex Learning Outcomes.
To the extent that instructional objectives require the student to organize information constructively to solve a problem, analyze and evaluate information, or perform other high-level cognitive skills, the essay test is an appropriate assessment tool.

Relatively Easy to Construct.
Although essay tests are relatively easy to construct, the items should not be constructed haphazardly; consult the table of specifications, identify only the topics and objectives that can best be assessed by essays, and build items around those and only those.

Emphasize Communication Skills as Essential in Complex Academic Disciplines. If developing communication skills is an instructional objective, it can be tested with an essay item. However, this assumes that the teacher has spent time in teaching communication skills pertinent to the course area, including special vocabulary and writing styles, as well as providing practice with relevant arguments for and against controversial points.

Guessing is Eliminated. Since no options are provided, the student must supply rather than select the proper response.

Naturally there is another side to the essay coin. These items also have limitations and disadvantages.

Disadvantages of the Essay Item

Difficult to Score. It is tedious to wade through pages and pages of student handwriting. Also, it is difficult not to let spelling and grammatical mistakes influence grading or to let superior abilities in communication cover up for incomplete comprehension of facts.

Scores are Unreliable. It is difficult to maintain a common set of criteria for all students. Two persons may disagree on the correct answer for any essay item; even the same person will disagree on the correctness of one answer read on two separate occasions.

Limited Sample of Total Instructional Content. Fewer essay items can be attempted than any objective type of item; it takes more time to complete an essay item than any other type of item. Students become fatigued faster with these items than with objective items.

Bluffing. It is no secret that longer essays tend to be graded higher than short essays, regardless of content! As a result, students may bluff.

The first two limitations are serious disadvantages. Fortunately, we do have some suggestions that have been shown to make the task of scoring essays more manageable and reliable. These will be discussed shortly. First, however, we will consider several situations in which the use of essay items is most appropriate.

WHEN SHOULD ESSAY QUESTIONS BE USED?

While each situation must be considered individually, there are certain situations that lend themselves well to the use of essay items. Among them are situations in which:

1. The instructional objectives specify high-level cognitive processes—they require supplying information rather than simply recognizing information. These processes often cannot be measured with objective items.
2. Only a few tests or items need to be graded. If you have thirty students and design a test consisting of six extended-range essays, you will spend a great deal of time scoring. Use essays when class size is small, or use only one or two essays in conjunction with objective items.
3. Test security is a consideration. If you are afraid test items will be passed on to future students and consequently decide not to reuse a test, it is better to use an essay test. In general, a good essay test takes less time to construct than a good objective test.

SCORING ESSAYS

As mentioned, essays tend to be difficult to score reliably. That is, the *same* essay answer may be given an A by one scorer and a B or C by another scorer. Or, the *same* answer may be graded A on one occasion, but B or C on another occasion by the *same* scorer! As disturbing and surprising as they may seem, these conclusions have long been supported by research findings (Coffman 1971). Why does this happen and what can be done to avoid such scoring problems?

Why Are Essay Scores Unreliable?

To understand the difficulties involved in scoring essays reliably, it is necessary to consider the difficulty involved in constructing good essay items. As you saw earlier, the clearer your instructional objective, the easier the essay item is to construct. Similarly, the clearer the essay item in terms of task specification, the easier it is to score reliably. Make sense? If you're not sure, look at the next two examples of essay items and decide which would likely be more reliably scored.

Example 1: Some economists recommend massive tax cuts as a means of controlling inflation. Identify at least two assumptions on which such a position is based, and indicate the effect that violating *each* assumption might have on inflation. Limit your response to one-half page. Organize your answer according to the criteria discussed in class. Although spelling, punctuation, and grammar will not be counted in your grade, try to attend to these factors to the best of your ability (8 points)

Example 2: What effect would massive tax cuts have on inflation? (100 points)

Which did you select? If you chose the first one, you are catching on.

Example 2 is a poor essay question. It is unstructured, unfocused, fails to define response limits, and fails to establish a policy for grammar, spelling, and punctuation. Thus, depending on the scorer, a lengthy answer with poor grammar and good content might get a high grade, a low grade, or an intermediate grade. Different scorers would probably all have a different idea of what a "good" answer to their question looks like. Questions like this trouble and confuse scorers and invite scorer unreliability. They do so for the same reasons that they trouble and confuse test-takers. Poorly written essay items hurt both students and scorers.

But the first example is different. The task is spelled out for the student, limits are defined, and the policy on spelling, punctuation, and grammar is indicated. The task for the scorer is to determine whether the student has included (1) at least two assumptions underlying the proposition, and (2) the likely effect on inflation if each assumption is violated. Granted, there may be some difficulty agreeing how adequate the statements of the assumptions and effects of violating of the assumptions may be, but there is little else to quibble over. Thus, there are *fewer* potential sources of scorer error or variability (that is, unreliability) in this question than in the second. Remember, essay scoring can never be as reliable as scoring an objective test, but it doesn't have to be little better than chance.

How to Improve Scoring Reliability (and Save Time!)

To improve essay scoring reliability: write good essay items, use several restricted-range items rather than a single extended-range item, and use a predetermined scoring scheme.

Write Good Essay Items.   Poorly written questions are one source of scorer unreliability. Questions that do not specify response length are another important source of unreliability. In general, long (say, two-page) essay responses are more difficult to score reliably than restricted-range essay responses (say, one-half page). This is due to student fatigue and subsequent clerical errors, as well as a tendency for grading criteria to vary from response to response, or for that matter, from page to page, or paragraph to paragraph in the same response.

Use Several Restricted-Range Items Rather Than a Single Extended-Range Item.   Writing good items and using restricted-range essays rather than extended-range essays will help improve essay scoring reliability. However, as we mentioned, sometimes extended-range essays are desirable and/or necessary. What do you do then? Use a predetermined scoring scheme.

Use a *Predetermined* Scoring Scheme.   This point is an important one. All too often essays are graded without the scorer having specified in advance what he or she is looking for in a "good" answer. In scoring an essay, you are making an evaluation. In making an evaluation, criteria are necessary. If a teacher does not determine and specify the relevant criteria beforehand, the reliability of scoring will be greatly reduced.

If the relevant criteria are not readily available for the teacher to refer to in scoring each question, the following may happen:

1. The criteria themselves may change (teacher grades harder or easier after a number of papers, even if the papers do not change).
2. The ability of the teacher to consistently keep these criteria in mind will be influenced by fatigue, distractions, frame of mind, and so on.

Since teachers and other essay scorers are only human, it is likely they will be subject to these factors. Referring to a predetermined set of criteria minimizes this likelihood. What do such criteria look like? Scoring criteria may vary from fairly simple checklists to elaborate combinations of checklists and rating scales. How elaborate your scoring scheme is depends on what you are trying to measure. If your essay item is a restricted-response item simply assessing mastery of factual content, a fairly simple listing of essential points would suffice. Table 7.1 illustrates this type of scoring scheme.

TABLE 7.1 An Essay Item Appropriate for a Tenth-Grade American Government Course, Its Objective, and a Simple Scoring Scheme

Scoring Scheme	*Description*
Objective	The student will be able to name and describe at least five important conditions that contributed to the industrial revolution, drawn from among the following: Breakdown of feudal ideas and social boundaries (rise of common man) Legitimization of individualism and competition Transportation revolution, which allowed for massive transport of goods (first national roads, canals, steamboats, railroads, etc.) New forms of energy (e.g., coal) that brought about factory system Slow decline of death rates due to improved hygiene and continuation of high birth rates resulted in rise in population Media revolution (printing press, newspapers, telegraph, etc.) Migration to urban areas
Test Item	Name and describe five of the most important conditions that made possible the industrial revolution. (10 points)
Scoring Criteria	1 point for each of the seven factors named, to a maximum of 5 points. 1 point for each appropriate description of the factors named, to a maximum of 5 points. No penalty for spelling, punctuation, or grammatical error. No extra credit for more than five factors named or described. Extraneous information will be ignored.

For most restricted-response items a similar scoring scheme would probably suffice. However, when items are measuring synthesis and evaluation skills, more complex schemes are necessary. Tuckman (1975) has identified three components that we feel are useful in evaluating high-level essay items: content, organization, and process. Let's consider these in more detail.

Scoring Criteria for High-Level Essay Items

Content.   Although essays often are not used to measure factual knowledge as much as thinking processes, the information included in an essay—the content—can and should be scored specifically for its presence and accuracy and not the way it is organized or otherwise used. This is what you would do in scoring the sample essay in the previous section. You are simply trying to determine whether a student has acquired prerequisite knowledge with such content criteria.

Organization.   Does the essay have an introduction, body, and conclusion? Let the students know that you will be scoring for organization to minimize rambling. Beyond the three general organizational criteria mentioned, you may want to develop specific criteria for your class. For example: Are recommendations, inferences, and hypotheses supported? Is it apparent which supporting statements go with which recommendation? Do progressions and sequences follow a logical or chronological development? You should also decide on a spelling and grammar policy and develop these criteria, alerting the students before they take the test.

Process.   If your essay item tests at the application level or above, the most important criteria for scoring are those that reflect the extent to which these processes have been carried out. Each process (application, analysis, synthesis, and evaluation) results in a solution, recommendation, or decision and some reasons for justifying or supporting the final decision, and so on. Thus, the process criteria should attempt to assess both the adequacy of the solution or decision and the reasons behind it.

When an essay requires a solution or conclusion, the solution or conclusion should be evaluated in terms of the following:

Accuracy/Reasonableness.   Will it work? Have the correct analytical dimensions been identified? Scorers must ultimately decide for themselves what is accurate but should be prepared for unexpected, but accurate, responses.

Completeness/Internal Consistency.   To what extent does it sufficiently deal with the problem presented? Again, the scorer's judgment will weigh heavily, but points should be logically related and cover the topics as fully as required by the essay item.

Originality/Creativity.   Again, it is up to the scorer to recognize the unexpected and give credit for it. That is, the scorer should expect that some students will develop new ways of conceptualizing questions, and credit should be awarded for such conceptualizations when appropriate.

Your criteria should be made known to students. This will maximize their learning experience. Knowing how you are going to score the test, students will be able to develop better and more defensible responses. Table 7.2 illustrates the application of these criteria to an extended-range essay item.

As the scorer reads through each response, points are assigned for each of the three major criteria of the scoring scheme. As you can probably guess, there are some disadvantages to this approach. It is likely to be quite laborious and time-consuming. Furthermore, undue attention may be given to superficial aspects of the answer. When used properly, however, such a scoring scheme can yield reliable scores for extended-range essay answers. Another advantage of this approach is that constructing such a detailed scoring scheme *before* administering the test can often alert the teacher to such problems in the item as unrealistic expectations for the students or poor wording. A third advantage is that discussion of a student's grade on such an item is greatly facilitated. The student can see what aspects of his or her response were considered deficient.

Keep in mind that Table 7.2 represents a scoring scheme for an extended-range essay item. When reliability is crucial, such a detailed scheme is vital. Scoring schemes for restricted-range items would be less complex, depending on what components of the answer the teacher felt were most critical. The point we have been making is that using some kind of scoring scheme is helpful in improving the reliability of essay scoring.

Another method that has gained considerable acceptance—although it runs contrary to our position that scoring criteria should be written down beforehand—is the rating method.

The Rating Method.   With the rating method, the teacher generally is more interested in the overall quality of the answer than in specific points. Rating is done by simply sorting papers into piles, usually five, if letter grades are given. After sorting, the answers in each pile are re-read and an attempt is made to ensure that all the A papers are of comparable quality (that is, that they do not include B and C papers) and so forth. This step is very important, since the problem of changing criteria mentioned above is always present in rating answers. It helps minimize the likelihood, for example, that an A paper gets sorted into the C pile because it was graded early while the teacher was maintaining "strict" criteria.

This method is certainly an improvement over simply reading each answer and assigning a grade based on some nebulous, undefined rationale. However, as we mentioned before, this method is still subject to the problem of unintentionally changing the criteria.

TABLE 7.2	An Essay Item Appropriate for a High School American History Course, Its Objectives, and a Detailed Scoring Scheme

Scoring Scheme	*Description*
Objectives	The student will be able to explain the forces that operated to weaken Southern regional self-consciousness between the Civil War and 1900. The student will consider these forces and draw an overall conclusion as to the condition of Southern self-consciousness at the turn of the century.
Test Item	The Civil War left the South with a heritage of intense regional self-consciousness. In what respects, and to what extent, was this feeling weakened during the next half century, and in what respects, and to what extent, was it intensified? Your answer will be graded on content and organization and on the accuracy, consistency, and originality of your conclusion and the quality of your argument in support of your conclusion. Be sure to identify at least seven weakening factors and seven strengthening factors. Although spelling, punctuation, and grammar will not be considered in grading, do your best to consider them in your writing. Limit your answer to two (2) pages. (32 points)
Detailed Scoring Criteria	*Content.* 1 point for each weakening factor mentioned, to a maximum of 7 points. 1 point for each strengthening factor mentioned—all factors must come from the following list: Forces weakening Southern regional self-consciousness: Growth of railroads and desire for federal subsidies Old Whigs join Northern businessmen in Compromise of 1877 Desire for Northern capital to industrialize the South Efforts of magazines and writers to interpret the South The vision of the New South Aid to Negro education by Northern philanthropists New state constitutions stressing public education Supreme Court decisions affecting Negro rights Tom Watson's early Populist efforts Booker T. Washington's "submissiveness" The Spanish-American War The white man's burden After 1890, new issues did not conform to a North-South political alignment World War I

TABLE 7.2	An Essay Item Appropriate for a High School American History Course, Its Objectives, and a Detailed Scoring Scheme (continued)

Scoring Scheme	*Description*

Forces strengthening Southern regional self-consciousness:
   Destruction caused by the war and its long-range effects
   Reconstruction policy of Congress
   One-crop economy, crop-lien system, and sharecropping
   Carpetbaggers, Ku Klux Klan, Red Shirts
   Waving the bloody shirt
   Memories of the lost cause
   Glorify the prewar tradition
   Continuing weakness of Southern education compared with
     the rest of the Union
   Populism
   Jim Crow laws after 1890
   Solid South
14 points possible

Organization
0 to 6 points assigned, depending on whether the essay has an introduction, body, and conclusion.
6 points possible.

Process
1. Solution: 0 to 6 points depending on whether the solution is:
  a. Accurate (0 to 2 points)
    Does the solution/conclusion fit?
  b. Internally consistent (0 to 2 points)
    Does the solution/conclusion logically flow?
  c. Originality/creativity
    Is the solution/conclusion novel or creative?
2. Argument: 0 to 6 points, depending on whether the argument is:
  a. Accurate (0 to 2 points)
    Dependent on whether the argument fits the situation.
  b. Internally consistent (0 to 2 points)
    Is the argument logical?
  c. Original/creative (0 to 2 points)
    Is the argument unique or novel in its approach?
32 points possible

Other Suggestions.   We have been discussing improving essay scoring reliability. Remember our first three suggestions?

1. Write good essay items.
2. Use restricted-range rather than extended-range items, if appropriate.
3. Use a predetermined scoring scheme.

Now let's consider several other suggestions to improve essay scoring reliability.

4. Use the scoring scheme consistently.

In other words, don't favor one student over another or get stricter or more lax over time. How can you do this?

5. Remove or cover the names on the papers before beginning scoring.

In this way you are more likely to rate papers on their merits, rather than on your overall impression of the student.

6. Score *each* student's answer to the *same* question before going on to the next answer.

In other words, do *all* of the answers to the first question before looking at the answers to the second. Why? First, to avoid having a student's score on an earlier question influence your evaluation of his or her later questions, and second, it is much easier to keep scoring criteria for one question in mind than it is to keep scoring criteria for all the questions in mind.

7. Try to keep scores for previous items hidden when scoring subsequent items for the same reason already mentioned.
8. Try to re-evaluate your papers before returning them. When you come across discrepant ratings, average them.

Well, there you have it! Eight suggestions for improving reliability of essay scoring. If you use essay items, try to incorporate as many of these suggestions as possible.

SUMMARY

Chapter 7 introduced you to the major issues related to the construction and scoring of essay items. Its major points were:

1. Essay items require that the student supply rather than select a response. The length and complexity of the response may vary, and essay items lend themselves best to the assessment of higher-level cognitive skills.

2. There are two main types of essay items that are differentiated by length of response: extended-response and restricted-response essay items.
   a. The extended-response item usually requires responses more than a page in length and may be used to assess synthesis and evaluation skills.
   b. The restricted-response item is usually answered in a page or less. It is often used to measure comprehension, application, and analysis.
3. The type of item written is determined by the cognitive skills called for in the instructional objective.
4. Suggestions for writing essay items include the following:
   a. Identify the cognitive processes you want the student to use before you write the item.
   b. State the task clearly (that is, focus the item), including any criteria on which the essay will be graded.
   c. Avoid beginning essay items with *what, who, when,* and *list,* unless you are measuring at the knowledge level.
   d. Ask for presentation of evidence for a controversial position, rather than asking the student simply to take a controversial position.
   e. Avoid using optional items.
   f. Establish reasonable time and/or page limits for each item.
   g. Use essays to measure learning outcomes that cannot be measured by objective items.
   h. Be sure the item matches the instructional objective.
5. Advantages of essay items over objective items include the following:
   a. Enable you to assess complex learning outcomes
   b. Are relatively easy to construct
   c. Enable you to assess communication skills
   d. Eliminate student guessing
6. Disadvantages of essay items include:
   a. Longer scoring time
   b. Scoring unreliability
   c. Limited content sampling
   d. Subjectivity to bluffing
7. Essay items should be used when:
   a. Objectives specify higher-level cognitive processes and objective items are inappropriate
   b. Few tests or items are necessary
   c. Test security is in question
8. Essay scoring reliability may be improved by:
   a. Writing good essay items
   b. Using restricted-range rather than extended-range essays whenever appropriate
   c. Using a predetermined scoring scheme
   d. Implementing the scoring scheme consistently with all students
   e. Removing or covering names on papers to avoid scoring bias
   f. Scoring all responses to one item before scoring the next item
   g. Keeping scores from previous items hidden when scoring subsequent items

  h. Rescoring all papers before returning them and averaging discrepant ratings
9. Essays may be scored according to:
  a. Simple scoring schemes that assign credit for content
  b. Detailed scoring schemes that assign credit for content, organization, process, and any other factors that the scorer deems desirable
  c. The rating method in which grades are assigned based on a global impression of the whole response.

For Practice

1. Write an essay-test item using both an extended-response format and a restricted-response format. Your extended-response question should be targeted to measure a synthesis or evaluation objective, while your restricted response question should be targeted to measure a comprehension, application, or analysis objective.
2. Prepare a scoring guide for your restricted-response essay item using the format shown in Table 7.1
3. Describe five scoring procedures from among those discussed in this chapter that will help ensure the reliability of scoring your essay question.
4. Give some pros and cons of the rating method in which grades are assigned based on global impressions of the whole response.

8

CHAPTER

ADMINISTERING, ANALYZING, AND IMPROVING THE TEST

|O| ver the last several chapters we have discussed various aspects of test planning and item construction. If you have written instructional objectives, constructed a test blueprint, and written items that match your objectives, then more than likely you will have a good test. All the "raw material" will be there. However, sometimes the raw material, as good as it may be, can be rendered useless because of poorly assembling and administering the test. By now, you know it requires a substantial amount of time to write objectives, put together a test blueprint, and write items. It is worth a little more time to properly assemble or package your test so that your efforts will not be wasted. Our goal for this chapter is to provide some suggestions to help you avoid common pitfalls in test assembly, administration, and scoring. Later in the chapter we will discuss considerations and techniques of test analysis. First, let's consider test assembly.

ASSEMBLING THE TEST

At this point let's assume you have:

1. Written measurable instructional objectives
2. Prepared a test blueprint, specifying the number of items for each content and process area
3. Written test items that match your instructional objectives.

Once you have done so you are ready to:

1. Package the test
2. Reproduce the test

These components constitute what we are calling *test assembly*. Let's consider each a little more closely.

Packaging the Test

There are several packaging guidelines worth remembering, including grouping together items of similar format, arranging test items from easy to hard, properly spacing items, keeping items and options on the same page, placing illustrations near the descriptive material, checking for randomness in the answer key, deciding how students will record their answers, providing space for the test taker's name and the date, checking test directions for clarity, and proofreading the test before you reproduce and distribute it.

Group Together All Items of Similar Format.
If you have all true-false items grouped together, all completion items together, and so on, then students will not have to "switch gears" to adjust to new formats. This will enable them to cover more items in a given time than if item formats were mixed throughout the test. Also, by grouping items of a given format together, only one set of directions per format section is necessary—another time-saver.

Arrange Test Items from Easy to Hard.
Arranging test items according to level of difficulty should enable more students to answer the first few items correctly, thereby building confidence and, hopefully, reducing test anxiety.

Space the Items for Easy Reading.
If possible, try to provide enough blank space between items so that each item is distinctly separate from others. When items are crowded together, students may inadvertently perceive a word, phrase, or line from a preceding or following item as part of the item in question. Naturally, this interferes with a student's capacity to demonstrate his or her true ability.

Keep Items and Options on the Same Page.
There are few things more aggravating to a test taker than to have to turn the page to read the options for multiple-choice or matching items, or to complete reading a true-false or completion item. To avoid this, do not begin an item at the bottom of the page unless you will have at least an inch left *after completing* the item. Not only will this help eliminate having to carry items over to the next page, it will also minimize the likelihood that the last line or two of the item will be cut off when you photocopy the test.

Position Illustrations Near Descriptions. Place diagrams, maps, or other supporting material immediately above the item or items to which they refer. In other words, if items 9, 10, and 11 refer to a map of South America, locate the map above items 9, 10, and 11—not between 9 and 10 or between 10 and 11 and not below them. Also, if possible, keep any such stimuli and related questions on the same page to save the test taker time.

Check Your Answer Key. Be sure the correct answers follow a fairly random pattern. Avoid true-false patterns such as T F T F, etc., or T T F F, etc., and multiple-choice patterns such as D C B A D C B A, etc. At the same time, check to see that your correct answers are distributed about equally between true and false and among multiple-choice options.

Determine How Students Record Answers. Decide whether you want to have students record their answers on the test paper or on a separate answer sheet. In the lower elementary grades it is generally a good idea to have students record answers on the test papers themselves. In the upper elementary and secondary grades, separate answer sheets can be used to facilitate scoring accuracy and to cut down on scoring time. Also, in the upper grades, learning to complete separate answer sheets will make students familiar with the process they will use when taking standardized tests.

Provide Space for Name and Date. Be sure to include a blank on your test booklet and/or answer sheet for the student's name and the date. This may seem an unnecessary suggestion, but it is *not* always evident to a nervous test taker that a name should be included on the test. Students are much more likely to remember to put their names on tests if space is provided.

Check Test Directions. Check your directions for each item format to be sure they are clear. Directions should specify:
1. The numbers of the items to which they apply
2. How to record answers
3. The basis on which to select answers
4. Criteria for scoring

Proofread the Test. Proofread for typographical and grammatical errors *before* reproducing the test and make any necessary corrections. Having to announce corrections to the class just before the test or during the test will waste time and is likely to inhibit the test takers' concentration.

Before reproducing the test, it's a good idea to check off these steps. The checklist in Figure 8.1 can be used for this purpose.

FIGURE 8.1   Test Assembly Checklist

Put a check in the blank to the right of each statement after you've checked to see that it applies to your test.

	Yes	No
1. Are items of similar format grouped together?	_____	_____
2. Are items arranged from easy-to-hard levels of difficulty?	_____	_____
3. Are items properly spaced?	_____	_____
4. Are items and options on the same page?	_____	_____
5. Are diagrams, maps, and supporting material above designated items and on the same page with items?	_____	_____
6. Are answers random?	_____	_____
7. Have you decided whether an answer sheet will be used?	_____	_____
8. Are blanks for name and date included?	_____	_____
9. Have the directions been checked for clarity?	_____	_____
10. Has the test been proofread for errors?	_____	_____
11. Do items avoid racial or sexual bias?	_____	_____

Reproducing the Test

Most test reproduction in the schools is done on ditto or photocopying machines. As you well know, the quality of such copies can vary tremendously. Regardless of how valid and reliable your test might be, poor copies will make it less so. Thus, it makes sense to take the following commonsense steps to ensure that the time you spend constructing a valid and reliable test does not end in illegible copies.

Know the Ditto or Photocopying Machine.   Be sure you or the person you designate to do the reproduction understands how to operate the ditto or photocopying machine. There is some variation across models, and a few minutes of "practice" on a new machine is a worthwhile investment.

Make Extra Copies.   Always make at least five extra copies of each page of the test, since ditto machines have a tendency to count pages they fail to print.

Specify Copying Instructions.   If someone else will do the reproducing, be sure to specify that the dittos are for a test and not simply an enrichment exercise. Ask the clerk or aide to inspect every tenth copy for legibility while running the copies and to be alert for blank or half-dittoed pages while collating, ordering, and stapling multi-page tests.

Avoid Common Pitfalls.   If your test is to be dittoed, avoid:

1. fine print
2. finely detailed maps or drawings
3. barely legible masters or originals—if you can barely read the original, you can't later blame the ditto machine.

File Original Test.   Finally, retain the original or master in case you want to reuse the test, or items within the test. Be sure you tell your clerk or aide to return the original to you—otherwise it may end up thrown away.

ADMINISTERING THE TEST

The test is ready. All that remains is to get the students ready and hand out the tests. Here is a series of suggestions to help your students psychologically prepare for the test:

Maintain a Positive Attitude.   Try to induce a positive test-taking attitude. Of course, this consideration must be kept in mind long before the test is actually distributed. It helps keep the main purposes of classroom testing in mind—to evaluate achievement and instructional procedures and to provide feedback to yourself and your students. Too often tests are used to punish ("Well, it's obvious the class isn't doing the readings, so we'll have a test today"), or are used indiscriminately ("It's Tuesday, I guess I may as well give my class a test"), or inappropriately ("I need a good evaluation from the principal; I'll give my class an easy test"). To the extent that you can avoid falling victim to such testing traps, you will be helping induce and maintain a positive test-taking atmosphere.

Maximize Achievement Motivation.   Try *not* to minimize the achievement aspect of the test. While you do not want to immobilize your students with fear, you do want them to try to do their best on the test. Encourage them to do so. If a student's grade will be influenced, avoid making comments such as "We're just going to have an easy little quiz today; it's no big deal." Such an approach will probably minimize anxiety in very nervous test takers, which might improve their performance, but it may also serve to impair the test performance of students who need to take tests seriously in order to be motivated enough to do their best. In your class you will likely have both types of students. Keep your general statement about the test accurate. The test is something to be taken seriously and this should be clear to the class. Remember, you can always make reassuring or motivational comments individually to students.

Equalize Advantages.

Try to equalize the advantages test-wise students have over nontest-wise students. Since you are interested in student achievement, and not how test-wise a student is (unless you are teaching a course in test-taking skills), the results will be more valid if the advantages of test-wiseness are minimized. You can do so by instructing the class when it is best to guess or not guess at an answer, and remind them about general test-taking strategies (for example: "Don't spend too much time on any difficult items"; "Try all items then return to those you are unsure of"; Cross off options you've ruled out on matching or multiple-choice items"; "Check your answers for accuracy before turning in the test").

You may even want to take guessing into consideration when scoring the test. If time allows each student to attempt every item, a total score that is equal to the number of right answers may be perfectly adequate. In this case, students should be told to make an "educated" guess, even if they are not certain of the answer. However, the case may arise in which different students will attempt different numbers of items. This sometimes occurs when the test has a strict time limit, which may prevent some students from finishing. In this situation you may want to discourage guessing, that is, discourage the random filling out of unfinished answers seconds before the time limit is up.

A correction-for-guessing formula can be used which penalizes the student for answering questions to which he or she does not know the answer. A student's score which has been corrected for guessing will be equal to the number of questions answered incorrectly divided by the number of answer choices for an item minus 1 and, then, this amount subtracted from the total number of right answers. Or,

$$\text{Score} = \text{Total Right} - \frac{\text{Total Wrong}}{\text{Number of Answer Choices} - 1}$$

For example, in a 50-item multiple-choice test where there are 4 possible answers and a student gets 44 answers correct, the student's score would be $44 - 6/3 = 42$. The student's score, corrected for guessing, is 42. When this formula is used, students should be encouraged to make "educated" guesses.

Avoid Surprises.

Be sure your students have sufficient advance notice of a test. "Pop" quizzes have little beneficial effect on overall academic achievement. They are especially problematic in junior-high and high school where students have five or six different teachers. If each teacher gave pop quizzes, students would be extremely hard pressed to be well-prepared for each class each day. This is not to say that you should avoid frequent quizzes, however. When students are tested frequently, learning or study takes place at more regular intervals rather than massed or crammed the night before a test. Retention is generally better following spaced rather than massed learning.

Clarify the Rules.   Inform students about time limits, restroom policy, and any special considerations about the answer sheet *before* you distribute the tests. Students often tune out the instructor after they receive their tests and may miss important information.

Rotate Distribution.   Alternate beginning test distribution at the left, right, front, and back of the class. This way, the same person will not always be the last one to receive the test.

Remind Students to Check Their Copies.   After handing out the tests, remind students to check page and item numbers to see that none has been omitted, and remind them to put their names on their papers.

Monitor Students.   While students are completing their tests, monitor them. While it would be nice to trust students not to look at each other's papers, it is not realistic. Inform students about penalties for cheating, and implement the penalties when cheating occurs. It is distasteful to do so, but so is cheating. After students learn they can't "get away with it," there should be little need for the penalties.

Minimize Distractions.   Try to keep noise and distractions to a minimum—for obvious reasons.

Give Time Warnings.   Give students a warning fifteen, ten, and five minutes before the time limit is up, so they are not caught by surprise at the deadline.

Collect Tests Uniformly.   Finally, have a uniform policy on collecting the tests. Indicate whether you want all papers or only some returned, where they are to be placed, and so forth. This not only saves time, but minimizes lost papers.

SCORING THE TEST

We discussed specific scoring recommendations for various types of objective test formats in Chapter 6 and for essay items in Chapter 7. Following are some general suggestions to save scoring time and improve scoring accuracy and consistency.

Prepare Answer Key.   Prepare your answer key in advance, which will save time when you score the test and will help you identify questions that need rewording or need to be eliminated. Also, when constructing the answer key, you should get an idea of how long it will take your students to complete the test and whether this time is appropriate for the time slot you have allocated to the test.

Check Answer Key.   If possible, have a colleague check your answer key to identify possible alternative answers or potential problems.

Score Blindly. Try to score "blindly." That is, try to keep the student's name out of sight to prevent your knowledge about, or expectations of, the student from influencing the score.

Check Machine-Scored Answer Sheets. If machine scoring is used, check each answer sheet for stray marks, multiple answers, or marks that may be too light to be picked up by the scoring machine.

Check Scoring. If possible, double-check your scoring. Scoring errors due to clerical error occur frequently. There is no reason to expect that you will not make such errors.

Record Scores. Before returning the scored papers to students, be sure you have recorded their scores in your record book! (Forgetting to do this has happened at least once to every teacher.)

ANALYZING THE TEST

Just as you can expect to make scoring errors, you can expect to make errors in test construction. *No* test you construct will be perfect—it will include inappropriate, invalid, or otherwise deficient items. In the remainder of this chapter we will introduce you to a technique called *item analysis*. Item analysis can be used to identify items that are deficient in some way, thus paving the way to improve or eliminate them, with the result being a better overall test. We will make a distinction between two kinds of item analysis, quantitative and qualitative. As you will see, qualitative item analysis is something with which you are already familiar. Quantitative item analysis is likely to be something new.

Quantitative Item Analysis

As mentioned, quantitative item analysis is a technique that will enable us to assess the quality or utility of an item. It does so by identifying *distractors* or response options that are not doing what they are supposed to be doing. How useful is this procedure for a completion or an essay item? Frankly, it is not very useful for these types of items, but qualitative item analysis is. On the other hand, quantitative item analysis is ideally suited for examining the usefulness of multiple-choice formats. The quantitative item analysis procedures that we will describe are most appropriate for items on a norm-referenced test. As you will see, we are interested in spreading out students, or discriminating among them, with such a test. When dealing with a criterion-referenced test, qualitative item analysis procedures are most appropriate.

Unfortunately, there is some terminology or jargon associated with quantitative item analysis that must be mastered. Figure 8.2, Item Analysis Terminology,

---

FIGURE 8.2   Item Analysis Terminology

Quantitative Item Analysis:	A numerical method for analyzing test items employing student-response alternatives or options.
Qualitative Item Analysis:	A non-numerical method for analyzing test items not employing student responses, but considering test objectives, content validity, and technical item quality.
Key:	Correct option in a multiple-choice item.
Distractor:	Incorrect option in a multiple-choice item.
Difficulty Index (p):	Proportion of students who answered the item correctly.
Discrimination Index (D):	Measure of the extent to which a test item discriminates or differentiates between students who do well on the overall test and those who do not do well on the overall test. There are three types of discrimination indexes.

1. **Positive discrimination index**—those who did *well* on the overall test chose the correct answer for a particular item more often than those who did poorly on the overall test.
2. **Negative discrimination index**—those who did *poorly* on the overall test chose the correct answer for a particular item more often than those who did well on the overall test.
3. **Zero discrimination index**—those who did well and those who did poorly on the overall test chose the correct answer for a particular item with equal frequency.

---

defines these terms. Study the definitions in the box and refer to them throughout this section.

Now that you have reviewed the terms and definitions, let's see how they apply to multiple-choice items. Consider the following example.

Suppose your students chose the options to a four-alternative multiple-choice item the following numbers of times: Three students chose option A, none chose B, eighteen chose the correct answer C, and nine chose D.

$$
\begin{array}{cccc}
\text{A} & \text{B} & \text{C}^* & \text{D} \\
3 & 0 & 18 & 9
\end{array}
$$

How does that help us? We can see immediately that B was not a very good option or distractor, since no one chose it. Also we can see that more than half the class answered the item correctly. In fact, by employing the following formula, we can compute p, the item's difficulty index, which is the first step in item analysis.

$$p = \frac{\text{Number of students selecting correct answer}}{\text{Total number of students attempting the item}}$$

$$p = \frac{18}{30} = .60$$

From this information we learn that the item was moderately difficult (60 percent of the class got it right) and that option B ought to be modified or replaced. This is useful information, but we can learn (and need to know) more about this item. Were the students who answerd it correctly those who did well on the overall test? Did the distractors fool those who did well or poorly on the test? The answers to these questions are important, because they tell us whether the item discriminated between students who did well and those who did not do well on the overall test. A little confused? Let's look at it another way:

Question: Why do we administer tests?

Answer: To find out who has mastered the material and who has not (that is, to discriminate between these two groups).

Question: Will a test discriminate between these groups better if each item on the test discriminates between those who did and did not do well on the test overall?

Answer: Absolutely! If more students who do *well* on the test overall answer an item correctly—positive discrimination index—that item helps the overall discrimination ability of the test. If this is true for all items (they are all positively discriminating), the test will do a good job of discriminating between those who know their stuff and those who don't. To the extent that students who do *poorly* on the overall test answer individual items correctly—negative discrimination index—the test loses its ability to discriminate.

Question: How can I tell whether the key for any question is chosen more frequently by the better students (i.e., the item is positively discriminating) or the poorer students (i.e., the item is negatively discriminating)?

Answer: Follow the procedure described next.

Discrimination Index.

To determine each item's discrimination index (D), complete the following steps:

1. Arrange the papers from highest to lowest score.
2. Separate the papers into an upper group and a lower group based on total test scores. Do so by including half of your papers in each group.
3. For each item, count the number in the upper group and the number in the lower group that chose each alternative.

4. Record your information for each item in the following form (the following is data from the previous example; again the asterisk indicates the keyed option):

Example for Item X
(Class size = 30)

Options	A	B	C*	D
Upper	1	0	11	3
Lower	2	0	7	6

5. Compute D, the discrimination index, by plugging the appropriate numbers into the following formula:

$$D = \frac{\text{(Number who got item correct in upper group)} - \text{(Number who got item correct in lower group)}}{\text{Number of students in either group (if group sizes are unequal, choose the higher number)}}$$

upper group
lower group

Plugging in our numbers we arrive at

$$D = \frac{11 - 7}{15} = .267$$

Our discrimination index (D) is .267, which is positive. More students who did well on the overall test answered the item correctly than students who did poorly on the overall test. Now, let's put it all together for this item.

Difficulty Index (p) = .60
Discrimination Index (D) = .267

An item with p = .60 and D = .267 would be considered a moderately difficult item that has positive (desirable) discrimination ability. When p levels are less than about .25, the item is considered relatively difficult. When p levels are above .75, the item is considered relatively easy. Test construction experts try to build tests that have most items between p levels of .20 and .80, with an average p level of about .50. All other factors being equal, the test's discrimination ability is greatest when the overall p level is about .50.

How high is a "good" discrimination index? Unfortunately, there is no single answer. Some experts insist that D should be at least .30, while others believe that as long as D has a positive value, the item's discrimination ability is adequate. Further complicating the issue is the fact that D is related to p. Just as a test tends to have maximum discrimination ability when p is around .50, so too does an individual item. It can be difficult to obtain discrimination indices above .30 when items are easy or difficult. Naturally, you want your items to have as high a discrimination index as possible, but our recommendation is that you consider seriously any item with a positive D value. Based on this information, we would conclude that, in general, the item is acceptable. But, we must also look at the item analysis data further to see if any distractors need to be modified or replaced.

We noted earlier that B would need to be replaced, since no one chose it. But what about A and D? Are they acceptable? The answer is yes, but can you figure out why? Because *more* people in the lower group chose them than people in the upper group. This is the opposite of what we would want for the correct answer, and it makes sense. If we want more students who do well on the overall test to choose the correct answer, then we also must want more students who do poorly on the overall test to choose the distractors. Let's look at the responses for another item.

Example for Item Y
(Class size = 28)

Options	A*	B	C	D
Upper	4	1	5	4
Lower	1	7	3	3

The following questions will help guide us through the quantitative item analysis procedure.

1. What is the difficulty level?

$$p = \frac{\text{Number selecting correct answer}}{\text{Total number taking the test}}$$

$$p = \frac{5}{28} = .18$$

2. What is the discrimination index?

$$D = \frac{\text{Number correct (upper)} - \text{Number correct (lower)}}{\text{Number in either group}}$$

$$D = \frac{4 - 1}{14} = .214$$

3. Should this item be eliminated? No, since it is positively discriminating. However, it is a difficult item; only 18% of the class got it right.
4. Should any distractor be eliminated or modified? Yes, distractors C and D have attracted *more* students who did *well* on the test overall. If these distractors are modified or replaced, a good item will be made even better. Remember, in order for an item to discriminate well, more students who do well on the test should choose the correct answer than do students who do

poorly (the correct answer should be positively discriminating) *and* fewer students who do well on the test should choose each distractor than students who do poorly (the distractors should be negatively discriminating).

Example for Item Z
(Class Size = 30)

Options	A	B*	C	D
Upper	3	4	3	5
Lower	0	10	2	3

Again, let's ask the four basic questions.

1. What is the difficulty level?

$$p = \frac{\text{Number selecting correct answer}}{\text{Total number taking the test}}$$

$$p = \frac{14}{30} = .467 \text{ (moderately difficult)}$$

2. What is the discrimination index?

$$D = \frac{\text{Number correct (upper)} - \text{Number correct (lower)}}{\text{Number in either group}}$$

$$= \frac{4 - 10}{15} = \frac{-6}{15} = -.40 \text{ (negatively discriminating)}$$

3. Should this item be eliminated? Yes! The item is moderately difficult (approximately 47 percent of the class got it right), but it discriminates *negatively* (D = −.40). Remember, one of the reasons for testing is to discriminate between those students who know their stuff and those who do not. On this item more students who knew their stuff (who did *well* on the overall test), chose the *incorrect* options than the correct answer. If the test were made mostly of or entirely of items like this, the students who score high on the test, who answered the most items correctly, would be those who did not know their stuff. This is clearly what we want to avoid. Thus, an item that discriminates negatively should be eliminated.

4. Should any distractor(s) be modified or eliminated? Since we have already decided to eliminate the item, this is a moot question. However, let's look at the distractors anyway. In the case of options A, C, and D, more students who did well on the test chose each of these options than students who did poorly on the test. Each distractor discriminates positively. We want our distractors to discriminate *negatively*. Thus, this item has nothing going for it, according to our quantitative item analysis. The correct answer, which should discriminate positively, discriminates negatively. The distractors, which should discriminate negatively, discriminate positively!

In addition to helping us decide which items to eliminate from a test before it is again administered, quantitative item analysis also enables us to make other decisions. For example, we can use quantitative item analysis to decide whether an item is miskeyed, whether responses to the item are characterized by guessing, or whether the item is ambiguous. To do so, we need only consider the responses of students in the upper half of the class. Let's see how.

Miskeying.   When an item is miskeyed, most students who did well on the test will likely select an option that is a distractor, rather than the option that is keyed. Consider the following miskeyed item:

Who was the first astronaut to set foot on the moon?
a. John Glenn
b. Scott Carpenter
c. Neil Armstrong
d. Alan Sheppard

Analyzing the responses for the *upper* half of the class, we find the following distribution:

	A	B	C	D*
Upper Half	1	1	9	2

Anytime most students in the upper half of the class fail to select the keyed option, consider whether your item is miskeyed. Remember, just as you are bound to make scoring errors, you are bound to miskey an item occasionally.

Guessing.   When guessing occurs, students in the upper half of the class respond in more or less random fashion. This is most likely to occur when the item measures content that is (1) not covered in class or the text, (2) so difficult that even the upper-half students have no idea what the correct answer is, or (3) so trivial that students are unable to choose from among the options provided. In such cases, each alternative is about equally attractive to students in the upper half, so their responses tend to be about equally distributed among the options. The following choice distribution would suggest that guessing occurred:

	A	B	C*	D
Upper half	4	3	3	3

Ambiguity.   So far we have discussed using quantitative item analysis to identify miskeying and guessing. We did so by looking at response distributions for the upper group. With miskeying, the upper group chooses a distractor more frequently than the key. With *guessing,* each option is chosen with about equal frequency. Ambiguity is suspected when, among the upper group, one of the distractors is chosen with about the same frequency as the correct answer. The following distribution suggests this item is ambiguous:

	A	B	C	D*
Upper half	7	0	1	7

In this item, students who do well on the test but miss the item are drawn almost entirely to one of the distractors. However, quantitative analysis data can only *suggest* ambiguity. In the preceding item, there is no way for us to tell whether the "good" students chose distractor A because the item is deficient, or whether it was because they were distracted by an option that was plausible, but not as correct as the key.

The only way to determine whether the root of the problem is lack of mastery or a poorly written item is through qualitative item analysis. Before leaving quantitative item analysis, however, a final point should be made. As you are by now aware, there can be considerable time and effort invested in quantitative item analysis by a teacher. This can be a "turn off" to some, resulting in a teacher failing to use this very useful test analysis tool. Fortunately, with the advent of microcomputers and item analysis computer software, the actual time spent in quantitative item analysis by the teacher may now be significantly reduced. We will discuss microcomputers and software in general and quantitative item analysis and other measurement-related software in more depth in Chapter 21.

We will turn to qualitative item analysis next. However, first review what we have learned about the application of quantitative item analysis by studying Figure 8.3, the Quantitative Item Analysis Checklist.

FIGURE 8.3   Quantitative Item Analysis Checklist

1. Item number   _____

2. Difficulty level: $p = \dfrac{\text{No. correct}}{\text{total}} =$ _____

3. Discrimination index:
   $$D = \dfrac{\text{Number correct (upper)} - \text{Number correct (lower)}}{\text{Number of students in either group}}$$ _____

4. Eliminate or revise item? Check:
   a. Does key discriminate positively?   _____
   b. Do distractors discriminate negatively?   _____
   If you answer yes to both a and b, no revision may be necessary. If you answer no to a *or* b, revision is necessary. If you answer no to a *and* b, eliminate the item.

5. Check for miskeying, ambiguity, or guessing. Among the choices for the *upper group only,* was there evidence of:
   a. miskeying (more chose distractor than key)?   _____
   b. guessing (equal spread of choices across options)?   _____
   c. ambiguity (equal number chose one distractor and the key)?   _____

Qualitative Item Analysis

As noted earlier, you already know something about qualitative item analysis. It's something you can and ought to do with items of *all* formats. Essentially, when we talk about qualitative item analysis, we are talking about matching items and objectives and editing poorly written items. These are activities we've discussed in Chapters 5, 6, and 7 in relation to improving the content validity of a test. We refer to them again simply because it is appropriate to edit or rewrite items and assess their content validity after a test, as well as before a test.

Let's face it. In spite of our best intentions, we end up pressed for time as the day for the test approaches. What do we do? Probably we work more quickly to assemble the test—overlooking such things as grammatical cues, specific determiners, double negatives, multiple defensible answers, and items that fail to match instructional objectives.

As a result, these faults creep into the final version of the test. It would be nice if quantitative item analysis pointed out such problems, but it does not. Quantitative item analysis is useful but limited. It points out items that have problems but doesn't tell us what these problems are. It is possible that an item that fails to measure or match an instructional objective could have an acceptable difficulty level, an answer that discriminates positively, and distractors that discriminate negatively. In short, quantitative item analysis is fallible. To do a thorough job of test analysis, one must use a combination of quantitative and qualitative item analysis, and not rely solely on one or the other. In other words, there is no substitute for matching test items with objectives and carefully scrutinizing and editing items in addition to performing a quantitative analysis of test items.

We've considered assembling, administering, scoring, and analyzing the test. What's left is returning the test to the students, something we like to call *debriefing*.

DEBRIEFING

Take a moment to think back to the times a test on which you did well was returned. Remember the happy, satisfied feeling you had? You felt good about yourself, your teacher, and the test. Of course, it was a good test because it proved that you knew your stuff. Now take a minute to think back to the times a test on which you did poorly was returned. Remember the unhappy, unsatisfied feeling you had? Were you angry or resentful? It's likely you weren't feeling very fond of yourself, your teacher, or the test—especially the test. Any time you give a test, it's likely that some students will do poorly and feel unhappy or angry as a result.

Teachers adopt their own ways of coping with complaints about a test. These range from, "Your score is final, and that's it," to "I'll give everybody ten extra points so that no one fails." We feel that neither of these positions is defensible. The first position denies or ignores reality. It is not just possible, but probable, that your test has deficiencies. Refusing to examine the test with your students robs you of the opportunity to get feedback that you can use to improve or fine-tune your test before you use it again. Furthermore, such an approach serves to antagonize and alienate students. Awarding extra credit or a make-up test may calm the angry students who did poorly but may be unfair to those who did well. As with the first approach, it robs you of the opportunity to get feedback on, and make appropriate modifications to, your test. Rather, we advocate having concern for the quality of your test and showing this concern by going over the test with your students each time you use it. Your students can actually save you time and effort by screening your test and identifying those items that are worth subjecting to the time-consuming processes of quantitative and qualitative item analysis.

If you are truly interested in improving the validity and reliability of your test, you can subject each item to both kinds of item analysis. Your reward will be a better test. Or you can find out which items your students found problematic and subject only those few items to analysis. Again, your reward will be a better test. The choice is yours, but, of course, we hope you choose to go over the test with your students later. Should you do so, consult the following suggested debriefing guidelines.

Debriefing Guidelines

Before handing back answer sheets or grades:

Discuss Problem Items.   Discuss any items you found problematic in scoring the test. This sets the stage for rational discussion and makes for more effective consideration of the item(s) in question. Also, you are more likely to have the attention of the students than you would if they were looking over their answer sheets or thinking about the grades they received.

Listen to Student Reactions.   Ask for student reactions to your comments and *listen* to their reactions. Again, you are setting the stage for rational discussion of the test by letting the students know you are interested in their feedback. Remember, your goal is to improve the validity and reliability of your test by improving on its weaknesses. When you or your students begin to respond emotionally, defensiveness is likely to replace listening and issues of power and control replace rational discussion. In short, improving the test may seem less important than asserting your authority. You will have plenty of opportunities to assert your authority and few opportunities to improve your test. Try to keep these issues separate, and use the few opportunities you do have for test improvement as advantageously as you can.

Avoid On-the-Spot Decisions.   Tell your students that you will consider their comments, complaints, and suggestions, but you will not make any decisions about omitting items, partial credit, extra credit, and so forth until you have had time to study and think about the test data. You may want to make it clear that soliciting their comments is only for the purpose of preparing the next test, not for reconsidering grades for the present test.

Be Equitable with Changes.

If you decide to make changes, let your students know that any changes in scoring will apply to all students, not just those who raise objections.

After handing back answer sheets or grades:

Ask Students to Double-Check.

Ask students to double-check your arithmetic, and ask any who feel clerical errors have been made to see you as soon as possible. Here you are presenting yourself as human by admitting that you can make errors.

Ask Students to Identify Problems.

If time permits, ask students to identify the items they find problematic and why they are so. Make note of the items and problems. Such items may then be discussed or worked into some new instructional objectives.

We have been suggesting that you use the time you spend returning your test as an opportunity to improve your test. To the extent that you can elicit relevant and constructive feedback from your class, you will be likely to reach this goal. In trying to remain emotionally detached from your test and nondefensive, it is useful to keep a few points in mind:

1. Your test will include at least some items that can be improved. You are human!
2. Students are criticizing your skill as a test constructor, not you as a person. Admittedly, though, frustrated students can get too personal. When this happens, try to remember what's behind it—frustration with your test.
3. The quality of an item is not necessarily related to the loudness with which complaints are made. At times, items that students loudly protest are indeed poor items. At other times they are simply difficult or challenging items. Use quantitative item analysis to determine which is the case.
4. When it appears necessary to rescore a test or award credit, keep in mind that research has shown that rescoring tends to be highly related to the original scoring. Thus, although some individual scores may change, one's rank in relation to others is not likely to change much. For all their protest, students seldom really gain much other than letting off steam.
5. Finally, keep in mind that the most important objectives for debriefing are to improve your test and to gain insight into the effectiveness and thoroughness of your instruction and to plan new objectives that can address the problems students had in learning the test content.

THE PROCESS OF EVALUATING CLASSROOM ACHIEVEMENT

Many of the various components of testing that have been presented in the last several chapters are specific and technical. You may wonder how important they are. Unfortunately, none of the major steps we have focused on can be considered optional because they are all components of a single process—the process of evaluating classroom achievement. It is important to keep this in mind since valid and reliable measurement of classroom achievement depends on *each* and *all* components. Remember, the general public is clamoring for accountability, and one of the factors for which teachers are likely to be held more and more accountable is classroom achievement. Spend the time now to master the skills involved in validly and reliably measuring classroom achievement. You will reap the benefits later. The process of measuring classroom achievement is depicted in Figure 8.4, which summarizes all of the important components of achievement testing that we have discussed thus far.

There's nothing for you to do now but go out and do it. If you've studied and worked at these chapters, you are ahead in the test-construction game. What that means for you is better tests that cause fewer students and parents to complain and are more valid and reliable measurements of achievement.

SUMMARY

In Chapter 8 many issues related to test assembly, administration, scoring, and analysis were covered. Major points mentioned were:

1. When assembling a test:
   a. Group all items of same or similar format together
   b. Arrange items so that item difficulty progresses from easy to hard
   c. Space items to eliminate overcrowding
   d. Keep items and options on the same page
   e. Place contextual material above the items to which they refer
   f. Arrange answers in a random pattern
   g. Decide how students are to record answers
   h. Be sure to include a space for the student's name
   i. Be sure directions are specific and accurate
   j. Proofread your master copy before reproducing it
2. Care must be taken in reproducing the test to avoid illegible copies that would impair test validity.
3. In administering a test, make an effort to:
   a. Induce a positive test-taking attitude

FIGURE 8.4 | The Process of Measuring Achievement in the Classroom

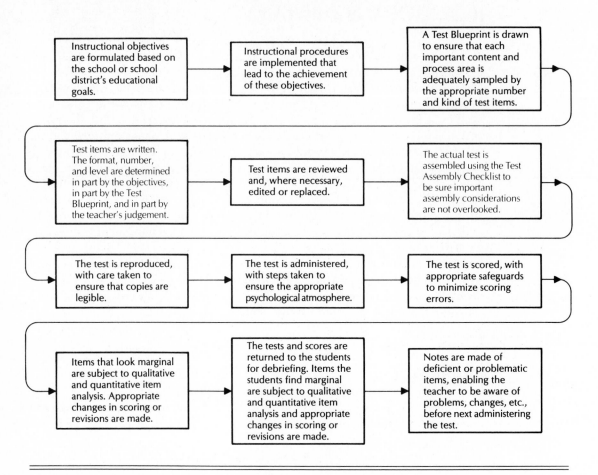

b. Maximize the achievement nature of the test
c. Equalize the advantages test-wise students have over nontest-wise students
d. Avoid surprise tests
e. Provide special instructions before the tests are actually distributed.
f. Alternate your test distribution procedures
g. Have students check that they have the entire test
h. Keep distractions to a minimum
i. Alert students to the amount of time left toward the end of the test
j. Clarify test collection procedures before handing out the test
4. In scoring the test, try to:
a. Have the key prepared in advance
b. Have the key checked for accuracy

c. Score blindly

d. Check for multiple answers if machine scoring is used

e. Double check scores, if scored by hand

f. Record scores before returning the tests

5. Quantitative item analysis is a mathematical approach to assessing an item's utility.

6. An item's difficulty level (p) is computed by dividing the number of students who answered correctly by the total number of students who attempted the item.

7. An item's discrimination index (D) is computed by subtracting the number of students who answered correctly in the low-scoring half of the class from the number of students who answered correctly in the high-scoring half of the class, and dividing the remainder by the number of students in the upper or lower group.

8. Keyed correct options should discriminate positively (positive D value), and incorrect options should discriminate negatively (negative D value).

9. Quantitative item analysis helps us decide whether to retain or eliminate an item, which distractor(s) should be modified or eliminated, whether an item is miskeyed, whether guessing occurred, and whether ambiguity is present.

10. Qualitative item analysis is a nonmathematical approach to assessing an item's utility.

11. Qualitative item analysis is performed by checking an item's content validity and inspecting it for technical faults, as outlined in Chapters 5, 6, and 7.

12. After the test has been scored, but before you give students their scores:

    a. Discuss any items considered to be problematic

    b. Listen to student concerns, trying to stay unemotional

    c. Let students know you will consider their comments but will not make any decisions affecting their scores until you have had time to reflect on their comments

    d. Let students know that any changes made will apply equally to all students

13. After the students are given their scores, ask them to check for clerical errors.

For Practice

*1. Compute p, the difficulty index, for the following items. Interpret your results. (The asterisk indicates the correct option.)

	Options		
A	B*	C	D
10	5	8	0

	Options		
A	B	C*	D
4	2	16	3

*2. Compute D, the discrimination index, for the following items. Interpret your results.

(Class size = 40)

Options

	A	B	C	D*
Upper	3	0	7	10
Lower	5	4	9	2

(Class size = 30)

Options

	A*	B	C	D
Upper	3	5	7	0
Lower	8	5	1	1

*3. Identify which of the following items are likely to be miskeyed, which are likely to be susceptible to guessing, and which are probably ambiguous.

	A*	B	C	D
a. Upper half	8	0	7	2

	A	B	C*	D
b. Upper half	10	2	4	3

	A	B*	C	D
c. Upper half	3	11	3	10

	A*	B	C	D
d. Upper half	9	8	11	9

	A*	B	C	D
e. Upper half	0	1	6	2

*4. Do a complete item analysis for the following item data. Use the Quantitative Item Analysis Checklist as your guide, answering each of the questions indicated.

Class size = 20

Options

	A*	B	C	D
Upper	3	2	3	2
Lower	2	3	1	4

*Answers for these questions appear in Appendix D.

Report Card Grades

MARKS AND MARKING SYSTEMS

After you have administered your test, you score it and assign a grade to the test. This grade is not what we will be referring to in this chapter. In this chapter we will discuss several issues related to the assignment of *marks*—cumulative grades that reflect academic achievement at the end of a six- or nine-week marking period, semester, or school year.

WHAT IS THE PURPOSE OF A MARK?

Marks are assigned to provide feedback about student achievement. We will reiterate this point several times in this chapter, not because it is so difficult to comprehend, but because it is so often forgotten. All too often marks have been assigned as rewards and punishments. This is not what they are intended for.

WHY BE CONCERNED ABOUT MARKING?

Marks have become an accepted and expected aspect of our culture. Students come to realize very early in their educational careers that they will be graded or marked depending on their performance in school. Parents of students, having been graded themselves, realize that the marks a student receives may well affect their child's educational, occupational, and financial status by opening or closing various opportunities. Parents know that children are compared with each other through their marks. Thus, marks have considerable meaning for both child and parent.

Educators also are strongly influenced by marks, often relegating pupils to faster or slower tracks, depending on their marks. Since marks carry a great deal of importance for many people, it seems sensible that care and objectivity be exercised in assigning marks. Unfortunately, this is often not the case. Rather than being assigned accurately, in hopes of presenting as valid a picture of student achievement as possible, marks are sometimes assigned in haste, or according to nebulous, undefined, and little-understood "marking systems." Different marking systems have different advantages and disadvantages—some of which the average teacher often does not know. We will acquaint you with various marking systems so that you may choose the system that best fits your situation. In general such systems compare students with other students or with established standards of knowledge or are based on aptitude, effort, and improvement.

WHAT SHOULD A MARK REFLECT?

What a mark should reflect depends on the subject or topic being marked. We generally talk about marks in relation to reading achievement, math achievement, and so on. However, marks are also assigned in areas like conduct, study skills, and responsibility. When marks are related to academic subjects, marks should reflect *academic achievement,* and nothing more!

Marks are assigned to provide feedback about academic achievement in order for students to be compared according to their achievement. If marks reflect *only* academic achievement and are assigned consistently according to a system, such marks may be compared with considerable validity (as long as the system according to which the marks are assigned is made clear). But when a single mark represents a hodgepodge of factors (for example, achievement, attitude, attendance, punctuality, or conduct) or systems (for example, comparisons with other students, comparisons with standards of effort, or improvement), interpretation or comparison of such marks becomes a hopeless task. Unfortunately, the latter case characterizes some marking practices today. Different schools employ different marking systems and weigh various nonachievement factors in assigning marks, making direct and meaningful comparisons of grades from two schools difficult at best.

We are *not* suggesting that information about nonachievement factors, such as conduct, punctuality, and so forth, should not be reported or is unimportant. We *are* suggesting that such information should *not* be mixed with test scores and other indicators of academic achievement in a single grade. In other words, don't mix apples with oranges in a single mark for an academic subject. All this may seem perfectly obvious, but strange things happen when marks are assigned. It's all too tempting to use marks as vehicles to reach, or try to reach, other ends. Consider the following dialogue:

PARENT: Mr. Stokes, Jack got a D in reading this six weeks, but he's had A's in reading all year. I don't understand. He seems to be reading better all the time, but I'm no teacher, what can I do to help him?

TEACHER: One thing you can do is tell him to stop looking out the window during oral reading. Some of these fifth-graders seem to think that what is going on outside is more important than reading!

PARENT: Do you mean Jack is being disruptive in class?

TEACHER: Yes, he looks out the window, then the next thing you know another one does, then another . . .

PARENT: Have you asked him why he's doing it?

TEACHER: Of course, but it's always the same excuse—"I'm bored, listening to the others read aloud what I've already read to myself."

PARENT: I see, but what about his reading ability—has it declined?

TEACHER: Oh no! Jack's one of the top readers in the class—there's nothing he can't read.

PARENT: So he's a top reader, but he got a D in reading for not paying attention—is that it?

TEACHER: Mrs. Burns! What do you think I am? I grade on achievement—not on conduct!

PARENT: Why *did* he get the D then? It sounds as though he was punished for not paying attention.

TEACHER: You've got it wrong. He failed to turn in two homework assignments. That's an automatic D in all my classes. Someone's got to teach these kids responsibility.

PARENT: Mr. Stokes, I know that Sarah Smith failed to turn in two homework assignments, and she got an A.

TEACHER: That's different, she pays attention during oral reading. So, it's obvious that she's getting more out of the class. She also tries harder, even though she's not as smart as Jack.

PARENT: Mr. Stokes, you certainly are an exceptional teacher.

TEACHER: Thank you, Mrs. Burns, but it won't work—Jack's D still stands.

Unfortunately, this type of dialogue is not uncommon. We agree with the teacher in that we feel grades should be based on achievement, not conduct. However, it is quite clear that Jack's D is unrelated to reading achievement. By the teacher's own admission, Jack is reading well, but his classroom *behavior* is not congruent with Mr. Stokes's expectations, and he failed to turn in some homework assignments—another behavioral deficiency that Mr. Stokes equates with poor reading achievement. To what is Mr. Stokes comparing Jack's reading achievement? We can't be sure, although effort and aptitude were mentioned.

It appears that the main function of the marks in this case is punishment. Rather than providing feedback to the student about *reading* achievement, Mr. Stokes is punishing Jack for off-task behavior during class and for less-than-perfect compliance with his homework expectations. The major problem we see here is that the main function of grades—to provide feedback about achievement—has been lost in Mr. Stokes's zeal to change Jack's behavior. In too many cases, a single grade is used to report achievement, conduct, homework compliance, tardiness, and so on. This would be *less* of a problem, if this were done consistently across schools. However, different schools weight each of these differently. The real point is that as long as grades continue to be based on factors other than achievement, we are robbing ourselves of the effective use of the main purpose of grading—evaluating *achievement*. Let's consider the different marking systems employed in schools.

MARKING SYSTEMS

Various types of marking systems have been used in the schools. They may be considered along two dimensions:

1. Type of comparison involved
2. Type of symbol used

Types of Comparisons

Often the type of symbol a teacher uses is determined at the school or district level—the teacher has little to say about whether an A–F, E–G–S–U, or numerical marking system is employed. However, the classroom teacher often has more flexibility and autonomy in deciding how to assign the marks. That is, teachers often have considerable control over *how* they decide who gets an A or B. As mentioned earlier, marks are based on comparisons, usually from among comparisons of students with:

1. Other students
2. Established standards
3. Aptitude
4. Actual versus potential effort
5. Actual versus potential improvement

Each of these systems has advantages and limitations. Our aim is to acquaint you with these so you may choose wisely. Whichever system you choose to employ, be sure to indicate it on the report card. Remember, the function of marking is to provide feedback on achievement. However, a grade of B based on effort versus a grade of B based on comparisons to established standards can reflect very different absolute levels of achievement. Indicating your marking system will minimize potential misinterpretations of a student's level of achievement.

Comparisons with Other Students.

Certainly you have had professors who have graded "on the curve." It almost sounds illegal, shady, or underhanded. It seems at times that this is some mysterious method by which test grades are transformed into semester marks. Basically, all that the expression "grading on the curve" means is that your grade or mark depends on how your achievement compares with the achievement of other students in your class. You may recall from Chapter 3 that such an approach is also called norm-referenced. Certain proportions of the class are assigned A's, B's, etc., regardless of their absolute level of performance on a test. In such a system a student who misses 50 percent of the items on a test might get an A, F, or any other grade on the test depending on how his or her score of 50 percent compared with the scores of the other students in the class. If the score was higher than those of 95 percent of the students, the student would likely get an A. Sometimes districts or schools encourage grading on the curve by specifying the percentages of students who will be assigned various grades. The following distribution is an example:

Grade	Percent of Students
A	10
B	25
C	40
D	20
F	5

The main advantage of such a system is that it simplifies marking decisions. The student is either in the top 10 percent or he or she doesn't get an A. There is no apparent need for deliberation or agonizing over what cut-off scores should determine if students get this grade or that.

There are several disadvantages in such a system. First, this type of marking system fails to consider differences due to the overall ability level of the class. Imagine the disappointment that would result if such a system were imposed on a class of intellectually gifted students—none of whom had ever earned less than a B. Suddenly 65 percent would be transformed into C through F students. Regardless of achievement, in such a system some students will always get A's, and some will always get F's.

Another problem involves the percentages—why not 5 percent A's, or 15 percent A's? These percentages are rather arbitrarily set. Furthermore, what does it mean when a student gets an A? Has the student mastered all course content? Or was the student lucky enough to be in with a class of slow learners? Such a system says nothing about *absolute* achievement, which makes comparisons across grades and schools difficult.

Finally, consider the teacher in such a system. No matter how well or poorly the teacher teaches, his or her students always get the same percentage of grades. There is little, if any, reward available through seeing grades on the whole improve following improved teaching. As a result a teacher may not feel quite as motivated to improve teaching.

Comparison with Established Standards.

In this marking system, it is possible for all students or no students to get A's or F's or any other grade in between. How much the rest of the students in the class achieve is irrelevant to a student's grade. All that is relevant is whether a student attains a defined standard of achievement or performance. We labeled this approach *criterion-referenced* in Chapter 3. In such a system, letter grades may be assigned based on the percentage of test items answered correctly, as the distribution below illustrates:

Grade	Percent of items answered correctly
A	85
B	75
C	65
D	55
F	less than 55

Thus, a student who answers 79 percent of the test items correctly earns a B, regardless of whether the rest of the class did better, poorer, or about the same. Obviously, such a system requires some prior knowledge of what level of achievement or performance is reasonable to expect and the difficulty of the test.

There are several advantages to such a system. First, it is possible, in theory, for all students to obtain high grades if they put forth sufficient effort (assuming the percentage cut-offs are not unreasonably high). Second, assignment of grades is simplified. A student either has answered 75 percent of the items correctly or hasn't. As with comparison with other students, there is no apparent need to deliberate or agonize over assigning grades. Finally, assuming that ability levels of incoming students remain fairly constant and that tests remain comparable in validity and difficulty, teachers who work to improve teaching effectiveness should see improvement in grades with the passage of time. Presumably, this would help motivate teachers to continue working to improve their effectiveness.

As you might expect, such a system also has its drawbacks. Establishing a standard is no small task. Just what is reasonable for an A may vary from school to school and from time to time, as a result of ability levels, societal pressures, and curriculum changes. Furthermore, should the same standards be maintained for a gifted or a special education class as for an average class? Another problem is that the public and administrators often have difficulty "adjusting" to a marking system that potentially allows everyone to make an A. It is a curious fact of life that everyone presses for excellence in education, but many balk at marking systems that make attainment of excellence within everyone's reach.

Comparisons with Aptitude.

Aptitude is another name for potential or ability. In such systems students are compared neither to other students nor to established standards. Instead, they are compared to themselves. That is, marks are assigned depending on how closely to their potential students are achieving. Thus, students with high aptitude or potential who are achieving at high levels would get high grades, since they would be achieving at their potential. Those with high aptitude and average achievement would get lower grades, since they would be achieving below their potential. But students with average aptitude and average achievement would get high grades, since they would be considered to be achieving at their potential. Such a system sounds attractive to many educators. However, serious problems exist as Table 9.1 shows.

Table 9.1 illustrates that the concept of assigning grades based on the congruence of a student's achievement with the student's aptitude is quite sensible for high-aptitude students. Look at what happens for the low-aptitude students, however. If a student's aptitude is low enough, the student would have a hard time achieving below his or her potential. Thus the student always would be achieving at or above the expected level. Would this be fair to the moderate- and high-ability students? Perhaps more important, can you see how such a system would greatly complicate interpreting grades? For example, a C for a high-aptitude student might indicate 70 percent mastery, while for an average-aptitude student it might indicate 60 percent, and perhaps 50 percent mastery for the low-aptitude student. The same grade may mean very different things in terms of absolute achievement.

TABLE 9.1 The Relationships Among Aptitude, Achievement, and Marks in Marking Systems Based on Comparisons of Achievement with Aptitude

Aptitude Level	Achievement Level	Marks
High	High	High
	Average	Average
	Low	Low
Average	High	High
	Average	High
	Low	Average
Low	High	High
	Average	High
	Low	High

Other drawbacks of such a system relate to statistical considerations beyond the scope of this text that affect the reliability of such comparisons. Another is the tendency for the achievement scores of slow learners to increase and the achievement scores of fast learners to decrease when tested again. Technically this phenomenon is called the *regression toward the mean* effect—the more extreme an achievement score, the greater it can be expected to "regress" or fall back toward the average or mean of all students at another testing. Finally, such a system requires more complex recordkeeping than the first two systems discussed. Such a system, as appealing as it is at first glance, is not practical.

Comparison of Achievement with Effort.

Systems that compare achievement with effort are similar to those that compare achievement with aptitude. Students who get average test scores but have to work hard to get them are given high marks. Students who get average scores but do not have to work hard to get them are given lower grades.

Several problems plague marking systems that are based on effort. First, we have no known measure of effort. Unlike aptitude, for which reliable and valid measures exist, effort is at best estimated by informal procedures. Second, within such a system children are punished for being bright and catching on quickly, while other children are rewarded for taking a long time to master concepts. Third, there is the old problem of the marks not representing academic achievement. Effort may cover up academic attainment, making marks all the more difficult to interpret. Finally, recordkeeping is once again complex.

The advantage cited for grading based on effort is that it serves to motivate the slower or turned-off students, but it may also serve to turn-off the brighter students who would quickly see such a system as unfair. Whatever the case, the primary function of marking—to provide feedback about academic achievement—is not well served by such a system.

Comparison of Achievement with Improvement.

Such systems compare the amount of improvement between the beginning (pretest) and end (posttest) of instruction. Students who show the most progress get the highest grades. An obvious problem occurs for the student who does well on the pretest. Improvement for such a student is likely to be less overall than for a student who does poorly on the pretest. In fact, bright students have been known to "play dumb" on pretests when such systems are in force. Other shortcomings of such systems include the statistical problems we mentioned before in regard to comparisons with aptitude (that is, unreliability of such comparisons and regression toward the mean) and unwieldy recordkeeping.

Which System Should You Choose?

We have seen that each system has significant drawbacks as well as advantages. Which should you choose? In our opinion, comparisons with established standards would best suit the primary function of marking—to provide feedback about academic achievement. Once standards are established, comparisons among schools and students may be more easily made. It seems to us that such a system has the best chance of reducing misinterpretation of marks.

In reality, many schools and districts have adopted multiple marking systems, such as assigning separate grades for achievement and effort or achievement, effort, and improvement. As long as the achievement portion of the grade reflects *only* achievement, such systems seem to be reasonable. Two disadvantages of such systems are worth noting, however. First, they double or triple the number of grades to be assigned and interpreted, leading to an increase in recordkeeping and interpretation time. Second, unless the purpose of each grade is explained very clearly on the report card, marking systems are often difficult for parents to decipher.

Types of Symbols

Within marking systems, a variety of symbols has been used. Some of the more common types are discussed in this section.

Letter Grades.

most popular

Using letter grades is the most common symbol system. According to Pinchach and Breland (1973), 68 percent of American high schools used the letters A–F to report marks in 1972. Often, plus and minus symbols are used to indicate finer distinctions between the letter grades. This system along with its variations (E, G, S, U) has several advantages that have led to its widespread adoption and continuing popularity.

First, the letter system is widely understood. Students, teachers, parents, administrators, and employers understand, at least in a general sense, that grades of A represent excellent or exceptional performance and grades of D or F represent marginal or poor performance. Second, such a system is compact, requiring only one or two spaces to report a summary mark of an entire semester's work. Third, such a system has just about the optimal number of levels of judgment humans can effectively exercise (Miller 1956). It can have as few as five or as many as fifteen if plus and minus signs are used.

Limitations of the system are worth considering. First, the specific meaning of letter grades varies from class to class and from school to school. Different schools and districts tend to use different marking systems and, as will be discussed later in this chapter, also tend to combine and weight the components of a mark differently. Consequently, a grade of A in one school or district may represent performance similar to a grade of B or even C in another. Second, letter grades fail to indicate clearly the student's actual level of mastery. There is often a considerable difference between the achievement of a "low-B" student and that of a "high-B" student. Finally, because of this, averaging of letter grades often results in a loss of information or misinterpretation of the student's actual achievement. When averaging letter grades, it is necessary to go back to the actual numerical grades to obtain the "correct" average.

Numerical Grades.

According to Pinchach and Breland (1973), the numerical symbol system was used by 16 percent of American high schools in 1972. Such systems usually employ 100 as the highest mark, and report cards often carry letter grade equivalents for the range of numerical grades. For example:

Numerical Grade	Letter Grade
90–100	A
80–89	B
70–79	C
60–69	D
below 60	F

Numerical grades have three main advantages. First, like letter grades, they provide a convenient summary mark for a semester's or year's work. Second, unlike letter grades, numerical grades are easily averaged to obtain the "correct" final marks. Third, they are widely understood—most pupils and parents realize there are substantial differences between a mark of 95 and one of 75.

There are also disadvantages to such a system. First, the discriminations are finer than humans can really make (Miller 1956). No one can make 40 reliable distinctions between grades from 61–100. Another way of saying this is that it is not possible to determine the real difference between a grade of 67 and a grade of 68 or between a grade of 95 and a grade of 96. Second, as with letter grades, we are never sure just what a grade means, since standards may vary considerably from school to school.

Other Symbols.

Pass-fail (P–F) grading reached its popularity peak about a decade ago. Few schools employ this approach today because of its many shortcomings, one of which is that such symbols do not provide enough information: P could mean the student exhibited anywhere from exceptional to marginal performance in the class. This makes it difficult for employers and admissions officers to evaluate applicants. Students themselves have complained about the same lack of information—they really do not know how well they did. Finally, students tend to do the minimum necessary to earn a P under such systems.

Checklists.

A common adjunct to a letter or numerical symbol system is a checklist. Since both letter and numerical symbol systems fail to define just what a student can or cannot do, many report cards now include skill checklists to go along with their grade symbols for each subject. Checklists are also used to provide information about nonacademic aspects of the child. For example, checklists often are provided to identify problems in the areas of conduct, social skills, responsibility, and organization. Properly utilized checklists represent useful supplements to letter or numerical grades and can convey much more detailed information about the student without contaminating or confusing the interpretation of a student's overall achievement level.

As mentioned at the beginning of this chapter, districts and schools usually decide which symbol system teachers must use. In such situations you have little choice but to employ the required system. It is more likely though that you will have some say about how the marks are actually assigned (that is, what you will compare student achievement with). Now that you have been exposed to the pros and cons of various systems, you should be able to make better use of any marking or symbol system you are required—or choose—to use. However, there are a number of technical considerations regarding the combining and weighting of the components of a mark that must be considered before we leave this topic. The following discussion covers points that, unfortunately, most classroom teachers are unaware of regarding marks. Master the points and procedures covered, and you will have yet another important tool to add to your growing expertise in classroom measurement and evaluation.

COMBINING AND WEIGHTING THE COMPONENTS OF A MARK

As we mentioned, the classroom teacher seldom has control over the symbol system employed but may have latitude insofar as deciding on the type of comparison used to assign marks at the end of a marking period. But how does a teacher go about combining the grades from two quizzes, one major test, several homework assignments, and a term paper into a mark without allowing one or more of these factors to influence the final mark too heavily or lightly? Recall the example at the beginning of this chapter. Mr. Stokes said that Jack's failure to turn in two homework assignments earned him "an automatic D," regardless of Jack's achievement on tests, oral reading, papers, etc. While Mr. Stokes later contradicted himself on this point, there are some teachers who do adhere to such or similar practices. This would be an example of allowing a component of a mark to influence that mark *too heavily*. Remember that the main purpose of marks is to provide feedback about student achievement.

It goes without saying that such feedback is beneficial only if it is accurate. To attain this goal, each component of a final mark (tests, quizzes, homework assignments, papers, etc.) should affect the final mark *only to the appropriate extent*. At first glance it might seem simple enough to do this by weighting components considered more important (e.g., a final test grade) more heavily than components considered less important (e.g., homework grades) in computing the final mark. While differential weighting of components is an important step in arriving at an accurate, fair, and just final mark, it is only *one* step of several that must be taken, and taken carefully, to prevent a final mark from misrepresenting student achievement. Unfortunately, failure to recognize this fact is widespread in classrooms today. As a result, feedback provided about student achievement through final marks is often distorted. It may be argued that distorted feedback is more troublesome than no feedback at all. To sensitize you to the complexity of what appears to be a simple issue, consider the following:

Who is the Better Teacher?

Mr. Nickels and Ms. Dimes, history teachers at different high schools in the same district, decided prior to the school year to collaborate in developing their instructional objectives, methods, tests, quizzes, and assignments for the upcoming school year. Since they always had similar students in the past, in terms of background and aptitude, they saw no problem in reducing their workload by using the same objectives, methods, and measurement instruments for both of their classes. They did have some concerns about students from the different schools "finding out" that they were using the same materials and sharing them, but they decided that this potential problem could be avoided by administering the quizzes and tests at the same time and by giving out assignments on the same day. Pleased that they had ironed out all the wrinkles, they agreed to meet at the end of the semester to compare marks. They expected that the marks would be about the same, on the average, for both classes, since the marking symbols and the marking system they were required to use by the district were the same in both of their schools, and they both considered quizzes and test grades to be more important than homework or term paper grades. Therefore, they agreed to weight their students' quiz and test grades twice as heavily in computing their final marks.

Mr. Nickels and Ms. Dimes both prided themselves on their ability and dedication as teachers. They decided that this would be a good opportunity to determine who was the "better" teacher. Since their classes would be similar, and since they would both be using the same objectives, methods, measurement instruments, and weights for the various components that would go into their students' marks, they agreed that any significant difference in the marks earned by their classes "must " reflect differences in teaching ability and/or effectiveness. To spice things up a bit, they agreed to wager a cheeseburger on the outcome. The competition was on, and both Mr. Nickels and Ms. Dimes anticipated their own students earning the higher marks. Each teacher expected to earn a cheeseburger at the end of the semester.

At their end-of-semester-meeting, Mr. Nickels was shocked, however, to find that on the average Ms. Dimes' students earned marks that were one-half to a full letter grade higher than those earned by his students. Not panicking, he applied what he had learned in his college tests and measurements class. Mr. Nickels compared aptitude test scores for the two classes, hoping that by chance there would be some difference in aptitude between these two classes and their previous classes. He expected he would find significantly higher aptitude scores for Ms. Dimes' class, which would explain why their semester marks were higher than those of his class. After comparing aptitude scores for the two classes, however, Mr. Nickels found them to be quite comparable. "I could have told you that," responded Ms. Dimes somewhat haughtily.

Unwilling to concede, and suspicious by nature, Mr. Nickels next suggested that Ms. Dimes must have "fixed" things by changing the curriculum—perhaps only covering two-thirds of the material he covered. This would have enabled her students to have more time to master the material and thereby earn higher grades. Offended by this challenge to her integrity, Ms. Dimes tossed her objectives, curriculum guide, and all the semester's assignments, quizzes, and tests to Mr. Nickels. "Read 'em and weep!" she exclaimed. And Mr. Nickels did . . . at first. After comparing the materials piece by piece with his own he found them to be identical. Next, however, he laboriously compared the test and quiz grades for both classes, since this is what both he and Ms. Dimes agreed would be the major basis for the marks of their students. To his relief he discovered that the scores from both classes on the tests and quizzes *were virtually the same.*

"Look here, Ms. Dimes! The test and quiz grades for both classes are the same—you must have made a mistake in computing your marks," said Mr. Nickels. "Impossible, I triple-checked all my computations," stated Ms. Dimes firmly. However, when she compared the grades herself she agreed that Mr. Nickels was correct. The test and quiz grades were almost identical, yet she had assigned marks that on the average were one-half to a full letter grade higher than those assigned by Mr. Nickels.

Both teachers were confused. Not only were they unable to settle their bet, they were puzzled as to how such a situation could occur. They decided to review the procedures they used to combine and weight the marks their pupils had obtained. What they learned from this review is described in the next section.

Combining Grades from Quizzes, Tests, Papers, Homework, etc., into a Single Mark

Let's consider a set of grades earned by a typical student in Mr. Nickels's class, who earned a mark of B, and a set of grades of a typical student in Ms. Dimes's class, who also earned a B over the semester (see Table 9.2). Remember, both teachers used the same measurement instruments and applied the same scoring schemes to these instruments. Also, consistent with good measurement practice, they included only *achievement* factors in assigning their marks, not *nonachievement* factors, such as attendance, conduct, appearance, effort, etc.

TABLE 9.2 | Grades of Nickels's and Dimes's Students

	Student (Nickels)	Student (Dimes)
semester test (75–100)	86	76
quiz No. 1 (5–10)	9	5
quiz No. 2 (5–10)	9	7
homework (15–25)	18	25
paper (15–25)	18	25
TOTAL POINTS EARNED	140	138

Note: the lowest and highest scores for each component are in parentheses.

Simply looking at the data in Table 9.2 indicates that the students' performance was different in an important way. Ms. Dimes' student obtained very low test and quiz grades but had very high homework and term paper grades, while Mr. Nickels' student displayed an opposite tendency. Yet both earned about the same number of overall points out of a possible 170, and both received B's. Since both teachers emphasize test and quiz grades over homework and term paper grades, this doesn't make sense, especially when one considers that Ms. Dimes' student had the lowest grade on one quiz and the second lowest grade on the final test—and yet still earned a mark of B! To understand how this happened we must consider how the obtained component scores were combined and weighted by the teachers.

Ms. Dimes, doing what most teachers commonly do in such situations, simply assigned double weight to the quiz and test scores and then added the scores:

$$(76 \times 2) + (5 \times 2) + (7 \times 2) + 25 + 25 = 226$$

Next she divided this number by the total number of points possible $[(100 \times 2) + (10 \times 2) + (10 \times 2) + 25 + 25 = 290]$ to arrive at the percentage of points earned by this student:

$$226/290 = 78\%$$

Since the district mandated that students who earn 78–88.99 percent of possible points be assigned a B, she assigned a mark of B to this student and followed the same procedure for all her students. Thus, even though Ms. Dimes herself believes that test and quiz performance is most important, and "weighted" these scores to reflect this belief, this student ended up with a grade of B in spite of having the lowest grade on one of the quizzes and close to the lowest grade on the final test! Unknowingly and unintentionally, Ms. Dimes is employing a combining and weighting procedure that contradicts her beliefs and her intent.

Mr. Nickels, assigned the *same weight* to the various components as did Ms. Dimes. However, he recalled that in his tests and measurements class his instructor emphasized over and over the importance of considering the *variation* or *range,* of the scores, not just the scores themselves, in combining component scores into a *composite score,* which is what a grading period or semester mark actually is. Mr. Nickels also recalled that the reason for this is that it is the *extent of the variability of the scores of each component that determines largely the extent of the component's contribution to the composite score, NOT simply the weight attached to the component.*

The variation, or range, of scores for each of the components is listed below. The range is obtained by subtracting the lowest score from the highest score. A more accurate estimate of variation, called the standard deviation (covered in Chapter 13), is actually preferable to the range when combining component scores into a composite score. However, the range is an adequate estimate for most classroom purposes and is less time consuming and easier to compute than the standard deviation. Here are the ranges for the five score components:

	RANGE
semester test	100−75=25
quiz No. 1	10−5 = 5
quiz No. 2	10−5 = 5
homework	25−15=10
paper	25−15=10

After determining the range for each of the components, Mr. Nickels avoided the problem Ms. Dimes had by realizing he had to *equate the variability of each component before he could double the weights of the quizzes and the tests*. Since the semester test had the greatest variability, 25 points, he did so by multiplying the quizzes by 5, the homework grade by 2.5, and the paper grade by 2.5. This procedure *equated* the variability of the scores (i.e., all components then had a range of 25 points). Only then did he *weight* the scores by multiplying the quiz and test scores by two. Table 9.3 illustrates the procedure followed by Mr. Nickels. The maximum number of points possible, *after equating and weighting,* is 525 (200 + 100 + 100 + 62.5 + 62.5 = 525). Dividing the points earned by the points possible gives us this student's percentage:

$$440/525 = 83.8\%$$

Recalling that the district's policy is to assign marks of B to all students who earn between 78 percent and 88.99 percent of possible points, Mr. Nickels as-

---

TABLE 9.3   Weighting Procedure Followed by Mr. Nickels

	score	×	equating factor	= equated score	×	weight	= weighted score
semester test	86	×	1	86	×	2	172
quiz No. 1	9	×	5	45	×	2	90
quiz No. 2	9	×	5	45	×	2	90
homework	18	×	2.5	44	×	1	44
paper	18	×	2.5	44	×	1	44
						TOTAL	440

signed a mark of B to this student—the same mark assigned by Ms. Dimes to her student, in spite of this student's significantly better test and quiz performance.

Which procedure best achieved the goals of the teacher, that is, to weight test and quiz performance twice as heavily as homework and term paper performance? Which procedure do you think is more fair? Which procedure is less likely to result in a storm of protest from the students, who will invariably compare their scores and marks?

In case you are still not clear as to why it is critical to *equate before you weight* in combining scores into a composite mark, let's consider one more example. This time let's compare the effects of Mr. Nickels's *correct* procedure on the mark earned by Ms. Dimes' student, as shown in Table 9.4. Dividing the total points earned after equating and weighting (397) by the total points possible (525) gives us the percentage of points earned:

$$397/525 = 75.6\%$$

According to the district's policy, this student mark would be a C. Clearly, it is more fair that this student, who has such low test and quiz grades, be assigned a lower semester mark than a student whose test and quiz grades are significantly higher.

We hope that this example has sensitized you to one of the most commonly overlooked and misapplied facets of classroom measurement and evaluation. Regardless of how good your instructional objectives, methods, and evaluation instruments are, no one benefits if you take a simplistic approach to combining scores into a composite mark. We wish that we could say that most teachers are aware of the necessity of equating scores for variability *before* weighting the

---

Table 9.4 | **Effect of Mr. Nickels's Correct Procedure on Ms. Dimes's Student's Mark**

	score	×	*equating factor*	=	*equated score*	×	*weight*	=	*weighted score*
semester test	76	×	1		76	×	2		152
quiz No. 1	5	×	5		25	×	2		50
quiz No. 2	7	×	5		35	×	2		70
homework	25	×	2.5		62.5	×	1		62.5
paper	25	×	2.5		62.5	×	1		62.5
							TOTAL		397.0

scores, but just the opposite is true. Most teachers arrive at marks pretty much as did Ms. Dimes, to the detriment of those teachers and their students.

Remember: *EQUATE before you WEIGHT* when combining scores to develop a composite mark!

SUMMARY

This chapter introduced you to various issues related to marks and marking systems. Its major points were:

1. Marks are used to provide information about student achievement.
2. Marks should reflect academic achievement and nothing more. Grades for attitude, effort, improvement, conduct, and so on should be recorded separately from marks.
3. Marks often reflect factors other than achievement and are often assigned according to a variety of marking systems. This makes valid comparisons of marks across schools, and even across teachers, difficult at best.
4. Several types of marking systems are employed in the schools today. These involve comparison of a student with:
   a. Other students (grade depends on how well the student did compared with other students)
   b. Established standards (grade depends on how well a student's performance compares with pre-established standards)
   c. Aptitude (grade depends on how consistent a student's actual achievement is with his or her achievement potential)
   d. Effort (grade depends on how hard the student works)
   e. Improvement (grade depends on how much progress a student makes over the course of instruction)
5. Each system has its advantages and disadvantages, but marking based on comparisons with established standards seems to fit best the main function of marks—to provide feedback about academic achievement.
6. The symbols most commonly used in marking systems are letter grades (A–F, E–U) and numerical grades (0–100). Such symbol systems are often combined with checklists to provide specific information about such factors as skill level, conduct, and attitude.

For Practice

1. List the pros and cons of each of the following types of marking systems:
   a. Comparison with other students
   b. Comparison with established standards
   c. Comparison of achievement with one's own aptitude

    d. Basing grades on effort

    e. Basing grades on improvement

2. Create a numerical scale for measuring effort and another for measuring improvement. Indicate, for each level of the scale, the type of behavior(s) you are looking for. What might be another way of measuring these two qualities?

3. Choose the most appropriate one from among the following pairs of symbol systems and give reasons for your choices.

    a. A–F and 0–100

    b. 0–100 and P–F

    c. E–U and P–F

4. The school in which you will teach will probably have an established marking system to report subject-matter grades. With what behaviors might you augment this marking system to report to students and parents additional information which you feel is important? How would you measure these additional behaviors?

10

CHAPTER

MEASURING ATTITUDES AND SOCIAL BEHAVIOR

"Just thinking about it makes me mad," said Bob. "I hate this class. The only reason I'm here is that the counselor told me to take it. Even though I like my other classes, this one ruins the whole semester for me. The teacher is OK, but the materials are useless, and the text is a waste of time. Sometimes I don't even attend class or do the readings. I told the teacher about my feelings. I thought she would see that some changes were needed. Guess what she said? She said that things wouldn't get better until my attitude changed! To top it off, she said she had suspected I had a bad attitude all along and listening to me just confirmed her suspicions. But it's *her* attitude that's bad. She has had a bad attitude about *me* all along and listening to her just confirmed *my* suspicions."

Have you ever felt like Bob? Well, most of us have at one time or another. No student enjoys, or is even neutral about, every class, teacher, or text. Similarly, no teacher is fortunate enough to have only interested and motivated students. Therefore, sometimes students are likely to develop negative attitudes about some classes, and sometimes teachers are likely to develop negative attitudes about some students. These are simply facts of life, but many can and should be resolved. One of the first steps toward resolving attitude problems is learning what attitudes are and what they are not.

In the situation just described, what do you think an attitude is? The teacher could tell Bob had a bad attitude from what she saw and heard. Bob could tell the teacher's attitude was negative from what he saw and heard. Seeing, looking, hearing, saying—these are what the teacher and Bob focused on to conclude that the other had a bad or negative attitude. In other words, based on what you see or hear, you draw conclusions about someone's attitude. You determine someone's attitude about something or someone from what they do or say. But just what are attitudes? Before defining what attitudes are, let's be sure we know what they are not. Attitudes are *not*:

descriptions of behaviors (you cannot see or hear them directly)
descriptions of what a person knows or understands
right or wrong, in a moral or ethical sense (although behaviors generated by attitudes may be!)
necessarily related to intelligence, age, ethnicity, social or financial status
directly measurable or observable

Attitudes *are*:

descriptions of how people typically feel about or react to other people, places, things, or ideas

Attitudes can be thought of as fairly consistent and stable ways that people feel, behave, and are predisposed to feel and behave in the presence of various stimuli.

HOW ARE ATTITUDES CLASSIFIED?

In our example, we referred to positive attitudes and negative attitudes. Others refer to attitudes as appropriate or inappropriate or as good or bad. However, we prefer to use *positive/negative,* since these terms do not necessarily imply value judgments about the attitude itself, at least not as clearly as do *good/bad,* or *appropriate/inappropriate.* We want to avoid making value judgments, since it is often not very clear whether attitudes are justified or sensible, especially for the individual in question.

Thus, we will classify attitudes as either positive or negative. But to do so, we need to decide on just what kinds of indicators or behaviors we will use to identify positive attitudes and negative attitudes. Fortunately, we can do this quite easily by considering what individuals with differing attitudes do or say in the presence of some stimulus. Consider the following:

Lisa and Lorrie are pupils in the fourth grade. As their teacher, you've noticed that Lisa:
has never missed math class
has never been late for math class
frequently is the first one to complete the math lesson
frequently is the first to finish math tests

often asks for extra math work

smiles often during math class

seldom, if ever, requires reminders to stay on task in math class

often tells you how much she likes math class

is often seen and heard explaining math concepts and procedures
to classmates

You've noticed that Lorrie:

frequently misses math class

frequently is late for math class

is usually the last to finish math lessons, on those few occasions she
does finish

has not finished a math test yet

has never asked for extra math work

constantly has a frown on her face during math class

needs constant reminders to stay on task during math

has told you several times how much she hates math

is often seen and heard telling classmates how much she hates math

Obviously, in this case the stimulus (math class) evokes different kinds of behaviors in Lisa and Lorrie. Those exhibited by Lisa may be called *approach* behaviors. Those exhibited by Lorrie may be called *avoidance* behaviors. Approach behaviors are those that result in more frequent, closer, or more intense contact with the stimulus. Such behaviors are considered to indicate a positive attitude toward the stimulus. Avoidance behaviors result in less frequent, more distant, or less intense contact with the stimulus. Such behaviors are considered to indicate a negative attitude toward the stimulus.

So far, we have considered what attitudes are—descriptions of how people typically feel about or react to other people, places, things, or ideas—and how attitudes are classified—positive if they lead to increased contact with the stimulus or negative if they lead to decreased contact with the stimulus.

WHY MEASURE ATTITUDES?

Attitude measurement can help most classroom teachers:

1. Identify early in the school year those students who are turned on or turned off to school, certain subjects, or certain teachers. Once this information is collected, the teacher may implement strategies to best utilize and challenge the turned-on students (those with positive attitudes) and to better motivate the turned-off students (those with negative attitudes).
2. Assess general changes that may take place in attitudes over time. Obviously, the teacher would prefer that students with positive attitudes get even more positive or at least maintain the same positive attitude. On the other hand,

the teacher would like to see students with negative attitudes develop more positive attitudes, or at least not develop more negative attitudes.

3. Determine the effect on student attitudes of specific aspects of the school or classroom experience. For example, it would be worthwhile to know whether a social studies unit on cultural differences alters student attitudes toward classmates from different cultures. All too often curricular or instructional innovations are implemented without really attempting to assess the effect they have on attitudes *as well as* on achievement.

Since attitudes are not directly measurable, what we will consider next are ways of measuring behaviors that are associated with positive or negative attitudes.

MEASURING ATTITUDES

Recall our example in which both the teacher and the student drew inferences about each other's attitudes based on what they saw and heard, that is, on what they observed. Indeed, one common way we assess attitudes is through observation. In the next section we will discuss two methods of carrying out observations. Afterwards we will consider several paper-and-pencil methods used to measure attitudes.

Observation

Observation can be classified into two categories, *structured* and *unstructured*. For our purposes, the difference between these two methods of assessing attitudes lies in the extent of the preparation we go through to "plan" an observation, and to record what we observe. Let's consider each method individually and then consider the pros and cons of observation as a means of assessing attitudes.

Unstructured Observation.   As the name implies, unstructured observation is open-ended. Essentially all that is done to prepare for an observation session is that the teacher identifies the time and place for the observation and how long it will last. Thus, very little preparation time is required. The teacher then observes the behavior of the pupils, recording as much as possible, or whatever appears to be useful, important, or unusual. Afterwards, an attempt is made to infer student attitudes based on the information recorded. The following illustrates data produced from an unstructured observation on the playground.

Class: 4th grade
Date: March 26
Time: 10:25 A.M.
Place: playground
Activity: recess

Notes: Sunny, cool, lots of energy, Jim on fringe of activity. Paul and Barb arguing, Mike running and yelling, Jim joins Dorothy and Mike on swings, Paula asks about math assignment, Jim leaves swing and wanders by self, Paul playing ball with Pat, Paula tells Mark about math assignment, much activity, but beginning to slow down, bell, time to line up, Paula is first, Jim last.

Once the data are recorded, the teacher's task is to make some sense of it. From this record, what conclusions can be drawn about student attitudes? Well, it seems that Paula is exhibiting approach behaviors (remember those?) related to math, and Jim exhibits avoidance behaviors related to his peers. Beyond these conclusions, little else that is useful is available. Unfortunately, this is often the case when unstructured observation is employed. Why is this so? Think for a moment about why the observation was conducted—to make inferences about student attitudes. But attitudes toward or about what or whom? About school? About math? About peers? About teachers? About playground equipment? Attitudes about what? Identifying the purpose of the observation too often is overlooked in unstructured observation.

By specifying the purpose of the observation *before* doing the observation, the task of the observer is focused. Now, rather than trying to record everything or all the important incidents, the observer can zero in on specific approach and avoidance behaviors that indicate positive and negative attitudes toward whatever or whomever has been identified. Thus, although focusing on *one aspect* of the playground interaction runs the risk of the observer overlooking potentially interesting events, the benefits in terms of reliability and relevance of the data obtained are substantial. In reality, clearly identifying the purpose of the observation is the first step in conducting a *structured* observation. Our recommendation is that you refrain from unstructured observation sessions and focus instead on structured observation sessions to measure student attitudes.

Structured Observation.   A structured observation requires more preparation time, often substantially more than an informal or unstructured observation session. It is necessary to determine *why* you are observing, *what* you expect to see or think you might see, and *how* you will record what you see. The following steps are useful in preparing for a structured observation session:

1.   Indicate why you are observing, for example:

     to determine whether students feel good about the new math curriculum

     to see whether cliques in the classroom have become more accepting of new students

     to determine whether students feel more positive about reading after your Fun-in-Reading program

2. Assemble an outline of approach and avoidance behaviors appropriate to why you are observing. To develop an appropriate list of approach and avoidance behaviors, it is often helpful to simply watch what a student does who is turned-on or turned-off to the person, thing, or activity in question and note the behaviors exhibited. For example, if you want to assess attitude toward reading following the Fun-in-Reading program, the following might be appropriate for an observation during free time:

Approach	*Avoidance*
Looks at books on table	Moves away from books on table
Picks up books on table	
Reads book(s)	Makes faces when looking at books
Tells others about a book recently read	Tells others not to read
	Expresses dislike for reading

3. If possible, list behaviors in terms of likelihood of occurrence, to save time scanning the list and recording the behavior. For example, "read books" would be further down the list than "looks at books on table" and "picks up books on table," since before you read a book you must first look at it and then pick it up. However, it is possible that someone could look at a book, pick it up, and then not read it.

4. Decide how to record the behaviors you observe. Two common methods are to:
   a. Place a checkmark to the right of the behaviors listed each time they occur, or
   b. Arrange five columns labeled "always," "often," "sometimes," "seldom," or "never" to the right of the behavior, and then put a check in the appropriate column for each behavior to indicate the approximate frequency of occurrence. These methods are illustrated in Figure 10.1.

The second checklist is most useful when the teacher is not able to devote sufficient attention to a student or students long enough to obtain valid frequency counts. Here, the teacher checks the appropriate column after observing for a while. Naturally, such an approach increases the chances of error. However, it is substantial improvement over an unstructured observation. If you have the opportunity, use the frequency approach, but the rating approach is normally an acceptable compromise.

The Likert Scale

This paper-and-pencil method of assessing attitudes was developed by and named after Rensis Likert (1932). The Likert scales have become one of the most widely used methods of attitude assessment. Likert scales consist of a series of attitude statements about some person, group, or thing. Respondents indicate the extent

FIGURE 10.1 | Two Checklists for a Structured Observation to Assess Attitudes Toward Reading

Checklist 1 *frequency Count*

Name	Date	Time

Behaviors   *Frequency*

1. Looks at books on table   _____
2. Picks up books on table   _____
3. Reads books   _____
4. Tells others about books read   _____
5. Moves away from books on table   _____
6. Makes faces when looking at books _____
7. Tells others not to read   _____
8. Expresses dislike for reading   _____

Checklist 2 *Rating scale   (although these are obs. beh.)*

Name	Date	Time

Behaviors   *Always* *Often* *Sometimes* *Seldom* *Never*
1. Looks at books on table
2. Picks up books on table
3. Reads books
4. Tells others about books read
5. Moves away from books on table
6. Makes faces when looking at books
7. Tells others not to read
8. Expresses dislike for reading

to which they agree or disagree with each statement, and the overall score then suggests whether the individual's attitude is favorable or unfavorable. Figure 10.2 illustrates a very brief Likert scale that might be used to assess attitudes toward a tests and measurement course.

Scoring Likert Scales.

To complete this scale, students would simply circle the appropriate letter for each item. In order to score the scale, weights are assigned to each letter, depending on whether the item is worded positively or negatively.

FIGURE 10.2 | A Five-Item Likert Scale to Assess Attitudes Toward a Tests and Measurement Course

DIRECTIONS: Indicate the extent to which you agree or disagree with each statement by circling the appropriate letter to the right of each statement.

	Strongly Agree	Agree	Uncertain	Disagree	Strongly Disagree
1. I have a hard time keeping awake in class.	SA	A	U	D	SD
2. This course should be required for teachers.	SA	A	U	D	SD
3. I like learning to write objective test items.	SA	A	U	D	SD
4. I daydream a lot in class.	SA	A	U	D	SD
5. I often feel like coming to this class.	SA	A	U	D	SD

For example, the weights assigned to the options for item 1, which is negatively worded, would be:

$$SA = 1$$
$$A = 2$$
$$S = 3$$
$$SD = 4$$
$$SD = 5$$

The weights assigned to the options for item 2, which is worded positively, would be:

$$SA = 5$$
$$A = 4$$
$$U = 3$$
$$D = 2$$
$$SD = 1$$

An individual's score for each item, then, would be the value assigned to the choice selected. For example, if an individual circled SA for item 1 (negatively worded), his or her score for that item would be 1. If the same individual circled SA for item 2 (positively worded), his or her score for that item would be 5. Figure

FIGURE 10.3 | Sample Likert Scale with Items Labeled as Positive or Negative, Options Circled, and Weights Assigned to Choices

	Strongly Agree	Agree	Uncertain	Disagree	Strongly Disagree
1. I have a hard time keeping awake in class. (negative)	SA	(A)	U	D	SD
	(1	2	3	4	5)
2. All teachers should have to take a course like this one. (positive)	SA	A	U	(D)	SD
	(5	4	3	2	1)
3. I like learning to write objective test items. (positive)	SA	A	U	D	(SD)
	(5	4	3	2	1)
4. I daydream a lot in class. (negative)	(SA)	A	U	D	SD
	(1	2	3	4	5)
5. I often feel like coming to this class. (positive)	SA	(A)	U	D	SD
	(5	4	3	2	1)

10.3 illustrates the attitude scale depicted in Figure 10.2 with items marked as either positive or negative, options circled, and weights assigned for the choices.

Scoring of the scale would simply require summing up the weights for the options selected and then dividing the total by the number of items. This provides the student's *mean attitude score.* The mean attitude score for our hypothetical student is 2.0 because $(2 + 2 + 1 + 1 + 4) \div 5 = 2.0$. Next, we would have to conclude whether the student's responses reflected a positive or negative attitude toward the course. Higher weights are associated with positive attitudes, and lower weights with negative attitudes. As a general rule, we draw the line at a mean rating of 3.0. That is, if the score is equal to or greater than 3.0, a positive attitude exists, and if the score is less than 3.0, as was the case for our hypothetical student in Figure 10.3, then a negative attitude exists. Let's look at one more example of scoring a Likert scale before moving on to a discussion of its advantages and disadvantages and some suggestions for writing attitude statements. Figure 10.4 again represents the Likert scale presented in Figure 10.2, but with another set of responses circled. This time, try to score the scale yourself, and conclude whether or not the mean attitude score represents a positive or negative attitude.

FIGURE 10.4 | Sample Likert Scale with Options Circled

	Strongly Agree	Agree	Uncertain	Disagree	Strongly Disagree
1. I have a hard time keeping awake in class.	SA	A	U	D	(SD)
2. All teachers should have to take a course like this one.	SA	(A)	U	D	SD
3. I like learning to write objective test items.	(SA)	A	U	D	SD
4. I daydream a lot in class.	SA	A	U	(D)	SD
5. I often feel like coming to this class.	SA	A	U	D	(SD)

What did you conclude? What is the hypothetical student's score? Does the score indicate a positive attitude? Check your answers against the solution provided.

Item	Positive/Negative	Weight of Option Selected
1	negative	5
2	positive	4
3	positive	5
4	negative	4
5	positive	1
	Total	19

$$19 \div 5 = 3.8$$

Since 3.8 is greater than 3.0, we would conclude that this student exhibits a positive attitude toward the course.

Advantages and Disadvantages of Likert Scales.

The following are probably the most salient advantages and disadvantages of Likert scales:

Advantages:
1. Quick and economical to administer and score
2. Adapts easily to most attitude measurement situations
3. Provides direct and reliable assessment of attitudes when scales are well-constructed
4. Lends itself well to item analysis procedures

Disadvantages:

1. Easily faked where individuals want to present a false impression of their attitudes (this can be offset somewhat by developing a good level of rapport with the respondents and convincing them that honest responses are in their best interests)
2. Intervals between points on the scale do not represent equal changes in attitude for all individuals (that is, the differences between SA and A may be slight for one individual and great for another)
3. Internal consistency of the scale may be difficult to achieve (care must be taken to have unidimensional items aimed at a single person, group, thing, or organization)
4. *Good* attitude statements take time to construct (it is usually best to begin by constructing several times as many attitude statements as you will actually need, then selecting only those that best assess the attitude in question, which takes time)

The last point, that attitude statements are time-consuming to construct, bears elaboration. In Chapter 6 you learned how to avoid common errors in constructing objective test items. Fortunately, many of the same guidelines apply to the construction of attitude statements, so it is not likely that you will have to start from scratch in learning how to write attitude statements.

Next we provide some suggestions for writing attitude statements. While some of these suggestions are straightforward, others are not. Examples of poorly written and well-written attitude statements are provided to clarify the suggestions.

Suggestions for Writing Attitude Statements

1. Write simple, clear, and direct sentences. Keep in mind that your goal is to assess *attitude* in as valid and reliable a fashion as possible. You are *not* trying to assess another person's intellectual ability, vocabulary, or reading comprehension or to demonstrate your own!
   Poor Item: In any kind of choice situation, we are likely to discover that different individuals will think and express themselves in ways that are idiosyncratic to them, and we should be willing to tolerate different kinds of behavioral manifestations, which by inference are related to their unobservable cognition and affect.
   Better Item: We should be tolerant of different kinds of behavior.
2. Write short statements. A general rule is that attitude statements should rarely, if ever, exceed twenty words. The item above is a good example of excessive wordiness. Another follows:
   Poor Item: When a person finds himself or herself in a situation in which he or she can take advantage of another person, he or she can usually be expected to do so.
   Better Item: Basically, people can't be trusted.

3. Avoid negatives, especially double negatives. The use of negatives like *no, not,* and *none* and especially the use of two negatives in one sentence confuses the reader.
   Poor Item: There isn't a teacher in this school that does not respect student rights.
   Better Item: Teachers in this school respect student rights.

4. Avoid factual statements. Remember that you are attempting to assess affective responses not cognitive responses.
   Poor Item: Career education programs require considerable developmental funds to begin.
   Better Item: The price tag for starting up career education programs is too high to be warranted.

5. Avoid reference to the past. Unless you are for some reason interested in retrospective accounts of *past* attitudes (which are likely to be less reliable than present-day attempts at attitude assessment), phrase your statements in the present tense.
   Poor Item: I have always gotten good grades when I wanted to.
   Better Item: I get good grades when I want to.

6. Avoid absolutes like *all, none, always,* and *never.* At best, such terms add little or nothing to the statement. At worst, they add either confusion or certainty.
   Poor Item: I never met a person I didn't like.
   Better Item: I like most people I meet.

7. Avoid nondistinguishing statements. Such statements fail to discriminate between various attitude positions. In other words they are statements with which most people either agree or disagree.
   Poor Item: I would rather go to school than do anything else.
   Better Item: School is one of my favorite activities.

8. Avoid irrelevancies. Such statements fail to address the real issue in question.
   Poor Item: My morning walk to school is pleasant.
   Better Item: I look forward to walking to school in the morning.

9. Use *only, merely,* and *just* sparingly. Although such terms do not always introduce ambiguity, in many instances they do. It is usually better to avoid them.
   Poor Item: Organized religion is the only way people can express their faith.
   Better Item: Organized religion is the best way for people to express their faith.

10. Use one thought per statement. If double-barreled statements are written, respondents will not know to which part of the statement to respond.
    Poor Item: A good teacher knows the subject matter and treats students fairly.
    Better Item: A good teacher treats students fairly.

Now you have some suggestions for writing attitude statements. See the boxed list that summarizes the suggestions to follow in writing attitude statements. However, these suggestions will be ineffective unless you thoroughly sample the *relevant* aspects of the attitudes to be measured. In other words, it is useful to consider several different kinds of statements that will enable you to tap the attitude in question adequately and avoid tapping irrelevant aspects of attitudes. You do this by focusing your Likert scale.

Focusing Your Likert Scale

Writing good attitude statements takes time. It makes sense to focus your writing on those aspects of the attitude in question that are relevant. What are they? The following suggestions should help you determine them:

1. List the attitudinal area in question (for example, attitudes toward space exploration).
2. List relevant approach and avoidance behaviors (as you did in the second step in developing a structured observation checklist). The list would include behaviors that lead to:
    a. Increased or decreased contact with the person, object, or group in question, or
    b. Exhibitions of support or disdain for the person, object, or group. (For example, approach behaviors may include the following: talks about the benefits of space exploration, takes a trip to Cape Kennedy, reads books

---

FIGURE 10.5   Suggestions to Follow in Writing Attitude Statements

In developing an attitude statement try to:

WRITE	simple, clear, and direct sentences or short statements
AVOID	negatives, especially double negatives
	factual statements
	reference to the past
	absolutes (*all, always, none, never*)
	nondistinguishing statements
	irrelevancies
USE	*only, merely, just,* and so on, sparingly
	one thought per statement
	equal numbers of positive and negative statements

about space exploration, and sends contributions to NASA. Avoidance behaviors could include: talks about the costs of space exploration, avoids Cape Kennedy while traveling down Florida's east coast, never reads books about space exploration, and is against public funding of NASA.)

3. Write your attitude statements. A good way to begin is to lump them into two categories, those that someone might:
   a. Say to indicate approach or avoidance tendencies ("A trip to Cape Kennedy would be interesting," "A trip to Cape Kennedy would be boring"), or
   b. Do to indicate approach or avoidance tendencies ("I intend to write a letter to the editor decrying the cost of space exploration," "I intend to write a letter to the editor extolling the benefits of space exploration").
4. Write several such statements for each approach or avoidance behavior listed in step 2.
5. Use the suggestions given for writing attitude statements to avoid common flaws.

You are now ready to begin constructing your own Likert scales. As with any skill, practice will be necessary if you want to be good at it. Thus far, we have discussed the Likert scale, which is only one of several paper-and-pencil attitude assessment approaches. In the next section, we will introduce two other commonly used attitude measures: the two-point scale and the bipolar adjective scale.

The Two-Point Scale

The two-point scale is simply a variation of the Likert scale. The only real differences between this scale and the Likert scale lie in the response options and in the scoring of the scale. Rather than selecting from among five degrees of agreement or disagreement, the respondent must choose between two options: *yes* to agree, or *no* to disagree. For this reason, this type of scale is often referred to as a *forced-choice scale*. In essence, the respondent is forced into an all or none indication of agreement or disagreement. Figure 10.6 is an example of a two-point scale measuring attitudes toward two-point scales.

Advantages and Disadvantages of Two-Point Scales.   The two-point scale has several advantages. It is simpler and more straightforward, responses are less likely to be inaccurately indicated, and many times a clearer indication of attitudinal preference is obtained than could be from the Likert scale. Its main disadvantage is that such a scale can rub people the wrong way. Most people do not have clear yes or no, black or white perceptions or attitudes, and they sometimes resent scales that suggest the world operates in such simplistic terms. Such individuals may purposely respond inaccurately in protest of such scales, damaging the validity of the attitude assessment. Problems like this can be defused somewhat by addressing the issues *before* administering the scale and giving individuals whose views differ the opportunity to voice their objections.

FIGURE 10.6 | A Two-Point Scale Measuring Attitudes Toward Two-Point Scales

DIRECTIONS: Circle *yes* or *no* to indicate whether you agree or disagree with each statement.

1. Two-point scales are underutilized.   yes   no
2. I prefer Likert scales to two-point scales.   yes   no
3. When I teach, I will use two-point scales.   yes   no
4. Likert scales are easier to use than two-point scales.   yes   no

---

Scoring Two-Point Scales. Coming up with an attitude score for a two-point scale follows much the same process as was used in scoring a Likert scale. The difference is that weights of +1 and −1 are assigned to the options depending on whether the statement contains positive or negative wording. After summing and averaging the weights for the entire scale, decisions are made as to whether the score indicates a positive or negative attitude according to the following rule.

Rule: If the average is greater than zero, a positive attitude is reflected. If the score is less than or equal to zero, a negative attitude is reflected.

Figure 10.7 illustrates the two-point scale presented in Figure 10.6 with options circled and scoring completed.

FIGURE 10.7 | A Scored Two-Point Scale with Weights Assigned to Options

DIRECTIONS: Circle *yes* or *no* to indicate whether you agree or disagree with each statement.

1. Two-point scales are underutilized.   (yes)   no
         (+ 1)   (− 1)

2. I prefer Likert scales to two-point scales.   (yes)   no
         (− 1)   (+ 1)

3. When I teach, I will use two-point scales.   (yes)   no
         (+ 1)   (− 1)

4. Likert scales are easier to use than two-point scales.   yes   (no)
         (− 1)   (+ 1)

Adding up the weights of the options selected, we have:

1. +1
2. −1
3. +1
4. +1

$$+2$$

Dividing by the number of items, we have:

$$2 \div 4 = .5$$

According to our rule, since .5 is greater than zero, this respondent has a positive attitude toward two-point scales.

The Bipolar Adjective Scale

The bipolar adjective scale differs from the previous two scales mainly because it does not use attitude statements. Instead, a word or phrase referring to the person, object, or group in question is presented, along with a list of adjectives that have opposite bipolar meanings. By circling one of the seven choices in the scale, respondents indicate the degree to which they feel the adjective represents their attitude. Figure 10.8 illustrates a bipolar adjective scale.

As you may have guessed, the major task in constructing a bipolar adjective scale is the selection of adjectives. A handy source of such adjectives is Osgood, Suci, and Tannenbaum (1957), which provides a lengthy list of bipolar adjectives. However, you are encouraged to think of adjectives that will be particularly relevant to what *you* want to measure. Many times this is better than borrowing from the lists of others.

Scoring the scale can be done in two ways. The first way is very similar to the procedures outlined for the Likert and two-point scales. Weights could be assigned, depending on whether the positive adjective was on the left (1 would get a weight of 7, and 7 a weight of 1), or on the right (1 would get a weight of 1, and 7 a weight of 7). The weights would then be summed and averaged, and a score of 3.5 or more would be indicative of a positive attitude. However, there are so many numbers involved that such an approach may become cumbersome, and the likelihood of clerical errors is greater. Consequently, we recommend an alternative procedure to score a bipolar adjective scale:

1. Assign weights of 7, 6, 5, 4, 3, 2, 1 to each option, regardless of whether the positive or negative adjective is on the left
2. Sum all the scores (weights) for the pairs with the positive adjective on the left
3. Sum all the scores (weights) for the pairs with the negative adjective on the left

FIGURE 10.8 | A Bipolar Adjective Scale

DIRECTIONS: Circle one of the numbers between each pair of adjectives to best indicate how closely one of the adjectives describes your attitude about essay questions.

Essay Questions

good	1	2	3	4	5	6	7	bad
unpleasant	1	2	3	4	5	6	7	pleasant
fair	1	2	3	4	5	6	7	unfair
ugly	1	2	3	4	5	6	7	beautiful
meaningful	1	2	3	4	5	6	7	meaningless
unimportant	1	2	3	4	5	6	7	important
positive	1	2	3	4	5	6	7	negative
painful	1	2	3	4	5	6	7	pleasurable

4. Subtract the score for the left negative adjective pairs from the score for the left positive adjective pairs
5. Divide the score by the number of adjective pairs
6. Make a decision as to the direction of the attitude according to the following rule: If the average is greater than zero, a positive attitude is reflected. If the average is equal to or less than zero, a negative attitude is reflected.

Figure 10.9 illustrates the bipolar adjective scale presented in Figure 10.8, with choices circled and scoring completed. Adding up the weights for the left positive adjectives we have $2 + 2 = 4$. Adding up the weights for the left negative items we have $7 + 4 = 11$. Subtracting the left negative sum from the left positive sum, we have $4 - 11 = -7$. Dividing this score by the number of adjective pairs, we have $-7 \div 4 = -1.75$. Since -1.75 is less than zero, according to our rule, these responses indicate a negative attitude toward essay questions.

|MEASURING BEHAVIORS

Thus far we have discussed the use of observation and paper-and-pencil questionnaires to assess or make inferences about attitudes. At times, however, we are interested in the behaviors themselves rather than the attitudes they may represent. We may be interested in what a student does rather than why he does it. The use of

FIGURE 10.9 | A Scored Bipolar Adjective Scale (Weights Assigned to Choices are in Parentheses)

Essay Questions

good	1	2	3	4	5	⑥	7	bad
(positive)	(7)	(6)	(5)	(4)	(3)	(2)	(1)	
unpleasant	①	2	3	4	5	6	7	pleasant
(negative)	(7)	(6)	(5)	(4)	(3)	(2)	(1)	
fair	1	2	3	4	5	⑥	7	unfair
(positive)	(7)	(6)	(5)	(4)	(3)	(2)	(1)	
ugly	1	2	3	④	5	6	7	beautiful
(negative)	(7)	(6)	(5)	(4)	(3)	(2)	(1)	

structured observation lends itself well to the assessment of behaviors in such cases. However, just as unstructured observation is not recommended for attitudinal measurement, it also is not recommended for behavioral measurement.

Although both teacher-made and standardized structured observation checklists have been used for many years, the typical classroom teacher often finds them too cumbersome and unwieldy for everyday use. What is a less cumbersome way for teachers to record student behavior? The answer is a compromise between the open-ended unstructured observation and the focused structured observation. We will refer to this compromise as the *anecdotal record.*

Anecdotal Records

Anecdotal records are sequential, usually brief reports that record a teacher's observation of a student's behavior. Such records are kept both for the benefit of the present teacher—so that better understanding of a student may be attained—and for the benefit of future teachers—so that they will have a better understanding of the student. However, most of what school personnel call anecdotal records are *not* all that useful. In fact, most of what are called anecdotal records may better be called *pseudoanecdotal records* (Thorndike & Hagen, 1977). Such records are often *not* sequential and are subjective, judgmental, and, too frequently, negatively phrased *opinions* about, rather than observations of, a student. The main difference between an anecdotal record and a pseudoanecdotal record is the presence or absence of statements referring to observed behaviors and the sequential or nonsequential character of the records. Consider the following examples:

EXAMPLE OF PSEUDOANECDOTAL RECORD

Jack has really not applied himself all year. He seems to have adequate social skills but can't overcome his laziness. I really tried to motivate him this year, but he was uncooperative. I wish his next teacher luck.

EXAMPLE OF ANECDOTAL RECORD

September 14. Jack returned from lunch talking with Mark and Jay. After the bell rang, Mark and Jay stopped talking, but Jack continued asking them questions. I asked the class to take out their math books. Everyone did except Jack, who said he was "too tired for math." I ignored his comment and began the lesson. Jack had his book open and was participating in the lesson within two minutes from the time we started the lesson. This is the third time this week an incident similar to this has occurred.

September 17. Today, Jack returned after lunch by himself. After the bell rang he was among the first to take out math books and went directly to work.

September 18. Jack, Mark, and Jay returned from lunch together. Jack and Jay continued talking after the bell. I asked the class to take out their books and all did, except Jack who continued to ask Jay questions for about three minutes. He then said, "Math is a drag." No one in the class responded, and he opened his book and went to work.

What is the difference between the two examples? In the second example (anecdotal record), only observable behaviors are described. The teacher does not speculate about why Jack does what he does, but describes what Jack was doing. In the first example (pseudoanecdotal record), the teachers speculates about the causes of Jack's behavior ("laziness," "he is uncooperative") and fails to describe any of the behaviors that are presumed to be caused by his personality or character traits. We are not suggesting that such comments or speculations are always incorrect, but how can one be sure the teacher is right?

Human behavior is complex and often difficult to explain. More important, the causes of human behavior are probably multiple. Rather than get involved in trying to explain behavior and never knowing whether you are right, it seems far more profitable and realistic to stick to descriptions of behavior. If you limit your records to descriptions of *observable* behavior, you are reporting, not interpreting, human behavior. Psychiatrists and psychologists are the experts in interpreting human behavior, and even they frequently disagree about why someone does what he or she does. Rather than get involved in the business of interpretation, stick to reporting. If Johnnie walks into class five minutes late and throws his book on the floor, describe his behavior in your anecdotal record. Avoid speculating about the causes of his behavior.

"Well, then," you may ask, "why bother?" For a couple of reasons. First, when you document a sequential description of behaviors over several days, it becomes possible to notice behavior patterns—patterns that perhaps may be altered and result in a decrease in undesirable or disruptive behavior. Anecdotal records can make your classroom management tasks easier. In the second example, it became evident, thanks to the anecdotal records, that Jack's behavior was markedly different after lunch, depending on whether he was engaged in conversation with Mark and Jay. When he was, his behavior after the bell was inappropriate. When he was *not,* his behavior was appropriate. As a result of this finding, you can develop a procedure to increase the likelihood of Jack engaging in appropriate behavior. The sequential descriptions of Jack's after-lunch behavior (anecdotal records) enabled you to identify a behavioral pattern that can be altered. Wouldn't a teacher notice such a pattern simply by being aware? Perhaps.

Writing about an incident and disciplining ourselves to describe only observable behavior are different from simply being aware. When we observe and try to synthesize everything we see happening, we can easily become overwhelmed by the amount of data we have access to (just like using an unstructured observation). As a result, we naturally limit the information we process. We risk making a decision on information that is too limited. And our memories are quite fallible. Trying to recall previous incidents over several days is difficult. Patterns fall victim to forgetting.

A second reason to keep a file of anecdotal records is to document your own and your student's responses to particular problems. Anecdotal records provide you with written, objective accounts of classroom incidents that you can refer to if needed. The following is a typical situation in which such documentation would be helpful:

> Mark has turned in less that 5 percent of his homework and in-school science assignments. You assign him a failing grade in science. His parents contact your principal and several school board members demanding that you be fired for not letting them know about the problem sooner. You have anecdotal records describing Mark's behavior and documenting the telephone calls you made to Mark's parents requesting a parent conference.

Another technique we employ to assess behavior is called a *sociogram*. This technique is used to measure social behavior and is discussed in the following section.

Measuring Social Interaction

Before we describe how to measure social interaction, consider the following interchange between Mr. and Mrs. White and their son's fifth-grade teacher, Mr. Kelley:

MR. WHITE: Thank you for taking time out to meet with us today.

MR. KELLEY: I'm pleased you both could make it.

MRS. WHITE: We're worried about our son Johnny. He just doesn't seem to have many friends around the house. We are afraid he is becoming a "loner." Is he like that at school?

MR. KELLEY: Uh . . . well . . . Johnny always does his work—he's never been a behavior problem.

MR. WHITE: We're happy to hear that, but what about socially? Does he have a friend or group of friends he pals around with?

MR. KELLEY: Oh, I've seen him talking with some of the other kids. He's never gotten in trouble though!

MRS. WHITE: Please. We're worried about his social development. We know he is a good student and that he has good conduct. We can see that from his report card. What we want to know is how well he "fits in" socially. Can you tell us that?

MR. KELLEY: I'm a teacher, not a sociologist. I have twenty-eight other kids to worry about and so much paperwork you wouldn't believe. All I know is that he's not a troublemaker and he gets good grades.

MRS. WHITE: But could we just get an idea of how Johnny is getting along with his classmates?

MR. KELLEY: If you want, come by during recess and lunch and watch. You're welcome to!

MR. WHITE: But couldn't you find out some other way? Is observation the only way to tell whether kids are developing socially?

MR. KELLEY: (looking annoyed) What else is there?

Is there no way other than through observation to obtain the information these parents wanted? While observation is one way to obtain information on social development or group behavior, a sociogram is another.

Sociograms.

A sociogram is one type of sociometric measure. *Sociometry* is the measurement of interaction patterns in groups. In the classroom, the following steps may be followed in developing a sociogram:

1. On a sheet of paper, ask each child to nominate two of his or her peers for a given activity (for example, "With whom would you like to play at recess?").
2. Construct a table to record "choosers" and "chosens," and record the choices on it. Such a table is illustrated in Table 10.1. In this table, choosers are listed vertically and their two choices are indicated by X's under the names of the students they chose (for example, Don chose Bob and Bill). By inspecting the row of totals, you discover the number of times each student was chosen—an index of popularity for the activity chosen.
3. Based on your table of choices, develop a sociogram, a graphical representation of the choice patterns in the group. A sociogram representing the choice pattern from Table 10.1 is illustrated in Figure 10.10. The sociogram is constructed by drawing arrows among the circles to indicate the direction of the choices.
4. Interpret the sociogram, which is done by inspecting the choice patterns and looking for cliques, cleavages, stars, mutual choices, and isolates. These terms are defined as follows:
   a. *Cliques*—Pupils select only each other and avoid selecting others in the group. In our example, Don, Bill, and Bob represent a clique.

TABLE 10.1 | Table Illustrating First and Second Choices

		Don	Marie	Pat	Joan	Bob	Bill	Mary	Ted
						Chosen			
	Don					X	X		
	Marie			X	X				
	Pat		X					X	
Choosers	Joan			X				X	
	Bob	X					X		
	Bill	X				X			
	Mary		X		X				
	Ted		X					X	
Totals		2	3	2	2	2	2	3	0

   b. *Cleavage*—Two or more groups in the class fail to nominate each other. In our example there is a cleavage, a split between Don, Bill, and Bob, and Pat, Joan, Marie, Mary, and Ted.

   c. *Stars*—Pupils most frequently selected. In our example there is no single star. Instead, both Marie and Mary may be considered stars, since each was chosen three times.

   d. *Mutual choices*—Two individuals who select each other. Don and Bill, Don and Bob, Bob and Bill, Joan and Mary, and Pat and Marie all represent mutual choices.

   e. *Isolates*—Individuals not selected by any other pupil. In our example, Ted would be the isolate.

After the sociogram has been interpreted, decisions can be made about possible interventions. For example, steps may be taken to get Ted more involved in the class, or an effort may be made to weaken the clique or bridge the cleavage. Care should be taken in interpreting sociograms, however. While they do have certain advantages, they also have their limitations, and these should be kept in mind when using sociograms. Some of these are listed next.

The limitations of sociograms

1. Only choices, not the reasons for the choices, are indicated.
2. Mutual choices and cliques do not necessarily indicate social acceptance or integration. For example, they may indicate common difficulties in being

FIGURE 10.10 | Sociogram Representing Choice Pattern in Table 10.1

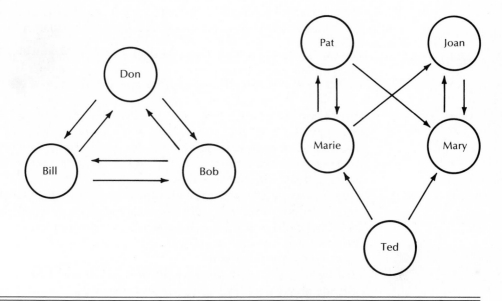

accepted or integrated into the class or some common advantage, depending on the situation. If the question "With whom would you like to sit during the math test?" were asked, the responses might indicate a hope to accidentally or intentionally "share" answers.

3. It is tempting to assume that isolates are actually rejected by the other pupils. Rather than being seen as undesirable, isolates may simply be new, shy, or not chosen for some other relatively minor reason. In general, however, isolates do tend to be less popular socially than nonisolates.

4. Popularity or isolation often depends on the situation. As mentioned before, choices may change depending on the kind of questions asked.

5. Finally, with a class of twenty-five to thirty pupils, a sociogram can be quite complicated and time consuming to construct. In general, use of a sociogram at the beginning and end of the school year, with perhaps one more administration at mid-year, is about the extent to which the average teacher can use this method of measurement.

While the techniques presented in this chapter will certainly not be used as frequently as teacher-made tests, they clearly have a role in the classroom to assess attitudes and social behavior. Use them to increase your understanding of your pupils and to further their development, and you will have moved a step closer to educating the whole child.

SUMMARY

Chapter 10 introduced you to a variety of teacher-made assessment instruments to measure attitudes, behaviors, and social interaction. Its major points were:

1. Attitudes are descriptions of how people typically feel about or react to other people, places, things, or ideas.
2. Attitudes are not directly measurable and are inferred from observable behaviors.
3. Attitudes are classified as positive or negative. Positive attitudes are inferred from approach behaviors—those that result in more frequent, closer, or more intense contact with the stimulus. Negative attitudes are inferred from avoidance behaviors—those that result in less frequent, more distant, or less intense contact with the stimulus.
4. Attitudes may be assessed through unstructured (open-ended) and structured (focused) observation. Structured observation is recommended.
5. The steps involved in conducting a structured observation are:
   a. Indicate why you are observing
   b. Outline relevant behaviors
   c. List behaviors, with those more likely to occur listed first
   d. Decide how you will record your observations
6. Attitudes may also be assessed with questionnaires: Likert scales, two-point scales, and bipolar adjective scales.
7. Likert scales consist of attitude statements to which respondents indicate the degree to which they agree or disagree with the statements, usually on a five-point scale.
8. Two-point scales are very similar to Likert scales, except that responses are made on a two-point scale. Respondents are "forced" to indicate their agreement or disagreement—they cannot take a neutral position as they could with a Likert scale.
9. Attitude statements should be short and written simply and clearly; should avoid negatives, and especially double negatives, factual statements, reference to the past, absolutes, nondistinguishing statements, irrelevancies; should use "only," "merely," "just," etc., sparingly; should have one thought per statement, and equal numbers of positive and negative statements.
10. The steps involved in developing a Likert or two-point scale are:
    a. List the attitudinal area in question
    b. List relevant behaviors
    c. Write attitude statements to reflect these behaviors (what someone would say or do)
    d. Write several statements for each behavior
    e. Edit your statements to avoid technical flaws
11. The bipolar adjective scale consists of a stimulus word or phrase and a list of several pairs of adjectives with opposite meanings. The respondent circles numbers from 1 to 7 to indicate the degree to which each adjective pair best represents his or her attitudes.

12. Behaviors may be measured through unstructured or structured observation and anecdotal records.
13. Anecdotal records are brief sequential reports of observations of a student's behavior, not presumed reasons for the student's behavior.
14. Social behavior or social interaction may be measured with a sociogram, a graphical representation of social patterns in a specific situation.
15. To develop a sociogram:
    a. Ask each child to nominate one or two of his or her peers
    b. Tabulate choices
    c. Graphically depict the choices
    d. Interpret the choice patterns to identify cliques, cleavage, stars, mutual choices, and isolates
16. Sociograms only indicate choice patterns, not the reasons for the choices.

For Practice

1. Make a list of observable approach and avoidance behaviors for a subject area you will be teaching. Arrange these in either a checklist or rating scale format.
2. Now develop a Likert scale for measuring student attitude in this same subject area.
3. Construct a bipolar adjective scale using ten bipolar adjectives of your own choosing. Try to make these adjectives as specific and meaningful as possible to the attitude you are measuring.
4. Make up a sociometric table similar to Table 10.1 using fictitious names. Now randomly place X's throughout the table. Practice converting the resulting data into a sociogram similar to that shown in Figure 10.10. Identify stars, mutual choices, and isolates.
5. The principal of a certain junior-high school schedules assemblies every Friday during the last period. For some time a few teachers have been telling him that the assemblies are not well received by the students or faculty. The principal asks for evidence that their opinion is shared by others. Develop an observation checklist. List 8 behaviors that you might observe from which could be inferred something about the students' attitude toward assemblies. Include 4 approach and 4 avoidance behaviors.
•6. Compute this person's attitude score for the following scale measuring attitude toward your class.
    a. I should have taken another course than this one.   SA   A   U   Ⓓ   SD
    b. I have a hard time keeping awake.   SA   A   U   Ⓓ   SD
    c. Class time should be lengthened.   SA   A   Ⓤ   D   SD
    d. I like writing objectives.   SA   Ⓐ   U   D   SD
    e. I daydream a lot in class.   SA   A   U   D   ⓈⒹ
•7. You are interested in determining attitudes toward utility companies, and you have generated the following list of behaviors that you feel will be helpful in assessing these attitudes. Classify these behaviors as either approach or avoid-

ance behaviors by placing an AP (for approach) or an AV (for avoidance) in the blank to the left of the behavior.

_____ a. Complaining about rising utility bills

_____ b. Volunteering to work for the utility company

_____ c. Picketing the central office

_____ d. Painting the glass on your electric meter black

_____ e. Paying utility bills the same day you are billed

_____ f. Including a $5.00 tip with each electric payment

_____ g. Writing a letter to your congressperson supporting utility rate hikes

_____ h. Defending utility companies in a debate

_____ i. Paying your utility bill in pennies

*8. The following statements were written as part of an attitude scale. In one sentence, explain what is wrong with each statement.

a. Mathematics in my school is fun to take, and my teacher teaches it well.

b. Classrooms in an open-education system often are without walls.

c. Last year I had some boring math assignments.

d. There is nothing I would rather do than make attitude scales.

e. I am often seized by an inexorable urge to engage in irrelevant rumination in math.

*Answers for questions 6, 7, and 8 appear in Appendix D.

11

CHAPTER

EVALUATING PRODUCTS, PROCEDURES, AND PERFORMANCES

In the last chapter we saw how to measure attitudes with measuring instruments of different "sizes and shapes." In this chapter we will see how many of these same measuring instruments can be used to evaluate student products, procedures, and performances.

Your students work hard in school, and their work often pays off on tests that assess their knowledge of what you've taught. But is knowledge all that you've taught? Probably not, if you are a typical teacher. In the course of teaching your curriculum, you directly and indirectly teach, and your students learn many behaviors that cannot adequately be measured with paper-and-pencil tests. Your students, for example, may be able to recite all the rules of grammar without hesitation but be unable to write about a simple event which they have experienced. They may understand the reasons behind world tensions but be unable to work with each other cooperatively. They may know a principal law of science but be unable to demonstrate how that principle works in real life. They may know the cellular structure of plant life but be unable to use a microscope to "see" what they know. And they may be enthusiastic and organized in communicating their thoughts to close friends but be "scared to death" to communicate these same thoughts in an oral presentation to the class. These are just some of the types of products, procedures, and performances which will concern us in this chapter. They are, to be sure, every bit the result of good teaching as are grades on tests.

We have divided this chapter into five areas representing some of the most important products, procedures, and performances that occur in classrooms. For each area we will present some practical ways of judging the quality of the behaviors which occur in them. Here is a preview of the five areas on which we will focus:

1. Evaluating themes and term papers
2. Evaluating group work and participation
3. Evaluating projects and demonstrations
4. Evaluating physical movements and motor skills
5. Evaluating oral performances

EVALUATING THEMES AND TERM PAPERS

Although the elements of good writing can often be tested with true-false and multiple-choice test formats, it would be impossible to measure in such a fashion the application and interrelationship of all the elements that go into making a good term paper. Nearly every subject matter that is taught can be evaluated by the coherent expression of ideas in the form of a theme or term paper. Judging the quality of a theme or term paper presents a special challenge to the teacher. Unlike a multiple-choice test, each product being judged differs from every other and reflects the personality and creativity of its author. Can such products be compared with some standard, and can different themes and term papers be compared with each other? The answer is "Yes, if . . . ." The "if" will be our way of introducing some important reminders for judging themes and term papers. We use the term "reminders" because, as you will see, these are very similar to suggestions we gave you in Chapter 7 to grade essay items more objectively.

The first reminder is that a theme or term paper can be evaluated fairly *if* some form of scale is devised ahead of time that captures the key dimension of the product that is to be judged. In the case of a theme or essay, we need to decide what elements of writing are important for our purposes and what weights may be assigned to them. For example, let's assume the following seven elements of writing are to be examined in each theme:

grammar	capitalization
punctuation	division of words
vocabulary	documentation and references
spelling	

Now we have a starting point for building an evaluation instrument.

Next we will need to decide if all the elements we wish to judge are of equal importance or if some are more important than others. More importance may be given to some than to others because more teaching time was spent on a particular element or because of a conviction that some elements are more critical to good writing than others. Let's say, for example, that because a great deal of care and time was taken in introducing your students to the library, documentation and references would be weighted twice as much as the others.

Next we will need to decide on a number scale to correspond with each of the elements to be judged. Three-, five-, or seven-point scales are typical alternatives. The most common is a five-point scale, since most raters feel fairly confident that distinctions can be made among the points on a scale of this size. The number of points—three, five or seven—is determined by how accurately the rater feels a rating of "1" can be distinguished from a rating of "2," and a "2" from a "3," and so on. If only gross distinctions are possible, for example, "bad," "ok," "good," a three-point scale should be used. If finer distinctions are possible, for example, "very good," "good," "acceptable," "poor," "very poor," then a five-point scale would be appropriate. The reason for the general practice of having odd numbered scales, for example, 3, 5, 7, is to have a center point in the scale that is halfway between the concepts positioned at the ends of the scale. Although this is not necessary, it adds a sense of balance to the scale and leaves a middle ground should the rater feel one is necessary.

Now we are ready to put our scale together. For our purposes, a five-point scale has been chosen. The format of the scale might be as shown in Figure 11.1.

Notice that in Figure 11.1 our scale for documentation and references is different. It runs 2, 4, 6, 8, 10 and not 1, 2, 3, 4, 5. Recall that we had decided to double-weight this element of our scale. By simply doubling the points for each blank, we do, in fact, count this scale twice as much as any of the others. A triple-weighted or even a quadruple-weighted scale could be accomplished in the same manner simply by multiplying the original scale points by 3, 4, or any other number, including fractions. If fractions are used, we might multiply each scale point by, say, .5, in which case that scale would be counted half as much as the other scales, that is, .5, 1, 1.5, 2, 2.5. Also, a 0-to-4 instead of 1-to-5 format could be used to reduce the effect of doubling a low rating on the double-weighted scale. The regular-weighted scales would then be scored 0, 1, 2, 3, 4, and the double-weighted scale, 0, 2, 4, 6, 8.

Finally, adding up the ratings given each element would result in a total number of points which then could be used to compare themes across pupils and to the maximum number of points attainable.

Themes and term papers in one subject may be scrutinized and rated quite differently than in another subject. The scale in Figure 11.1, for example, might be suitable to a class in English, writing, or reading but not to a class in social studies. In the latter, other, more general dimensions of the theme, essay, or term paper may take on greater importance, and concern for the more specific, mechanical aspects of writing less importance. Also, some dimensions of writing, such as the use of documentation and references, will lose importance when one is judging themes from the lower grades. Likewise, generally, the mechanical aspects of writing occupy less attention in the higher grades, since these skills presumably have already been attained and the focus of the instruction at this level is on the development of ideas, organization, style, wording, and phrasing, etc. This should remind us that the dimensions to be rated should be flexible, varying with both subject matter and grade level. For example, Figure 11.2 shows another rating scale for judging themes, essays, and term papers that taps quite different aspects of writing than did our first scale. Here emphasis is on the more

FIGURE 11.1 | Format for Scale for Judging Elements of Writing in a Term Paper

Degrees of quality

For evaluating form or style

Grammar

1	2	3	4	5
very poor	poor	adequate	good	very good

Punctuation

1	2	3	4	5
very poor	poor	adequate	good	very good

Vocabulary

1	2	3	4	5
very poor	poor	adequate	good	very good

Spelling

1	2	3	4	5
very poor	poor	adequate	good	very good

Capitalization

1	2	3	4	5
very poor	poor	adequate	good	very good

Division of words

1	2	3	4	5
very poor	poor	adequate	good	very good

FIGURE 11.1 | Format for Scale for Judging Elements of Writing in a Term Paper (continued)

Documentation and references

2	4	6	8	10
very poor	poor	adequate	good	very good

interpretative aspects of writing or how different aspects of writing, such as organization, style, and wording, come together to communicate ideas clearly and with impact.

Notice that for the five-point scale in Figure 11.2, only three descriptors are included. These descriptors are intended to give the rater a sense of the specific behavior without being overly restrictive. This scale, in addition to rating the integration of many different aspects of writing, offers the possibility of providing specific feedback to the pupil about what was "wrong" and "right" with the essay and serves to remind the teacher why the essay was rated as it was. As was true in our earlier example, specific dimensions and descriptors for any scale should be flexible and changed according to subject, grade, and the objectives of your instruction.

Before leaving the evaluation of themes and term papers, it is important to mention a few tips for evaluating what sometimes can be the most difficult of all dimensions to evaluate in this area: neatness and handwriting. Since standards for neatness and handwriting are not always available, this dimension of writing is often overlooked or measured poorly. Handwriting and neatness is best measured against some existing examples that can be displayed to your students. For example, displaying to your students three term papers from last year varying in neatness (e.g., "messy and unacceptable"; "acceptable and about average"; "excellent and deserving of extra points") would be one way in which your students' writing samples could be judged against an existing standard. This would take some of the guess work out of grading neatness as well as provide your students with a concrete target to shoot for.

Handwriting can be judged in a similar fashion, but since standards here are far more definitive, we recommend that you keep on hand one of several nationally published scales of handwriting. As in the case of the display of term papers, these scales provide handwriting samples at various grades and ages. One of these handwriting scales is shown in Figure 11.3. This scale is used by moving a sample of the pupil's handwriting along the scale until the quality of the writing matches a particular sample. The pupil's handwriting is then assigned the value indicated on the scale. This general type of measuring procedure is called a "product scale," since an example of the pupil's work is compared to existing products of varying quality.

FIGURE 11.2 | Rating Scale for Themes and Term Papers that Emphasizes Interpretation and Organization

Quality and accuracy of ideas

1	2	3	4	5
Very limited investigation; little or no material related to the facts		Some investigation and attention to the facts are apparent		Extensive investigation; good detail and representation of the facts

Logical development of ideas

1	2	3	4	5
Very little orderly development of ideas; presentation is confusing and hard to follow		Some logical development of ideas but logical order needs to be improved		Good logical development; ideas logically connected and build upon one another

Organization of ideas

1	2	3	4	5
No apparent organization. Lack of paragraphing and transitions		Organization is mixed; some of the ideas not adequately separated from others with appropriate transitions		Good organization and paragraphing; clear transitions between ideas

Style, individuality

1	2	3	4	5
Style bland and inconsistent; or "borrowed"		Some style and individuality beginning to show		Good style and individuality; personality of writer shows through

Wording and phrasing

1	2	3	4	5
Wording trite; extensive use of clichés		Some word choices awkward		Appropriate use of words; words and phrasing work to sharpen ideas

FIGURE 11.3 | Handwriting Scale for the California Achievement Tests

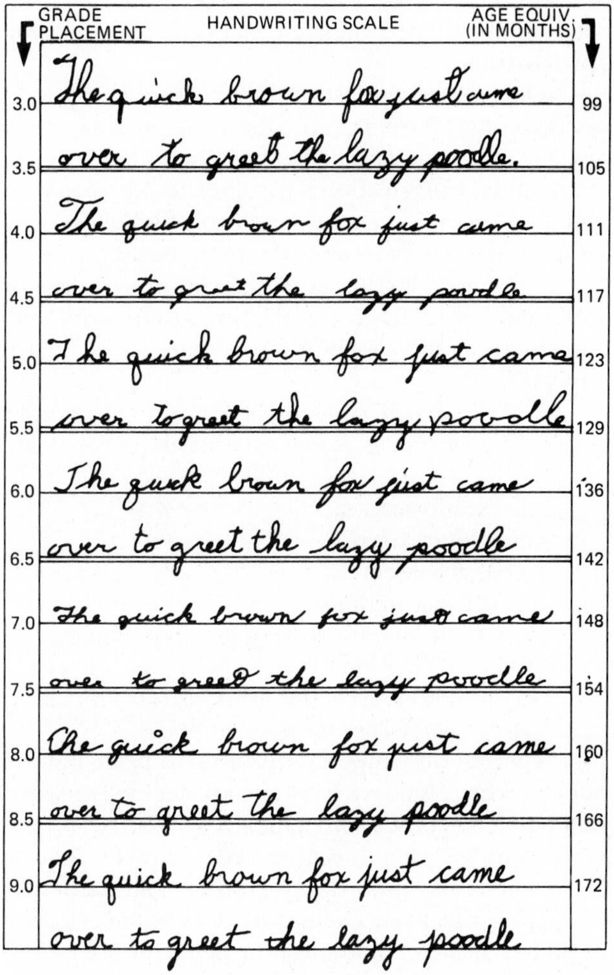

*a product
scale =
pupil's work
compared to existing
products of varying
quality.*

GRADE PLACEMENT	HANDWRITING SCALE	AGE EQUIV. (IN MONTHS)
3.0	*The quick brown fox just came*	99
3.5	*over to greet the lazy poodle.*	105
4.0	*The quick brown fox just came*	111
4.5	*over to greet the lazy poodle*	117
5.0	*The quick brown fox just came*	123
5.5	*over to greet the lazy poodle*	129
6.0	*The quick brown fox just came*	136
6.5	*over to greet the lazy poodle*	142
7.0	*The quick brown fox just came*	148
7.5	*over to greet the lazy poodle*	154
8.0	*The quick brown fox just came*	160
8.5	*over to greet the lazy poodle*	166
9.0	*The quick brown fox just came*	172
	over to greet the lazy poodle	

EVALUATING GROUP WORK AND PARTICIPATION

Good teaching often engages students in problem-solving activities. These activities can be intended as exercises for individual students to be completed independently or as learning experiences for groups of students working together. When problem-solving exercises are group oriented, behavior such as sharing of ideas, cooperating with others, consideration of others' viewpoints, and working as a team will be important to the goals of your instruction. In this section, we will present some ideas and examples for measuring group work and participation.

One of the simplest ways to measure group work and participation is with a checklist. Recall from the previous chapter that a checklist measures behavior in a Yes/No or Present/Absent manner. Therefore, only two discriminations need to be made, and no information regarding the *degree* to which the behavior is present or absent is sought. When the degree to which a given behavior is present or absent is either difficult to determine or cannot be determined with accuracy, the checklist is the most appropriate measurement format. Let's follow the same steps in constructing a checklist for evaluating group work and participation as we did in constructing our five-point rating scale for evaluating essays, themes, and term papers.

First recall that we identified the dimensions of the behavior to be observed. For our current focus, some suitable dimensions might be:

> shares information
> contributes ideas
> listens to others
> follows instructions
> shows initiative in solving group problems
> gives consideration to viewpoints of others
> accepts and carries out group-determined assignments

There is one important caution to make before we proceed in developing our checklist. Since we have already decided on the checklist format, our system for coding responses automatically will be "0" when the behavior cannot be observed and "1" when it is observed. However, there will be times when the rater may not have the opportunity to observe all the behaviors on the checklist. In this case a "0" or lack of a checkmark does not necessarily represent the inability of a pupil to satisfactorily display the behavior but rather the absence of an opportunity for the pupil to show the behavior. For example, if observation is made when a pupil is discussing his or her own ideas, there would be no opportunity to determine if *that pupil* "listens to others" or "gives consideration to the viewpoints of others," and absence of a checkmark should not be taken as a sign that the pupil does not engage in the behavior. The answer to this dilemma is a slightly revised format for our checklist. This format should take into account the rater's opportunity to observe the behavior being rated as well as the presence or absence of the behavior.

Using our original seven dimensions of group work and participation, our checklist format might look like that in Figure 11.4.

Notice in Figure 11.4 that two types of information are being requested of the rater. The first requires the rater to indicate whether conditions permit the behavior to be observed, while the second indicates whether the behavior was ac-

FIGURE 11.4 | Checklist that indicates whether behavior has been observed and whether there has been an opportunity to observe it

group participation

no opportunity to observe	observed	
☑	☐	Shares information
☐	☑	Contributes ideas
☐	☑	Listens to others
☑	☐	Follows instructions
☐	☐	Shows initiative in solving group problems
☐	☐	Gives consideration to viewpoints of others
☑	☐	Accepts and carries out group-determined tasks

tually observed. When the "no opportunity" column is checked, a rating of that behavior would not be warranted, as illustrated for the first, fourth, and seventh ratings above. In this manner, observation of a behavior will always be associated with whether conditions at the time of the observation permitted the behavior to be observed.

Checklists are not the only means of evaluating group work and participation. As was seen elsewhere, three-, five-, and even seven-point scales may be appropriate when finer distinctions among levels of the behavior can be made. These finer distinctions are usually possible as a result of longer periods of observation permitting a greater range of behavior to occur and be noticed. Unlike the single observation period in which most checklists are used, three-, five-, and seven-point scales sometimes summarize the results from a number of observations or a single observation period over a long period of time. For example, a five-point scale, measuring the degree to which a pupil gives consideration to the viewpoints of others, might take either of the two forms in Figure 11.5.

The two scales in Figure 11.5 differ in subtle but important ways. The first scale requires the rater to precisely place the student in one of the five categories. The second allows the rater some flexibility in placing a mark either directly over a descriptor or between adjacent descriptors. If the observer is uncertain as to which two adjacent categories the pupil's behavior belongs, a checkmark may be placed somewhere between the two. In the coding of that item, the division half-way between the categories marks the start of the next code. Keeping track of just where a student's behavior falls within a category (e.g., low, middle, high) can be useful for providing feedback to the student and for recording small changes in behavior that may not be reflected in the numbers assigned to each category.

FIGURE 11.5 | Two scales to measure the extent to which a pupil gives consideration to the viewpoints of others

Does the student give consideration to the viewpoints of others?

_____ very little

_____ seldom

_____ occasionally

_____ frequently

_____ very often

Does the student give consideration to the viewpoints of others?

| Never considers others' viewpoint | Infrequently gives considera-tion to others' viewpoint | Sometimes gives consideration to others' view-point | Frequently gives consideration to others' view-point | Always considers others' view-points |

In addition to these methods, a scheme suggested by Thomas (1960) can be helpful for keeping track of the quality and quantity of the contribution to group work made by individual students during an observation period. Thomas divides the quality of a contribution into four types, defined as follows:

Superior contribution: introduction of significant idea
Secondary contribution: introduction of important, but minor idea
Uncertain or doubtful   contribution needs clarification
   contribution:
Detracting contribution: contribution detracts from discussion

These definitions are then placed into the following format and tally marks placed below each individual according to the number of times a particular type of contribution is observed.

	Kathy	*Damon*	*Brandy*	*Gary*
Superior	III	II	╫	II
Secondary	II			I
Uncertain	I		I	I
Detracting		III		

In this fashion, both the quality as well as the quantity of group work can be recorded during a single observation or over multiple observations. The longer such a record can be maintained, the more accurate will be the record of the quality and quantity of each individual's contribution to group work.

EVALUATING PROJECTS AND DEMONSTRATIONS

If you are like most teachers, you will encourage your students to explore and demonstrate the concepts and principles you have taught them. Likewise, your students will enjoy seeing what otherwise might be considered dull school work come "alive" by applying what they've learned. These practical applications to the real world can take the form of science projects, biology experiments, life-like renderings, graphic illustrations, scale models, and the like which require your students to apply the concepts and principles you have taught. Since projects and demonstrations are often individual "creations" of the students own choosing, they pose a special challenge when it comes time for their evaluation. Several useful ways of judging projects and demonstrations are presented in this section.

Among the most popular and practical methods of evaluating projects and demonstrations are product scales, rankings, and peer ratings.

Earlier we saw a product scale applied to the evaluation of handwriting. At that time a student's handwriting was compared with a number of different handwriting samples, which had been previously scored according to grade level. This same general idea can be an effective tool for evaluating projects and demonstrations. Recall that a product scale measures the comparability of a product to carefully graded examples of varying quality. Let's assume the assignment you gave to your students was to illustrate a scientific principle you've taught by showing an example of it and demonstrating how it works.

First, you will want to give guidelines to your students as to what will be expected. You will want to make these guidelines specific enough to ensure that the projects conform to the assignment, fit within space limitations, and are safe but not so specific that creativity and individuality are restricted. Planning these guidelines in advance and communicating them clearly to your students are crucial steps in your evaluation of projects and demonstrations.

Next you will want to divide the projects into one of several categories which indicates your evaluation of the projects in terms of what might typically be expected from students of that age and experience. These categories can be quite broad, representing, for example, projects that are "insufficient, below expectations," "adequate, meets expectations," "good, more than expected." There may be, of course, more or fewer categories, depending upon your ability to confidently make the discriminations implied by larger scales. Three to five categories, however, generally provide for sufficient range of quality without becoming too complex and difficult to use. A rating of 0, 1, and 2 (e.g., representing "poor," "average," "good") or 0 points, 10 points, and 20 points could be assigned to a three-point scale, depending upon the importance of the assignment. These points could then be added to the total number of points received from tests and other assignments for the grading period.

So far, so good, but with what are the projects compared? Actually, for this grading period there may not be any products with which to compare your student's work. However, you can select and preserve some of the projects this time to become examples with which other students' projects in other classes later in the year can be compared. The point is that you will need to select at least one and, preferably, a few projects from each of your initial categories (e.g., poor, average, good) as representing that category. You may ask selected students to donate their project for a time as an example for other classes, or you may ask if you can photograph their displays. These examples or photographs can then be made available to other classes as a guide and reference point as to the completeness and quality of the projects that characterize each of your rating categories. For teachers teaching multiple classes of the same subject in high school and junior high, simply staggering the time the assignment is given among your classes will allow example projects from the first class to form the product scale for the next and subsequent classes.

A second frequently used method for evaluating projects and demonstrations is rankings. With this method, *each project* is given one of several specific ranks. Typically, only the ranks "1st," "2nd," "3rd" are used, so that more than a single student will receive the same rank. The advantage of this approach compared with ranking all projects from first to last is that some students are not placed in the potentially embarrassing situation with their peers of having the last or close to last rank. Also, it is often the case that when rank ordering twenty or so projects, small and often trivial differences may have to be used to separate the ranks, particularly at the higher (less desirable) ranks, making some of the ranks more or less meaningless. In the classroom, as in the real world, effort should count, and an extremely undesirable rank could sufficiently discourage some students from trying or participating in the activity the next time. Often city, regional, and state-wide competition in the form of science fairs, speech tournaments, and music recitals use this ranking method, which may be another reason for getting your students accustomed to it.

A final approach to evaluating projects and demonstrations is one which can be used in conjunction with either of the previous two methods or alone, depending on how important the resulting grade will be in your final semester evaluation of a pupil. This approach is called *peer rating* and involves students evaluating each other. Obviously, if a great deal of instructional time has been spent in preparing students for their projects and, hence, their grade on it represents a major sample of your students' work, peer rating should be used with other teacher-oriented methods of evaluation or not at all. If, on the other hand, the purpose of the assignment is more to stimulate, excite, activate, and motivate your students than to test them, peer rating can be fun and rewarding to your students. For students there is something about being rated by their classmates that promotes excitement and motivation, sometimes far exceeding that which can be produced by other evaluation methods. The need to "show off" is part of all of us, and having a product of our own scrutinized and rated by peers ensures that a captive audience of those we respect will be there to witness us at our best. Assembling a collection, gathering specimens, building scale models, producing life-like renderings, showing examples, etc., all provide opportunities to be creative and imaginative. If the energy exerted by your students in a peer-rating situation can be focused in ways that result in a meaningful evaluation of their work, you will have accomplished what many other testing situations have not.

The types of scales that can be used in peer ratings include both rating and ranking methods. A four-point rating scale, designated simply as "excellent," "very good," "good," "fair" might be used, in which each student is asked to rate the project of each other student using one of these four categories. With peer-rating scales, the simpler the scale the better, since students will be more qualified to provide their global impressions of a project than to rate it on its "fine points." The numbers *4, 3, 2, 1* could be assigned to each scale response, and an average score calculated for each student's project. The top five or so could then be ordered and given special recognition.

The use of rankings can be equally appropriate for judging projects and demonstrations. Here, as in our earlier example, a complete prioritized ranking which assigns a consecutive rank to each project should be avoided, since students, especially young students, have difficulty keeping track of the ranks when more than a few projects are ranked at a time. Using the top three ranks for a small class, the top five for an average class, and the top seven for a large class could be suitable alternatives. Ranks assigned to each individual project (e.g. *1, 2,* or *3*) could be averaged to determine the top five or so projects for the class.

EVALUATING PHYSICAL MOVEMENTS AND MOTOR SKILLS

There may be times in your classroom in which physical movements and motor skills will be an integral part of your objectives. In many cases, your curriculum objectives cannot be met unless your students are able to exhibit dexterity in their physical movements and other motor skills. Using tools and equipment in the classroom; painting and drawing; being able to operate an electronic calculator; using a microscope; taking a picture; showing a movie; and drawing, cutting and pasting all require that certain physical movements and motor skills be mastered before the activity can be performed. When relevant to your objectives, you will want to evaluate those physical movements and motor skills required for learning to take place. In this section, we present some simple suggestions for measuring these types of behaviors.

Two types of scales are readily adapted to measuring physical movements and motor skills. The first, with which you are already well acquainted, is the checklist; the second is called a Guttman Scale.

Since physical movements and motor skills usually are thought of as either present or absent, the checklist is a "natural" for measuring these types of behaviors. You already know quite a bit about checklists from this and the previous chapter, so we will limit our discussion to examples illustrating their use in this context. Let's begin by looking at the checklist in Figure 11.6.

Notice that we have included both a "no opportunity to observe" and an "observed" column. Often you will be observing several students simultaneously. In this case, the back-and-forth scanning that may be necessary may not provide you with the opportunity to observe each step on the checklist for every student. Rather than penalize the student, you can check the "no opportunity to observe" box. For complex movements and skills, the checklist is a convenient way of judging the presence or absence of a large number of independent acts which contribute to some general skill or behavior. Two other example checklists for measuring physical movements and motor skills appear in Figures 11.7 and 11.8.

You may have noticed that there is often an implied sequence to the physical movements and motor skills you wish to observe. The accuracy with which your students can perform a skill is often related to the order of the physical movements that make up the skill. It may be important to consider not only whether a set of movements occurs, but whether it occurs in the order necessary for a skill to be performed successfully. This brings us to our second method of measuring physical movements and motor skills—the Guttman Scale.

Named for its inventor, the Guttman Scale arranges checklist-type items hierarchically, that is, with the assumption that if a particular behavior at the top of

---

FIGURE 11.6 | Checklist for Using a Microscope

no opportunity to observe	*observed*	
☐	☐	Wipes slide with lens paper
☐	☐	Places drop or two of culture on slide
☐	☐	Adds few drops of water
☐	☐	Wipes off surplus fluid
☐	☐	Places slide on stage
☐	☐	Turns to low power
☐	☐	Looks through eyepiece with one eye
☐	☐	Adjusts mirror
☐	☐	Turns to high power
☐	☐	Adjusts for maximum enlargement and resolution

the hierarchy is accurately performed, all behaviors lower in the hierarchy can also be performed. An example will help make this concept clear.

Let's take our first checklist in this section pertaining to the use of the microscope. If we were to follow the Guttman concept, several of the items on this original checklist could be arranged accordingly:

- ☐ Can find a blank slide
- ☐ Can place slide on stage
- ☐ Can see slide through eyepiece with one eye
- ☐ Can adjust high and low power to focus specimen
- ☐ Can identify specimen

Notice how this scale differs from a simple checklist. The five items are not just any items taken from our checklist but items that have been carefully chosen so as to represent a hierarchy of behavior, from simple to complex, with an implied order. The first behavior, "can find a blank slide," represents the simplest and first behavior that would be expected to occur in this sequence, while "can identify specimen" is the most complex and final behavior that would be expected to occur. All behaviors in between follow a logical stairstep pattern to complete the hierarchy. The idea behind this type of scale is that if all the behav-

---

FIGURE 11.7 | Checklist for Using an Electronic Calculator

no opportunity to observe	*observed*	
☐	☐	Knows how to turn calculator on
☐	☐	Can "key in" ten numbers consecutively, without hitting adjacent keys
☐	☐	Can quickly add three two-digit numbers, without error
☐	☐	Knows how to position keyboard and to rest arm and elbow for maximum comfort and accuracy
☐	☐	Knows how to reposition display screen to reduce reflection and glare, when necessary
☐	☐	Pushes keys with positive, firm motions
☐	☐	Can *feel* when a key touch is insufficiently firm to activate calculator

FIGURE 11.8 | Checklist for Drawing, Cutting, and Pasting

no opportunity to observe	*observed*	
☐	☐	Arranges work space neatly
☐	☐	Can draw a straight line with ruler
☐	☐	Can cut material with scissors
☐	☐	Can cut along a straight line
☐	☐	Can cut along a circle
☐	☐	Can apply glue slowly and evenly
☐	☐	Mounts objects squarely

iors taken together represent a stairstep pattern, a single checkmark at the highest level of behavior observed would indicate whether all other behaviors in the scale were present or absent, even though they may not have been directly observed. The point of the Guttman Scale is that one checkmark at any one behavior reveals equal amounts of information about all the other behaviors in the scale, if the individual items comprising the scale have been chosen and ordered hierarchically. For example, if the highest level of behavior observed was "can adjust the high and low power to focus specimen," we could safely conclude that this student could also perform the three behaviors below, whether or not they were directly observed. For "spot" observing large numbers of students, a Guttman Scale is a handy tool, since students do not have to be observed performing each item on the scale. Instead, only the highest level of behavior attained need be noted.

The Guttman Scale can be tricky to build because each item must successfully represent steps in the hierarchy. This is not always easy to accomplish, and this is why Guttman Scales usually represent no more than five individual behaviors on a single scale, although any number of different scales may appear on the same instrument. Guttman Scales are scored with the usual ordered points, for example, 1–5, with the higher number representing the more complex behavior.

EVALUATING ORAL PERFORMANCE

Our last topic in this chapter deals with evaluating the oral behavior of your students. Oral competence—the ability to express oneself through speaking and recitation—is expected in almost every subject area. Although oral performances may not be the primary teaching objective in some subjects, few of your objectives in any subject will be met if the results of your teaching cannot be seen and evaluated orally. English, social studies, science, and even math require to varying degrees some type of oral performance. The type of oral performance required of students can vary considerably depending on the subject, but most often it will take the form of reading aloud, reciting, giving a speech, performing in a skit, play, or demonstration, and the like.

The main tools for evaluating oral performance have been the rating scale and anecdotal report, although other forms of measurement, such as a checklist, may be equally appropriate for a given purpose.

When a single grade represents many different types of behavior, it becomes less effective in pinpointing particular areas of strength and weakness. This is never more true than when your evaluation of students involves both their knowledge and their organization of content as well as their delivery of this content in the form of some oral performance. For example, recitation of an original poem involves both knowledge of the structure of poetry *and* the ability to deliver it orally in ways that communicate and emphasize its meaning. The ability to represent a character in a skit or play involves knowing how the character might dress and act, remembering the lines he or she is to speak, *and* being able to convey this characterization orally to others so as to create a feeling of empathy. Giving a good speech to the class involves both having something to say *and* saying it in a way that promotes acceptance and understanding of a particular point of view. Each of these examples could be cited as examples of mixed grading, if each major component of the product being sought were not identified and rated separately. This is the purpose of rating oral performance in areas other than speech and public speaking—to separate content and process and to give each its proper emphasis.

Giving each its proper emphasis can be accomplished by organizing your evaluation into two broad categories: (1) Content and Organization and (2) Delivery.

At this point, a separate rating instrument should be constructed for each of these two areas. Some example performance categories that could be rated under the general topic of delivery are:

> Enunciation
> Pronunciation
> Loudness
> Word usage
> Pitch
> Rate
> Gestures

A number of different types of rating scales can be used with these and similar categories. For example, the rating shown in Figure 11.9 uses a five-point format and three descriptors per item to identify degrees of the behavior rated.

Notice that for some of these "five-point scales" the center point is the most acceptable behavior. In these cases the scale may be scored with a *5* at the center

---

FIGURE 11.9 | Rating Scale for Speaking

1. Enunciation

```
|_____|_____|_____|
```

most words   some words   all words
inarticulate   inarticulate   clearly
                                            articulated

2. Pronunciation

```
|_____|_____|_____|
```

freq.

few words   some words   all words
pronounced   pronounced   pronounced
accurately   incorrectly   accurately

3. Loudness

```
|_____|_____|_____|
```

too soft,   appropriate   too loud,
difficult to   level of   distracting
hear   volume

4. Word Usage

```
|_____|_____|_____|
```

often chooses   word choice   always
wrong word   adequate but   chooses
                      could be   right word
                      improved

5. Pitch

```
|_____|_____|_____|
```

too low   just right   too high

quality

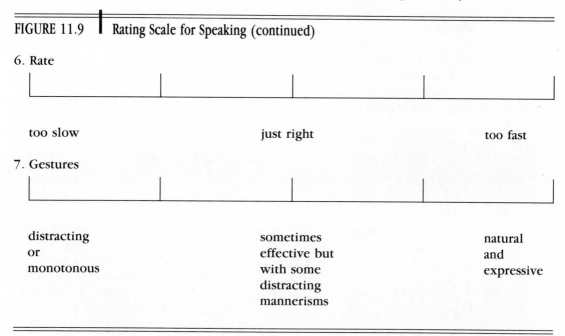

FIGURE 11.9 | Rating Scale for Speaking (continued)

6. Rate

too slow　　　　　　　　just right　　　　　　　　too fast

7. Gestures

distracting　　　　　　sometimes　　　　　　natural
or　　　　　　　　　　effective but　　　　　　and
monotonous　　　　　　with some　　　　　　　expressive
　　　　　　　　　　　distracting
　　　　　　　　　　　mannerisms

point, two *3*'s to the left *and* right of center and two *1*'s representing the extremes. A rating of *4* or *2*, therefore, would not be possible for these scales, but scores from them could be added to others in the scale to determine an average score for the entire instrument. One other suggestion is to leave space after each scale for comments. These might include instances of poorly articulated or mispronounced words that later could be practiced by the student or recommendations as to how to correct the problem, as when "take a breath at each punctuation mark" is suggested after a low rating is given on scale *6*.

Another technique that can be useful in evaluating an oral performance is the anecdotal record. This method of collecting information about an oral performance generally is considered appropriate when a critical incident presents itself that provides insight into a particular student's strength or weakness. The word "critical" is important because the incident to be recorded should provide special meaning as to the reason why the student performed orally the way he or she did. Anecdotal reports typically expand and make clear extreme or unusual scores that have been recorded for students on other types of rating forms. Since performing orally is often an emotional experience, particularly in the early grades, critical incidents are likely to occur frequently before, during, and after oral performances, and when recorded, these incidents can be an effective means of explaining *why* a particular level of performance occurred.

As noted in the previous chapter, anecdotal reports describe in everyday natural language the nature of the incident that occurred. An anecdotal record is a brief, factual account of the situation leading up to the incident, the incident itself, and the situation immediately following the incident. This factual description is then usually followed by a brief interpretation of the incident and any recommendation that might be possible for remedying the situation if it is negative or for providing conditions conducive for its reoccurrence if it is positive. The following is an example of an anecdotal record that might have been made during an oral reading assignment:

SAMPLE: ANECDOTAL RECORD

Class: Fifth Grade   *Pupil:* John Smith
Date: *Place:* Classroom   *Observer:* Hawkins

INCIDENT

As class started, John asked if he could be first to read his story. I gave him permission and he came to the front of the room. John began to read the story in a very low and uncertain voice, and when he had been reading for about thirty seconds, Sharon, who was sitting in a seat at the back of the room, spoke up and asked John to read louder. At this point John tore up the pages he was reading and went back to his seat.

INTERPRETATION

John appears to enjoy writing and sharing his creations with other people. It seems, however, that he is very nervous and gets very easily upset when he receives the slightest criticism, as noted by his tearing up of his story and refusing to continue. John might be asked to read one of his stories to a smaller group to gain more confidence before coming before the full class again.

John's scores on a five-point rating scale for this oral performance probably would not reflect the special circumstances revealed by this anecdotal report. Those scores would not tell the whole story, which the anecdotal report might place in perspective. Perhaps most important will be any suggestions or recommendations you might make to yourself or other teachers for handling John's sensitivity in the future.

Contrary to popular belief, anecdotal reports need not always be negative. Critical incidents can be positive as well, as the following record indicates:

Class: Seventh Grade   *Pupil:* Brandy
Date: *Place:* Auditorium   *Observer:* Brown

INCIDENT

The class play was in its second act. King Lear had just begun his speech to his daughter, played by Brandy, when he forgot all but his opening line. Realizing this, Brandy ad-libbed a sequence which provided King Lear with enough clues to his lines that he picked up where he left off and continued according to the script, with few in the audience ever realizing what had happened.

INTERPRETATION

Brandy's ad-libbed speech was so spontaneous and consistent with the character she was playing that even I didn't realize at the time what was happening. Her quickness of thought and ability to "live" the character she was playing, even without a formal script, speaks to her ability in speaking and acting. This ability should be encouraged with extemporaneous speaking and improvisations during next semester's speech class.

In both of these examples, the incident was separated from its interpretation. This is important in order to allow the factual description to dictate the interpretations—not the other way around, as sometimes happens. Also, the factual description can be returned to at a later, less emotional time to check on the appropriateness of the interpretation and recommendation.

SOME ADVANTAGES AND DISADVANTAGES OF THE METHODS USED TO MEASURE PRODUCTS, PROCEDURES, AND PERFORMANCES

We began this chapter by suggesting that the effect of your teaching may be realized in many different ways. The cognitive behavior and attitudes of your students will always be important outcomes of your teaching. However, the objective of this chapter has been to show that these are not the only outcomes your instruction can have. Your students will work hard in your classroom and will want to be observed and graded in all the ways that represent their hard work. Their performance in writing, their work in groups, their work on demonstrations and projects, their motor skills and oral performances are other important areas in which your impact as a teacher can be seen and the work of your students evaluated. We conclude our discussion of this topic with a brief summary of some of the advantages and disadvantages of some of the most popular measurement methods presented in this chapter. These measurement methods are the rating scale, checklist, anecdotal record, and Guttman Scale. Use these methods wisely by keeping in mind the strengths and weaknesses noted here:

RATING SCALES

Advantages

1. Directs observation toward specific and clearly defined aspects of behavior.
2. Provides a common frame of reference for comparing all individuals on the same set of characteristics.

Disadvantages

1. Tendency to rate all individuals at approximately the same position on the scale.
2. Rater's general impression of the person may influence how that person is rated on individual characteristics.
3. Usually allows for relative judgments only, that is, allows for relative comparisons among individuals but not absolute judgments that a particular behavior was or was not attained.

CHECKLIST

Advantages

1. Useful in evaluating those performance skills that can be divided into a series of clearly defined, specific actions.
2. Can provide absolute judgments of the presence or absence of specific learning outcomes.

Disadvantages

1. Not useful in recording general impressions of behaviors that are customarily seen as continuous, for example, personality, achievement, attitude.
2. Can provide inaccurate data when the opportunity to observe the behavior is not recorded at the time of scoring.

ANECDOTAL RECORDS

Advantages

1. Provides a description of actual behavior in natural situations.
2. Can be used to collect information on very young pupils and on others who may not be able to respond in a self-report format.
3. Can provide data about persons without their being aware that they are being observed.

Disadvantages

1. Amount of time required to maintain an adequate system of records.
2. Objectivity when observing and recording behavior.
3. Obtaining an adequate sample of an individual's behavior requires considerable time and effort.

GUTTMAN SCALE

Advantages

1. Can provide information as to whether different behaviors have been attained without actually having observed all of them.

2. Provides the opportunity for "spot" observing.

Disadvantages

1. Requires considerable knowledge of the behaviors being measured in order to arrange them into a hierarchy.
2. Applicable only to those behaviors that can be related to one another in a hierarchical, stairstep fashion.

SUMMARY

This chapter has introduced you to the measurement of products, procedures, and performances. Its major points were:

1. Some of the areas in which student learning can be observed, in addition to formal cognitive tests and attitude assessments, are
   a. themes and term papers
   b. projects and demonstrations
   c. group work and participation
   d. physical movements and motor skills
   e. oral performances
2. A product scale measures the comparability of a product, for example, a term paper, with carefully graded examples of varying quality.
3. Five-point rating scales and product scales are appropriate means of measuring themes and term papers.
4. Checklists, five-point rating scales, and observation records are appropriate means of measuring group work and participation.
5. Product scales, rankings, and peer ratings are appropriate means of evaluating projects and demonstrations.
6. A Guttman Scale arranges behaviors in a hierarchy, or stairstep, pattern from simple to complex so that behavior attained at one point in the hierarchy implies the attainment of all behaviors lower in the hierarchy.
7. Checklists and Guttman Scales are appropriate means of evaluating physical movements and motor skills.
8. Five-point rating scales and anecdotal records are appropriate means of evaluating oral performance.

For Practice

1. Create and appropriately weight a five-point scale for evaluating a term paper in your teaching area.
2. For evaluating group work and participation, create a checklist which incorporates an "opportunity to observe" response.
3. Describe a procedure for developing a product scale for evaluating projects, such as science fair projects, experiments, or demonstrations of a principle or concept.

4. Describe a method you would use to rank student projects and demonstrations in a class of thirty honor students.
5. Develop a checklist for evaluating physical movements and motor skills that are required in your subject area or a related area.
6. Develop a Guttman Scale for measuring simple arithmetic achievement.
7. Identify the unique advantage of the Guttman Scale over other types of rating scales.
8. Explain the disadvantages of a mixed multiple concept grade and suggest an appropriate alternative.
9. Describe in what situations an anecdotal report is most appropriate and provide an example of how it would be used in a parent-teacher conference.
10. List the advantages and disadvantages for each of the following scales: rating scale, checklist, anecdotal record, Guttman scale.

12

CHAPTER

SUMMARIZING DATA AND MEASURES OF CENTRAL TENDENCY

|F|or many, the term *statistics* forebodes evil. It is probably one of the most misunderstood terms in education. A statistician, or statistical expert, is stereotypically seen as a social isolate who lacks a sense of humor, speaks in strange tongues, and knows how to make numbers say whatever he or she desires them to say. Indeed, in some doctoral programs, courses in statistics are acceptable as substitutes for foreign languages! Having taught statistics courses, both authors are keenly aware of the anxiety and/or resentment many students feel when they are required or encouraged to take their first statistics course. As we mentioned in Chapter 1, however, fewer than 1 percent of the students we have taught fail courses in tests and measurement because of statistics. Then why are students so anxious about statistics?

The answer, we believe, lies in the misconceptions students have about statistics and statisticians. Let's clarify some things. We do not intend that you become full-fledged statisticians after completing this section of the text. In fact, a complete course of graduate study is usually necessary before one can call oneself a statistician. Perhaps you know students who suffered through an introductory statistics course. Will you have to undergo the trauma they may have undergone? Again, the answer is no. Even courses in introductory statistics treat this topic in much greater depth than is necessary for a course in tests and measurement. If you did well on the self-test and review in Appendix A, you have little to fear. If you failed to do well, brush up on the fundamentals presented in Appendix A until you do perform well. After completing the review it should have been apparent that the four basic functions—addition, subtraction, multiplication, and division—will suffice for the statistics we will deal with. Master these operations and with a little work (and an open mind), mastery of statistics at the tests and measurement level will soon follow.

WHAT ARE STATISTICS?

Thus far we have been talking about statistics in general. In reality, there are two types of statistics: descriptive and inferential. For our purposes we will deal entirely with the "easy" side of statistics, descriptive statistics. Inferential statistics are more complicated and are best taught in more advanced courses.

Descriptive statistics are simply numbers, for example, percentages, numerals, fractions, and decimals. These numbers are used to describe or summarize a larger body of numbers. For example, if you wanted to give someone an indication of how your grades have been in college, you could list all your courses and the grade you received in each course, or you could simply report your grade-point average (GPA). Both approaches have advantages and disadvantages, of course, but we think you will agree that reporting your GPA would normally be the most useful approach. In this example, the GPA is a descriptive or summary statistic, since it describes or summarizes extensive data.

In the classroom the typical teacher has from 25 to 30 pupils. When a test is administered to the class, 25 to 30 test scores result. If a teacher gives ten tests over the year, 250 to 300 test scores result. Naturally, these scores would be recorded in the teacher's grade book, but when it comes time to report grades to parents at the end of the year, are they *all* reported? Obviously not. Instead, teachers report descriptive or summary statistics—that is, grades—probably without realizing they are reporting statistics!

Anytime you deal with averages (GPA, batting averages), rates (death rates, birth rates), or other numbers used to describe or summarize a larger body of numbers, you are dealing with descriptive or summary statistics. All of us deal with statistics daily. One of our goals for this chapter is to make you better users and consumers of such information. We hope to do this by going a little beyond common-sense statistics and looking at statistics and their uses more systematically.

WHY STATISTICS?

As we said, the term *statistics* is frequently misunderstood. Although some people want nothing to do with statistics, statistics are important and appear to be an increasingly important aspect of our personal as well as professional lives. Anytime you read, hear, or see "a 70 percent chance of rain" or "82 percent of doctors surveyed recommend" or "an EPA average of 32 miles per gallon," you are being exposed to statistics. Exposure to statistics will not go away. The ability to understand and profit from everyday statistics is well within your reach. You will become a better interpreter of educational data (and thus a better teacher) by mastering the statistical concepts presented in this section of the text. You will also become a better consumer of everyday data presented in advertising, public relations, opinion polls, and so forth. Much of what you learn in teacher training may seem to have little application outside the classroom. This is not the case for statistics. Master the concepts in this chapter and they will serve you throughout your personal and professional life.

With increasing calls for accountability, it will become all the more important that classroom teachers understand the statistics reported to them and the statistics they report to others. Needless to say, the teacher who understands the uses and limitations of various kinds of statistical data will have a decided advantage over the teacher who lacks such understanding. While your professional survival and development may not depend entirely upon a working knowledge of statistics, they may certainly be enhanced by it.

TABULATING FREQUENCY DATA

The classroom teacher normally deals with a large amount of data, usually in the form of test scores. As more and more scores accumulate, it gets more and more difficult to make sense of the data. It becomes more and more difficult to answer questions such as:

How many people are above average?
How many scored above the cut-off passing score?
Did most of the class do well on the test?
What is the highest or lowest score?

Keeping these questions in mind, consider the following set of scores obtained by 25 sixth-grade children on a math test:

36	63	51	72	93
54	48	84	36	45
57	45	48	96	66
54	72	81	30	27
45	51	57	63	88

Without doing anything to these test scores, are you able to answer the above questions? Naturally, you cannot answer the first two questions until you compute the average score and establish the cut-off or passing score. But what about the last two questions?

You can eventually answer these questions, but it takes a lot of time to do so. In arriving at answers to the last two questions, you probably resorted to some sort of strategy to organize the data so they make sense. For example, to determine whether "most of the class did well" you may have crossed off and counted the number of scores in the 80's and 90's.

Whatever the strategy you used, you used it because the 25 scores, as they stood, were difficult to make sense of or to interpret. Next, we will consider several systematic ways of making sense of an unwieldy group of numbers. We will be organizing or introducing some sort of order to unorganized, unordered test scores. The first method is to simply list the scores in ascending or descending numerical order.

The List

```
96   72   54   48   43
93   66   54   47   36
88   63   51   45   36
84   63   51   45   30
81   57   48   45   27
```

Introducing some order or "sense" into this group of scores makes trends, patterns, and individual scores easier to find and to interpret. At a glance we can now determine the highest score, lowest score, and even the middle score. We can easily see that only five students scored above 80 on the test. Thus, listing has helped us organize this set of scores. But, what if we had 50 scores, or 100 scores, or 1,000 scores?

As the number of scores increases, the advantage of simply listing scores decreases. Many scores will repeat themselves several times. It becomes more and more difficult to make sense of data when the number of scores would require a lot of paper. Also, when you list data there are usually many missing scores (for example, 95, 94, 92, 91, 90, 89, 86, and so on in the above example). Failure to consider these missing scores can sometimes result in a misrepresentation of the data.

To sum up, a simple list summarizes data conveniently if N, the number of scores, is small. If N is large, however, lists become difficult to interpret. Trends are not always very clear, numbers tend to repeat themselves, and there are usually a lot of missing scores. Next, we will consider a *simple frequency distribution*. This approach to tabulating data considers all scores, including those that are missing.

The Simple Frequency Distribution

Inspecting the simple frequency distribution in Table 12.1 may cause as much, or more, confusion as the original group of 25 unorganized scores. Usually, for classroom purposes, a simple frequency distribution is too unwieldy. Unless your tests yield a narrow spread of scores, simple frequency distributions tend to be so lengthy that it is difficult to make sense of the data, which is what we are trying to do. Seldom will a simple frequency distribution prove useful in the average classroom.

TABLE 12.1	Simple Frequency Distribution		
X (score)	f (frequency)	X (score)	f (frequency)
96	1	61	0
95	0	60	0
94	0	59	0
93	1	58	0
92	0	57	2
91	0	56	0
90	0	55	0
89	0	54	2
88	1	53	0
87	0	52	0
86	0	51	2
85	0	50	0
84	1	49	0
83	0	48	2
82	0	47	0
81	1	46	0
80	0	45	3
79	0	44	0
78	0	43	0
77	0	42	0
76	0	41	0
75	0	40	0
74	0	39	0
73	0	38	0
72	2	37	0
71	0	36	2
70	2	35	0
69	0	34	0
68	0	33	0
67	0	32	0
66	1	31	0
65	0	30	1
64	0	29	0
63	2	28	0
62	0	27	1

In summary, a simple frequency distribution will summarize data effectively *only* if the spread of scores is small. If there is a large amount of variation in test scores, a simple frequency distribution usually results in a table similar to Table 12.1, full of zeros in the frequency column and with so many categories that it becomes difficult to interpret the data. Fortunately, a variation of the simple frequency distribution, called the *grouped frequency distribution,* eliminates these shortcomings and can be quite useful in the classroom. Let's consider this variation.

The Grouped Frequency Distribution

The grouped frequency distribution method of tabulating data is very similar to the simple frequency distribution, except that ranges or intervals of scores are used for categories rather than considering each possible score as a category. The following is a grouped frequency distribution for the 25 scores we've been talking about:

Interval	f
91–97	2
84–90	2
77–83	1
70–76	1
63–69	3
56–62	1
49–55	4
42–48	7
35–41	2
28–34	1
21–27	1

Contrast this grouped frequency distribution with the simple frequency distribution and with the listing of scores. The grouped frequency distribution has two major advantages over the listing and the simple frequency distribution. It compresses the size of the table and makes the data much more interpretable. At a glance it becomes apparent that most of the class (as indicated by the numbers in the *f* or frequency column) obtained scores of 55 or below. If we add the numbers in the *f* column, we can see specifically that 15 $(4 + 7 + 2 + 1 + 1 = 15)$ of the 25 students in the class scored 55 or below. That is, 4 students scored between 49 and 55, 7 scored between 42 and 48, 2 scored between 35 and 41, 1 scored between 28 and 34, and 1 scored between 21 and 27.

Since most of the class scored 55 or lower, one interpretation the grouped frequency distribution helps us make is that the test may have been too difficult. However, at least three other possible interpretations are suggested: perhaps the students simply failed to prepare for the test; perhaps the students need more instruction in this area because they are "slower" than the teacher expected them to be; perhaps the instruction was ineffective or inappropriate.

Whichever of these interpretations is correct is irrelevant to us at the moment. What is important is that once we construct a grouped frequency distribution, it quickly becomes apparent that the class did not do well on the test. We may have arrived at the same conclusion after looking at the listing of scores or simple frequency distribution, but it certainly would take longer. Thus, a grouped frequency distribution does help us make sense of a set of scores. But there are also disadvantages to using a grouped frequency distribution.

The main disadvantage of a grouped frequency distribution is that information about individual scores is lost. As a result, the information we deal with becomes less accurate. Consider the interval of scores 49–55 in the previous grouped frequency distribution. We see that four scores fell in this interval. However, exactly what were these scores? Were they 49, 51, 53, and 55? Or were they 49, 50, 51, and 54? Or were all four scores 49? Or were two scores 52 and two scores 53? Or 51? The four scores could be any conceivable combination of scores. Without referring to the original list of scores, we cannot tell.

Thus, while a grouped frequency distribution compresses table size and makes data easier to interpret, it does so at the expense of accuracy and information about individual scores. Usually, the advantages of constructing grouped frequency distributions are great enough to offset the disadvantages. Next, we will consider the steps involved in actually constructing a grouped frequency distribution.

Steps in Constructing a Grouped Frequency Distribution

Step 1. Determine the range of scores (symbolized by R). The range (or spread) of scores is determined by subtracting the lowest score (L) from the highest score (H).

Formula	*Application*
R = H − L	R = H − L
	R = 96 − 27
	R = 69

The range of scores for the 25 sixth-graders is 69.

Step 2. Determine the appropriate number of intervals. The number of intervals or categories used in a grouped frequency distribution is somewhat flexible or arbitrary. Different authorities will suggest that you select from among 5, 10, or 15 intervals, or 8, 10, 12, or 15 intervals, and so on. In our example we used 11 intervals. Well, then what is "correct"?

As we said, this decision is somewhat arbitrary. In making such decisions though, be sure to *use as many categories or intervals as are necessary to demonstrate variations in the frequencies of scores.* In other words, if you decide to use five intervals and find that for an N of 25 scores there are frequencies of 5 in each interval, the number of intervals is too small. Increasing the number of intervals to ten in this case should result in different frequencies for each interval. Selecting too many intervals is also a possibility. Generally, if you find more than one interval with zero in the frequency column you have decided on too many intervals. If this all sounds confusing, that's because in some ways it is. The bottom line is that sometimes it is necessary to experiment a little. You may have to vary the number of intervals until you find the number you feel best represents your data. Generally, it is best to begin with 8 or 10 intervals when constructing a grouped frequency distribution for a group of 25 to 30 scores, the typical number of scores resulting from a classroom test. Increase the number of intervals for larger score sets.

Step 3.   Divide the range by the number of intervals you decide to use and round to the nearest odd number. This will give you *i*, the interval width.

Formula	*Application*
$i = \dfrac{R}{\text{number of intervals}}$	$i = \dfrac{69}{10}$
	$= 6.9$ (rounded to nearest odd number $= 7$)

The width of the interval is 7. If we decided to use 8 for our number of intervals we would arrive at a wider interval width, or *i*.

Formula	*Application*
$i = \dfrac{R}{\text{number of intervals}}$	$i = \dfrac{69}{8}$
	$= 8.6$ (rounded to nearest odd number $= 9$)

If we decide to use 15 intervals, we would arrive at a narrower interval width than we would with 10 or 8 intervals.

Formula	*Application*
$i = \dfrac{R}{\text{number of intervals}}$	$i = \dfrac{69}{15}$
	$= 4.6$ (rounded to nearest odd number $= 5$)

You can see there is an inverse relationship between the number of intervals and the width of each interval. That is, as fewer intervals are used, the width of each interval increases; as more intervals are used, the interval width decreases. Also, keep in mind that as *i*, the interval width, increases, we lose more and more information about individual scores.

Step 4.   Construct the interval column making sure that the lowest score in each interval, called the lower limit (LL), is a multiple of the interval width (*i*). The upper limit of each interval (UL) is one point less than the lower limit of the next interval. All this means is that the lowest score of each interval should be a value that is equal to the interval width times 1, 2, 3, etc. With an interval width of 7, the LL of each interval could be 7, 14, 21, etc. (7×1; 7×2; 7×3). However, we eliminate those intervals below and above the intervals that include or "capture" the lowest and highest scores. Consider the following sets of intervals for which the highest score was 96 and the lowest score was 27:

Lower Limit	Upper Limit	
112	118	
105	111	
98	104	
91	97	← highest score captured,
84	90	eliminate all intervals
77	83	above
70	76	
63	69	
56	62	
49	55	
42	48	
35	41	
28	34	
21	27	← lowest score captured,
14	20	eliminate all intervals
7	13	below

We retain only the intervals 21–27 through 91–97. Thus, the interval column of our grouped frequency distribution should look like this:

Intervals
91–97
84–90
77–83
70–76
63–69
56–62
49–55
42–48
35–41
28–34
21–27

Step 5. Construct the *f,* or frequency, column by tallying the number of scores that are captured by each interval.

Intervals	Tally	f
91–97	||	2
87–90	||	2
77–83	|	1
70–76	|	1
63–69	|||	3
56–62	|	1
49–55	||||	4
42–48	‖‖‖ ||	7
35–41	||	2
28–34	|	1
21–27	|	1

Next, simply eliminate the tally column and you have a grouped frequency distribution.

However, didn't we decide we wanted ten intervals? How is it we ended up with eleven? The answer to the first question is yes, but it is not unusual to end up with one more or one less interval than you intended. This happens because of what we often end up doing at Step 3. We round to the nearest odd number. The inaccuracy we introduce by rounding to the nearest odd number is multiplied by the number of intervals (since in effect we do this for each interval). The result is that the range from the upper limit of the highest interval to the lower limit of the lowest interval is greater than the range from the highest score to the lowest score. In our example:

Upper limit of highest interval	97
Lower limit of lowest interval	− 21
	76

High score	96
Low score	− 27
	69

Notice the difference between 76 and 69. The extra interval is needed to include the extra values. Fortunately, ending up with one more or one less interval than we intended is not a serious problem. We need only be aware of it, not unduly concerned with it.

Before we leave grouped frequency distributions, let's clarify one more point. In Step 3 we said "round to the nearest odd number." There is no sound mathematical reason for this recommendation. Rather, it is to simplify determining the midpoint of the interval. While the midpoint is of little importance for grouped frequency distributions, it is important in the construction of a *frequency polygon*, a graphical representation of a grouped frequency distribution, which we will consider next.

GRAPHING DATA

"A picture is worth a thousand words" is a well-worn expression, but especially applicable to statistics. Some of you may have the ability to extract meaning from groups of numbers, but others, the authors included, need to see graphical representations before such data can be meaningful. In any case, a graph will almost always clarify or simplify the information presented in a grouped frequency distribution. There are three types of graphs we will consider: the *bar graph,* or *histogram,* the *frequency polygon,* and the *smooth curve.*

The Bar Graph or Histogram

The bar graph, or histogram, is the type of graph used most frequently to convey statistical data. The histogram in Figure 12.1 is based on the grouped frequency distribution used earlier to represent the scores of 25 sixth-graders.

In constructing a histogram, or bar graph, several guidelines should be followed, which are listed in Figure 12.2.

The interpretation of bar graphs is straightforward. The higher the column, the greater the number of scores falling in that interval. The lower the column, the lesser the number of scores falling in that interval.

The Frequency Polygon

Technically, a frequency polygon is best used for graphically representing what are called *continuous data,* such as test scores. Continuous data usually represent entities that can be expressed as fractions or parts of whole numbers, for

---

FIGURE 12.1 | Histogram Based on a Grouped Frequency Distribution

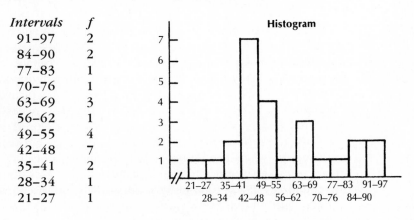

Intervals	f
91–97	2
84–90	2
77–83	1
70–76	1
63–69	3
56–62	1
49–55	4
42–48	7
35–41	2
28–34	1
21–27	1

FIGURE 12.2   Guidelines for Constructing a Histogram

1. The vertical axis should be two-thirds to three-fourths as long as the horizontal axis to help prevent misrepresenting the data.

2. Scores are listed along the horizontal axis and increase from left to right. Frequencies are listed along the vertical axis and increase from bottom to top.

3. Double slash marks (//) are used to indicate breaks in the sequence of numbers (horizontal axis) or in the sequence of frequencies (vertical axis).

4. Points in the scales along the axes are expanded or compressed so that the range of scores and frequencies fit within the "two-thirds to three-fourths" guideline given above.

5. If an interval or intervals with frequencies of zero occur, these *must not* be omitted from the horizontal axis. To do so misrepresents the data. The following example illustrates this point:

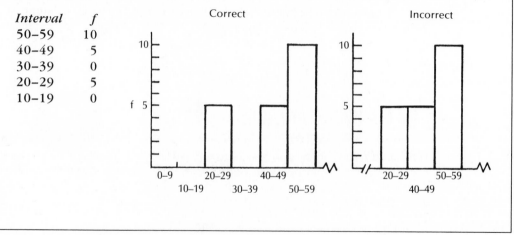

Interval	*f*
50–59	10
40–49	5
30–39	0
20–29	5
10–19	0

example, achievement test scores and grade point averages. Histograms are best used for graphically representing *discrete* or *noncontinuous data*. Discrete or noncontinuous data represent entities that usually cannot be expressed as fractionated parts of anything and, hence, signify different dimensions, for example, Catholics, Protestants, and Jews. However, we need not be overly concerned with discriminating between continuous and discrete data, because much overlap exists in the actual ways these two types of graphs are used.

For our purposes, what is the critical difference between a histogram and a frequency polygon? The answer is that a frequency polygon is an alternative way of representing a grouped frequency distribution. It uses straight lines to connect the midpoint (MP) of each interval rather than bars or columns to show the frequency with which scores occur. The grouped frequency distribution with midpoints and the frequency polygon shown in Figure 12.3 represent the same group of scores we have been considering:

FIGURE 12.3 | A Grouped Frequency Distribution and Frequency Polygon

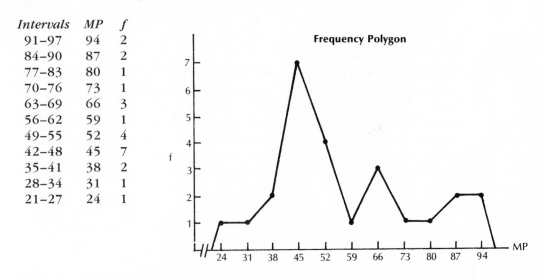

Intervals	MP	f
91–97	94	2
84–90	87	2
77–83	80	1
70–76	73	1
63–69	66	3
56–62	59	1
49–55	52	4
42–48	45	7
35–41	38	2
28–34	31	1
21–27	24	1

Interpretation of the frequency polygon is similar to that of the histogram. The higher or lower the dots, the greater or lesser the number of scores in the interval.

Comparing the frequency polygon with the histogram demonstrates the same pattern of scores. This is a perfectly logical finding, since they were both constructed from the same grouped frequency distribution, except that we add a midpoint column to construct a frequency polygon.

Determining the MP is straightforward and results in a whole number if the interval width is an odd number. Its determination results in a fractional number if the interval width is an even number. In either case, the midpoint is simply the middle score in each interval. If you mistrust your ability to determine the middle score in an interval, you can check yourself mathematically. Simply add the lower limit (lowest score in the interval) to the upper limit (highest score in the interval) and divide the sum of these two scores by 2.

Formula

$$MP = \frac{LL + UL}{2}$$

Application

Top interval

$$MP = \frac{91 + 97}{2} = \frac{188}{2} = 94$$

Second from top

$$MP = \frac{84 + 90}{2} = \frac{174}{2} = 87$$

Guidelines for constructing a frequency polygon appear in Figure 12.4. Notice that they are similar to those for histograms.

The Smooth Curve

Thus far we have discussed two graphical ways of depicting data represented by a grouped frequency distribution, the histogram and the frequency polygon. Our topic for this section, the *smooth,* or *smoothed, curve,* is not really an appropriate way to represent data from grouped frequency distributions, since an accurate smooth curve requires that advanced mathematical calculations be computed. Nevertheless we will make great use of a smooth curve as a general representation of groups of scores. An example of a smooth curve is provided in the following graph:

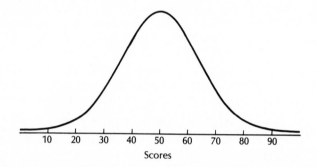

This curve represents a set of data. Note that it closely resembles a frequency polygon except that the *f,* or frequency, axis is omitted and curved rather than straight lines are used. Although the *f* column is omitted, we can still make decisions about the frequency of occurrence of certain scores based on the height of the curve. That is, scores in the 40–60 range were obtained by large numbers of students, while very few students obtained scores below 20 and/or above 80. With a histogram or frequency polygon we could determine *exactly* how many students scored between 40 and 60 or above 80 and/or below 20 by referring to the *f* axis. However, we are willing to sacrifice this accuracy when dealing with smooth curves because we use these curves to depict the *shape* of a distribution rather than to accurately represent the data.

Smooth curves can easily be developed from existing histograms or frequency polygons by connecting the high points of the bars or midpoints of the intervals, as shown in Figure 12.5.

Follow these two guidelines in constructing smooth curves:

1. Be sure your score axis increases from left to right
2. Be sure the "tails" or ends of the curves come close to, but do not touch, the baseline

FIGURE 12.4   Guidelines for Constructing a Frequency Polygon

1. Construct the vertical axis two-thirds to three-fourths as long as the horizontal axis.

2. List scores along the horizontal axis, increasing from left to right, and list frequencies along the vertical axis, increasing from bottom to top.

3. Double slash marks (//) are used to indicate breaks in the sequence of numbers between scores and/or frequencies and zero points.

4. Points in the scales along the axes are expanded or compressed to fit the two-thirds to three-fourths guideline.

5. When intervals of zero frequency occur, the midpoints *must not* be omitted from the horizontal axis, and the lines connecting the dots must be brought down to the baseline to represent zero frequencies.

6. The lines should also be brought down to the baseline halfway into the intervals above and below the highest and lowest intervals, as noted in the diagram below:

Interval	*MP*	*f*
50–59	55	10
40–49	45	5
30–39	35	0
20–29	25	5

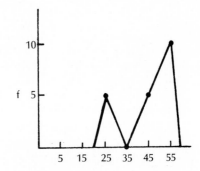

This guideline represents more of an aesthetic than a statistical consideration. A frequency polygon "tied" to the baseline has a better or more complete appearance, as shown below.

Incorrect
Frequency Polygon "Floating"

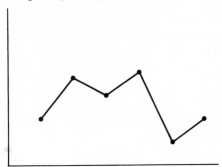

Correct
Frequency Polygon "Tied Down"

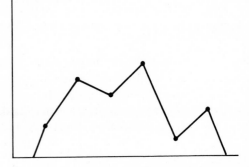

FIGURE 12.5 | Smooth Curves

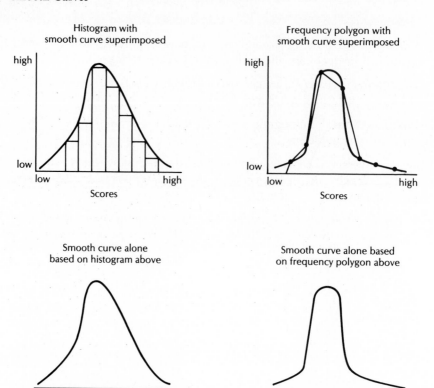

Remember, although we use smooth curves to give us an idea of the shape of a distribution, they also enable us to make general statements about the frequency of scores. The higher the curve, the more frequently the scores listed above occur. The lower the curve, the less frequently the scores listed above occur. Next, let's consider two major characteristics of distributions: symmetry and skewness.

Symmetrical and Asymmetrical Distributions.

There are two major types of distributions: symmetrical and asymmetrical. In a symmetrical distribution each half or side of the distribution is a mirror image of the other side. An asymmetrical distribution, on the other hand, has nonmatching sides or halves. Both types of distributions are illustrated in the following graphs:

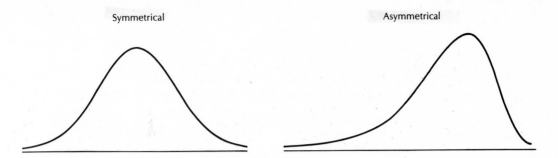

Symmetrical distributions can come in a variety of configurations. As illustrated, they may appear peaked, flattened, or somewhere in between:

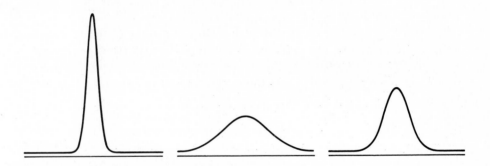

All three of these are symmetrical distributions. The distribution on the right, however, has special significance. It is a special kind of symmetrical distribution called a *normal distribution*. It has some unique characteristics that make it the most important distribution in statistics. Practice drawing this distribution. You will be called on to draw it many times before leaving this section of the book. Technically, the normal distribution follows very precise mathematical rules, but as long as you can approximate the illustration you need not worry about its precise mathematical properties. We will have more to say about the normal curve later.

Positively and Negatively Skewed Distributions.

There are also two types of skewness: positive skewness and negative skewness. A positively skewed distribution results from an asymmetrical distribution of scores. In this case, the majority of scores fall *below* the middle of the score distribution. There are many low scores, but few high scores. A positively skewed distribution is illustrated as follows:

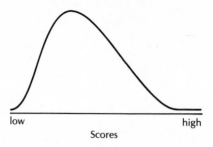

In a classroom testing situation a positively skewed distribution indicates the class did poorly on the test (a majority of low scores and few high scores). The reasons for such poor performance could include that the test was too difficult, teaching was ineffective, the students didn't study, or not enough time was allowed. A positively skewed distribution does *not* tell you why the class did poorly; it only informs you of the fact that they did.

A negatively skewed distribution also results from an asymmetrical score distribution. In this type of distribution the majority of scores fall *above* the middle of the score distribution. There are many high scores, but few low scores. A negatively skewed distribution is illustrated as follows:

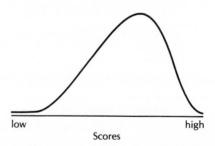

One interpretation attached to a negatively skewed distribution is that the class did well on the test (a majority had high scores and few had low scores). Again, there could be many reasons for this. The test may have been too easy, too much time may have been allowed, the class may be exceptionally bright, and so forth. Distributional shapes only describe data. They do not explain why the data take their shape.

We have discussed the what and why of statistics and have described methods for tabulating and depicting data. Next, we will discuss what are probably the most widely used (and frequently misunderstood) summary statistics, *measures of central tendency.*

MEASURES OF CENTRAL TENDENCY

There are three measures of central tendency: the mean, the median, and the mode. We will define each in turn, give an example or examples of its computation, and discuss its characteristics. The main point to remember about these measures is that they represent our best bet when we must rely on a single score to represent an entire distribution. Since we have three measures of central tendency, it may occur to you that each is more or less applicable in different situations. But before we go any further, test yourself to see if you are on top of the statistical jargon we have already presented. If you can define the terms listed in Figure 12.6, the Jargon Checklist, you are in good shape. If not, review these terms and commit them to memory to build your vocabulary and to prepare yourself to learn more terms later.

The Mean

Have you ever computed your grade average in elementary school, your GPA in college, your field-goal average in basketball, or any other average? The mean is nothing more than the average of a group of scores.

Average = Mean

FIGURE 12.6   JARGON CHECKLIST

Statistics	Frequency (*f*)
List	Midpoint (MP)
Simple Frequency Distribution	Histogram
Grouped Frequency Distribution	Frequency Polygon
N	Smooth Curve
Range (R)	Symmetrical Distribution
Interval (*i*)	Normal Distribution
Lower Limit (LL)	Positively Skewed Distribution
Upper Limit (UL)	Negatively Skewed Distribution

The symbol we will use for the mean is $\overline{X}$ (pronounced "X bar"). Some texts use M rather than $\overline{X}$ to symbolize the average or mean score, but most use $\overline{X}$, and so will we. Just in case you have forgotten how, we will compute a mean (our sneaky way of introducing a formula with a couple of other unfamiliar symbols). The formula and its plain English interpretation appear here:

Formula	*Plain English Version*
$\overline{X} = \dfrac{\Sigma X}{N}$	$\text{average} = \dfrac{\text{sum of all the scores}}{\text{total number of scores}}$

The formula looks impressive. But, as you can see, it (like all mathematical formulas) is only a shorthand way of describing the process you go through to compute an average. Let's have a closer look at the terms in the formula:

$\overline{X}$ symbol for the mean or arithmetic average
Σ sigma symbol used in mathematics that tells you to sum up whatever follows it
X   symbol we will use from now on to represent a test score
N   total number of scores in a distribution

Thus, ΣX tells you to sum up the test scores, and $\Sigma X/N$ tells you to sum up the test scores and divide this value by the total number of scores in the distribution. Let's work an example for the following set of scores: 90, 105, 95, 100, and 110.

Example	*Application*
$\overline{X} = \dfrac{\Sigma X}{N}$	$\overline{X} = \dfrac{\Sigma X}{N}$
	$\overline{X} = \dfrac{90 + 105 + 95 + 100 + 110}{5}$
	$\overline{X} = \dfrac{500}{5}$
	$\overline{X} = 100$

The mean has several characteristics that make it the measure of central tendency most frequently used. One of these characteristics is stability. Since each score in the distribution enters into the computation of the mean, it is more stable over time than other measures of central tendency, which consider only one or two scores.

Another characteristic is that the sum of each score's distance from the mean is equal to zero. Presently, this is probably quite meaningless to you. However, it is a key concept in more advanced statistical operations. We will discuss this characteristic and its importance shortly.

A third characteristic of the mean is that it is affected by extreme scores. This means that a few very high scores in a distribution composed primarily of low scores (a positively skewed distribution) or a few very low scores in a distribution composed primarily of high scores (a negatively skewed distribution) will "pull" the value of the mean down or up toward the extreme score or scores. Table 12.2 illustrates this point. Since the mean is affected by extreme scores it is usually *not* the measure of choice when dealing with skewed distributions. In such cases a measure that is more resistant to extreme scores is required. Our next topic for discussion, the median, represents such a measure.

The Median

The median is the second most frequently encountered measure of central tendency. The median is the score that splits a distribution in half: 50 percent of the scores lie above the median, and 50 percent of the scores lie below the median. Thus, the median (abbreviated MDN) is also known as the fiftieth percentile. You may also think of the median as the middle score, since it falls in the middle of the distribution of scores.

The methods used to determine the median are simple. When the score distribution contains an odd number of scores, the median is the score that has equal numbers of scores above and below it. The following example describes the steps

TABLE 12.2 | The Effect of Extreme Scores on the Mean

original set of scores	*add an extremely low score*	*add an extremely high score*
90	90	90
105	105	105
95	95	95
100	100	100
+ 110	110	110
ΣX = 500	+ 20	+ 200
	ΣX = 520	ΣX = 700

$$\overline{X} = \frac{\Sigma X}{N} \qquad \overline{X} = \frac{\Sigma X}{N} \qquad \overline{X} = \frac{\Sigma X}{N}$$

$$\overline{X} = \frac{500}{5} \qquad \overline{X} = \frac{520}{6} \qquad \overline{X} = \frac{700}{6}$$

$$\overline{X} = 100 \qquad \overline{X} = 86.67 \qquad \overline{X} = 116.67$$

involved in determining the median when N, the total number of scores in the distribution, is odd.

EXAMPLE: Determine the median for the following set of scores: 90, 105, 95, 100, and 110.

STEPS:

1. Arrange the scores in ascending or descending numerical order (don't just take the middle score from the original distribution).
2. Circle the score that has equal numbers of scores above and below it; this score is the median.

APPLICATION:

110
105
(100) = MDN
95
90

When N is even, the procedure is only a bit more complicated. In this case, select the *two* scores in the middle that have equal numbers of scores above and below them. Taking the average of these two scores will give you the median. These steps are illustrated in the following example.

EXAMPLE: Determine the median for the following set of scores: 90, 105, 95, 100, 110, and 95.

STEPS:

1. Arrange the scores in numerical order.
2. Circle the *two* middle scores that have equal numbers of scores above and below them.
3. Compute the average of these two scores to determine the median.

APPLICATION:

110
105
(100
95) 2 middle scores $\frac{95 + 100}{2} = \frac{195}{2} = 97.5 = $ MDN
95
90

Notice that Step 1 is the same regardless of N. *Always* arrange your data in numerical order before determining the median. Next, let's consider one more example of determining the MDN when N is even.

EXAMPLE: Determine the median for the following set of scores: 90, 105, 95, 100, 110, and 100.

STEPS:

1. Arrange the scores in numerical order.
2. Circle the *two* middle scores that have equal numbers of scores above and below them.
3. Compute the average of these two scores to determine the median.

APPLICATION:

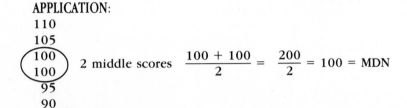

$$\begin{array}{l} 110 \\ 105 \\ \boxed{100} \\ \boxed{100} \\ 95 \\ 90 \end{array} \quad \text{2 middle scores} \quad \frac{100 + 100}{2} = \frac{200}{2} = 100 = \text{MDN}$$

In this case the median is a whole number and the same value as the two middle scores, a common occurrence.

The main characteristic of the median is that it is not affected by extreme scores. This is because only the middle or two middle scores are considered in determining the median. Let's consider the following examples:

Original set of scores	*Substitute an extremely high score*	*Substitute an extremely low score*
X	X	X
110	**600**	110
105	105	105
100	100	100
100	100	100
95	95	90
90	90	**5**

$$\text{MDN} = \frac{100 + 100}{2} \qquad \text{MDN} = \frac{100 + 100}{2} \qquad \text{MDN} = \frac{100 + 100}{2}$$

$$= 100 \qquad\qquad\qquad = 100 \qquad\qquad\qquad = 100$$

Since the median is not affected by extreme scores, it represents central tendency better than the mean when distributions are skewed. In skewed distributions the mean is "pulled" toward the extremes, so that in some cases it may give a falsely high or falsely low estimate of central tendency. Since the median, on the other hand, is the score above and below which half the scores lie, it always indicates the center of the distribution, as illustrated by the following diagrams:

Positively Skewed Distribution

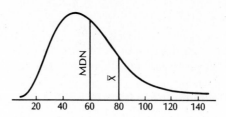

Negatively Skewed Distribution

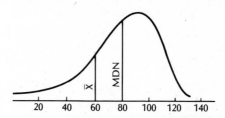

In the positively skewed distribution the few scores of 100 or above pull the $\overline{X}$ toward them. The mean presents the impression that the typical student scored about 80 and passed the test. However, the MDN shows that fully 50 percent of the students scored 60 or below. In other words, not only did the typical students fail the test (if we consider the middle student typical), but the *majority* of students *failed* the test.

In the negatively skewed distribution the few scores of 40 or below pull the mean down toward them. Thus, the mean score gives the impression that the typical student scored about 60 and failed the test. Again, the median contradicts this interpretation. It shows that fully 50 percent of the students scored 80 or above on the test and that actually the *majority* of students *passed* the test.

As you can see, it is important that the median be considered when skewed distributions are involved. Too often, however, only the average or mean is reported when statistics are presented, without regard for the shape of the distribution.

Percentile.   Now that we have introduced the idea of the median as the fiftieth percentile, it is only a small step to finding out how to determine the score that represents any desired percentile in a frequency distribution. Although a percentile is not considered a measure of central tendency unless it is the fiftieth percentile, the calculation of other percentiles is very similar to that of the median. A percentile is a score below which a certain percent of the scores lie. In the case of the median, we saw that 50 percent of the cases were lower (and higher) than the median. Percentiles divide a frequency distribution into 100 equal parts. Percentiles are symbolized $P_1, P_2 \ldots P_{99}$. P_1 represents that score in a frequency distribution below which 1 percent of the scores lie. P_2 represents that score in a frequency distribution below which 2 percent of the scores lie. P_{99} represents that score in a frequency distribution below which 99 percent of the scores lie. A score can be calculated for each percentile from P_1 to P_{99} in a manner similar to the way the median—or fiftieth percentile—was calculated for a distribution with an even number of scores. That is:

1. Arrange the scores in numerical order
2. Counting up from the bottom, find the point below which the desired percent of scores falls
3. Circle the two scores that surround this point
4. The average of this pair of scores will be the percentile of interest

For example, for the following data, P_{25} would be determined in the following manner:

$$\begin{array}{c} 115 \\ 110 \\ 110 \\ 110 \\ 105 \\ 100 \\ 100 \\ 95 \end{array}$$

$$P_{25} \cdots \quad \boxed{\begin{array}{c} 95 \\ 90 \end{array}} \; \frac{95 + 90}{2} = 92.5$$

$$\begin{array}{c} 90 \\ 85 \end{array}$$

(handwritten: $\frac{1}{4}$ of $12 = 3$ $\frac{3^{ed}, 4^{th}}{2} =$)

Finally, we will consider the last of the measures of central tendency—the mode.

The Mode

The mode is the least reported measure of central tendency. The *mode,* or *modal score,* in a distribution is the score that occurs most frequently. However, a distribution may have one score that occurs most frequently (unimodal), two scores that occur with equal frequency and more frequently than any other scores (bimodal), or three or more scores that occur with equal frequency and more frequently than any other scores (multimodal). If *each* score in a distribution occurs with equal frequency, the distribution is called a rectangular distribution, and it has *no mode.*

The mode is determined by tallying up the number of times each score occurs in a distribution and selecting the score that occurs most frequently. The following examples are illustrative:

EXAMPLE: What is the mode of this score distribution: 90, 105, 95, 100, and 100?

X	Tally	
105	|	
100	||	Mode = 100
95	|	This is a unimodal distribution.
90	|	

EXAMPLE: What is the mode for this set of scores: 90, 110, 95, 100, 110, 90, 105, 100, 110, and 95?

X	Tally	
110	|||	
105	|	
100	||	Mode = 110
95	||	This is a unimodal distribution.
90	||	

EXAMPLE: What is the mode for this set of scores: 6, 9, 1, 3, 4, 6, and 9?

X	Tally	
9	||	
6	||	
4	|	Modes = 6 and 9
3	|	This is a bimodal distribution.
1	|	

The mode has the advantage of being easy to determine. If you know how to count you can determine a mode! However, it is the least used of the measures of central tendency because of a serious shortcoming. The mode is the *least* stable measure of central tendency. A few scores can influence the mode considerably. Consider the following:

Original set of scores			*Add a few scores (e.g., 90, 70, 70, 70, and 90)*		
X	Tally			X	Tally
105	|			105	|
100	||			100	||
95	|			95	|
90	|			90	|||
				70	|||
Mode = 100				Modes = 70 and 90	

Because of this unfortunate characteristic, the mode usually is not used as the only measure of central tendency. An exceptional case, however, is the normal distribution because in a normal distribution all three measures of central tendency have the same value.

The Measures of Central Tendency in Various Distributions

As was mentioned, the mean, median, and mode all have the same value in a normal distribution, which is illustrated here:

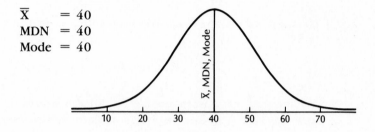

$$\overline{X} = 40$$
$$MDN = 40$$
$$Mode = 40$$

In a positively skewed distribution the $\overline{X}$ usually has the highest value of all the measures of central tendency, the mode the lowest, and the median the middle or intermediate value.

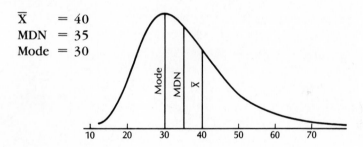

$$\overline{X} = 40$$
$$MDN = 35$$
$$Mode = 30$$

Just the opposite occurs in a negatively skewed distribution. In a negatively skewed distribution, the mean usually has the lowest value, the mode the highest, and the median the middle or intermediate value.

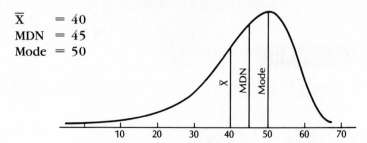

$$\overline{X} = 40$$
$$MDN = 45$$
$$Mode = 50$$

Knowing the relationships of the measures of central tendency to these distributions enables you to place these measures in their appropriate position when a distribution's shape is known. The opposite is also true. Knowing the values of the measures of central tendency enables you to determine the shape of the distribution. For example, if the $\overline{X} = 47$, MDN = 54, and mode = 59, what is the shape of the distribution? You know it is not normal (since the values are different). But, before you *guess* at whether it's positively or negatively skewed, take the uncertainty or guesswork out of the question. How? The answer to this and many other questions concerning statistical principles is to draw a picture.

EXAMPLE: What is the shape of a distribution with a mean of 47, median of 54, and mode of 59?

STEPS:

1. Examine the relationship among the three measures of central tendency.
2. Draw a picture (baseline first) then mark the measures of central tendency in the appropriate spaces. Draw in the curve. Remember the high point of the curve is above the mode.
3. Answer: negatively skewed.

APPLICATION:

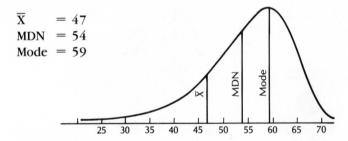

$$\overline{X} = 47$$
$$\text{MDN} = 54$$
$$\text{Mode} = 59$$

We've been discussing estimates of one important aspect of a distribution. Estimates of central tendency represent good bets about the single value that best describes a distribution. But some good bets are better than others. In the next chapter we will consider statistics that indicate how adequate our good bets really are. These are estimates of variability.

|SUMMARY

This chapter introduced you to various methods of tabulating and graphing data and to the measures of central tendency. Its major points are:

1. Descriptive statistics are numbers used to describe or summarize a larger body of numbers.

2. Data are tabulated to introduce some order to the data and make them more interpretable. Three methods of tabulating data are listing, simple frequency distributions, and grouped frequency distributions.

3. While each method has its advantages and disadvantages, for classroom use the grouped frequency distribution is usually most appropriate.

4. The following steps are followed in constructing a grouped frequency distribution:

   a. Determine the range

   b. Determine the number of intervals

   c. Divide the range by the number of intervals and round to the nearest odd number to get the interval width (i)

   In statistics this was decimal value

   d. Develop the interval column, being sure the lower limit of each interval is a multiple of i

   e. Tally the scores in each interval to get f, the frequency column

5. Data from grouped frequency distributions may be graphically represented by histograms or frequency polygons.

6. Histograms or bar graphs use columns of varying height to represent the frequencies in each interval.

7. Frequency polygons use straight lines to connect the midpoints of each interval, which vary in height depending on the frequency of scores in the interval.

8. The following general guidelines apply to the construction of both histograms and frequency polygons:

   a. Make sure the vertical axis is two-thirds to three-quarters as long as the horizontal axis

   b. List scores along the horizontal axis, frequencies along the vertical axis

   c. Use double slash marks (//) to indicate breaks in any number sequences

   d. Do *not* omit intervals with frequencies of zero

9. A smooth curve is usually drawn to represent a distribution's shape, although decisions about frequency of occurrence of scores or scores in intervals can be made by looking at the height of the curve. The f axis is omitted in a smooth curve.

10. In a symmetrical distribution, each half or side of the distribution is a mirror image of the other, unlike in an asymmetrical distribution.

11. A normal distribution is a special type of symmetrical distribution.

12. An asymmetrical distribution in which most scores are low is called a positively skewed distribution. The tail in such a distribution is toward the high scores.

13. An asymmetrical distribution in which most scores are high is called a negatively skewed distribution. The tail in such a distribution is toward the low scores.

14. One of the measures of central tendency (mean, median, and mode) is used to represent a distribution when a single value must be used. Such a measure is our "best bet" about the overall distribution.

15. The mean, or the arithmetic average, of a set of scores is determined by summing all the scores and dividing by the number of scores.

16. The mean has several important characteristics. Of the measures of central tendency it is the most stable, the sum of the deviations of each score from the mean always equals zero, and it is affected by extreme scores.
17. Since the mean is affected by extreme scores, it is not the measure of central tendency of choice for skewed distributions.
18. The median is the score that splits a distribution in half. It is also known as the middle score, or the fiftieth percentile.
19. The median is determined by finding the score or value that has equal numbers of scores above or below it.
20. The most important characteristic of the median is that it is not affected by extreme scores. Thus, it is the measure of central tendency of choice in a skewed distribution.
21. The mode is the score in a distribution that occurs most frequently.
22. The mode is determined by counting the number of times scores occur and selecting the score(s) that occur(s) most frequently. A distribution may have more than one mode.
23. The major characteristic of the mode is its instability. Seldom is the mode, by itself, acceptable as a measure of central tendency.
24. In a normal distribution, the mean, median, and mode have the same value.
25. In a positively skewed distribution, the mean has the highest and the mode the lowest value of the measures of central tendency. The median has an intermediate value.
26. In a negatively skewed distribution, the mean has the lowest value and the mode the highest value of the measures of central tendency. Again, the median has an intermediate value.

For Practice

*1. An achievement test designed to measure the level of arithmetic achievement among students in the middle of the third grade is administered to three classes of equal size. There is one first-grade class, one third-grade class, and one fifth-grade class. The test is administered in the middle of the school year. Other things being equal, what sort of distribution would you predict for each of the three classes? Sketch a distribution of the shape you would expect for each grade. On each of your three sketches, indicate the probable location of the three measures of central tendency.

*2. Mr. Martin's best reading group obtained the following scores on an achievement test:

$$85, 90, 90, 92, 94, 94, 96, 97, 97, 98$$

Mr. Scott's best reading group obtained the following scores on the same achievement test:

$$61, 85, 90, 90, 92, 93, 94, 97, 97, 97$$

For each group, determine the following:

a. N =
b. R =

c. $\overline{X}$ =

d. MDN =

e. Mode =

f. Why is there so much difference in means?

g. Which measure of central tendency should be used to compare these distributions?

*3. For the following group of 30 scores, construct three grouped frequency distributions with different numbers of intervals. Graph your data, using both a histogram and a frequency polygon. Decide which frequency distribution best represents the data?

60, 60, 63, 68, 70, 72, 75, 75, 75, 76, 76, 77, 78, 80, 83, 83, 84, 88, 93, 93, 93, 94, 94, 94, 94, 95, 97, 98, 100, 100

*4. Match the terms in Column B with the characteristics listed in Column A. The options from Column B may be used more than once.

Column A	*Column B*
_____ 1. least stable measure of central tendency	a. mean
_____ 2. more than one possible in same distribution	b. median
_____ 3. most influenced by extreme scores	c. mode
_____ 4. also known as the 50th percentile	
_____ 5. measure of choice in skewed distributions.	

*5. Find P_{25} and P_{50} in the following distribution of scores:

115, 112, 110, 108, 106, 104, 100, 100, 98, 96, 96, 94, 93, 91, 90, 88

*6. Indicate the type of distribution to which each of these sets of data refer:

a. $\overline{X}$ = 78.37   b. $\overline{X}$ = 374.3   c. $\overline{X}$ = 109.5

MDN = 78.37   MDN = 379.7   MDN = 107.4

Mode = 78.37   Mode = 391.3   Mode = 107.4

*7. For the following sets of data, which method of tabulating data would be most appropriate? Why?

a. 70, 70, 70, 71, 72, 72, 73, 73, 73, 73, 74

b. 39, 47, 67, 51, 92, 60, 75

c. 35, 88, 85, 45, 49, 52, 69, 71, 49, 50, 90, 72, 79, 36, 43, 52, 92, 81, 80, 47, 55, 60, 72, 94, 91, 53, 48, 72

*Answers for these questions appear in Appendix D.

13

CHAPTER

VARIABILITY, THE NORMAL DISTRIBUTION, AND CONVERTED SCORES

In Chapter 12 we learned that measures of central tendency can be used to describe a distribution. However, an estimate of the variability, or spread, of scores is needed before we can compare scores within and between distributions. For example, suppose we have the following data: $\overline{X} = 160$, MDN = 170, Mode = 180. After drawing a curve, we know that the distribution is negatively skewed. What we don't know is how spread out, dispersed, or variable the scores are. For this we would at least need to know the range of obtained scores. Were all the scores between 100 and 200? 50 and 250? 150 and 190? Without an estimate of variability, we don't know which of the following three negatively skewed distributions best fits the data:

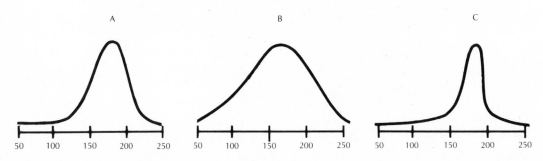

In A, the scores vary between about 100 and 200; in B, between 50 and 250; and in C between 150 and 190. In other words, it's possible for two or more distributions to have the same values for the mean, median, and mode but be different in the way their scores are spread out around these measures. This is why we must have an estimate of variability. This estimate helps us determine how "compressed" or "expanded" the distributions are.

THE RANGE

The easiest estimate of variability to compute is one we've already been exposed to: the range (R). The range is determined by subtracting the lowest score from the highest score.* This is what you did as the first step in constructing a grouped frequency distribution. Ease of computation does not offset the major drawbacks of the range as an estimate of variability, however. Since the range is dependent only on the low and high scores, it is often unstable and useful only for gross ballpark estimates of variability. If an extreme score is present, R can be very misleading. Consider the following example:

DIRECTIONS: Compute the range for the following set of data: 11, 11, 11, 11, 12, 12, 13, 14, 14, 14, 15, 15, 15, 15, 16, 17, 18, 18, 18.

$$R = H - L$$
$$R = 18 - 11$$
$$R = 7$$

Now substitute one extreme score, 96, for one of the scores of 18 and compute the range: 11, 11, 11, 11, 12, 12, 13, 14, 14, 14, 15, 15, 15, 15, 16, 17, 18, 18, 96.

$$R = H - L$$
$$R = 96 - 11$$
$$R = 85$$

This single extreme score increased R by 78 points and gives the impression that there is a large spread of scores when, with the exception of the single extreme score, there is actually very little.

THE SEMI-INTERQUARTILE RANGE (SIQR)

The semi-interquartile range (SIQR) compensates for the sensitivity of the range to extreme scores by eliminating extreme scores from its computation. The SIQR is determined solely by the middle 50 percent of the scores in a distribution. The

---

*Sometimes the range is defined as the lowest score subtracted from the highest score plus one. This is called the *inclusive range*. It is the statistic most often referred to in introductory statistics texts and is based upon mathematical concepts that need not concern us here.

lower 25 percent and upper 25 percent do not enter into its computation. The formula for the SIQR is presented here:

$$SIQR = \frac{Q_3 - Q_1}{2}$$

In this formula Q_3 stands for the third quartile and Q_1 stands for the first. Quartiles, like the median, are points in a distribution below which a certain percentage of scores lie. In fact the median, or fiftieth percentile, is the same as Q_2, or the second quartile.

Q_1 is the point below which 25 percent of the scores lie, and Q_3 is the point below which 75 percent of the scores lie. The same process we used in Chapter 12 to determine a percentile is used to determine Q_1 and Q_3, as illustrated by the following example:

EXAMPLE: Determine the semi-interquartile range for the following set of scores: 85, 115, 90, 90, 105, 100, 110, 110, 95, 110, 95, 100.

PROCESS:

1. Determine Q_1 and Q_3 by employing the steps used to determine the median (Q_2) for a distribution with an even number of scores.
   a. Arrange scores in numerical order.
   b. Counting up from the bottom, find the points *below which* 25 percent of the scores and 75 percent of the scores fall.
   c. Circle the two scores that "surround" these points.
   d. The averages of each of these two pairs of scores are Q_1 and Q_3.

$$
\begin{array}{l}
 \quad 115 \\
 \quad 110 \\
Q_3 \cdots \left(\begin{array}{c} 110 \\ 110 \end{array}\right) \quad \frac{110 + 110}{2} = 110 \\
 \quad 105 \\
 \quad 100 \\
 \quad 100 \\
 \quad 95 \\
Q_1 \cdots \left(\begin{array}{c} 95 \\ 90 \end{array}\right) \quad \frac{95 + 90}{2} = 92.5 \\
 \quad 90 \\
 \quad 85
\end{array}
$$

2. Plug Q_1 and Q_3 into the formula and determine the SIQR.

Formula	*Application*
$SIQR = \dfrac{Q_3 - Q_1}{2}$	$SIQR = \dfrac{Q_3 - Q_1}{2}$

$$= \frac{110 - 92.5}{2}$$

$$= \frac{17.5}{2}$$

$$= 8.75$$

Although the SIQR has the advantage of not being influenced by extreme scores, it has the disadvantage of being determined by only *half* the scores in a distribution. Anytime *all* scores in a distribution do not enter the computation of a statistic, an element of error is introduced. Thus, although the SIQR is a better estimate of variability than the range, it is not as good, or as stable, as the estimate of variability known as the standard deviation. The standard deviation, like the mean, considers all scores in its computation. As a result, it is the most commonly used estimate of variability. When the SIQR is reported it usually accompanies the median, which is not surprising since they share part of the same computational process. Next we will consider the standard deviation.

THE STANDARD DEVIATION

As mentioned, the standard deviation (SD) includes all scores in a distribution in its computation. The mean must be computed before the SD can be computed. Thus, you normally see the SD reported as the estimate of variability that accompanies the mean in describing a distribution.

Remember, we said an estimate of variability tells us how poor our best bet is as a single value with which to describe a distribution. Consider the following three distributions:

A	B	C
38	20	25
34	20	24
26	20	23
24	20	22
20	20	21
20	20	19
16	20	18
14	20	17
6	20	16
2	20	15
$\Sigma X = 200$	$\Sigma X = 200$	$\Sigma X = 200$

$$\overline{X}_A = \frac{\Sigma X}{N} \qquad \overline{X}_B = \frac{\Sigma X}{N} \qquad \overline{X}_C = \frac{\Sigma X}{N}$$

(continued)

$$= \frac{200}{10} \qquad = \frac{200}{10} \qquad = \frac{200}{10}$$

$$= 20 \qquad\quad = 20 \qquad\quad = 20$$

Although the distributions are composed of many different scores, they all have the same mean value. In distribution B, this best bet is right on the mark. Our mean value of 20 perfectly represents each and every score in the distribution, simply because each score in the distribution is 20. What about our best bets in A and C? How good or poor are they?

From these cases we can easily see that the mean is a better estimate of the scores in distribution C than in distribution A. We know this because none of the scores in C is more than 5 points away from the mean. Distribution A, on the other hand, has six of its ten scores 6 or more points away from the mean. Using this information, we can conclude that there is less variability, spread, or dispersion of scores in C. But just how much less variable is C than A? And what if there were less of a discrepancy in scores between A and C? How could we determine which was more or less variable?

With only this information, it would be difficult, if not impossible, to answer these questions. We need a reliable index of variability that considers all scores. Let's develop one by putting down on paper what we did when we compared A and C.

First, we looked at each distribution to see how far away each score was from the mean. We can do this more formally by subtracting the mean from each score $(X - \overline{X})$. We'll call this distance the score's *deviation* from the mean and use the symbol x (lower case) to represent such deviation scores. Thus, $X - \overline{X} = x$, which is illustrated here:

A				C		
X	$-\ \overline{X}$	$=$	x	X	$-\ \overline{X}$	$=$	x
38	$-\ 20$	$=$	18	25	$-\ 20$	$=$	5
34	$-\ 20$	$=$	14	24	$-\ 20$	$=$	4
26	$-\ 20$	$=$	6	23	$-\ 20$	$=$	3
24	$-\ 20$	$=$	4	22	$-\ 20$	$=$	2
20	$-\ 20$	$=$	0	21	$-\ 20$	$=$	1
20	$-\ 20$	$=$	0	19	$-\ 20$	$=$	-1
16	$-\ 20$	$=$	-4	18	$-\ 20$	$=$	-2
14	$-\ 20$	$=$	-6	17	$-\ 20$	$=$	-3
6	$-\ 20$	$=$	-14	16	$-\ 20$	$=$	-4
2	$-\ 20$	$=$	-18	15	$-\ 20$	$=$	-5

This is just what we did before, except it was done in our heads. Since we want a single number or index to represent the deviations, why don't we just sum the x column, being careful to note the sign of the number, and then average the result? Let's do this.

A	C
x	*x*
18	5
14	4
6	3
4	2
0	1
0	−1
− 4	−2
− 6	−3
−14	−4
−18	−5
$\frac{\Sigma x}{N} = 0$	$\frac{\Sigma x}{N} = 0$

Because the positive and negative numbers cancel each other out, the sum of both *x* columns is zero. Remember the characteristics of the mean? One of these stated that the sum of the deviations from the mean always equals zero. Now you can see what is meant by this characteristic. This characteristic holds true for all shapes and sizes of distributions without exception. Thus, we cannot use Σx or even the average deviation, $\frac{\Sigma x}{N}$, as our index of variability, as promising as these two indices might appear at first glance.

Fortunately, mathematics provides us with a way out of this dilemma. An index of variability based on deviation scores that we can use is computed in much the same fashion. There are two differences, however. First, let's square all the individual deviation scores and then sum them, as illustrated here:

	A				C		
X	− $\overline{X}$	= *x*	x^2	X	− $\overline{X}$	= *x*	x^2
38	20	18	324	25	20	5	25
34	20	14	196	24	20	4	16
26	20	6	36	23	20	3	9
24	20	4	16	22	20	2	4
20	20	0	0	21	20	1	1
20	20	0	0	19	20	−1	1
16	20	−4	16	18	20	−2	4
14	20	−6	36	17	20	−3	9
6	20	−14	196	16	20	−4	16
2	20	−18	324	15	20	−5	25
			$1144 = \Sigma x^2$				$110 = \Sigma x^2$

The next step is to find the average of the sum of the squared deviation scores.

$$\frac{1144}{10} = 114.4 \qquad\qquad \frac{110}{10} = 11.0$$

These estimates of variability are useful in more advanced statistical computations and have a special name. The average of the sum of the squared deviation scores is called the *variance*. By themselves these estimates are not very useful because they represent squared units, not the units we started with. To return these values to units representative of our original data we must extract their square roots:

A   C

$\sqrt{114.4} = 10.7$ $\sqrt{11.0} = 3.32$

These values—10.7 for distribution A and 3.32 for distribution C—are the indices we've been looking for. They are based on *all* the scores in a distribution and are on the *same scale* of units as our original set of data. These values are the standard deviations for distributions A and C. The following formula is simply a shorthand mathematical way of representing what we have just done for distributions A and C.

$$SD = \sqrt{\frac{\Sigma(X - \overline{X})^2}{N}} \quad \text{or, since } X - \overline{X} = x, \; SD = \sqrt{\frac{\Sigma x^2}{N}}$$

These formulas are equivalent. In other words, they tell you that to find the standard deviation you must square each deviation score, sum the squares of the deviation scores, divide this value by the number of scores in the distribution, and find the square root of this value. Just to be sure you understand the process we will work one more example, listing each of the steps.

The Deviation Score Method for Computing the Standard Deviation

EXAMPLE: Determine the standard deviation for the following set of scores: 92, 100, 90, 80, 94, 96.

PROCESS:

1. Determine the mean.

100	$\overline{X} =$	$\dfrac{\Sigma X}{N}$
96		
94		
92	$\overline{X} =$	$\dfrac{552}{6}$
90		
80		
$\overline{552} = \Sigma X$	$\overline{X} =$	92

2. Subtract the mean from each raw score to arrive at the deviation scores. (As a check on your computations, sum the x column to see if it equals zero.)

$$
\begin{array}{ccc}
X & - \; \overline{X} \; = & x \\
100 & 92 & 8 \\
96 & 92 & 4 \\
94 & 92 & 2 \\
92 & 92 & 0 \\
90 & 92 & -2 \\
80 & 92 & \underline{-12} \\
& & 0 \; = \Sigma x
\end{array}
$$

3. Square each deviation score and sum the squared deviation scores.

$$
\begin{array}{cccc}
X & - \; \overline{X} \; = & x & x^2 \\
100 & 92 & 8 & 64 \\
96 & 92 & 4 & 16 \\
94 & 92 & 2 & 4 \\
92 & 92 & 0 & 0 \\
90 & 92 & -2 & 4 \\
80 & 92 & -12 & \underline{144} \\
& & & 232 = \Sigma x^2
\end{array}
$$

4. Plug the x^2 into the formula and solve for the SD.

$$
SD = \sqrt{\frac{\Sigma x^2}{N}} = \sqrt{\frac{232}{6}} = \sqrt{38.67} = 6.22
$$

The Raw Score Method for Computing the Standard Deviation

The following formula is another, easier way of representing what we have just done for distributions A and C. It is called the *raw score* formula for the standard deviation, since it uses only the raw scores and does not require the more laborious process of finding deviations from the mean. Here is the raw score formula for calculating SD:

$$
SD = \sqrt{\frac{\Sigma X^2 - (\Sigma X)^2 / N}{N}}
$$

where:

ΣX^2 = each score squared and then summed
$(\Sigma X)^2$ = the square of the sum of the scores (i.e., add the scores then square the total)
N = the number of pupils.

Both the more cumbersome deviation method and the shorter raw score method of computing the standard deviation will give you the exact same result, keeping in mind that the raw score formula will be easier to use. Just to be sure you understand the process of obtaining a standard deviation, we will work one more example. This time let's use the raw score formula and follow the following steps.

EXAMPLE: Determine the standard deviation for the following set of scores: 10, 12, 15, 13, 20, 14, 15, 16, 18, 13.

PROCESS:

1. Determine the square of each X score.

X	X^2
10	100
12	144
15	225
13	169
20	400
14	196
15	225
14	196
18	324
13	169

2. Sum both the scores (X) and the *squared* scores (X^2).

X	X^2
10	100
12	144
15	225
13	169
20	400
14	196
15	225
14	196
18	324
13	169
$\Sigma X = 144$	$\Sigma X^2 = 2,148$

3. Square the sum of all the scores.

$$\Sigma X = 144$$
$$(\Sigma X)^2 = 20,736$$

4. Find N, the number of scores.

$$N = 10$$

5. Plug ΣX^2, $(\Sigma X)^2$, and N into the formula and solve for the SD.

$$SD = \sqrt{\frac{\Sigma X^2 - (\Sigma X)^2/N}{N}}$$

$$= \sqrt{\frac{2148 - (20{,}736)/10}{10}}$$

$$= \sqrt{\frac{2148 - 2{,}074}{10}}$$

$$= \sqrt{\frac{74}{10}}$$

$$= \sqrt{7.4}$$

$$= 2.72$$

Since the SD is an estimate of score variability or spread, it stands to reason that large SD values indicate greater score variability than do small SD values. In other words, when the SD is small, scores tend to cluster closely around the mean. Such a distribution is said to be *homogeneous* and tends to have a compressed shape, whether it is symmetrical or skewed. Three examples of the homogeneous distributions with compressed shapes are pictured here:

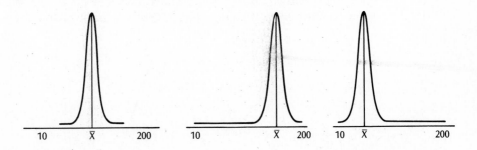

In these examples the $\overline{X}$ is a very good best bet as the single value that represents all the scores in each distribution. Our best bet is much poorer when distributions have large standard deviations. Such distributions have a lot of variability or spread of scores and all have an expanded appearance. These are called *heterogeneous distributions*. Three examples follow.

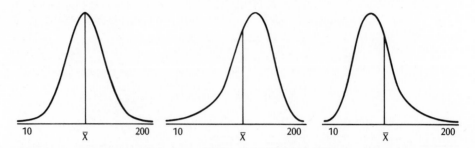

To sum up, measures of central tendency help us determine whether a distribution is symmetrical or skewed. Measures of variability help us determine more precisely whether these distributions appear compressed (small SD) or expanded (large SD). The SD also has a very important role in a special kind of symmetrical distribution. This is called the *normal distribution,* and it is to this topic that we now turn.

THE NORMAL DISTRIBUTION

The normal distribution is a special kind of symmetrical distribution that represents specific mathematical properties. This distribution has special importance for us because it is the model we use to make comparisons among scores or to make other kinds of statistical decisions. It is important, however, to note that the normal distribution is hypothetical. No distribution of scores matches the normal distribution perfectly. However, many distributions or scores in education *come close* to the normal distribution, and herein lies its value. The following example shows a distribution of Stanford-Binet IQ scores for a large number of students:

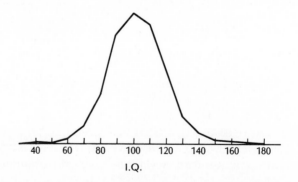

Looking at this figure you can see that although the IQ distribution differs somewhat from the symmetrical normal distribution, it is close enough that we do not lose too much accuracy by using the normal distribution as a model for the actual distribution. Many other characteristics of individuals also come close enough to the normal distribution for it to be used as a model for these distributions. Besides IQ, examples of these include most kinds of achievement and physical characteristics (for example, height and weight). The accuracy we sacrifice by employing a slightly inaccurate model is offset by the advantages of being able to make statistical and measurement decisions based on a *single* standard for comparison, the normal distribution. Before we can make such decisions, though, we must become familiar with the fixed properties of the normal distribution.

Properties of the Normal Distribution

The curve drawn here represents the normal distribution. Notice in the curve that the mean, median, and mode all coincide. This, of course, will occur whenever a distribution is normal. The percentages show the percent of cases that fall under portions of the curve.

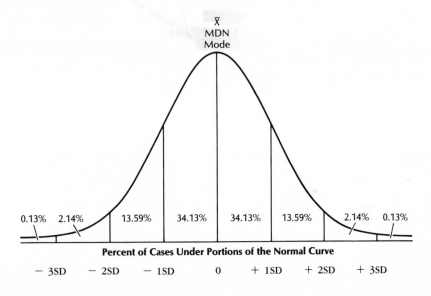

Percent of Cases Under Portions of the Normal Curve

Now add up the percentages you see above the baseline between three SD units below and three SD units above the mean. Notice that more than 99.9 percent or almost all scores in the normal distribution fall between three standard deviation units below the mean and three standard deviation units above the mean. Now, look at the area of the curve between the mean and one SD above the mean. The 34.13 percent you see in this area is a constant and indicates the percentage of cases that fall between the mean value and the value of the mean *plus* the value of one standard deviation unit. For example, if we were using the normal curve as a model for a distribution with a mean of 61 and a standard deviation of 7, we would know that 34.13 percent (or about 34 percent) of the scores in this distribution fall between 61 and 68, as the following illustration shows.

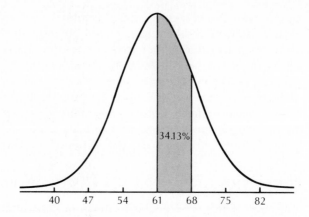

Notice also that for a distribution with a mean equal to 61 and a standard deviation equal to 7, seven points are added for each standard deviation unit above the mean (68, 75, 82), and seven points are subtracted from the mean for each standard deviation unit below the mean (54, 47, 40). Thus, we can see that about 68 percent of the scores in this distribution fall between 54 and 68, as shown here:

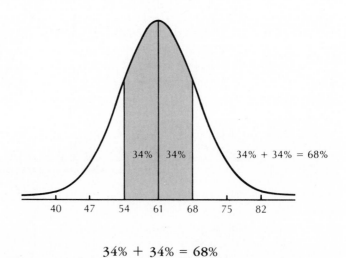

$$34\% + 34\% = 68\%$$

The interval between the mean and 75 represents what percent of scores? The answer is about 48 percent, as shown in the following illustration:

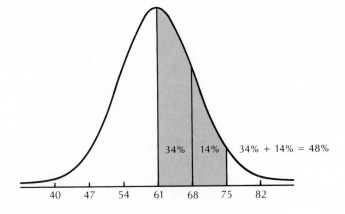

$$34\% + 14\% = 48\%$$

We can also use the normal curve to determine the percentage of scores above or below a certain score. The interval above 47 represents what percent of scores? The answer, 98 percent, is illustrated next:

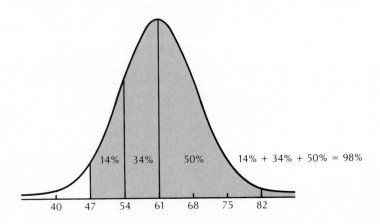

$$14\% + 34\% + 50\% = 98\%$$

The interval below 68 represents what percent of scores? The answer is about 84 percent, as shown in the following illustration:

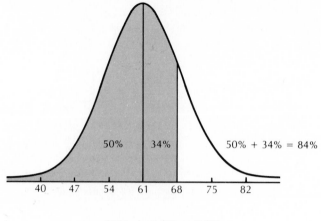

$$50\% + 34\% = 84\%$$

In other words, in a distribution with a mean of 61 and a standard deviation of 7, a score of 68 is at the eighty-fourth percentile. Recall that a percentile, like a quartile, is the point *below* which a given percentage of scores lie. So, if you wanted to determine the score at the sixteenth percentile, you would find that score below which there is 16% of the area under the normal curve, as illustrated here:

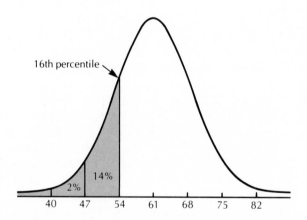

Assuming that test scores for a group of students were normally distributed—that is, if they conformed to a normal curve or close approximation of it—the standard deviation of that group could be converted to numbers and percentages of students scoring above or below certain score points. Before illustrating this concept, however, we must know how to accomplish this conversion.

CONVERTED SCORES

Thus far, we have talked about scores that come directly from tests. These actual or obtained scores are called *raw* scores. Consider the following:

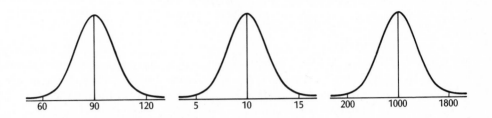

In these illustrations all three distributions have the same shape, but their means and standard deviations are different, which is often what happens because tests have different ranges of scores. The example illustrates what we are up against when we try to compare scores from different tests. The following example shows the process necessary to compare scores from distributions with different means and standard deviations.

John obtained a score of 85 on his psychology mid-term and 90 on his history mid-term. On which test did he do better, compared to the rest of the class?

At first glance you might say he did better in history. Well, this may be true, but how do you know? If you did say history, chances are you're treating these raw scores as percentages. Most of us are accustomed to test scores being converted to percentages before they are reported to us—but this is not always the case. John's score of 85 *may* mean he answered 85 out of 100 correctly, or it *may* mean he answered 85 out of 85 correctly, or 85 out of 217! Similarly, his history score may indicate he answered 90 out of 100, 90 out of 90, or 90 out of 329 items correctly. The point is that, without additional information, we can't say which of these scores is higher or lower. With only raw scores reported, we *cannot* determine whether these scores are low, high, or intermediate. We need more information. Raw scores, by themselves, are *not* interpretable. This is an important but often overlooked point. Let's add some information.

The information we have—the raw scores—exists as part of two distributions: one for psychology and one for history. The distributions consist of the raw scores obtained by all the students who took these tests. If we can determine where John's scores fall in these distributions, we should be able to answer our question. The answer, then, is that we need information that describes each distribution. As we now know, the mean and standard deviation are necessary to describe a distribution. Thus, if we have the mean and the standard deviation for each distribution, we should be able to answer our question. Let's add the information we need, but one piece at a time. First, we will add the means. The mean in psychology was 75, and the mean in history was 140. Before we go any further, let's organize our data and examine them carefully.

Psychology	*History*
X = 85	X = 90
$\overline{X}$ = 75	$\overline{X}$ = 140

We see that John's score was 10 points above the class mean in psychology and 50 points below the class mean in history. Clearly, he performed better compared with the rest of the class in psychology than in history. We have answered our question without even using the standard deviation of these distributions. Well, then, of what value is the standard deviation? As we will soon see, the standard deviation will enable us to pinpoint the percentage of scores above or below each of these scores. At first glance it may appear that John's history score is far below average, maybe even the lowest in the class. however, we don't know for sure because we have no idea how spread out or variable the history scores were. Consider the following illustrations:

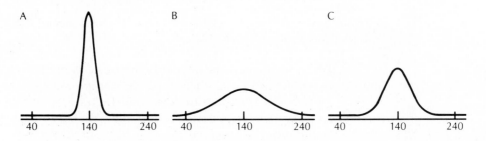

If the history scores are distributed as they are in A, then a score of 90 may indeed be the lowest in the class. If the distribution looks like B, 90 will not be the lowest score. In distribution C, we can expect a fair percentage of scores to be lower than 90. Similarly, we don't know if John's psychology score of 85 is far above average or only a little above average, simply because we don't know how spread out this distribution is. We will now add the standard deviations and pinpoint the locations of John's scores in their respective distributions.

The standard deviation in psychology was 10, and the standard deviation in history was 25. Again, let's organize our data before we do anything else.

Psychology	*History*	
X = 85	X = 90	
$\overline{X}$ = 75	$\overline{X}$ = 140	given?
SD = 10	SD = 25	

Next, let's construct curves to represent these data, assuming the scores are normally distributed.

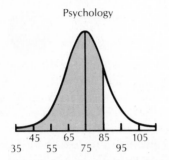

Psychology

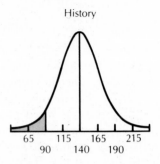

History

The shaded area in each distribution represents the proportion of scores below John's score. We can see that his psychology score is one standard deviation *above* the mean, and his history score is two standard deviations *below* the mean. To determine exactly what percentage of scores is lower than John's scores, all we need to do is consult the normal curve diagram to determine the percentage of cases lower than one standard deviation unit *above* the mean (for psychology) and two standard deviation units *below* the mean (for history).

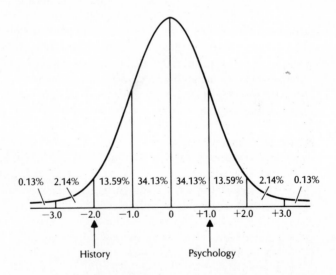

This diagram is identical to the normal curve presented in the section "Properties of the Normal Curve." The normal curve is used when we need a common basis on which to compare scores from distributions with different means and standard deviations. Examining this distribution we can see that about 84 percent of the class scored lower than John in psychology, while only about 2 percent scored lower in history. As compared with the rest of the class, his performance in psychology was far better than his performance in history. In psychology he scored at the eighty-fourth percentile, and in history he scored at the second.

Z-Scores

Now we have very specific information about John's performance. We had to collect the proper data (means and standard deviations for each distribution) and determine how far above or below the mean in standard deviation units each score was in order to determine the percentage of scores below (or above) the obtained raw scores. It took a while, but we got there! Fortunately, there is a mathematical shortcut. A relatively simple formula enables us to determine a score's exact position in the normal distribution quickly. The formula is called the *z*-score formula, and it converts raw scores into what are called *z*-scores. These are scores that tell us how far above or below the mean in standard deviation units scores lie.

Formula	*Translation*
$z = \dfrac{X - \overline{X}}{SD}$	z = *z*-score
	X = obtained score
	$\overline{X}$ = mean score
	SD = standard deviation

This formula enables us to convert raw scores from any distribution to a common scale, regardless of its mean or standard deviation, so that we can easily compare such scores. This eliminates the confusion that would ordinarily result from such comparisons. As we mentioned above, this formula is a shortcut method of doing what we just did in step-by-step fashion. In case you don't believe us, let's work through the same example, this time using the *z*-score formula.

John obtained a score of 85 on his psychology mid-term and 90 on his history mid-term. On which test did he do better compared to the rest of the class?

The first thing we should do is to organize the relevant information. We begin with the raw scores themselves.

Psychology	*History*
X = 85	X = 90

Clearly, we need more information—namely, the mean and standard deviation. Let's add them.

Psychology	*History*
X = 85	X = 90
$\overline{X}$ = 75	$\overline{X}$ = 140
SD = 10	SD = 25

Once we have all the necessary data, the obtained score, mean, and standard deviation for each distribution, we are ready to plug the data into the z-score score formula, obtain z-scores for each raw score, and compare these using the z-score distribution:

$$\text{\textit{Psychology}} \qquad \text{\textit{History}}$$

$$z = \frac{X - \overline{X}}{SD} \qquad z = \frac{X - \overline{X}}{SD}$$

$$= \frac{85 - 75}{10} \qquad = \frac{90 - 140}{25}$$

$$= \frac{10}{10} \qquad = \frac{-50}{25}$$

$$= +1.0 \qquad = -2.0$$

As you can see, we were able to get the same results as before quite quickly using the mathematical formula. We can now use the properties of the normal curve to quickly answer a variety of questions about these scores. For example:

What percentage of scores fall higher? lower?
At what percentile do the scores lie?
How much better than average were the scores? How much poorer?

Just to make sure you understand the z-score concept, let's work through two examples.

EXAMPLE: On a 70-item test Mary obtained a score of 49. The test had a mean of 40 and a standard deviation of 3. What percentage of the class scored higher than Mary?

STEP 1: Organize the relevant information.

$$X = 49$$
$$\overline{X} = 40$$
$$SD = 3$$

STEP 2: Convert to z-scores.

$$z = \frac{X - \overline{X}}{SD}$$

$$= \frac{49 - 40}{3}$$

$$= \frac{9}{3}$$

$$= +3.0$$

STEP 3: Use the normal curve to answer questions about comparisons, percentages, or percentiles.

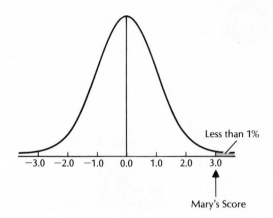

The shaded area in the z-score distribution indicates the percentage of obtained scores that were higher than Mary's. In other words, less than 1 percent (or, more accurately, less than .1 percent) of the individuals who took the test scored higher than Mary.

EXAMPLE: On the verbal portion of the Scholastic Aptitude Test (SAT) Pete obtained a score of 350. The mean of the SAT-V is 500, and its standard deviation is 100. The college Pete wants to go to will *not* accept applicants who score below the eighth percentile on the SAT-V. Will Pete be accepted by this college?

STEP 1:
$$X = 350$$
$$\overline{X} = 500$$
$$SD = 100$$

STEP 2:
$$z = \frac{X - \overline{X}}{SD}$$

$$= \frac{350 - 500}{100}$$

$$= \frac{-150}{100}$$

$$= -1.5$$

STEP 3:

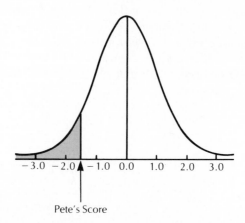

Pete's Score

So far, we have not had to deal with *z*-scores containing decimals. We can see though that the shaded area in the curve represents the percentage of scores *below* Pete's score. The question is, does this shaded area represent at least 8 percent of the scores obtained by others? If it does, Pete's score is at or above the eighth percentile, and he will be accepted. If it represents less than 8 percent, Pete's score is below the eighth percentile, and he will not be accepted.

In an introductory statistics course you would learn to determine *exactly* what percentage of the *z*-score distribution falls below a *z*-score of -1.5, but we will settle for an estimate. Let's go ahead and estimate, considering the following illustration:

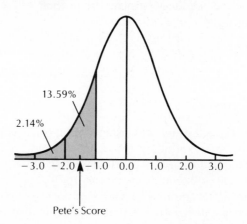

Pete's Score

We know that about 2 percent of the scores fall below two *z*-score units below the mean and that about 14 percent fall between one and two *z*-score units below the mean. A common mistake is to erroneously assume that since −1.5 is halfway between −1.0 and −2.0, about 7 percent of the scores fall between −1.0 and −1.5 and another 7 percent fall between −1.5 and −2.0. This reasoning would be correct *if* the proportion of the curve between −1.0 to −1.5 and −1.5 to −2.0 were the same. The following illustration shows, however, that a greater proportion of scores falls between −1.0 to −1.5 than falls between −1.5 and −2.0.

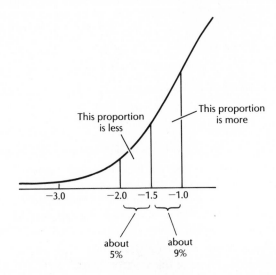

Remember, we are dealing with a curve, not with a bar graph! If we were, then splitting the percentage in half would be correct. Since we are not dealing with a bar graph, we must estimate the proportions any time we have a z-score that results in a decimal number.

Now, returning to our example, we see that about 7 percent (2 percent below $z = -2.0$, and 5 percent between $z = -1.5$ and $z = -2.0$) of SAT-V scores fall below 350. Pete's score is *below* the eighth percentile.

T-Scores

In working through this last example, you may have been confused about the negative numbers at times, or forgot that you were dealing with negative numbers. To avoid this difficulty, statisticians often convert z-scores to T-scores. T-scores are identical to z-scores, *except* that the T-score distribution has a mean of 50 and a standard deviation of 10. Our z, or normal curve distribution, had a mean of 0 and a standard deviation of 1.0. In the T-score distribution, negative numbers are eliminated except in those extremely rare cases where raw scores more than five standard deviations below the mean are obtained. To convert a raw score to a T-score you must first convert to a z-score. The formula for a T-score is:

$$T = 10z + 50$$

This formula says multiply the z-score by 10 and add 50 to this value to obtain the equivalent T-score. Let's convert John's psychology z-score of +1.0 and history score of −2.0 to T-scores.

Psychology	*History*
T = 10z + 50	T = 10z + 50
= 10(1.0) + 50	= 10(−2.0) + 50
= 10 + 50	= (−20) + 50
= 60	= 30

Thus, a z-score of 1.0 is equivalent to a T-score of 60, and a z-score of −2.0 is equivalent to a T-score of 30. Notice that the negative number has been eliminated. The following illustration shows the relationship between z-scores and T-scores:

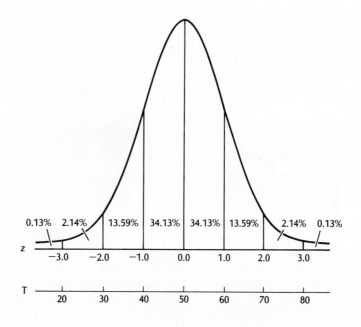

Thus far, we have considered statistical methods of tabulating and graphing data, the measures of central tendency and variability, and converted scores. In the next chapter we will consider another statistic, one that enables us to indicate how closely related or associated different sets of scores are.

SUMMARY

This chapter introduced you to the concept of score variability, methods to compute estimates of variability, the normal distribution, and converted scores. Its major points were:

1. *Variability* is the term we use to describe how spread out or dispersed scores from a distribution are.

2. The range, a gross estimate of variability, is determined by subtracting the lowest score from the highest score in the distribution.

3. The semi-interquartile range, which is usually reported along with the median, is determined by subtracting the value for the first quartile from the value for the third quartile and dividing the remainder by 2.

4. The standard deviation (SD) is usually reported along with the mean, and is our best estimate of variability. It is determined by subtracting the mean from each raw score to obtain a deviation score (x), squaring each deviation score, summing the squared deviation scores, dividing the total by the number of scores, and then determining the square root of this value.

5. Distributions with small standard deviations have a compressed appearance and are called *homogeneous distributions*.

6. Distributions with large standard deviations have a more expanded appearance and are called *heterogeneous distributions*.

7. The normal distribution is a specific type of symmetrical distribution that is mathematically determined, and has fixed properties.

8. Although the normal distribution is hypothetical, it approximates the distribution of many test scores, enabling us to use it as a model on which to base statistical decisions.

9. We use the normal distribution as our basis for comparing scores from distributions with different means and standard deviations.

10. We do so by converting raw scores from different distributions to either z-scores or T-scores and using these converted scores as the baseline for the normal distribution. This enables us to compare scores from different distributions on a single distribution with a single mean and standard deviation.

11. Determine z-scores by subtracting the mean for the distribution from the raw score and dividing by the standard deviation of the distribution.

12. Determine T-scores by first computing the corresponding z-score for a raw score, multiplying the z-score by 10, and adding 50 to the product.

13. The main advantage of the T-score over the z-score is the elimination of negative numbers.

For Practice

*1. For this set of scores (5,6,6,4,5,1,2,3,5,3), compute the following:
   a. N
   b. Mode
   c. Median

    d. Mean

    e. Standard deviation

    f. Variance

    g. Range

•2. Given $\overline{X} = 100$ and SD = 10

    a. Convert these raw scores into *z-scores:* 120, 132, 140, and 145.

    b. Convert these *z*-scores into *raw scores:* −2.5, 0.6, 1.25, and 2.15.

    c. Convert these T-scores into *raw scores:* 75, 38, 35, and 28.

    d. What percentages of scores lie between these scores?

     75–90

     90–120

    100–110

    112–125

•3. A score distribution has a mean of 100 and a standard deviation of 15.

    a. What *z*-score is the equivalent of a raw score of 120?

    b. What raw score is most equivalent to a T-score of 33?

    c. Approximately what percentage of scores lie below a score of 85?

•4. A pupil obtains a raw score of 82 on a test with a mean of 100 and a standard deviation of 12. His score corresponds to what T-score?

•5. The mean for the following distribution is 80 and the standard deviation is 12. Assuming a normal distribution, compute or determine the *z*-score and T-score for the following students:

Student	Score
John	68
Mary	104
Jim	86
Claire	62

•6. The following are the means and standard deviations of some well-known standardized tests, referred to as Test A, Test B, and Test C. All three yield normal distributions.

	Mean	Standard Deviation
Test A	500	100
Test B	100	15
Test C	60	10

    a. A score of 325 on Test A corresponds to what score on Test C? A score of 640 on Test A corresponds to what score on Test B?

    b. The counselor told Sally that she had scored so high on Test A that only 2 people out of 100 would score higher. What was Sally's score on Test A?

•Answers for questions 1 to 6 appear in Appendix D.

14

CHAPTER

CORRELATION

|O| ur last statistical topic is correlation. Thus far we have discussed statistics that are used to describe distributions and the position of individual scores within a distribution. There are times, though, when we are interested in the extent to which an individual's position or rank in one distribution is similar or dissimilar to his or her position or rank in a *different* distribution. That is, at times we want to determine how closely scores in different distributions are related to each other. Or, simply, we wish to know if individuals with high scores in distribution A tend also to obtain high scores in distribution B.

These and similar issues are concerned with the extent to which two different distributions of scores correlate. A statistic called a *correlation coefficient* (symbolized by r) helps us address general issues like those just mentioned or answer specific questions like those that follow:

Are athletes really poor scholars?
If you do poorly on the verbal portion of the SAT, are you likely to do poorly on the quantitative portion?
Do students with high grades in high school really tend to get high grades in college?

In this first question what is being asked is whether individuals who score high in a distribution of ratings pertaining to physical ability tend to score low in a distribution of ratings pertaining to intellectual ability. Using information gained from the previous chapter we can illustrate this as follows:

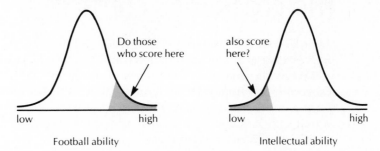

This question asks whether there is a *negative* correlation between the two. Are high scores in one distribution associated with low scores in the other?

The next question asks whether those who score low in the SAT-V distribution also score low in the SAT-Q distribution. Here, too, we can illustrate the question being asked, but note the difference from our previous illustration:

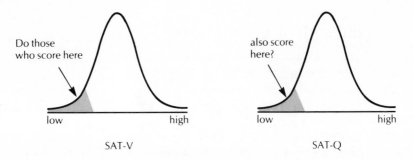

This question asks whether there is a *positive* correlation between the two distributions of scores.

Our last question asks whether students with high grades in high school tend also to receive high grades in college. This issue could be illustrated in the same manner as before:

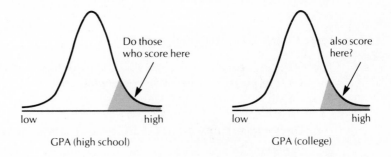

It asks whether there is a *positive* correlation between the two distributions. In other words, are high scores in one distribution associated with high scores in the other distribution?

THE CORRELATION COEFFICIENT

As we have seen, distributions can correlate positively or negatively. They may also *not* correlate at all! The correlation coefficient (*r*) tells us at a glance the strength and direction (positive or negative) of the relationship between distributions. Correlation coefficients range from −1.0 to +1.0. The closer a coefficient gets to −1.0 *or* to +1.0, the stronger the relationship. The sign of the coefficient tells us whether the relationship is positive or negative. The following examples are illustrative of correlation coefficients:

Coefficient	Strength	Direction
$r = -.85$	strong	negative
$r = +.82$	strong	positive
$r = +.22$	weak	positive
$r = +.03$	very weak	positive
$r = -.42$	moderate	negative

Strength of a Correlation

The previous coefficients are described as ranging from very weak to strong. You may ask yourself, "How high must *r* be for it to be strong?" Well, there is no cut-and-dried answer to this question, because an $r = .40$ may be considered strong for one set of data (for example, correlation of IQ scores and "happiness") and very weak for another (for example, correlation of scores from two standardized achievement tests). In other words, we must always consider the distributions with which we are dealing before deciding whether an *r* is weak, moderate, or strong. If our distributions are composed of scores arrived at by fairly objective means, such as standardized achievement tests, we would require *r*'s to be fairly high (for example, .80 or more) before we would call them strong. When distributions are composed of scores arrived at by subjective means, such as ratings of happiness, job success, or maturity, we would probably consider much lower *r*'s (for example, .50 to .60) as indicative of the presence of a strong relationship between the distributions in question.

Direction of a Correlation

The following illustrates the possible relationships between distributions that will result in positive or negative correlation coefficients. A positive correlation exists when:

1. High scores in distribution A are associated with high scores in distribution B, and
2. Low scores in distribution A are associated with low scores in distribution B.

A negative correlation exists when:

1. High scores in distribution A are associated with low scores in distribution B, and
2. Low scores in distribution A are associated with high scores in distribution B.

An everyday example of a positive correlation is the relationship between height and weight. As people *increase* in height they tend to *increase* in weight, and vice versa. A real-life example of negative correlation is the relationship between the number of cigarettes smoked per day and life expectancy. As the number of cigarettes smoked per day *increases,* life expectancy *decreases,* and vice versa. Fortunately, for those who are smokers, the correlation is not "very strong."

When there is no systematic relationship between two distributions, correlation coefficients around .00 are found. These indicate that high scores in distribution A are likely to be associated with *both* high and low scores in distribution B, and vice versa. In other words, there is no consistent pattern.

Scatterplots

As we have noted, the strength and direction of a relationship between two distributions can be determined by a correlation coefficient. Scatterplots also enable us to determine the strength and direction of a correlation, but in a less formal manner. A scatterplot is nothing more than a graphical representation of the relationship between two variables representing the scores in two distributions. Suppose we are interested in determining whether there is a relationship between number of touchdowns scored and academic achievement. To do so, we randomly select five running backs from past football teams, count up the number of touchdowns they scored, and obtain copies of their transcripts. Although it would not be necessary to do so, for illustrative purposes we will then rank each player on the two variables in question: touchdowns scored and GPA.* The results might look something like those in Figure 14.1.

This graph is a scatterplot of the data for each individual player. It indicates there is a *perfect negative* correlation ($r = -1.0$) between rank in touchdowns and rank in GPA. The player ranked highest in touchdowns is ranked lowest in GPA, and vice versa. There is a *perfect* correlation because all the plotted points can be connected by a straight line. We can tell it is a *negative* correlation because the slope of the scatterplot descends from left to right.

Let's collect the same data from another school, one that emphasizes academics and not athletics. These data are represented in Figure 14.2, with a graphical representation.

*We could also have used the unranked, or raw score, data. Our choice of data will determine the type of correlation coefficient that we compute and the symbol used to denote it, as will be noted later.

FIGURE 14.1 A Scatterplot Indicating a Perfect Negative Correlation

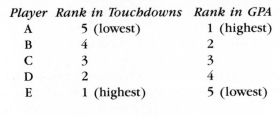

Player	Rank in Touchdowns	Rank in GPA
A	5 (lowest)	1 (highest)
B	4	2
C	3	3
D	2	4
E	1 (highest)	5 (lowest)

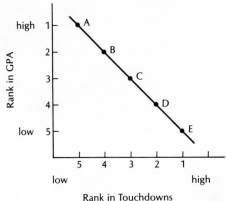

The scatterplot in Figure 14.2 indicates a *perfect positive* correlation (*r* = 1.0) between these variables. The player ranked lowest in touchdowns was also ranked lowest in GPA. The player ranked highest in touchdowns was also ranked highest in GPA. This is a *perfect* correlation because, again, the points are connected by a straight line. However, this time we can see the correlation is *positive* because the slope of the scatterplot ascends from left to right.

As you might have suspected, both of these examples are unrealistic. Perfect correlations, whether positive or negative, seldom occur. Normally one ends up with *r*'s somewhere *between* −1.0 and +1.0. Consider in Figure 14.3 data collected from a third school. The scatterplot in this figure represents a *positive* correlation. However, it is not a perfect correlation, because the points are "scattered" around the line rather than falling on the line. The line drawn through the points, called the regression line, is mathematically determined and is included here only to highlight the degree to which the data points slope upward or downward.

These data yield an *r* of .42. You can estimate the position of a regression line by drawing a straight line through the scattered points that best fits the movement of data upward (positive correlation) or downward (negative correlation). This movement is actually the rate at which rank in touchdowns changes relative to rank in GPA as we move from one individual to another. You may also enclose scattered data points with an ellipse, as we have done, to highlight the *strength* of

FIGURE 14.2 | A Scatterplot Indicating a Perfect Positive Correlation

Player	Rank in Touchdowns	Rank in GPA
A	5 (low)	5 (low)
B	4	4
C	3	3
D	2	2
E	1 (high)	1 (high)

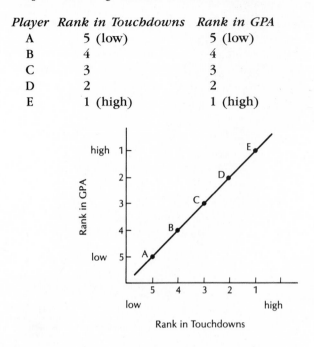

the relationship. As the data points form a tighter and tighter ellipse, the correlation gets stronger. This is illustrated by the scatterplots in Figure 14.4. Notice that when *r* approaches zero, a circle rather than an ellipse is needed to "capture" all the data points. As these examples illustrate, we often deal with correlations less than −1.0 or +1.0 because people do not conform to strict rules governing relationships among their abilities and other characteristics. Instead, relationships occur according to general trends with lots of exceptions. For example, there is a positive relationship between height and weight. Tall people tend to weigh more than short people. However, there are reversals to this trend (or exceptions to the rule): tall, skinny folks and short, stout folks. The more reversals or exceptions present in relationships, the weaker the correlation between the variables.

Where Does *r* Come From?

The correlation is determined through any one of a variety of mathematical formulas. One of these uses data that have been ranked, rather than raw scores—data like those presented in Figure 14.1. This type of correlation coefficient is called a rank difference correlation, which has the formula*:

*The rank difference correlation is one of several different types of correlations. The Greek letter rho (ρ) usually is used to identify a rank difference correlation.

FIGURE 14.3 | A Scatterplot Indicating a Weaker Positive Correlation

Player	Rank in Touchdowns	Rank in GPA
A	5 (low)	5
B	4	2
C	3	4
D	2	1
E	1 (high)	3

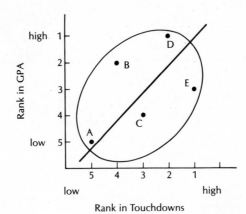

$$r_\rho = 1 - \frac{6\Sigma D^2}{N(N^2-1)}$$

r_ρ = rank difference coefficient of correlation
Σ = sum of
D = difference between a pair of ranks
N = number of pupils

The results of this formula for the rank difference coefficient when applied to the data presented in Figure 14.1 are as follows:

Rank in Touchdowns	Rank in GPA	Difference Ranks	D^2
5	1	4	16
4	2	2	4
3	3	0	0
2	4	2	4
1	5	4	16
			$\Sigma D^2 = 40$

FIGURE 14.4 | Scatterplots for a Variety of Correlations

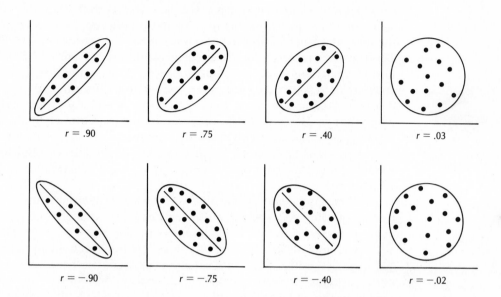

$$r_\rho = 1 - \frac{6(40)}{5(25-1)}$$

$$= 1 - \frac{240}{120}$$

$$= 1 - 2$$

$$= -1.0$$

The calculation of another type of correlation, called the Pearson-Product Moment Correlation, is illustrated with an example in Appendix B. The advantage of the rank difference correlation is that it can be used with small numbers of subjects, whereas the Pearson-Product Moment Correlation must be used with larger numbers of scores, usually about 30 or more pairs of scores. Generally, when this number of scores is obtained, the Pearson-Product Moment Correlation (symbolized simply as r) is easier to use and more accurate. However, since few teachers are ever called on to actually compute a correlation coefficient, especially on large numbers of students, we will not concern ourselves with computations for the Pearson-Product Moment Correlation in this chapter. More important is your ability to understand and interpret correlation coefficients. Thus far we have described what a correlation is and we have considered the numerical and graphical representations of correlations. Next, let's consider a frequently misunderstood aspect of correlation.

Causality

Correlation does not imply causality. That is, a correlation only indicates that some sort of relationship or association exists between two distributions. It does not mean that one distribution of scores *causes* the other distribution of scores. This may seem perfectly logical and sensible to you. Yet, one of the most frequent misinterpretations in statistics (and in education) is to infer that because two variables are correlated with each other, one variable causes the other. It is possible that one variable may cause another, and thus account for the relationship between the two. However, it is just as possible, and usually more likely, that the two variables are correlated with each other because of the effects of some *third* unidentified variable. That is, a third variable is actually causing one or both variables, thus making it only appear as though the first variable is causing the second.

For example, there is a negative correlation between air temperature and frequency of colds. As air temperature decreases, the number of people who catch colds increases. Thus, one might infer, incorrectly, that a drop in air temperature will cause colds. While this is a *possibility,* it is much more likely that the effect is the result of the effects of a third variable. That is, rather than a drop in air temperature causing an increase in colds, it may be that a drop in air temperature causes people to stay indoors and come in contact with each other more frequently, which causes an increase in colds. Figure 14.5 illustrates the probable sequence of events:

Two variables may also correlate with each other because a third variable affects both variables. For example, head size correlates with mental age. However,

---

FIGURE 14.5 | One way a third variable may affect conclusions about causality

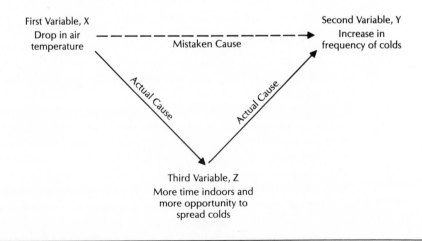

this does not mean that increases in head size cause increases in mental age. Both of these are affected by a third variable, chronological age, shown in Figure 14.6.

To sum up, in and of themselves, correlation coefficients alone can *never* be used to prove causality. Now that we are aware of this common misinterpretation, let's consider some other cautions.

Other Interpretive Cautions

A correlation coefficient of .83 is referred to as "point eight three," *not* as 83 percent. Furthermore, to make comparative decisions about the relative strength of correlation coefficients, it is insufficient to simply compare the coefficients themselves. Instead, it is necessary to square the coefficient and multiply the result times 100. The result of this operation is called the *coefficient of determination*. The coefficient of determination is the percent of variability (see Chapter 13) in one variable that is associated with or determined by the other variable. The following computations of the coefficient of determination demonstrate that a correlation coefficient of .80 is four times as strong as a coefficient of .40 and sixteen times as strong as a coefficient of .20.

Correlation Coefficient (r)	$r^2 \times 100$		Coefficient of Determination
.80	.64	64	64%
.40	.16	16	16%
.20	.04	4	4%

(r^2) usually referred as this — see in research

The coefficient of determination is an important concept in more advanced statistical operations. For our purposes we need to keep in mind only that correlation coefficients are not percentages and that we must convert correlation

---

FIGURE 14.6 | Another way a third variable may affect conclusions about causality

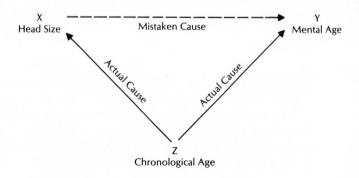

coefficients to the coefficient of determination *before* we can make decisions about their *relative* strength.

Curvilinearity.

All the scatterplots we have discussed thus far are plots of variables that have *linear* relationships with each other. In a linear relationship, scores on variables A and B either increase or decrease at approximately the same rate throughout the entire range of scores. That is, they progressively move up or down together in the same way regardless of whether they are at the low end, middle, or high end of the score continuum. In a curvilinear relationship, scores on variables A and B may increase together at first, and then decrease, or they may decrease at first, and then increase, depending on whether the scores are at the low, middle, or high end of the score distribution. The curvilinear relationship between anxiety and test performance is depicted in the scatterplot here:

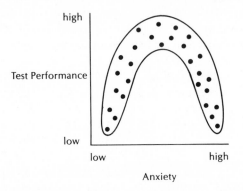

When data are related to each other in curvilinear fashion, a curved regression line, rather than a straight regression line, best fits the data. When plotted, such data take on a boomerang shape. While it is possible to compute a correlation coefficient for such data, the coefficient is of a special type. For curvilinear data, computing a coefficient like that which we've been discussing will yield an artificially low *r*. Thus, it is always a good idea to plot data *before* computing a correlation coefficient. Otherwise, a falsely low *r* will result if the data are curvilinear.

Truncated Range.

Normally, we compute correlation coefficients across the range of all possible values for variables A and B. At times, though, we may desire or be forced to consider only a part of all the possible values (for example, just low-ranked or high-ranked individuals). Here we are dealing with a truncated range of scores. When only a portion of the entire range of scores is considered, the strength of the correlation coefficient *goes down*. The following scatterplots illustrate this conclusion. The first scatterplot illustrates the relationship between IQ scores and standardized test scores.

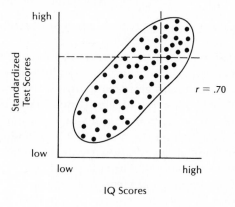

IQ Scores

However, let's say that we are concerned only with the relationship between high scores on both tests (indicated by the broken lines demarcating the upper, right section of the scatterplot). The correlation between only the high scores is much weaker than the correlation between scores across the entire range. This is illustrated in the next scatterplot, which is an enlargement of the upper, right section of the previous scatterplot.

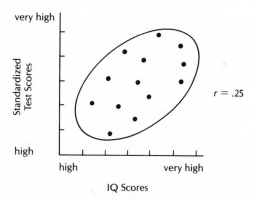

IQ Scores

This completes our chapters on statistics. We trust you now have a good working knowledge of the concepts and methods presented. If so, you are ready to apply some of these concepts and methods in the following chapters. If not, now is the time to review. The remainder of the text will be a lot easier to understand if you take the extra time to review.

SUMMARY

In this chapter you were introduced to a number of considerations related to the topic of correlation. The major points made were:

1. Correlation refers to the extent to which two distributions are related or associated. That is, it refers to the extent to which scores in one distribution vary depending on the variation of scores in the other distribution.

2. The extent of correlation is indicated numerically by a correlation coefficient (r), and graphically by a scatterplot.

3. When high scores in one distribution tend to be associated with low scores in another distribution, and vice versa, the correlation is negative.

4. When high scores in one distribution tend to be associated with high scores in another distribution (with the same being true for low and moderate scores), the correlation is positive.

5. Correlation coefficients may range from −1.0 (perfect negative correlation) to +1.0 (perfect positive correlation). A correlation of .00 indicates an absence of relationship or association.

6. The size of the number of the correlation coefficient indicates the strength of the correlation (higher numbers indicate stronger correlation), and the sign indicates the direction (positive or negative).

7. Scatterplots range from straight lines indicative of a perfect correlation to ellipses that approach circles. The tighter the ellipse, the stronger the correlation: the more circular the ellipse, the weaker the correlation.

8. Two variables correlated with each other does *not* mean that one variable causes the other. Often the correlation is the result of the effects of a third variable.

9. To compare the relative strength of correlation coefficients it is necessary to square the coefficients, resulting in coefficients of determination. Correlation coefficients are not percentages: coefficients of determination are.

10. When two distributions are linearly related, scores increase or decrease across the range of scores.

11. When two distributions have a curvilinear relationship, scores in one distribution may increase and then decrease, or vice versa, while scores in the other distribution consistently increase or decrease.

12. Since a linear correlation coefficient will underestimate the strength of a curvilinear relationship, it is wise to construct a scatterplot before computing a correlation coefficient.

13. When only a portion of the entire range of scores for a distribution is considered (for example, only high or low scores) in computing a correlation coefficient, the strength of the correlation coefficient decreases. This effect is due to use of a truncated range of scores, rather than the entire range of scores.

For Practice

1. After pairing each X score with each Y score in the order given below, construct a scatterplot of the data:

   X: 15, 15, 15, 15, 30, 30, 30, 30, 45, 45, 45, 45, 60, 60, 60, 60, 75, 75, 75, 75.

   Y: 1, 2, 1, 3, 12, 10, 13, 15, 19, 18, 20, 21, 15, 11, 12, 12, 2, 3, 1, 2.

*2. Does the scatterplot in question 1 indicate that the data are linear or curvilinear? If X represents age and Y represents average annual income in thousands of dollars, describe this relationship in words.

*3. Using the formula given in Appendix B, compute a Pearson Product-Moment correlation for the following data.

   X: 10, 8, 14, 6, 4, 8, 7, 3, 7, 10.
   Y: 12, 7, 13, 8, 7, 6, 6, 4, 9, 11.

   How would you describe the direction and size of this relationship?

*4. Compute the coefficient of determination for the data in question 3.

*5. In the following matching exercise, Column A contains scatterplots and Column B contains correlation coefficients. Indicate which of the correlation coefficients in Column B most closely approximates the scatterplots in Column A. Each of the options may be used only once or not at all.

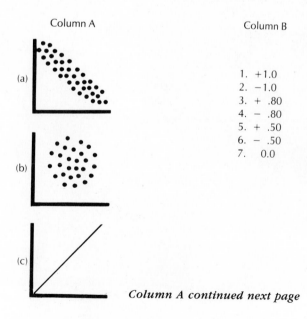

Column A

(a)

(b)

(c)

Column B

1. +1.0
2. −1.0
3. + .80
4. − .80
5. + .50
6. − .50
7.   0.0

Column A continued next page

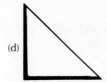

(d)

*6. A researcher finds a high positive correlation between shoe size and vocabulary size in elementary school pupils. The researcher concludes that "big feet cause big vocabularies." Do you agree or disagree? If so, why? If not, why not?

*7. Explain why the use of a truncated range of scores will result in a low correlation between the variables in question.

*Answers for questions 2 to 7 appear in Appendix D.

15

CHAPTER

VALIDITY

In the last three chapters we introduced you to the field of statistics. In this and subsequent chapters we will show how to use some of this newly acquired knowledge to evaluate tests. In short, we will show you how statistical tools are applied to test results to determine the degree of confidence we can place in them.

WHY EVALUATE TESTS?

If a test shows that 60 percent of the students in our third-grade class are reading below grade level, should we be seriously concerned? Your initial response might be an unqualified yes, but we would say not necessarily. We would be worried only if we had confidence in the results of our test. We have such confidence only when we are reasonably sure a test measures the skill, trait, or attribute it is supposed to measure, when it yields reasonably consistent results for the same individual, and when it measures with a reasonable degree of accuracy. That is, we should seriously consider using test results only from tests that are valid, reliable, and accurate. These terms can be defined as follows:

1. Validity: Does the test measure what it is supposed to measure?
2. Reliability: Does the test yield the same or similar scores (all other factors being equal) consistently?
3. Accuracy: Does the test approximate fairly closely an individual's true level of ability, skill, or aptitude?

To be a "good" test, a test ought to have adequate validity, reliability, and accuracy. In this chapter we will see how statistics help us determine the extent to which tests possess validity.

TYPES OF VALIDITY

A test is valid if it measures what it says it measures. For instance, if it is supposed to be a test of third-grade arithmetic ability, it should measure third-grade arithmetic skills, not fifth-grade arithmetic skills and not reading ability. If it is supposed to be a measure of ability to write behavioral objectives, it should measure that ability, not the ability to recognize bad objectives. Clearly, if a test is to be used in any kind of decision making, or indeed if the test information is to have any use at all, it is essential that the test be valid.

Content Validity

There are several ways of deciding whether a test is sufficiently valid to be useful. The simplest is content validity. The content validity of a test is established by examination. Test questions are inspected to see whether they correspond to what the user feels should be covered by the test. This is easiest when the test is in an area such as achievement, where it is fairly easy to specify what should be included in the content of a test. It is more difficult if the concept being tested is a personality or aptitude trait, for which it is sometimes difficult to specify beforehand what a relevant question should look like. Another problem with content validity is that it gives information about whether the test *looks* valid, but not whether the reading level of the test is too high or the items are poorly constructed. A test can sometimes look valid but measure something entirely different than what is intended, such as guessing ability, reading level, or skills that may have been acquired before instruction. Content validity is, therefore, more a minimum requirement for a useful test than it is a guarantee of a good test.

Content validity answers the question "Does the test measure the instructional objectives?" In other words, a content-valid test matches or fits the instructional objectives.

Criterion-Related Validity

A second form of validity is criterion-related validity. In establishing criterion-related validity, scores from a test are correlated with an external criterion. There are two types of criterion-related validity: concurrent and predictive.

Concurrent Criterion-Related Validity.
Concurrent criterion-related validity deals with measures that can be administered at the same time as the measure to be validated. For instance, the Stanford-Binet and the Wechsler Intelligence Scale for Children-Revised (WISC-R) are well known, widely accepted IQ tests. Therefore, a test publisher designing a short screening test that measures IQ might show that

the test is highly correlated with the WISC-R or the Binet, and thus establish concurrent criterion-related validity for the test. Unlike content validity, criterion-related validity yields a numeric value, which is simply a correlation coefficient, sometimes called a validity coefficient. The concurrent validity for a test is determined by administering both the new test and the established test to a group of respondents, then finding the correlation between the two sets of test scores. If there exists an established test (criterion) in which most people have confidence, criterion-related validity provides a good method of estimating the validity of a new test. Of course, usually there is some practical advantage of having a new test—it is cheaper to give, or shorter, or can be administered to groups. Otherwise, it would be easier simply to use the established test. The following example illustrates how concurrent validity might be established for a new third-grade math test.

The Goodly Test of Basic Third-Grade Math has been around a long time, but it takes 60 minutes to administer. Being pressed for teaching time, you develop another test that takes only 20 minutes to administer and call it the Shorter and Better Test of Basic Third Grade Math. You send it off to a test publisher with visions of fame and wealth.

   The publisher writes back to say that he wants to know whether the test is as good as the Goodly Test. "No point marketing a test that isn't at least as good as the Goodly," he says.

To address this challenge, you would determine the test's concurrent validity by giving both the Goodly and the Shorter and Better to the same group of students and calculating a correlation coefficient between scores on the two tests. If the same students score similarly on both tests, indicated by a high correlation, the new test could be said to have concurrent validity. Consider the following hypothetical data:

Student	*Scores on Goodly*	*Scores on Shorter and Better*
Jim	88	37
Joan	86	34
Don	77	32
Margaret	72	26
Teresa	65	22
Victor	62	21
Veronica	59	19
Wilson	58	16

Since the correlation in this instance is likely to be very high (notice that, for the data shown, everyone maintains the same rank across tests), the concurrent validity of the Shorter and Better Test has been established. The publisher will be impressed, and you are soon to be famous.

Predictive Validity.

Predictive validity refers to how well the test predicts some future behavior of the examinee. This form of validity is particularly useful for aptitude tests, which attempt to predict how well the test taker will do in some future setting. The Scholastic Aptitude Test, or SAT, for instance, is frequently used to help decide who should be admitted to college. It would be desirable, therefore, for it to do a good job of predicting success in college. If a personality test is used to choose among various types of therapy for mental patients, then it is desirable that it have good predictive validity. That is, it should predict who will do well with what kind of therapy. The predictive validity of a test is determined by administering the test to a group of subjects, then measuring the subjects on whatever the test is supposed to predict after a period of time has elapsed. The two sets of scores are then correlated, and the coefficient that results is called a *predictive validity coefficient*.

If a test is being used to make predictions, then an effort should be made to find its predictive validity for the setting in which it will be used. High predictive validity provides a strong argument for the worth of a test, even if it seems questionable on other grounds. In such a situation you might argue about whether it is being used to predict something worthwhile, but you can't argue about whether the test does a good job of predicting. The following example illustrates the concept of predictive validity:

"Psychics predict blizzard for Houston on July 4th!" You have likely seen similar predictions on various tabloids while waiting in check-out lines at supermarkets. Are they valid? Initially, you'd probably say no, but how can you be sure? The only answer is to wait and see if the predictions come true. With a test, similar reasoning applies. Just because a test is named the Test to Predict Happiness in Life doesn't mean it can (or cannot). More likely than not, we would be inclined to say it can't. But again, the only way to be sure is to wait for a period of time and see if the individuals for whom the test predicts "happiness" are actually happy.

Both predictive and concurrent criterion-related validity yield numerical indices of validity. Content validity does not yield a numerical index, but instead yields a logical judgment as to whether the test covers what it is supposed to cover. However, all three of these methods—content, concurrent, and predictive—assume that some criterion exists external to the test that can be used to anchor or validate the test. In the case of content validity, it was the instructional objectives that provided the anchor or point of reference; in the case of concurrent validity, it was another well-accepted test measuring the same thing; and in the case of predictive validity, it was some future behavior or condition which we were attempting to predict. However, if a test is being developed to measure something not previously measured, or not measured well, and no criterion exists for anchoring the test, another kind of validity must be used. This type of validity is called *construct validity*.

Construct Validity

A test has construct validity if its relationship to other information corresponds well with some theory. A theory is simply a logical explanation or rationale that can account for the interrelationships among a set of variables. Many different kinds of theories can be used to determine the construct validity of a test. For instance, if it is supposed to be a test of arithmetic computation skills, you would expect scores on it to improve after intensive coaching in arithmetic. If it is a test of mechanical aptitude, you might expect that mechanics would, on the average, do better on it than poets. You might also expect that it would have a *low* correlation with scores on a reading test, since it seems reasonable to assume that reading ability and mechanical ability are not highly related. In general, any information that lets you know whether results from the test correspond to what you would expect (based on your own knowledge about what is being measured) tells you something about the construct validity of a test. It differs from concurrent validity in that there is no good second measure available of what you're trying to test, and from predictive validity in that there is no measure of future behavior available.

Already in this chapter we have had to introduce some new terms and concepts. Before proceeding, be familiar with these terms and concepts, and, if necessary, reread our presentation on validity. Before you do, though, let's try to understand at a commonsense level what we've been saying.

What Have We Been Saying? A Review

A test should ideally do the job it's written to do. That is, it should measure what it's supposed to measure. In other words, it should be valid. The three questions here are equivalent:

1. Is the test valid?
2. Does the test measure what it is supposed to measure?
3. Does the test do the job it was designed to do?

It makes no sense to prepare or select for the classroom a test designed to measure something other than what has been taught. If we wanted to measure someone's height, does it make sense to use a scale? A ruler, yardstick, or a tape measure would certainly be more appropriate. Similarly, if we are interested in knowing whether our students can multiply two-digit numbers, would it make sense to administer a test that focuses *only* on addition of two-digit numbers? The appropriate measure would be a test that includes items on two-digit multiplication. Such a test would *do the job it's supposed to do*. It would have content validity.

For achievement tests, content validity is most important because the "job" of an achievement test is to measure how well the content taught has been mastered. The best way to ensure that a test's content is valid is to be sure its items match or measure the instructional objectives. Recall that in Chapter 5 we discussed ways to check whether items match objectives. Now, let's review predictive validity.

Consider a situation in which the purpose of a test is to identify those individuals who are likely to stay with a company for at least three years. A valid test in this case would accomplish this purpose. But, just what is the purpose? Is it to measure how well certain content has been mastered? No, the purpose is to *pre-dict* who will last three years and who won't. A different kind of validity is in order—predictive validity.

In this situation we are interested only in finding a measuring instrument that correlates well with length of time on the job. We don't care whether it is an IQ test, math test, reading test, vocational test, visual-motor integration test, or whatever. The purpose is to predict who will last three years. If the math test correlates .75 with length of time on the job and the vocational test correlates .40 with length of time on the job, which test has the *better predictive* validity? The math test, of course, because it would provide us with the most accurate predictions of future behavior.

In the case of concurrent validity, the purpose of a test is to approximate the results that would have been obtained had a well-established test been used. In other words, if the ranking of students with the new or shorter test *concurs* with the rankings of students on the older, standard test, then the new or shorter test has concurrent validity. Remember, unless a new test does something more easily or better than an established measure, there is no point in constructing a new test!

Finally, let's think about construct validity. Construct validity is important in establishing the validity of a test when we cannot anchor our test either to a well-established test measuring the same behavior or to any measurable future behavior. Since we do not have these anchoring devices to rely on, we can only create verbal and mathematical descriptions or theories of how our test behavior (called a *construct*) is either likely to change following or during certain situations, or likely to be related to other constructs. If a test of our theory reflects or demonstrates the relationships specified, then the new measure has construct validity. Unlike predictive and concurrent validity, not one but many correlation coefficients emerge from a construct-validation study. The actual process used to assess construct validity can be lengthy and complex and need not concern us here. Figure 15.1, Review of Validity, summarizes our discussion of validity thus far.

Thus far, we've discussed test validity. Our presentation, believe it or not, has been quite superficial as far as measurement theory goes. If you are interested in a more intensive discussion of any of these topics you can consult one or more of the measurement texts listed in Appendix C. Next, we will discuss the role of validity coefficients in evaluating tests.

INTERPRETING VALIDITY COEFFICIENTS

Now that we have discussed and reviewed the concepts of content, concurrent, and predictive validity, we can begin to put these concepts to use in evaluating tests. Remember, validity coefficients enable us to estimate the extent to which a test measures what it is supposed to measure. Let's consider the role of validity coefficients in making decisions about tests.

FIGURE 15.1 Review of Validity

	Asks the question:	*To answer the question:*
• Content Validity	Do test items match and measure objectives?	Match items with objectives.
• Concurrent Criterion-Related Validity	How well does performance on the new test match .performance on an established test?	Correlate new test with an accepted criterion, for example, a well-established test measuring the same behavior.
• Predictive Criterion-Related Validity	Can the test predict subsequent performance, for example, success or failure in the next grade?	Correlate scores from the new test with a measure of some future performance.

Remember: Predictive validity involves a time interval. A test is administered and, after a period of time, a behavior is measured which the test is intended to predict. For example:

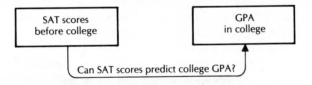

Remember: Concurrent validity does not involve a time interval. A test is administered, and its relationship to a well established test measuring the same behavior is determined. For example:

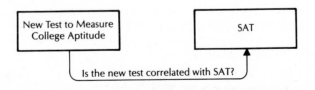

Content Validity

If you are wondering why content validity is included in this section, you are probably grasping more of what has been presented than you may realize. Procedures to determine a test's content validity do *not* yield validity coefficients. Content validity is established by comparing test items with instructional objectives (with, for example, the aid of a test blueprint) to determine whether the items match or measure the objectives. After such an examination takes place, a test is judged either to have or not to have content validity. No correlation coefficient is computed. Instead, human judgment is relied upon.

Concurrent and Predictive Validity

Concurrent and predictive validity require the correlation of a predictor or concurrent measure with a criterion measure. Thus, these types of validity *do* yield numerical coefficients. Using our interpretation of these coefficients, we can determine whether a test is useful to us as a predictor or as a substitute (concurrent) measure. In general, the higher the validity coefficient, the more valid the test will be. However, several principles must be considered in evaluating validity coefficients.

PRINCIPLE 1: Concurrent validity coefficients are generally higher than predictive validity coefficients. This does *not* mean, however, that the test with the higher validity coefficient is more suitable for a given purpose.

The rational for this principle is that, in establishing concurrent validity, no time interval (or a very small time interval) is involved between administration of the new test and the criterion or established test. Thus, the chances that the behavior of individuals measured on both the new test and the criterion test has changed between testings is negligible. On the contrary, predictive validity coefficients are by definition susceptible to such changes. Life-style, personality, and attitudinal or experiential changes may alter an individual's rank on a criterion measure two years from now from what it was at the initial testing. Thus, a *decline* in the size of the correlation between the test and a measure of future performance would be expected as the time interval between the two testings increases.

Generally, concurrent-validity coefficients in the .80-and-higher range and predictive-validity coefficients in the .60-and-higher range are considered encouraging. Thus, if a new achievement test reports a concurrent-validity coefficient of .60 with an established achievement test, we probably would not consider using the new achievement test. On the other hand, if a new college selection test correlated .60 with college GPA, the new test might be considered suitable for use as a college selection test. In other words, the *purpose* of the test as well as the size of the validity coefficient must be considered in evaluating the test.

PRINCIPLE 2: Group variability affects the size of the validity coefficient. Higher validity coefficients are derived from heterogenous groups than from homogeneous groups.

If the college selection test mentioned before was administered to *all* high-school seniors in a district (a heterogeneous group) and if *all* these students went to the same four-year college, the obtained validity coefficient would be higher for this group than if the test were administered only to high-school seniors in the top 10 percent of their class (a homogeneous group). At first glance this may not seem to make sense. The picture becomes clear, however, if we think about how changes in the rankings of individuals on the two measures are affected by the variability of these distributions. In the heterogeneous group, students who are at the top of their high-school class are likely to score high on the test and have high college GPA's. Students at the bottom of the class are likely to score low and have low college GPA's. That is, the likelihood of major shifting in ranks occurring is small. It's not likely that students who score low on the test will have high GPA's and vice versa, as is illustrated in Figure 15.2.

FIGURE 15.2 | Comparison of probable rankings between college selection test scores and college GPA for four students from a heterogeneous group

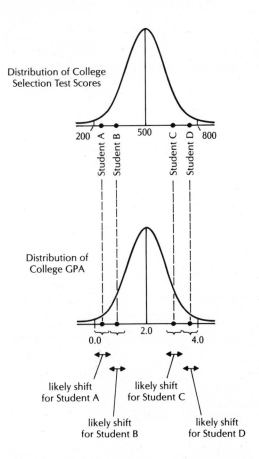

Although some shifting in ranks or position might be expected, as indicated by the arrows in Figure 15.2, dramatic shifts would be unlikely. While it might be possible for our lowest-scoring student on the selection test (Student A) to obtain a 3.5 GPA, it would be unlikely. But what happens when the variability of the group is greatly reduced, creating a homogeneous group composed only of the top 10 percent of the high-school seniors? Now we would expect a pronounced shifting of ranks or positions to take place. This is likely to occur because the students are all ranked *so closely together* on the selection test that even small differences between their ranks on GPA and their ranks on the selection test will lower the size of the validity coefficient. This is illustrated in Figure 15.3.

FIGURE 15.3   Comparison of probable rankings between college selection test score and college GPA for four students from a homogeneous group (upper 10% of senior class)

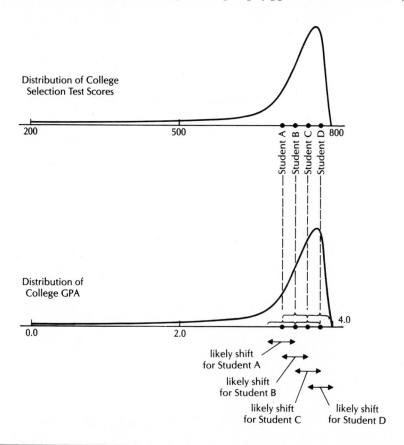

Compare the overlap, or possible shifting in ranks, for this group to the possible shifting in ranks for the heterogeneous group. The width of the arrows has not changed, but their significance has. There is much more likelihood of dramatic shifts occurring among the students in this homogeneous group. They are so much alike in ability that the test is unable to discriminate among those individuals in the high-ability group who will rank low, middle, or high in their GPA's, since the range of GPA's for this group is only about 3.5 to 4.0. When test scores or criterion measures are more heterogeneous, however, the test is able to discriminate among those who will rank low, moderate, or high in GPA's. In such a case, GPA's might range from 0.0 to 4.0. Thus, in evaluating a test's validity coefficient, it is necessary to consider the variability of the group from which the coefficient was derived. For example, critics who discourage using the Scholastic Aptitude Test (SAT) as a criterion for college admission often point out that its predictive validity coefficient is only about .40. What they may fail to consider, however, is that the coefficient is not based on all high-school students, but only on those who took the test and actually went to college. This is a far more homogeneous group than the entire body of high-school students. Thus, its predictive validity coefficient is smaller than would be expected if it were based on *all* high-school students.

PRINCIPLE 3: The relevance and reliability of the criterion should be considered in the interpretation of validity coefficients.

Wherever predictive validity is being considered, it is necessary to be aware that the size of the resulting coefficient is dependent on both the reliability of the predictor *and* the criterion measure. If you are using a test to predict whether someone will last for three years on a job, your criterion is easy to measure, and your criterion measure would be dependable. For this measure you need simply to determine whether someone is employed after three years. Unfortunately, in many cases criterion measures are not so clear cut. For example, let's say you want to establish the predictive validity of a test to predict job success, rather than simply whether someone is or is not employed after three years. What does job success mean? Herein lies the problem of selecting a criterion measure. Is it best measured by salary scale? Number of promotions? Amount of sales? Merchandise produced? Supervisor ratings? Peer ratings? All of these? We could probably go on and on, but the point is that criterion measures that are meaningful are often difficult to identify and agree upon. Each of the criterion measures mentioned may be an important *aspect* of job success, but none is *equivalent* to job success. Ideally, you would want to collect many measures of job success and determine their relationship to the test. In reality, however, such a thorough approach might be impossible due to financial or time constraints. What typically happens in a predictive-validity investigation is that one or two of what are considered to be relevant criterion measures are selected and correlated with the predictor. Naturally, such a compromise limits somewhat the weight that one might attach to predictive-validity coefficients, since not all relevant aspects of the criterion are considered.

If a test has a predictive-validity coefficient of .60 with salary after three years, but coefficients of .20 with supervisor ratings, and .16 with peer ratings, we would seriously question the test's validity. Since salary typically increases from year to year, often independent of success on the job, the correlation with salary might not be very meaningful, since salary may not be all that *relevant*. On the other hand, supervisor and peer ratings may be more relevant measures. However, our test's correlation with these measures is little more than what might occur by chance. Thus, since the test does not correlate highly with more relevant criteria, we might question its predictive validity. However, to do so without considering the dependability of the criterion measure we have chosen would be a mistake. To correlate highly or even moderately with each other, measures must be dependable or fairly stable (that is, *reliable*). If ratings by supervisors or peers vary greatly from rating period to rating period, then any attempt to correlate such ratings with a predictor will yield low-correlation coefficients—even if the predictor is highly reliable. Thus, if an employee gets a high rating from one peer or supervisor and a low rating from another, how can the predictor possibly predict a rating? The answer is that it can't. Some evidence of stability or reliability in a criterion measure is necessary before we can conclude that a predictor that correlates poorly with a criterion measure is actually a poor predictor and not the result of an unreliable criterion measure.

We have intended this discussion to alert you to the importance of studying carefully any and all statistical data presented in test manuals. Where predictive validity coefficients are reported, check the adequacy (the relevance) of the criterion measure and its dependability (the reliability) before drawing any conclusions about the validity of the predictor.

|SUMMARY

This chapter introduced you to the major types of validity and some principles to be considered in interpreting validity coefficients. The following major points were covered:

1. To be considered seriously, test results should be valid and reliable.
2. A valid test measures what it is supposed to measure.
3. Content validity is assessed by comparing a test item with instructional objectives to see if they match. Content validity does not yield a numerical estimate of validity.
4. Criterion-related validity is established by correlating test scores with an external standard or criterion to obtain a numerical estimate of validity.
5. There are two types of criterion-related validity: concurrent and predictive.
   a. Concurrent validity is determined by correlating test scores with a criterion measure collected at the same time.

b. Predictive validity is determined by correlating test scores with a criterion measure collected after a period of time has passed.
6. Construct validity is determined by finding whether test results correspond with scores on other variables as predicted by some rationale or theory.
7. In interpreting validity estimates, the following principles should be kept in mind:
   a. The adequacy of a validity estimate depends on both the strength of the validity coefficient and the type of validity being determined.
   b. Group variability affects the strength of the validity coefficient.
   c. Validity coefficients should be considered in terms of the relevance and reliability of the criterion or standard.

For Practice

*1. A teacher who is a friend of yours has just developed a test to measure the content in a social studies unit you both teach. His test takes 30 minutes less time to complete than the test you have used in the past, and this you decide is a major advantage. You decide to evaluate the new test by giving it and the old test to the same class of students. Using the data below, determine if the new test has concurrent validity.

Scores on the new test: 25, 22, 18, 18, 16, 14, 12, 8, 6, 6.
Scores for the same students on the old test: 22, 23, 25, 28, 31, 32, 34, 42, 44, 48.

*2. Indicate how and with what types of tests you would evaluate the predictive and construct validity of this new social studies test in question 1.
*3. Examine the validity coefficients of the following tests and, assuming they are content valid, determine which are suitable for use. State your reasons. What is unusual about Test C?

	Test A	Test B	Test C
concurrent validity coefficient	.90	.50	.75
predictive validity coefficient	.72	.32	.88

*4. Assuming the following tests measure the same content and assuming all other things are equal, rank them in terms of their overall acceptability for predicting behavior in upcoming years.

	Test A	Test B	Test C
concurrent validity coefficient	.90	.80	.85
predictive validity coefficient (one month interval)	.50	.65	.60
predictive validity coefficient (six month interval)	.40	.10	.55

*5. What types of validity go with the following procedures?
   a. Matching test items with objectives.
   b. Correlating a test of mechanical skills after training with on-the-job performance ratings.
   c. Correlating the short form of an IQ test with the long form.
   d. Correlating a paper-and-pencil test of musical talent with ratings from a live audition completed after the test.
   e. Correlating a test of reading ability with a test of mathematical ability.
   f. Comparing lesson plans with a test publisher's test blueprint.
6. The principal is upset. The results of the four-year follow-up study are in. The correlation between the grades assigned by you to your gifted students and their college GPA is lower than the correlation between grades and college GPA for nongifted students. The principal wants to abandon the gifted program. How would you defend yourself and your program?

*Answers for questions 1 through 5 appear in Appendix D.

16
CHAPTER

RELIABILITY

|T| he reliability of a test refers to the consistency with which it yields the same rank for an individual taking the test several times. In other words, a test (or any measuring instrument) is reliable if it consistently yields the same, or nearly the same, ranks over repeated administrations during which we would not expect the trait being measured to have changed. For instance, a bathroom scale is reliable if it gives you the same weight after five weighings in a single morning. If the five weights differ by several pounds, then the scale is not especially reliable. If the five weights differ by 25 pounds, then it is extremely unreliable. In the same manner, educational tests may be very reliable, fairly reliable, or totally unreliable. For instance, if a multiple-choice test given to a class is so difficult that everyone guesses at the answers, then a student's rank would probably vary quite a bit from one administration to another, and the test would be unreliable.

If any use is to be made of the information from a test, then it is desirable that the test results be reliable. If the test is going to be used to make placement decisions about individual students, you wouldn't want it to provide different data about students if it were given again the next day. If a test is going to be used to make decisions about the difficulty level of your instructional materials, you wouldn't want it to indicate that the same materials are too difficult one day and too easy the next. In testing, as in our everyday lives, if we have use for some piece of information, we would like that information to be stable, consistent, and dependable.

METHODS OF ESTIMATING RELIABILITY

There are several ways to estimate the reliability of a test. The three basic methods most often used are called *test-retest, alternative form,* and *internal consistency.*

Test-Retest

Test-retest is a method of estimating reliability that is exactly what its name implies. The test is given twice and the correlation between the first set of scores and the second set of scores is determined. For example, suppose a math test given to six students on Monday is given again on the following Monday without any math having been taught in between these times. The six students make the following scores on the test:

Student	First Administration Score	Second Administration Score
1	75	78
2	50	62
3	93	91
4	80	77
5	67	66
6	88	88

The correlation between these two sets of scores is .96. Thus it could be concluded that this test is quite reliable. The main problem with test-retest reliability is that there is usually some memory or experience involved the second time the test is taken. That means that the scores may differ not only because of the unreliability of the test, but also because the students themselves may have changed in some way. For example, they may have gotten some answers correct on the retest by remembering or finding answers to some of the questions on the initial test. To some extent this problem can be overcome by using a longer interval between test administrations, to give memory a chance to fade. However, if the interval is too long, the students may have changed on the trait being measured because of other factors, for example, reading in the library, instruction in other courses, seeing a film, and so on. Thus, in considering test-retest reliability coefficients, the interval between testings *must* also be considered. Test-retest reliability is illustrated in Figure 16.1.

Alternate Forms

If there are two equivalent forms of a test, these forms can be used to obtain an estimate of the reliability of the test. Both forms are administered to a group of students, and the correlation between the two sets of scores is determined. This

FIGURE 16.1   Test-Retest Reliability

To determine test-retest reliability, the same test is administered twice to the same group of students, and their scores are correlated. Generally, the longer the interval between test administrations, the lower the correlation. Since students can be expected to change with the passage of time, an especially long interval between testings will produce a "reliability" coefficient that is more a reflection of student changes on the attribute being measured than it is a reflection of the reliability of the test.

This time interval reflects the reliability of the test.	January 1 Test A	February 1 Test B
	Correlation, $r = .90$	
This time interval reflects the reliability of the test plus unknown changes in the students on the attribute being measured.	January 1 Test A	June 1 Test B
	Correlation, $r = .50$	

estimate eliminates the problems of memory and practice involved in test-retest estimates. Large differences in a student's score on two forms of a test which supposedly measures the same behavior would indicate an unreliable test. To use this method of estimating reliability, there must be two equivalent forms of the test available, and they must be administered under conditions as nearly equivalent as possible. The most critical problem with this method of estimating reliability is that it takes a great deal of effort to develop *one* good test, let alone two. Hence, this method is most often used by test publishers who are creating two forms of their test for other reasons (for example, to maintain test security). Figure 16.2 illustrates alternate-forms reliability.

Internal Consistency

If the test in question is designed to measure a single basic concept, then it is reasonable to assume that people who get one item right will be more likely to get other, similar items right. In other words, items ought to be correlated with each other, and the test ought to be internally consistent. If this is the case, then the reliability of the test can be estimated by the internal-consistency method. One approach to determining a test's internal consistency, called *split-halves,* involves splitting the test into two equivalent halves and determining the correlation between them. This can be done by assigning all items in the first half of the test to

FIGURE 16.2   Alternate-Forms Reliability

To determine alternate-forms reliability of a test, two different versions of the same test are administered to the same group of students in as short a time period as possible, and their scores correlated. Efforts are made to have the students complete one form of the test in the morning and another, equivalent form of the test in the afternoon or the following day.

June 1, morning   June 1, afternoon
Test A (Form X)   Test A (Form Y)

Correlation, $r = .80$

one form and all items in the second half of the test to the other form. An equivalent approach would be to divide test items by placing all odd numbered items into one half and all even numbered items into the other half. When this latter approach is used the reliability is more commonly called the *odd-even reliability*.

Split-Half Methods.

To find the split-half (or odd-even) reliability, each item is assigned to one half or the other. Then, the total score for each student on each half is determined and the correlation between the two total scores for both halves is computed. Essentially, a single test is used to make two shorter alternative forms. This method has the advantage that only one test administration is required, and, therefore, memory or practice effects are not involved. Furthermore, it does not require two tests. Thus, it has several advantages over test-retest and alternate-form estimates of reliability. Because of these advantages, it is the most frequently used method of estimating the reliability of classroom tests. This method is illustrated in Figure 16.3.

Internal consistency calculated by this method is actually a way of finding alternate-form reliability for a test half as long. However, since a test is usually more reliable if it is longer, the internal consistency method *underestimates* what the actual reliability of the full test would be. Thus, the split-half (or odd-even) reliability coefficient should be corrected or adjusted upward to reflect the reliability that the test would have if it were twice as long. The formula used for this correction is called the Spearman-Brown Prophecy Formula. It is:

$$r_w = \frac{2r_h}{1 + r_h}$$

where r_w is the correlation for the *whole* test, and r_h is the correlation between the two *halves* of the test. The result of applying this formula gives the predicted split-half (or odd-even) reliability coefficient for a test twice as long as either of its halves. In almost all cases, it will increase the size of the reliability coefficient from that computed for the two half tests.

FIGURE 16.3   Internal Consistency Reliability (Odd-Even Method)

The internal consistency of a test is determined from a *single* test administration. Hence, it does not involve a time interval as do the test-retest and alternate-form methods. The test is split into two equal parts and the total scores for each student on each half of the test are correlated. The internal-consistency method of determining reliability is appropriate only when the test measures a unitary, homogeneous concept (for example, addition or finding the least common denominator) and not a variety of concepts.

<table>
<tr><td align="center">Half of Test A
(e.g., even-numbered items)</td><td align="center">Half of Test A
(e.g., odd-numbered items)</td></tr>
</table>

Correlation, $r = .75$

Kuder-Richardson Methods. Another way of estimating the internal consistency of a test is through one of the Kuder-Richardson methods. These methods measure the extent to which items within one form of the test have as much in common with one another as do the items in that one form with corresponding items in an equivalent form. The strength of this estimate of reliability depends on the extent to which the entire test represents a *single,* fairly consistent measure of a concept. Normally Kuder-Richardson techniques will yield somewhat lower estimates of reliability than split-halves, but higher than test-retest or alternate-form estimates.

There are several ways to determine the internal consistency of a test using Kuder-Richardson procedures. Of these, two are frequently seen in test manuals. The first is more difficult to calculate, since it requires the percentage of students passing each item on the test. It is, however, the most accurate and has the name KR20 (Kuder-Richardson Formula 20). The resulting coefficient is equal to the average of all possible split-half coefficients for the group tested. The second formula, which is easier to calculate but slightly less accurate, has the name KR21. It is the least cumbersome of the KR formulas and requires a knowledge only of the number of test items (n), the mean of the test $(\overline{X})$ and its standard deviation(s). The formula for the KR21 is

$$KR21 = \frac{n}{n-1} \left(\frac{1-\overline{X}(n-\overline{X})}{ns^2} \right)$$

The KR21 formula tends to produce a smaller (less accurate) coefficient than KR20 but has the advantage of being easier to calculate. Test publishers often report a Kuder-Richardson coefficient, so it is important that you recognize it and know something about it.

Before leaving the topic of internal consistency one other coefficient needs to be mentioned because of its frequent use. This coefficient, called coefficient Alpha, is closely related to Kuder-Richardson procedures but has the advantage of being applicable to tests that are multiple-scored, that is, that are not scored right or wrong or according to some other all-or-none system. For example, on attitude or personality surveys the respondent may receive a different numerical score on an item depending on whether the response "all," "some," "a little," or "none" is checked. In such cases our previous methods of determining internal consistency would not be applicable and the coefficient Alpha should be used. Coefficient Alpha is laborious to compute, and, therefore, its computation is best left up to the test publisher. Its interpretation is not difficult, however, because it is interpreted the same as the Kuder-Richardson methods and, therefore, may be taken as an index of the extent to which the instrument measures a single, unified concept.

Problems with Internal Consistency Estimates.

Internal consistency techniques are useful measures of reliability in that they involve only one test administration and are free from memory and practice effects. However, there are some problems with these methods. First, they can only be used if the entire test consists of similar items measuring a single concept. Thus, they *would* be appropriate for use on a spelling test, but *not* a language test involving a spelling section, a reading comprehension section, and a composition section.

A second problem is that measures of internal consistency yield inflated estimates of reliability when used with *speeded tests*. A speeded test consists entirely of easy or relatively easy items or tasks with a strict time limit. On such a test, test takers are expected to answer correctly most items attempted. Ranks or grades are usually assigned mostly on the basis of the number of items attempted (since the items are easy, most attempts are successful), rather than on mastery of the subject areas, written expression, and so forth. Examples of speeded tests are typing tests or such manual dexterity tests as screwing nuts on bolts or putting square pegs in square holes.

Speeded tests may be thought of in contrast to *power tests*. Power tests have difficult items, or items varying in difficulty, but have such generous time limits that most students have an opportunity to attempt most or all of the items. With a power test, ranks or grades are assigned based mostly on the quality or "correctness" of answers, rather than on the number of items attempted. Examples of power tests are essay tests, word problems, and reasoning tasks. In reality, *most* tests are a combination of power *and* speed tests. The typical classroom or standardized achievement test is partially a speeded test (for example, some easy items, fairly strict time limits) and partially a power test (for example, items range in difficulty, most students are expected to attempt most items in the allotted time).

Why is this important? Recall that we said that measures of internal consistency yield inflated estimates of reliability when used with speeded tests. Therefore, since most achievement tests are partially speeded, estimates of internal consistency reliability that are computed for such tests will also be somewhat inflated. Naturally, they will not be as falsely high as they would be for a *pure* speeded test, but they will be high enough to suggest that the test is more reliable than it actually is. For this reason, it is always preferable to use a second estimate of reliability (for example, test-retest, or alternate-form) when using the internal consistency method.

INTERPRETING RELIABILITY COEFFICIENTS

In Chapter 15 we discussed several principles relevant to the interpretation of validity coefficients. These were provided to give you some guidelines with which to consider the validity of a test. In this chapter we will discuss several principles related to the interpretation of reliability coefficients, which should prove useful as guidelines in evaluating the reliability of a test.

Our first principle relates to the effect of group variability on the size of the reliability coefficient. It should sound familiar, since we considered this concept in discussing the interpretation of validity coefficients.

PRINCIPLE 1: Group variability affects the size of the reliability coefficient. Higher coefficients result from heterogeneous groups than from homogeneous groups.

Rather than present our rationale for this principle, you might want to refresh your memory by reviewing Principle 2 from the previous chapter. The concept applied here is exactly the same, except that it refers to repeated administrations of the same test, or to alternate forms of the same test, rather than predictor and criterion measures. Figures 16.4 and 16.5 illustrate Principle 1 applied to test-retest reliability.

PRINCIPLE 2: Scoring reliability limits test reliability.

If tests are scored unreliably, error is introduced that will limit the reliability of the test. A test cannot have reliability higher than the reliability of the scoring. Recall that in Chapter 7 we stressed how important it is to make essay scoring as reliable as possible. If there is little agreement among scorers about the "correctness" of an answer, an otherwise good test may not have sufficient reliability. Stated another way, if scoring reliability is .70, then .70 becomes the *maximum* possible reliability of the test. In reality, it would be even lower, since other sources of error would add to the unreliability of the test. This is why objectivity in scoring and clerical checks are important. Thus, before dismissing a test as too unreliable for your purposes, check its scoring reliability. It may be that improvements in scoring procedures will result in a reliability increment large enough to make the test usable.

PRINCIPLE 3: All other factors being equal, the more items included in a test, the higher the test's reliability.

FIGURE 16.4 ┃ Comparison of probable rankings for repeated administrations of the same test (or alternate forms of the same test) for four students from a heterogeneous sample

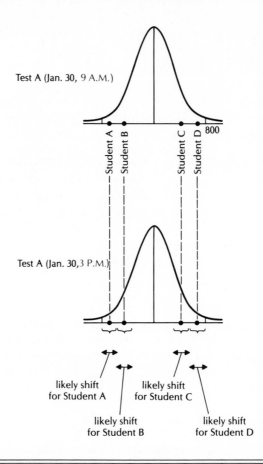

There are several reasons for this principle. First, the number of items increases the potential variability of the scores (that is, group variability will increase). According to Principle 1, this will lead to an increase in the stability of ranks across administrations, and increased reliability. Second, when more items are added to a test, the test is better able to sample the student's knowledge of the attribute being measured. For example, a ten-item test about the presidents of the United States will provide a more reliable and representative sample of student knowledge of United States presidents than a two-item test. With a two-item test, a student might get lucky and guess correctly twice, earning a perfect score. Furthermore, such a limited sample may penalize better prepared students, since its narrow focus may

FIGURE 16.5 | Comparison of probable rankings for repeated administrations of the same test (or alternate forms of the same test) for four students from a homogeneous sample

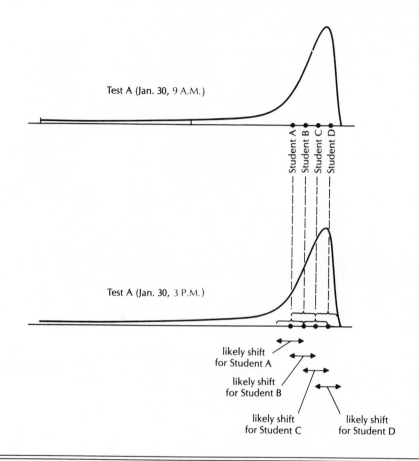

miss much of what they have mastered. It should be noted that Principle 3 is the basis of the Spearman-Brown Prophecy Formula we introduced earlier. A caution is in order, however. Simply increasing the number of items on a test will *not necessarily* increase a test's reliability. For example, if the extra items are ambiguous or otherwise poorly written items, then test reliability would likely *decrease*. Only if the added items are at least the equivalent of those in the original test will reliability *increase*. Thus, in interpreting a test's reliability, always consider its length. A very short test with a reliability of .80 may, with only a few more items added, turn out to measure some trait just as well as or better than a longer test with a reliability of .90.

PRINCIPLE 4: Reliability tends to decrease as tests become too easy *or* too difficult.

As tests become very easy (nearly everyone answers all of the items correctly) or very difficult (nearly everyone answers all of the items incorrectly), score distributions become homogeneous, which is illustrated by Figure 16.6.

By referring to Principle 1, we can conclude that when distributions are homogeneous, significant shifting of ranks and a lowering of the correlation coefficient will occur. Another factor worth considering is that when tests are made very difficult, guessing is encouraged. This is another source of error that serves to lower reliability even further. Hence, both very easy and very difficult tests will have low reliabilities. Because of error due to guessing, very difficult tests will be even *less* reliable than very easy tests.

SUMMARY

This chapter introduced you to the concept of reliability, various methods of estimating reliability, and several principles to be considered in interpreting reliability coefficients. Its major points were:

1. Reliability refers to the stability of a test score over repeated administrations. A reliable test will yield stable scores over repeated administrations, assuming the trait being measured has not changed.
2. Test-retest estimates of reliability are obtained by administering the same test twice to the same group of individuals, with a small time interval between testing, and correlating the scores. The longer the time interval, the lower test-retest estimates likely will be.

FIGURE 16.6 | Score distributions for very easy and very difficult tests

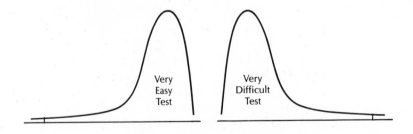

Very Easy Test   Very Difficult Test

3. Alternate form estimates of reliability are obtained by administering two alternate or equivalent forms of a test to the same group and correlating their scores. The time interval between testings is as short as possible.

4. Internal consistency estimates of reliability fall into two general categories: split-half or odd-even estimates and item-total correlations, such as the Kuder-Richardson approaches. These estimates should be used only when the test measures a single or unitary trait.

5. Split-half and odd-even estimates divide a test into halves and correlate the halves with each other. Because these correlations are based on half tests, the obtained correlations underestimate the reliability of the whole test. The Spearman-Brown Prophecy Formula is used to correct these estimates to what they would be if they were based on the whole test.

6. Kuder-Richardson methods determine the extent to which the entire test represents a single, fairly consistent measure of a concept.

7. Internal consistency estimates tend to yield inflated reliability estimates for speeded tests.

8. Since most achievement tests are at least partially speeded, internal consistency estimates for such tests will be somewhat inflated.

9. In interpreting reliability coefficients the following principles should be considered:
    a. Group variability affects test reliability
    b. Scoring reliability limits test reliability
    c. Test length affects test reliability
    d. Item difficulty affects test reliability

For Practice

*1. All other things being equal, which test—A, B, or C—would you use?

Type of Reliability	Test A	Test B	Test C
split-half reliability coefficient	.80	.90	.85
test-retest reliability coefficient	.60	.60	.75
parallel form reliability	.30	.60	.60

*2. If the unadjusted odd-even reliability for a test is .60, what is its true reliability? *(.75)*

*3. What reliability coefficient would be *least* appropriate in each of the following situations?
    a. The test is speeded. *internal*
    b. The test measures heterogeneous topics. *internal*
    c. Students can easily learn the answers from taking the test. *test-retest*

*4. Assuming that the following tests all had exactly the same internal consistency reliability coefficient of .75, and assuming all other things are equal, which test—A, B, or C—would you use?

Aspects of Test	Test A	Test B	Test C
content	homogeneous	heterogeneous	homogeneous
test length	50 items	25 items	100 items
difficulty	average	difficult	average
speed/power	speeded	speed and power	power

*5. For each of the following statements indicate which type of reliability is being referred to from among the four alternatives which follow:

test-retest
alternate-forms

alternate-forms (long interval)
split-half

a. "Practice effects" could most seriously affect this type of reliability. *test/retest*

b. This procedure would yield the lowest reliability coefficient. *alt. f. (LI)*

c. Requires the use of a formula to adjust the estimate of the reliability to that for a total test. *split-half*

d. Should be used by teachers who want to give comparable (but different) tests to students. *alt. forms*

e. Changes due to item sampling will not be reflected. *test/retest*

*6. Test A and Test B both claim to be reading achievement tests. Test A reports a test-retest reliability of .88, and Test B reports split-half reliability of .91. Test B has content validity with Mr. Burns's classroom objectives. Test A has concurrent validity with a recognized reading test, but measures several skills not taught by Mr. Burns. If Mr. Burns wishes to evaluate progress over his course of instruction, which test should be used for both his pretest and posttest?

*7. Test A and Test B both claim to be reading readiness tests for use in placing children in first-grade reading groups. Neither test reports validity data. Test A reports an internal consistency reliability of .86, and Test B reports a test-retest reliability of .70. If a first-grade teacher came to you for advice on test selection, what would be your recommendation? *neither test should/need to report validity —*

*Answers for these questions appear in Appendix D.

17

CHAPTER

ACCURACY AND ERROR

W|hen is a test score inaccurate? Almost always. Surprised? If you are, you have reason to be. We have learned (or have been "programmed") to put a great deal of faith in test scores. In fact, test results to some individuals represent the ultimate truth. Our position is that tests are fallible. They come with varying degrees of "goodness," but *no test* is completely valid or reliable. In other words, all tests are imperfect and are subject to error.

If most or all tests were perfectly reliable, then we could put a great deal of confidence in a person's score from a single test. If student A scores 75 on a perfectly reliable test, then 75 is his or her "true" score. However, most tests are *not* perfectly reliable—in fact, most tests are a long way from being perfectly reliable. Therefore, when student A scores 75 on a test, we only hope that his or her true score—his or her actual level of ability—is somewhere around 75. The closer the reliability of the test is to perfect, the more likely it is that the true score is very close to 75.

Later in this chapter we will introduce a special statistic that will enable you to estimate the *range* of scores within which lies an individual's true score or true level of ability. This is the extent of the precision we can realistically arrive at in interpreting test scores. In other words, a score from any test is our best *guess* about an individual's true level of knowledge, ability, achievement, and so forth, and, like all guesses, the guesses we make can be wrong.

All tests are subject to various sources of error that impair their reliability and, consequently, their accuracy. Logically, if we understand these sources of error in test scores, we should be able to minimize them in constructing tests and thereby improve test reliability. But, just what is "error" in testing?

ERROR—WHAT IS IT?

"I've made a mistake." We have all said this aloud or to ourselves at one time or another. In other words, we've made an error—we have failed to do something perfectly, or as well as we would like to have done it. The notion of error in testing is very similar. No test measures perfectly, and many tests fail to measure as well as we would like them to. That is, tests make "mistakes." They are always associated with some degree of error. Let's look at a test score more closely.

Think about the last test you took. Did you obtain exactly the score you felt or knew you deserved? Was your score higher than you expected? Was it lower than you expected? What about your *obtained* scores on all the other tests you have taken? Did they *truly* reflect your skill, knowledge, or ability, or did they sometimes underestimate your knowledge, ability, or skill? Or did they overestimate? If your obtained test scores did not always reflect your true ability, they were associated with some error. Your obtained scores may have been lower than they should have been, or higher than they should have been. In short, an *obtained* score has a *true* score component (actual level of ability, skill, knowledge) and an *error* component (which may act to lower or raise the obtained score).*

Can you think of some concrete examples of a type of error that lowered your obtained score? Remember when you couldn't sleep the night before the test, or you were sick but took the test anyway, or the essay test you were taking was so poorly constructed it was hard to tell what was being tested, or the test had a 45-minute time limit but you were allowed only 38 minutes, or the time you took a test that had multiple defensible answers? Each of these examples illustrates various types of error. These and perhaps other sources of error prevented your "true" score from equaling your obtained score. Another way of saying this is simply that your obtained score equaled your true score *minus* any error.

Now, what about some examples of situations in which error operated to *raise* your obtained score above your actual or "true" level of knowledge, skill, or ability? In short, what about the times you obtained a higher score than you deserved? Never happened, you say! Well, what about the time you just happened to "see" the answers on your neighbor's paper, or the time you got lucky guessing, or the time you had 52 minutes for a 45-minute test, or the test that was so full of clues that you were able to answer several questions based on the information given in other questions? Each of these examples also illustrates error. Again, because of this error your true score was not reflected in your obtained score. You received a higher score than you deserved! In these cases your obtained score equaled your true score *plus* any error.

Then how does one go about discovering one's true score? Unfortunately, we do not have an answer. The true score and the error score are both theoretical or hypothetical values. We never actually know an individual's true score or error score. Why bother with them then? They are important concepts in that they allow

---

*A "true" score is more correctly defined as the expected value of the observed score. Because of the complexity of this topic and the insignificance of this more psychometrically correct definition in actual practice, especially with regard to norm-referenced tests (Lord and Novick, 1968), we have chosen to take a more intuitive approach.

us to illustrate some important points about test reliability and test accuracy. For now, simply keep in mind:

$$obtained\ score = true\ score \pm error\ score$$

Table 17.1 illustrates the relationship among obtained scores, true scores, and error. In considering the table, remember that the *only* value in the table we are sure about is the obtained score value. We *never* know what the exact true scores are or what the exact error scores are. This is probably one of the most difficult concepts you have had to master.

According to Table 17.1, Donna, Gary, and Marsha each obtained higher scores than they should have. These students had error work to their advantage in that their obtained scores were higher than their true scores.

On the other hand, Jack, Phyllis, and Milton each obtained lower scores than they should have. These students had error work to their disadvantage in that their obtained scores were *lower* than their true scores. Unfortunately, as noted earlier, we never actually know what an individual's true and error scores are. The values shown in our table are hypothetical values used to impress upon you the fact that *all* test scores contain error. If you understand the notion of test error, you already have an intuitive understanding of our next topic, the standard error of measurement.

THE STANDARD ERROR OF MEASUREMENT

The standard error of measurement of a test (abbreviated S_m) is the standard deviation of the *error scores* of a test. In the calculations following, S_m is the standard deviation of the error score column. It is determined in the same manner you

---

TABLE 17.1 | The Relationship Among Obtained Scores, Hypothetical True Scores, and Hypothetical Error Scores for a Ninth-Grade Math Test

Student	Obtained Score	True Score*	Error Score*
Donna	91	88	+3
Jack	72	79	−7
Phyllis	68	70	−2
Gary	85	80	+5
Marsha	90	86	+4
Milton	75	78	−3

*Hypothetical values

would determine a standard deviation of any score distribution. Review the following calculations to confirm this.

Error scores from Table 17.1   +3, −7, −2, +5, +4, −3

STEP 1: Determine the mean.

$$\overline{X} = \frac{\Sigma X}{N} = \frac{0}{6} = 0$$

STEP 2: Subtract the mean from each error score to arrive at the deviation scores. Square each deviation score, and sum the squared deviations:

X −	$\overline{X}$ =	x	x^2
+3	0	3	9
−7	0	−7	49
−2	0	−2	4
+5	0	5	25
+4	0	4	16
−3	0	−3	9

$$112 = \Sigma x^2$$

STEP 3: Plug the x^2 into the formula and solve for the standard deviation.

$$\text{Error Score SD} = \sqrt{\frac{\Sigma x^2}{N}} = \sqrt{\frac{112}{6}} = \sqrt{18.67} = 4.32$$

Thus, the standard deviation of the *error score distribution,* also known as the standard error of measurement, is 4.32. If we could know what the error scores are for each test we administer, we could compute S_m in this manner. But, of course, we never know these error scores. If you are following so far, your next question should be, "But how in the world do you determine the standard deviation of the error scores if you never know the error scores?"

Fortunately, a rather simple statistical formula can be used to *estimate* this standard deviation (S_m) without actually knowing the error scores:

$$S_m = SD\sqrt{1 - r}$$

Where *r* is the reliability of the test.

Using the Standard Error of Measurement

Error scores are assumed to be random. As such, they cancel each other out. That is, obtained scores are inflated by random error to the same extent as they are deflated by error. Another way of saying this is that the mean of the error scores for a test is zero. The distribution of the error scores is also important, since it approxi-

FIGURE 17.1 ┃ The Error Score Distribution

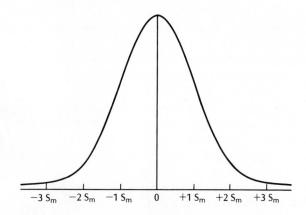

$-3\ S_m$ $-2\ S_m$ $-1\ S_m$ 0 $+1\ S_m$ $+2\ S_m$ $+3\ S_m$

mates a normal distribution closely enough for us to use the normal distribution to represent it. In summary, then, we know that error scores (1) are normally distributed, (2) have a mean of zero, and (3) have a standard deviation called the standard error of measurement (S_m). These characteristics are illustrated in Figure 17.1

Returning to our example from the ninth-grade math test depicted in Table 17.1 we recall that we obtained an S_m of 4.32 for the data provided. Figure 17.2 illustrates the distribution of error scores for these data.

FIGURE 17.2 ┃ The Error Score Distribution for Test Depicted in Table 17.1

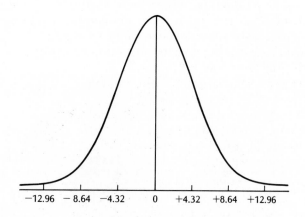

-12.96 -8.64 -4.32 0 $+4.32$ $+8.64$ $+12.96$

What does the distribution in Figure 17.2 tell us? Before you answer, consider this: The distribution of error scores is a *normal* distribution. This is important since, as you learned in Chapter 13, the normal distribution has characteristics that enable us to make decisions about scores that fall between, above, or below different points in the distribution. We are able to do so because fixed percentages of scores fall between various score values in a normal distribution. Figure 17.3 should refresh your memory.

In Figure 17.3 we listed along the baseline the standard deviation of the error score distribution. This is more commonly called the *standard error of measurement* (S_m) of the test. Thus we can see that 68 percent of the error scores for the test will be no more than 4.32 points higher, or 4.32 points lower than the true scores. That is, if there were 100 obtained scores on this test, 68 of these scores would *not* be "off" their true scores by more than ±4.32 points. Another way of saying this is that we are 68 percent sure that any *individual's* obtained test score will *not* be more than 4.32 points higher or lower than his or her true test score. This point is worth considering more closely.

Let's use the number line following to represent an individual's obtained score, which we will simply call X.

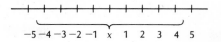

That is, X plus or minus 4.32 (±4.32) defines the range or band, which we are 68 percent sure contains this individual's true score.* Extending this reasoning, we can construct a similar band around *any* obtained score to identify the range of scores that, at a certain level of confidence, will capture or span an individual's true score. Stated another way, if a student obtains a score of X on a test, the student's true score on the test will be within ±1 S_m of X, 68 percent of the time. We know this to be the case since error (the difference between obtained and true scores) is normally distributed. We can conceptualize what we have been describing by considering error to be normally distributed around any obtained score. Returning once again to our ninth-grade math test (Table 17.1), we see that Marsha had an obtained score of 90. We also know that the S_m for the test was 4.32. Knowing the data, and that error is normally distributed, we can graphically depict the distribution of error around Marsha's obtained score of 90, as shown in Figure 17.4. Figure 17.5 illustrates the distribution of error around an obtained score of 75 for the same test.

Why all the fuss? Remember our original point. All test scores are fallible; they contain a margin of error. The S_m is a statistic that estimates this margin for us. We are accustomed to reporting a single test score. Considering the S_m, that is, re-

*Strictly speaking, the standard error of measurement would be used in this manner to construct a band around a true score in which lies a certain percentage of observed scores, not around an observed score as indicated here. As noted previously, however, due to the insignificance of this more appropriate expression in actual practice, we have chosen to take a more intuitive approach customary to texts of this nature.

FIGURE 17.3 | The Ninth-Grade Math Test Error Score Distribution with Approximate Normal Curve Percentages

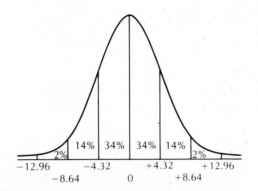

porting a range of scores that spans or captures an individual's true score, helps us present a more realistic picture of someone's obtained scores. From our last two examples we could conclude with 68 percent certainty that for a distribution with a standard error of measurement of 4.32, each student's true score would be captured by a range of scores ± 4.32 from his or her obtained score. Left unsaid

FIGURE 17.4 | The Error Distribution Around an Obtained Score of 90 for a Test with $S_m = 4.32$

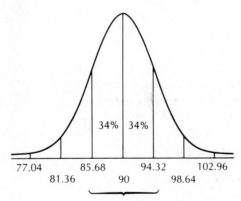

We are 68% sure that Marsha's true score lies between 85.68 and 94.32.

FIGURE 17.5 | The Error Distribution Around an Obtained Score of 75 for a Test
with $S_m = 4.32$

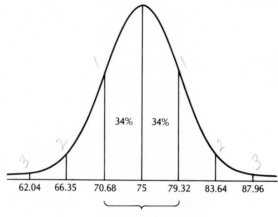

We are 68% sure that
someone with an obtained score
of 75 has a true score
between 70.68 and 79.32

was the fact that we would probably be wrong in drawing such a conclusion 32 percent of the time! Even though we report a band of scores 8.64 points wide around a single score, we will still draw an incorrect conclusion 32 percent of the time.

This is *not* an exceptional case. Even the *best* tests often have S_m of from 3 to 5 points (more or less, depending on the scale). In education we have long had a tendency to *overinterpret* small differences in test scores since we too often consider obtained scores to be completely accurate. Incorporating the S_m in reporting test scores *greatly* minimizes the likelihood of overinterpretation and forces us to consider how fallible our test scores are. After considering the S_m from a slightly different angle, we will show how to incorporate the S_m to make comparisons among test scores. This procedure is called *band interpretation*. First, however, let's sew up a few loose ends about S_m.

More Applications

Let's look again at the formula for the S_m:

$$S_m = SD \sqrt{1 - r}$$

We know that an obtained score, $X \pm 1S_m$, will span or capture the true score 68 percent of the time. Extending this thinking further we know that the range of scores covered by $X \pm 2 \, S_m$ will capture the true score 95 percent of the time. Finally, we know that the range of scores covered by $X \pm 3 \, S_m$ will capture the true score more than 99 percent of the time. Figure 17.6 illustrates these relationships.

Let's work an example. A test has a standard deviation of 5 points and a reliability of .75. The standard error of measurement of the test is

$$S_m = 5 \sqrt{1 - .75} = 5\sqrt{.25} = 2.5$$

If a student obtains a score of 80 on the test, the student knows that his or her true score lies between:

$$
\begin{array}{lll}
77.5 \text{ and } 82.5 \ (68\% \text{ of the time}) & X \pm 1 \, S_m \\
75 \text{ and } 85 \ (95\% \text{ of the time}) & X \pm 2 \, S_m \\
72.5 \text{ and } 87.5 \ (99\% \text{ of the time}) & X \pm 3 \, S_m
\end{array}
$$

The expressions "68 percent of the time," "95 percent of the time," and so on refer to the hypothetical situation in which the student is given the test many times. In this case, the student could expect that his or her true score would be within the interval a certain percentage of the total number of times the test was taken.

FIGURE 17.6   The Area or Bands for a Given Obtained Score that are 68%, 95%, and 99% Sure to Span the True Score

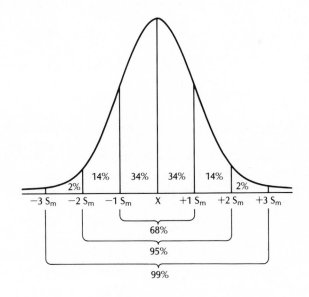

Here's another example. A teacher gets back the results of her class IQ tests. The IQ test given to the students has a standard deviation of 15 and a test-retest reliability of .84. Therefore, the test has a standard error of measurement of 6. The teacher then knows that of the children who made an IQ score of 100, about 68 percent of them have a true score of 94 and 106; 95 percent of them have a true IQ score between 88 and 112; and 99 percent of them have a true IQ score between 82 and 118. For one particular child with an IQ of 100, she knows that probably his true IQ is between 94 and 106, but 32 percent of the time (100% − 68% = 32%) it will be even further than that from 100. Thus, the teacher has some idea of just how much confidence to place in the score. That is, she has an idea about the accuracy of the score.

If the test is perfectly reliable ($r = 1.0$), then a student will always get exactly the same score. In this case the S_m is 0, as can be seen by substituting a coefficient of 1.0 in the formula for S_m. If the test is very close to perfectly reliable, the S_m will be very small, and we can assume the student's obtained score is very close to his or her true score. If the test is not reliable, the S_m will be nearly as big as the standard deviation, and we can assume the student's obtained score is not a good approximation of his or her true score. The relationships among true scores, error scores, obtained scores, and reliability are illustrated next.

Test K Is Perfectly Reliable ($r = 1.00$).

In other words a student's ranking on repeated administrations of Test K *never changes*. There is no error, and as a result the student's true score equals the obtained score *and* there is *no* error score distribution. Thus S_m is zero. Proof:

$$S_m = SD \sqrt{1 - r}$$
$$= SD \sqrt{1 - 1.0}$$
$$= SD \sqrt{0}$$
$$= 0$$

Test L Is Totally Unreliable ($r = .00$).

In other words, a student's ranking on repeated administrations of Test L is *likely to vary across the range of possible rankings*. If the student is ranked first on one administration, he or she could easily be ranked last on the next administration. Thus, because there is *so much error* present, the S_m will be the same as the SD of the test. Proof:

$$S_m = SD \sqrt{1 - r}$$
$$= SD \sqrt{1 - .00}$$
$$= SD \sqrt{1}$$
$$= SD \, (1)$$
$$= SD$$

In reality, neither of the examples presented here actually occur. So, the S_m typically takes on a value greater than 0 and smaller than the test's standard deviation. As reliability increases, S_m decreases, and as reliability decreases, the S_m increases.

In summary, the S_m can be thought of as a measure of the accuracy of a test score. The larger the S_m, the less accurate the score. The smaller the S_m, the more accurate the score.

Standard Deviation or Standard Error of Measurement?

Until you have a working familiarity with these concepts, you can expect to confuse the standard deviation (SD) with the standard error of measurement (S_m). Don't despair! The two have some similarities, but are very different. Both are measures of score variability, but of different kinds of scores. The standard deviation is a measure of variability of *raw* scores for a *group* of test takers. It tells you how spread out the scores are in a distribution of raw scores. You learned to compute and interpret standard deviations in Chapter 13. The standard error of measurement, however, is the standard deviation of the hypothetical *error* scores of a distribution. This is what you learned to compute and interpret in *this* chapter. Think about what you have just read:

Standard deviation (SD) is the variability of *raw* scores.
Standard error of measurement (S_m) is the variability of *error* scores.

The standard deviation is based on a group of scores that *actually exist*. The standard error of measurement is based on a group of scores that is *hypothetical*.

WHY ALL THE FUSS ABOUT ERROR?

In reality, an individual's obtained score is the best estimate of an individual's true score. That is, in spite of the foregoing discussion, we usually use the obtained score as our best guess of a student's true level of ability. Well, why all the fuss about error, then? For two reasons: first, we want to make you aware of the fallibility of test scores and, second, we want to sensitize you to the factors that can affect scores. Why? So they can be better controlled. Now you know how to determine how wide a range of scores around an obtained score must be to be 68 percent sure that it captures the true score. Controlling error can help narrow this range, thereby increasing the utility of test results. So, let's consider error more closely.

The sources of error can be classified into the following categories:

1. test takers — w/ individual
2. the test itself — item sample
3. test administration
4. test scoring — environmental

Error Within Test Takers

This source of error could be called intra-individual error. Earlier, we talked about several within-student factors that would likely result in an obtained score lower than a student's true score. The examples we used were fatigue and illness. We also noted that accidentally seeing another student's answer could be a factor that might result in an individual's obtained score being higher than his or her true score. Situations such as these are undesirable since they have unpredictable effects on test performance, and as a result the reliability and accuracy of the test suffers. They are usually temporary situations, affecting a student on one day, but not on another. Any temporary and unpredictable change in a student can be considered intra-individual error or error within test takers. Remember, we are *not* saying anything about actual errors or mistakes test takers make in responding to test items. Rather, we are talking about factors that change unpredictably over time and, as a result, impair consistency and accuracy in measurement.

Error Within the Test

We may refer to this source of error as an intra-test or within-test error. The poorly designed essay test that results in an obtained score lower than a true score and the poorly written test replete with clues that results in an obtained score higher than a true score are both examples of this source of error.

There are many, many ways to *increase* error within the test. The following is only a partial list:

> trick questions
> reading level that is too high
> ambiguous questions
> items too easy or too difficult
> poorly written items

To the extent that test items and tests are poorly constructed, test reliability and accuracy will be impaired.

Error in Test Administration

Misreading the amount of time to be allotted for testing is an example of error in test administration that could raise or lower obtained scores in relation to true scores. There are, however, a variety of other direct and indirect test administration factors to be considered, including physical comfort, instructions and explanations, and test administration attitudes.

Physical Comfort. Room temperature, humidity, lighting, noise, and seating arrangement are all potential sources of error for the test taker.

Instructions and Explanations. Different test administrators provide differing amounts of information to test takers. Some spell words, provide hints, or tell whether it's better to guess or leave blanks, while others remain fairly distant. Naturally, your score may vary depending on the amount of information you are provided.

Test Administrator Attitudes.   Administrators will differ in the notions they convey about the importance of the test, the extent to which they are emotionally supportive of students, and the way in which they monitor the test. To the extent that these variables affect students differently, test reliability and accuracy will be impaired.

Error in Scoring

With the advent of computerized test scoring, error in scoring has decreased significantly. However, even when computer scoring is used, error can occur. The computer, being a highly reliable machine, is seldom the cause of such errors. But teachers and other test administrators prepare the scoring keys and directions that are provided to the programmers and operators, thus introducing possibilities for error. And students sometimes fail to use #2 pencils or make extraneous marks on answer sheets, introducing another potential source of scoring error. Needless to say, when tests are hand scored, as most classroom tests are, the likelihood of error increases greatly. In fact, you can be sure that you will make some scoring errors in grading the tests you give. You can be sure because you are human.

These four sources of error—the test takers, the test, the test administration, and the scoring—are factors that increase the discrepancy between an individual's obtained score and his or her true score. To the extent that these sources of error are present, individual and group scores will be prone to error, and therefore less accurate. We can take measures to minimize error within the test, the test administration, and the scoring, but we can never eliminate such error completely. Generally, error due to within-student factors is beyond our control.

These sources of error also affect the different types of reliability coefficients we have discussed. This notion is worth considering further, since different estimates of reliability may be spuriously high (if they fail to account for important sources of error) or spuriously low (if they account for unimportant sources of error). Next we consider the extent to which our four sources of error influence the test-retest, alternate-forms, and internal consistency methods of estimating reliability.

SOURCES OF ERROR INFLUENCING VARIOUS RELIABILITY COEFFICIENTS

Test-Retest

If test-retest reliability coefficients are determined over a short time, few changes are likely to take place *within students* to alter their test scores. Thus, short-interval test-retest coefficients are not likely to be affected greatly by within-student error. However, as the time interval involved increases, it becomes more and more likely that significant changes will occur in the test takers. Correspondingly, test scores will be increasingly affected by these changes and the test-retest reliability will be lowered. This lowered reliability may be more a result of new learning on the part of the students than it is an indication of the unreliability of the test.

Since the *same* test is administered twice in determining test-retest reliability, error within the test itself (for example, from poorly worded or ambiguous items) does not affect the strength of the reliability coefficient. Any problems that do exist in the test are present in both the first and second administrations, affecting scores the same way each time the test is administered. As long as similar administration and scoring procedures are followed, administration and scoring errors are likely to contribute only minimally to error. However, if there are significant changes in either or both, these can contribute significantly to error, resulting in a lower estimate of test-retest reliability.

Alternate Forms

Since alternate-forms reliability is determined by administering two different forms or versions of the same test to the same group close together in time, the effects of within-student error are negligible. Generally, students do not change significantly between morning and afternoon, or from one day to the following day. Granted, students may be more fatigued when taking Form B of a test immediately after taking Form A. However, these factors can be controlled by splitting the test administration across groups of students, as suggested in Table 17.2

Error within the test, however, has a significant effect on alternate-forms reliability. Unlike test-retest reliability, error within the test is *not* the same between test administrations. Error within Form A combines with error within Form B to have an effect on alternate-forms reliability. By now you are aware of how difficult it is to construct one good test, much less two! Yet, this is just what is necessary for acceptable alternate-forms reliability.

As with test-retest methods, alternate-forms reliability is not greatly affected by error in administering or scoring the test, as long as similar procedures are followed. Since within-test error is considered by alternate-forms estimates, they normally have the lowest numerical index of reliability.

TABLE 17.2	Splitting Same-Day Alternate-Form Administrations Across Groups	
	A.M. Group	*P.M. Group*
	Students whose last names begin with A–K get form A.	Students whose last names begin with A–K get form B.
	Students whose last names begin with L–Z get form B.	Students whose last names begin with L–Z get form A.

Internal Consistency

With test-retest and alternate-forms reliability, within-student factors are taken into account by the method of estimating reliability, since changes in test performance due to such problems as fatigue, momentary anxiety, illness, or just having an "off day" are recorded by having two separate administrations of the test. If the test is sensitive to these problems, it will record different scores from one test administration to another, lowering the reliability (or correlation coefficient) between them. Obviously, we would prefer that the test *not* be sensitive to these problems. But if it is, we would like to know about it.

With internal consistency reliability, neither within-student nor within-test factors are taken into account by the method of estimation. Since there is a single test administered, no changes in students should occur, and any errors within the test will occur only once. Similarly, since there is but a single administration and scoring procedure, administration and scoring errors are held to a minimum.

Measures of internal consistency, then, are influenced by the fewest of four sources of error affecting test reliability. Thus, we would expect such measures to yield higher reliability coefficients than test-retest or alternate-forms estimates. This is important in evaluating test data presented in standardized test manuals. If a test publisher presents only internal consistency estimates of reliability, the publisher has failed to indicate how consistent the obtained scores from the test are likely to be over time. Also unknown is whether any parallel or alternative forms being offered are equivalent to each other. Simply *saying* there are two alternate, equivalent, or parallel forms is not sufficient. To evaluate their equivalence there *must* be an estimate of alternate-forms reliability.

By itself, then, an internal consistency reliability coefficient—high though it may be—does not provide sufficient evidence of a test's reliability. When you must have an estimate of a test's reliability and can give only a single administration (such as with a typical teacher-made test), measures of internal consistency can be useful. However, any well-constructed standardized test must provide more than just information on the test's internal consistency. Generally, there must be provided a measure of the test's reliability over time (that is, test-retest reliability) and, if it advertises alternate forms, an estimate of the equivalence of the forms being offered (that is, alternate-forms reliability).

The influence of the four sources of error on the test-retest, alternate forms, and internal consistency methods of estimating reliability are summarized in Table 17.3.

BAND INTERPRETATION

Thus far, we have learned how to use the standard error of measurement, S_m, to more realistically interpret and report single test scores. In this section we will show you how to use the standard error of measurement to more realistically interpret and report *groups* of test scores. Let's consider the following example:

TABLE 17.3	Extent of Error Influencing Test-Retest, Alternate Forms, and Internal Consistency Methods of Reliability

| *Type of Test* | *Type of Error* | | | |
	Within Student	*Within Test[1]*	*Administration*	*Scoring*
Test-Retest, Short Interval	minimal	minimal	minimal[2] or moderate[3]	minimal[4] or moderate[5]
Test-Retest, Long Interval	extensive	minimal	minimal[2] or moderate[3]	minimal[4] or moderate[5]
Alternate-Forms, Short Interval	minimal	moderate[2] or extensive[3]	minimal[2] or moderate[3]	minimal[4] or moderate[5]
Alternate-Forms, Long Interval	extensive	moderate[2] or extensive[3]	minimal[2] or moderate[3]	minimal[4] or moderate[5]
Internal Consistency	minimal	minimal	minimal	minimal

1. Assuming test is well constructed.
2. If test is standardized.
3. If test is teacher made.
4. If test is objective.
5. If test is subjective.

John obtained the following scores on an end-of-year achievement test:

Subtests	*Converted Score*
Reading	103
Listening	104
Writing	105
Social Studies	98
Science	100
Math	91

Note: $\overline{X} = 100$ and SD = 10 for all subtests

Now, suppose you have a parent conference coming up, and John's parents want you to interpret his scores to them. What would you say? Would you say that he did best in writing and poorest in math? Would you say that the differences among the scores are likely due to measurement error, or do they represent actual differences in achievement?

It seems likely that John's parents would know from looking at the scores what John did best in and what he did poorest in. If they had some statistical sophistication, as you now have, they might even be able to conclude that his math score is at about the nineteenth percentile and that his reading score is at about the sixty-ninth percentile—a difference between the two tests of 50 percentile points. This appears to be a rather dramatic difference indicating a real difference in achievement. But how can we be sure the difference is not due to error? Granted it seems to be so large a difference that it probably is a "real" difference rather than a "chance" (that is, due to error) difference. But what about the difference between Writing (sixty-ninth percentile) and Science (fiftieth percentile)? Is this difference a "real" or a "chance" one? In short, how large a difference do we need between test scores to conclude that the differences represent real and not chance differences? As you might have guessed, we can employ the standard error of measurement to help us answer these questions. The specific technique we will be discussing is called *band interpretation*. This technique lends itself quite well to the interpretation of scores from test batteries. Here is a step-by-step approach to band interpretation.

Steps: Band Interpretation

List Data.   List subtests and scores, and the $\overline{X}$, SD and reliability (r) for each subtest. For purposes of illustration, let's assume that the mean is 100, the standard deviation is 10, and the reliability is .91 for all the subtests.

Subtests	Converted Scores
Reading	103
Listening	104
Writing	105
Social Studies	98
Science	100
Math	91

Determine S_m for Each Subtest.   Since in our example SD and r are the same for each subtest, S_m will be the same for each subtest.

$$
\begin{aligned}
S_m &= SD\sqrt{1 - r} \\
&= 10\sqrt{1 - .91} \\
&= 10\sqrt{.09} \\
&= 3
\end{aligned}
$$

Add and Subtract S_m.   To identify the band or interval of scores that has a 68-percent chance of spanning or capturing John's true score, add and subtract S_m to each subtest score. If the test could be given to John 100 times (without John learning from taking the test), 68 out of 100 times John's true score would be within the following bands:

Subtest	Converted Score	68% band
Reading	103	100–106
Listening	104	101–107
Writing	105	102–108
Social Studies	98	95–101
Science	100	97–103
Math	91	88–94

Graph the Results.   On each scale, shade in the bands to represent the range of scores that has a 68-percent chance of capturing John's true score.

Interpret the Bands.   Interpret the profile of bands by visually inspecting the bars to see which bands overlap and which do not. Those that *overlap* probably represent differences that occurred by *chance*. For example, reading, listening, writing, and science may differ from each other only by chance—in spite of the fact that John's science grade of 100 was 5 points lower than his writing grade of 105–a difference of ½ a standard deviation. We arrive at this conclusion because there is at least some overlap among the bands for each of these subtest scores. Thus, we could say John's level of achievement is similar in each of these subjects.

However, we can see a large difference in John's math achievement compared to these same four subtests. Since there is no overlap, we will consider this difference a *real,* not a chance, difference. Social studies shows a *real* difference compared to writing (again no overlap), but only a *chance* difference compared to reading, listening, and science (again, because there is overlap).

Getting the hang of it? Band interpretation is one of the most realistic and appropriate ways to interpret scores from test batteries, since it considers the error that is always present in testing. Work with it and you will reduce the natural tendency to put too much weight on small or chance differences among scores.

So far we have used the subtest score plus and minus the standard error of measurement to identify whether a real difference exists among subtest scores. We have constructed ranges of scores around each obtained score in which we are 68 percent sure the individual's true score lies. Recall from our earlier discussion of S_m, though, that by adding and subtracting two times S_m to the obtained subtest score, we can construct an interval or range of scores within which we are 95 percent sure the individual's true score lies. Naturally this would create a much wider band for each obtained score that has the effect of making overlap much *more* likely. This means "real" differences would be less likely to appear. That is, if we use the 95-percent rule by adding and subtracting two times the standard error of measurement to each score instead of adding and subtracting only the standard error of measurement to each score, we may have very different interpretations of the same test scores. Let's see what kind of difference this makes. Figure 17.7 compares and contrasts the 68-percent and 95-percent approaches.

Now let's compare conclusions. At the 68-percent level, we concluded that there was a significant discrepancy between John's math achievement and all his other subjects (there is no overlap between his math score interval and any other subtest score interval). We also concluded that there was a real difference (that is, no overlap) between John's social studies achievement and his writing achievement. All other differences were attributed to chance (that is, there was overlap).

Now look at the 95-percent profile in Figure 17.7. In essence we have doubled the width of each band in order to become more confident that we have really captured John's true score within each interval. As a result of this more conservative approach to test interpretation, the real differences decline sharply. We use the word *conservative* with the 95-percent approach since the odds of John's true score falling outside the band are only 1 in 20 or .05 with the 95-percent approach, but 1 in 3 or about .32 with the 68-percent approach. We are, therefore, more confident that John's true score is within the band with the 95-percent approach. Since the bands will be larger, the only real differences we find at the 95-percent level are between John's math achievement and his achievement in listening and writing. All the other bands overlap, suggesting that at the 95-percent level the differences in obtained scores are due to chance. Thus, if we employ the more conservative 95-percent approach, we would conclude that even though the difference between John's obtained reading and math scores is 12 points (103 − 91 = 12, a difference of 1.2 standard deviations), the difference is due to chance, not to a real difference in achievement.

Why bother with the 95-percent level, then? Well, if you are going to make important decisions about a student, a conservative approach appears warranted. In short, if you are concerned about the effects of a "wrong" decision (that is, saying a real difference in achievement exists when it is really due to chance), take the conservative approach. On the other hand, if little is at risk for the student (or yourself), then the less conservative 68-percent approach is probably warranted.

FIGURE 17.7 | Comparison of the 68% and 95% Methods of Band Interpretation

Subtest	Converted Score*	68% range $(X \pm S_m)$	95% range $(X \pm 2 S_m)$
Reading	103	100–106	97–109
Listening	104	101–107	98–110
Writing	105	102–108	99–111
Social Studies	98	95–101	92–104
Science	100	97–103	94–106
Math	91	88–94	85–97

*$\overline{X} = 100$
$SD = 10$

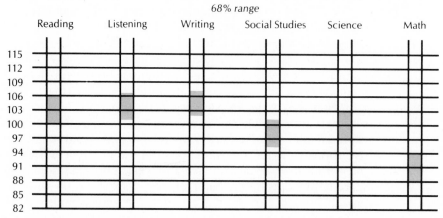

Profiles

To make it simpler yet, let differences at the 68-percent level be a signal to you; let differences at the 95-percent level be a signal to school and parents.

In the next chapter, we will describe an application of band interpretation in which we believe the more conservative 95-percent approach should typically be employed. This will be in relation to determining real differences between a student's potential for achievement, called *aptitude,* and actual achievement.

A Final Word

Technically, there are more accurate statistical procedures for determining real differences between an individual's test scores than the ones we have been able to present here. These procedures, however, are time-consuming, complex, and overly specific for the typical teacher. Within the classroom, band interpretation, properly used, makes for a practical alternative to these more advanced methods, which is superior to simply comparing individual scores.

Before we complete this chapter, answer the questions—using the 95-percent approach—that we raised at the beginning of this section. To refresh your memory here they are:

Is there a real difference between John's reading score and his math score?
Is there a real difference between John's writing score and his science score?*

|SUMMARY

Chapter 17 presented the concepts of accuracy and error, the statistic used to represent error (the standard error of measurement), and the four sources of error in measurement. Its major points were:

1. No test is perfectly reliable, and therefore no test is perfectly accurate. All tests are subject to error.
2. Error is any factor that leads an individual to perform better or worse on a test than the individual's true level of performance.
3. An obtained score for a test contains two components: One reflects the individual's true level of performance, the other reflects the error associated with the test that prevents the individual from performing at exactly his or her true level of ability.
4. An individual's true score and error score are hypothetical. We can never be sure exactly what they are.
5. The standard error of measurement (S_m) is the standard deviation of the error score distribution of a test.
6. The standard error of measurement for a test can be determined mathematically if we know the test's standard deviation and reliability.

*Answer appears in Appendix D.

7. The error distribution is normally distributed, has a mean of zero, and its standard deviation is the standard error of measurement.
8. We can be 68-percent sure an individual's true score lies in the range between one S_m above and one S_m below an individual's obtained score.
9. We can be 95-percent sure a true score lies in the range of scores between two S_m above and two S_m below the obtained score.
10. We can be 99-percent sure a true score lies in the range of scores between three S_m above and three S_m below the obtained score.
11. Using the S_m in interpreting scores helps us avoid overinterpreting small differences among test scores.
12. As reliability increases, accuracy increases and the S_m decreases.
13. The S_m refers to the variability of error scores; the SD refers to the variability of raw scores.
14. By controlling the sources of error in testing, test accuracy can be improved.
15. Error is classified into four categories, within:
    a. test takers
    b. the test
    c. the test administration
    d. scoring
16. Error within the test takers refers to changes in the student over which the test administrator has no control.
17. Error within the test refers to technical problems in the test. The test developer has considerable control over this source of error.
18. Error within the test administration refers to physical, verbal, and attitudinal variables that vary from administration to administration and affect test scores. By standardizing administration procedures, the administrator can minimize this source of error.
19. Error in scoring typically refers to clerical errors that influence test scores. The test administrator can control this source of error by using objective items and clerical checks or using computer scoring.
20. Different estimates of reliability are differentially affected by the various sources of error.
21. Test-retest reliability is most susceptible to error within test takers.
22. Alternate-form reliability is most affected by error within the two forms of the test. As a result, it usually yields lower reliability estimates than test-retest or internal consistency estimates.
23. Since only one administration and one test are necessary for internal consistency estimates, this approach is least affected by error. As a result, internal consistency estimates of reliability typically will be higher for the same test than test-retest or alternate-form reliability estimates.
24. Band interpretation is a technique that the teacher can use to help separate real differences in student achievement from differences due to chance. This approach helps prevent overinterpretation of small differences among subtests in achievement test batteries.

For Practice

*1. Calculate the standard error of measurement for a test with a standard deviation of 10 and a reliability of .84. Draw a normal curve picturing the error score distribution in units of the standard error of measurement.

*2. Suppose an individual received a score of 16 on the above test. Calculate the range or band within which we could be 95-percent sure that this individual's true score is contained. What would this range or band be if we wanted to be 99 percent sure this individual's true score is contained within it? To be 68 percent sure?

*3. What are the four sources of error that increase the discrepancy between an individual's obtained score and his or her true score? Give a specific example of each.

*4. Indicate the extent to which (a) within-student, (b) within-test, (c) administration, and (d) scoring error affects each of the following methods of determining reliability:

   a. Test-retest, short interval
   b. Test-retest, long interval
   c. Alternate forms, short interval
   d. Alternate forms, long interval
   e. Internal consistency

*5. Construct a subtest profile with bands for each of the following subtests taken by a particular student. Assume the mean is 50, the standard deviation is 8, and the reliability is .91 for all the tests. Construct your bands so that they have a 68-percent chance of capturing this individual's true scores. How would you interpret the differences between subtests to this student's parents?

Subtests	Corrected Scores
Reading	56
Listening	50
Writing	61
Social Studies	35
Science	60
Math	56

*6. The following table lists the scores obtained from five different tests by Tom and Mary. At the 99-percent level, indicate which tests showed real differences in performance between Tom and Mary.

Test	S_m	Tom	Mary
A	5.5	80	60
B	16.0	150	165
C	3.4	32	35
D	30.0	620	679
E	8.0	89	103

*7. The following reliability coefficients were reported for a single test adminis-
tered to a single class. How do you account for the differences?

Test-retest (30 days) $r = .90$
Alternate-forms $r = .84$
Split-half (corrected using the $r = .93$
  Spearman-Brown formula)

Expected diff. because each test type is affected by error categories [handwritten margin note]

*8. Consider the following information from two tests:

Test	Mean	Reliability	SD
A	100	.91	20
B	100	.75	10

[handwritten:] $SEM = SD\sqrt{1-r}$

$lg. SEM$ $20\sqrt{.09}$

$20 . 3 = 6$

$10\sqrt{1-.25} = 5$

On which test would an individual's score fluctuate the most on repeated test administrations? Explain why.

*Answers for these questions appear in Appendix D.

18

CHAPTER

STANDARDIZED TESTS

|S| o far, we have limited our discussion of testing and measurement to teacher-constructed tests—and with good reason. The average teacher uses teacher-made tests for most classroom testing and decision making. However, teachers are also required at least once a year to administer *standardized* tests, evaluate the results of such tests, and interpret the results to curious and sometimes concerned parents. Thus, it is necessary that we spend time getting to know the advantages, limitations, and uses of standardized tests and how to interpret their results. Before we consider these issues, however, let's find out what a standardized test is.

WHAT IS A STANDARDIZED TEST?

Standardized tests are tests constructed by test-construction specialists, usually with the assistance of curriculum experts, teachers, and school administrators, for the purpose of determining a student's level of performance relative to the performance of other students of similar age and grade. Such tests often take years to construct as opposed to a few days for a teacher-made test. They are called *standardized* because they are administered and scored according to *specific* and *uniform* (that is, standard) procedures. In other words, a standardized test administered and scored today in Buffalo, New York, would be administered and scored in exactly the same manner whether it is administered in New York City, Chicago,

Los Angeles or anywhere else in the United States. Because of these standardization procedures, measurement error due to administration and scoring is reduced.

When standardized tests are employed, test results from different students, classes, schools, and districts can be more easily and confidently *compared* than would be the case with different teacher-made tests. Imagine the difficulty in comparing teacher-made test results from Mrs. Smith's fifth-grade class in Orlando, Florida with Mrs. Wilson's fifth-grade class in Portland, Oregon. Not only would the test items be different; the length of the test, the amount of time allowed, the instructions given by the teacher, and the scoring criteria would also be different. In short, there would be little or no basis for comparison. Table 18.1 compares standardized achievement tests with teacher-made achievement tests. We have emphasized the word *achievement* because there are actually various types of standardized tests. *Standardized test* is a general term that includes not only achievement tests, but also aptitude tests, interest inventories, and various personality assessment instruments, which we will discuss later. Now that we have a basic idea of what a standardized achievement test is, let's consider the uses of such tests.

USES OF STANDARDIZED ACHIEVEMENT TESTS

In Chapter 2 we discussed educational decision making. We concluded that teacher-made measurement instruments are useful for most educational decisions. In the classroom, standardized achievement tests are administered once, or perhaps twice, each school year. These tests are used when it is necessary to *compare* test scores over time or across students, classes, schools, or districts. In some cases standardized achievement tests are used diagnostically, to help educators identify student strengths and weaknesses or for evaluating specific programs and curricula. For the most part, though, standardized tests are used for comparative purposes. This is quite different from the main uses of teacher-made tests, which are to determine pupil mastery or skill levels, to assign grades, and to provide students and parents with feedback. Why, then, would the classroom teacher administer a standardized test? To compare this year's students with last year's? To compare class A with class B? Yes, but the most accurate answer is more likely that the classroom teacher administers standardized achievement tests because he or she is required to do so. This is the case in many, if not most, school districts in the country today.

Part of the reason for this is the current trend toward increasing accountability. As teacher salaries and school taxes increase, taxpayers demand more justification for how their tax dollar is spent. By and large, taxpayers will support higher teacher salaries if teacher effectiveness increases, or at least remains constant. One indicator of teaching effectiveness, limited though it is, is standardized

TABLE 18.1	A Comparison of Standardized and Teacher-Made Achievement Tests	
	Standardized Achievement Tests	*Teacher-Made Achievement Tests*
Learning outcomes and content measured	Measure general outcomes and content appropriate to the majority of schools in the United States. They are tests of general skills and understanding that tend not to reflect specific or unique emphases of local curricula.	Well-adapted to the specific and unique outcomes and content of a local curriculum; they are adaptable to various sizes of work units, but tend to neglect complex learning outcomes.
Quality of test items	Quality of items generally is high. Items are written by specialists, pretested, and selected on the basis of the results of a quantitative item analysis.	Quality of items is often unknown. Quality is typically lower than that of standardized tests due to the limited time of the teacher.
Reliability	Reliability is high, commonly between .80 and .95, and frequently above .90.	Reliability is usually unknown, but can be high if items are carefully constructed.
Administration and scoring	Procedures are standardized; specific instructions are provided.	Uniform procedures are possible, but usually are flexible and unwritten.
Interpretation of scores	Scores can be compared to norm groups. Test manual and other guides aid interpretation and use.	Score comparisons and interpretations are limited to local class or school situation. Few, if any, guidelines are available for interpretation and use.

achievement test scores. As long as the public wants standardized achievement tests administered in the schools, the public will elect school board members who feel similarly, who will in turn choose school administrators who feel similarly, and who will, in turn, tell their teachers they have to administer standardized achievement tests in their classrooms.

Accountability also includes evaluation of various federal and state programs. Most, if not all, such programs require that standardized achievement tests be administered as part of the program's evaluation. Further funding may depend on the results of these tests.

What this boils down to is that citizens, school administrators, special project personnel, and administrators of federal programs want to be able to compare students, schools, and districts with each other in order to make judgments concerning the effectiveness of school-wide or district-wide programs and practices. Standardized achievement tests enable them to do so. As long as this objective remains, standardized test administration and interpretation will be a necessary part of teaching. Hence, the classroom teacher must learn to administer and interpret these tests.

ADMINISTERING STANDARDIZED TESTS

Recall our discussion of reliability and error in Chapters 16 and 17. We identified four major sources of error associated with measurement:

1. Within the test (poor items)
2. Within the student (illness, fatigue)
3. In administration (too little time, too many "hints")
4. In scoring (clerical errors)

A standardized test, because it has been carefully prepared over several years, generally will have carefully constructed items, thereby minimizing error within the test. Since such tests usually are machine scored, clerical errors in scoring are minimized. Little can be done in standardized test situations to minimize within-student error, but standardized tests do minimize error in test administration. Figure 18.1 provides an example of how a standardized test minimizes error in test administration. Notice the specific directions that are given the test administrator as to what to say, how to give out pencils, and what to do during the test. The best way to guard against error in test administration is to instruct *everyone* to administer the test in exactly the same way. Instructions such as these attempt to promote uniformity in how the test is administered across teachers, schools, and districts. Figure 18.2 also provides some helpful hints to keep in mind when administering standardized tests.

The last point in the box bears further emphasis. It is not uncommon for classroom teachers to "individualize" the test administration by helping slower students, or by pushing faster students. This is a violation of standardized testing procedure. The test and its administration and scoring are called *standardized* because everyone gets the same treatment. This sameness is what allows reliable comparisons to be made. Helping or pushing some students means those students are not getting the same treatment as other students. Thus, any comparisons we make will be less reliable.

| FIGURE 18.1 | Directions read aloud to students taking the Comprehensive Tests of Basic Skills (CTBS) |

Before the first test session, distribute to each student the copy of CTBS/S, Level B, with his or her name on it and a pencil (No. 2 or softer) with an eraser attached.

SAY: In this book are some tests. I will tell you a few things to remember while you are taking the tests.

Listen carefully to all directions I give and make sure you know what to do before you begin. Raise your hand if you do not understand. Do not begin to work on a test until I tell you to do so.

For some tests, I will read the questions out loud to you. On other tests, you will work by yourselves. When you are working by yourselves, work as fast as you can.

There may be some questions that you are not able to answer, because they test things you have not yet been taught. If you cannot answer a question, do not spend too much time on it. Make the most careful choice you can, and go on to the next one. When you come to the word "WAIT" or "STOP," do not go any farther. If you finish before I tell you to stop, you may go back over the test you have been working on.

Each question has only one right answer. Each answer choice has a circle that goes with it. When you have decided which answer is right, fill in the circle that goes with that answer. Mark only one answer for each question. Make your marks clear and dark. Do not let your marks go outside the circle.

Mark all your answers in your book, but do not make any other marks in the book. If you think you have made a mistake and want to change an answer, erase the first mark completely and then fill in the circle that goes with the one you think is right.

If you are not beginning the testing session with Test 1, see the Table of Contents for the page number of the test being given.

The directions in this manual for administering each test may also be used for the Reading tests as a separate; the page numbers are the same.

TYPES OF SCORES OFFERED FOR STANDARDIZED ACHIEVEMENT TESTS

In this section we will consider the types of scores offered for standardized tests: grade equivalents, age equivalents, percentiles, and standard scores.

Grade Equivalents

Grade-equivalent scores are probably the most widely used vehicle to report test results. They are likely also to be those most often misinterpreted. Grade equivalents are deceptively simple to interpret, on the surface. Consider the following statement:

FIGURE 18.2   Do's and Don'ts About Administering Standardized Tests

Do

- Read the manual *before* test administration day.
- Be sure you have been given the correct form for your grade level.
- Adhere strictly to the administration instructions.

Don't

- Try to minimize the achievement nature of the test.
- Deviate from the standardized administration instructions (i.e., do *not* allow more time, give hints, spell words, define words, etc.)

Danielle obtained a Math Computation grade-equivalent score of 7.6 (seventh grade, sixth month) on the CAT. That means that even though she's only in fourth grade, she can do seventh-grade level math!

Do you agree with this statement? If you do, you have fallen victim to the most common kind of misinterpretation regarding grade-equivalent scores. Danielle's obtained score is the score that the publisher estimates would be obtained by the *average* seventh grader during the sixth month of school. It does *not* mean that Danielle is *ready* for seventh-grade math! She may not necessarily have mastered the prerequisites for success in seventh grade or even sixth grade! All we know for sure is that a fourth grader who obtains a math grade equivalent of 7.6 is *well above average* in math. This is not the same as saying the student is ready for seventh-grade math work. In fact, we don't even know how seventh graders would do on this test since it is unlikely that any seventh grader took the test! To understand this statement, we must consider the way in which grade-equivalent scores are determined.

Usually a test is administered to the targeted grade (for example, fourth grade) plus the grades immediately below and above the targeted grade (for example, third and fifth grades). Thus, grade equivalents are based on actually obtained scores only for students one grade level below to one grade level above the grade being tested. Scores appearing in grade-equivalent norms tables that are more than one grade level below or above the grade being tested are *estimated*— they are extrapolated from the obtained scores. This is where the problem lies. Much higher or lower grade equivalents than average represent only relative degrees of performance. They say nothing about specific skills mastered or deficiencies.

Unfortunately, the problems related to grade equivalents do not end here. Others are listed below.

1. Apparently equal differences in scores do not necessarily reflect equal differences in achievement. For example, growth in reading comprehension

from 2.6 to 3.6 will likely not mean the same degree or amount of growth as growth in reading comprehension from 7.6 to 8.6. It is likely that the one year's improvement is attributable to different factors in each case.

2. Grade equivalents are meaningless unless a subject is taught across all grades. Why report a physics grade equivalent of 6.2 when physics is taught only during the twelfth grade? What does it mean to say your performance in physics is equivalent to that of a beginning sixth grader?

3. Grade equivalents are often misinterpreted as *standards* rather than norms. That is, teachers often forget that grade equivalents are averages—about half the students will score above and below grade placement (depending on aptitude, of course!).

4. Grade equivalents may not be directly comparable across school subjects. That is, a fifth grader who is one year behind grade placement in reading is not necessarily as far behind in reading as he or she may be in math, even though he or she is one year behind in math too. This is because growth in different subjects occurs at different rates. Equal levels of growth or deficiency, as indicated by grade-equivalent scores, may mean quite different things.

In spite of these shortcomings, grade equivalents continue to be popular. Our recommendation is that if you use them, consider carefully the cautions we have outlined above. In general, they are more useful for the elementary grades, where they can be used to compare growth across a common core of subjects. In spite of this, remember that we cannot be very confident in the equality of the units, their equivalence across subjects, or their meaningfulness when grade equivalents far above or below grade placement are obtained.

Age Equivalents

Age-equivalent scores are very similar to the grade-equivalent scores just discussed. Age-equivalent scores are determined in a fashion similar to that described for grade equivalents. That is, samples of seven-, eight-, and nine-year-olds might be tested and average scores for each age determined. Scores for younger or older students would then be estimated or extrapolated from these scores. Problems similar to those affecting grade equivalents affect age equivalents as outlined here:

1. Equal differences in scores may not reflect equal differences in achievement. In other words, does growth from age six to age seven represent the same amount of growth as from age ten to eleven? It may or may not, depending on the trait being measured. Furthermore, growth in most traits slows down or stops during the teens or early twenties. In other words, a year's growth in reading after age seventeen is likely to be very different from a year's growth in reading at age seven.

2. Age equivalents are only meaningful if subjects are taught across all grades. It makes little sense to say someone has an age equivalent of 16.9 in subtraction.
3. Age equivalents may be misinterpreted as standards, rather than averages or norms.
4. Growth across subjects may vary greatly, even if age equivalents show equal growth. A year's increase in language age equivalent does not necessarily mean the same thing as a year's increase in science age equivalent.

Unlike grade equivalents, age equivalents have *not* attracted widespread acceptance in the schools. Like grade equivalents, they are most useful in the elementary grades to compare growth across a common core of subjects. The above-mentioned shortcomings should always be considered in interpreting age equivalents.

Percentile Ranks

With grade- and age-equivalent scores we indicate the grade or age group in which a student's test performance would be considered average. That is, if a student obtains a grade equivalent score of 4.5, we can say the student did as well on the test as an average fourth grader during the fifth month of school. At times, however, we are not interested in making such comparisons. In fact, we would go so far as to say that in most cases we are more interested in determining how a student's performance compares with that of students in his or her own grade or of the same age. Percentile ranks enable us to make such comparisons.*

Percentile ranks are a substantial improvement over grade- and age-equivalent scores in that they do not suffer from the many limitations of the latter. Since comparisons are within-grade, it does not matter whether subjects are taught across grades, and since growth is only relative to others in the grade, the problem of growth being unequal at different grade levels is avoided. In addition, percentile ranks are less likely to be considered as standards for performance. However, percentile ranks *do* have two major shortcomings, which are listed below:

1. Percentile ranks are often confused with *percentage correct.* In using percentile ranks, be sure you are communicating that a percentile rank of 62, for example, is understood to mean that the individual's score was higher than 62 percent of the people who took the test. Commonly, a score at the sixty-second percentile is misinterpreted to mean the student answered only 62 percent of the items correct. A score at the sixty-second percentile

---

Percentiles and *percentile ranks* have slightly different meanings. In finding *percentiles,* one starts with the percentage of cases desired (e.g., P_{25}, P_{50}, P_{75}, etc.) and then finds the score value below which there is that percent of cases. In finding *percentile ranks* the reverse direction is taken: one starts with a score value and, then, finds the percent of cases falling below that particular score. Generally, percentile ranks are determined for all scores in a distribution at the same time.

might be equivalent to a B or a C, whereas a score of 62 percent would likely be an F.

2. Equal differences between percentile ranks do *not* necessarily indicate equal differences in achievement. To refresh your memory, review the relevant section of Chapter 13. Briefly, in a grade of 100 pupils, the difference in achievement between the second percentile and fifth percentile is substantial, whereas the difference between the forty-seventh and fiftieth is negligible—assuming a normal distribution. Interpretation of percentile ranks has to consider that units toward the tails of the distribution tend to be spread out, while units toward the center tend to be compressed, as illustrated in Figure 18.3.

As long as these limitations are considered, percentiles represent a useful type of score to employ in interpreting standardized test results.

Standard Scores

Like percentile ranks, standard scores compare a student's performance to that of other students at the same grade level. The problem of equal differences between units not representing equal differences in achievement is overcome through the use of standard scores. Computation of such scores was discussed in Chapter 13, and you might want to review the relevant sections of that chapter. Recall that the z-score is the basic type of standard score, and all other standard scores are derived

---

FIGURE 18.3 | Normal curve (approximate percentile ranks indicated along baseline)

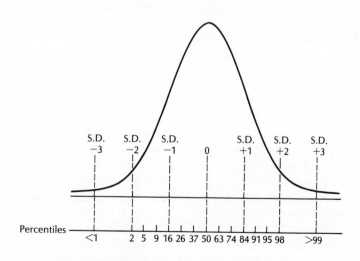

from it. This is an important consideration to keep in mind since many test publishers "create" new types of standard scores with various means and standard deviations when they publish new tests. You need not be overwhelmed by such scores since conceptually they are identical to *z*-scores.

Similar to, but different from, *z*-scores are a special type of standard score called *stanines*. Stanines are ranges or bands within which fixed percentages of scores fall. They are determined by dividing the normal curve into nine portions, each being one-half standard deviation wide. Stanines and the percentage of cases within each stanine are indicated here:

Stanine	Percent of cases
1	4% (lowest)
2	7
3	12
4	17
5	20
6	17
7	12
8	7
9	4 (highest)

Stanines have a mean equal to 5 and a standard deviation equal to 2. Each stanine is one-half standard deviation wide. Interpreting stanines is straightforward in that a student is simply described as being "in" the second stanine, ninth stanine, etc. A major advantage of stanines is that, since they are intervals or bands, they tend to minimize overinterpretation of data. Also, since they only require single-digit numbers, they are useful for situations where recording space is limited.

Standard scores represent the ultimate in standardized test score interpretation. However, there is one factor that limits their widespread adoption—most educators, parents, and students do not understand how to use standard scores. As a result, few schools or districts request standard scores from test publishers. As we will demonstrate, however, standard scores can be time and effort savers in determining aptitude-achievement discrepancies. They also allow for easy comparison of scores both within and across pupils, either over time or across subjects.

Having had a course in tests and measurements, you are now able to make use of standard scores to make sense out of standardized test scores. Keep in mind that such scores are not understood by most parents and students and as a result are not a good medium to use in reporting standardized test results. What should you use then? In our opinion, grade and age equivalents lend themselves too easily to misinterpretation and have too many limitations. As we mentioned, standard scores would be our choice but may be too complicated for use by the general public. We recommend, therefore, that you use percentile ranks when reporting and interpreting standardized test results to parents. Be sure, however, to consider the limitations we mentioned regarding percentile ranks in making such interpretations.

INTERPRETING STANDARDIZED TEST RESULTS TO PARENTS AND STUDENTS

Standardized tests, although less useful for day-to-day instructional decision making than teacher-made tests, can be very useful for placement and diagnostic decisions and for providing feedback to parents and students. Unfortunately, standardized test interpretation is by no means a straightforward task. Standardized or not, tests are fallible and require thoughtful and considerate use. To acquire the skill of properly using standardized tests, certain factors must be considered. These factors can be classified into two categories: test-related and student-related.

Test-Related Factors

Test-related factors can limit the interpretability of the test's results due to problems inherent in the test itself, its use, or its administration. They can be addressed by asking the following questions: Does the test have acceptable reliability and criterion-related validity? Does the test have content validity for my instructional objectives? Was the test's norm group composed of students similar to my class? Were the standardized procedures followed? Let's consider each of these questions.

Does the test have acceptable reliability and criterion-related validity?

This question highlights the need to know how valid, reliable and accurate a test is. In Chapters 15, 16, and 17 we discussed validity, reliability, and accuracy. We can determine whether a test is reliable, accurate, and valid from information contained in the administrator's manual or the technical manual accompanying the standardized test. Let's consider this information.

Reliability.   An acceptable standardized test should have reliability coefficients of about:

.95 for internal consistency
.90 for test-retest
.85 for alternate forms

If your test has coefficients this high, you can feel confident that the test is reliable. Of course, there is nothing sacred about these particular coefficients. If your test has .92 test-retest reliability, .93 internal consistency, and .82 alternate forms, your test will still have good reliability.

Accuracy.   If the test is reliable, then it is also accurate. That is, it is likely to yield obtained results close to an individual's true level of achievement. In the administrator's or technical manual for a test under the section "Standard Error of

Measurement" you will find a numerical value that will enable you to determine the range of scores within which an individual's true score is likely to lie. Recall from Chapter 17 that this range of scores can be determined at the 68-, 95-, and 99-percent levels of confidence.

Criterion-Related Validity.

Recall that criterion-related validity may be of two types: predictive and concurrent. Since standardized achievement tests are used to assess past learning, it makes little sense to report predictive validity coefficients for them. However, concurrent validity coefficients are often reported. These are numerical estimates of the extent to which a test correlates with another established test or tests. However, using such coefficients to determine an achievement test's validity is difficult. Since the content and specificity of the different tests will vary, a valid achievement test may yield a concurrent validity coefficient of .60 with Test X, and .90 with Text Y, and still be a good achievement test. The reason for the discrepancy would likely reflect a closer match in content and specificity between your test and Test Y, and less of a match with Text X. For this reason, it is *most* important to evaluate the content validity of standard achievement tests. Concurrent validity is of secondary importance. Of course, one would be very suspicious of an achievement test that yielded a concurrent validity coefficient of less than .50 with an established standardized achievement test.

Does the test have content validity for my instructional objectives?

A numerical estimate of validity, showing that test A correlates highly with test B, does *not* mean that either test A *or* test B has content validity for your instructional objectives. *Only* by matching items with your objectives can you determine whether a standardized achievement test has content validity for your class. Furthermore, remember that just because a test is reliable does not necessarily mean it is valid. If the test has several items covering dictionary skills and you have not taught such skills, the case for content validity of the test for your class has been weakened. That is, if the test does not measure or match your objectives and your instruction, the test's results will be ambiguous, regardless of that test's reliability or accuracy.

As the person on whom the burden of test interpretation is likely to fall, it is your responsibility to assess the test's content validity. You can do so by matching each item with your objectives. If there is a high degree of correspondence between your objectives and the test items, the content validity of the test has been affirmed.

Was the test's norm group composed of students similar to my class?

When the pilot or preliminary version of a standardized test is constructed, it is often administered to a test or pilot group of students. Revisions are made as indicated, and then it is administered to a *norming group* or *norming sample*. A norms table for the test is then compiled, based on the performance of this sample on the test. The norms table tells us what proportion of the test takers scored above, at, or below the different possible scores on the test. A typical norms table is reproduced in Table 18.2.

Knowing what kind of students the norm group was composed of is of utmost importance. This is the group with which you will be comparing your students in interpreting their scores. If the test you administer to your upper-income class was normed on a sample of low-income children from impoverished backgrounds who were malnourished, and your class scored somewhat higher than 50 percent of the norm group, would you interpret the findings to mean exceptional performance? Hopefully not. Since children who were malnourished and raised in impoverished, low-income families tend to score low on standardized tests, we would expect children from upper-income families to score considerably higher regardless of instructional method or the academic potential of the children involved. Such a comparison would be inappropriate. Similarly, it would be inappropriate to compare the performance of low-income children to a norm group composed entirely of upper-income children. The low-income group would be expected to fare poorly in comparison, again, regardless of instructional methods or academic potential.

Fortunately, most norm groups are not composed of such homogeneous groups of students. Most standardized test publishers attempt to administer their tests to norm groups that are representative of the general United States population. This means the sample is scientifically chosen to be as similar to the general United States population as possible in terms of sex, ethnicity, region, and income. This increases the usefulness of the test for making comparisons with your class. Often a compromise must be reached in creating a norms table. In trying to closely represent the United States norm, we create a norms table that may not represent the unique characteristics of an individual classroom. To the extent your class fails to approximate the United States population in general, the comparisons you make to the norm will be less valid.

Trying to assess progress in a class for the intellectually gifted by comparing test scores to a national norm, therefore, would not be appropriate. All or most students would score high in comparison. This is *not necessarily* because the students are working hard, or their teachers are effective. It may simply be the result of choosing an inappropriate standard for comparison, in this case a norm group composed of the general population of students, not gifted students. Although the gifted students may seem to be doing very well by comparison, it would be difficult to discriminate among them, since all or most would score at or near the "ceiling" for the test.

A similar case could be made for the inappropriateness of comparing a class composed entirely, or mainly, of low-income, low-achieving students to a norm group representative of the national population. Such a class would score very low by comparison—probably so low as to make discrimination among students in the class difficult.

TABLE 18.2 | Norms table to convert raw score to percentile rank and stanines for fourth graders who take the CTBS from September to November

Table 6
RAW SCORE to EXPANDED STANDARD SCORE (SCALE SCORE)

Form Q ,   Level 2

RAW SCORE	READING			LANGUAGE				ARITHMETIC				TOTAL BAT-TERY	STUDY SKILLS			RAW SCORE
	VOCAB	COMPR	TOTAL	MECH	EXPR	SPELL	TOTAL	COMPU	CNCPT	APPLI	TOTAL		REF	GRAPH	TOTAL	
00	186	132	127	163	179	175	132	211	195	187	176	108	177	182	140	00
01	214	167	143	201	216	211	145	228	220	231	186	112	236	214	160	01
02	233	188	156	236	239	239	155	242	240	265	194	116	277	235	176	02
03	248	202	166	268	258	261	165	254	259	294	201	119	309	253	191	03
04	261	215	174	295	277	280	174	264	276	319	207	122	336	272	205	04
05	274	228	182	319	297	296	182	272	291	341	213	125	360	292	219	05
06	287	242	189	340	316	310	190	280	306	361	218	128	381	312	234	06
07	299	258	196	358	325	322	198	287	319	378	223	131	401	331	249	07
08	310	274	203	373	352	333	207	293	332	393	229	134	418	349	263	08
09	321	291	211	387	367	343	216	300	344	406	234	137	434	366	278	09
10	332	307	219	400	354	352	224	306	354	418	239	139	449	380	292	10
11	341	323	227	412	354	361	233	311	364	431	244	142	464	392	306	11
12	349	337	236	423	405	368	242	317	373	443	249	145	479	403	319	1/2
13	356	349	245	423	417	376	251	323	381	454	254	147	496	413	331	13
14	363	360	254	443	428	383	260	328	388	471	259	150	514	422	343	14
15	369	370	262	454	439	391	269	334	395	487	265	152	534	431	353	15
16	375	378	271	464	450	399	277	339	403	505	270	155	554	440	363	16
17	381	385	280	476	462	408	285	344	410	524	275	157	576	449	372	17
18	386	392	288	488	473	417	293	349	417	549	280	160	601	458	380	18
19	392	398	296	502	485	427	301	354	425	581	285	162	631	467	388	19
20	398	404	304	518	497	438	308	359	434	628	290	165	673	477	395	20
21	404	410	311	538	510	450	314	364	443		295	167		488	402	21
22	410	415	318	562	524	463	321	368	453		299	170		500	408	22
23	416	421	325	594	540	477	326	373	464		304	173		513	414	23
24	423	428	331	635	556	493	332	377	476		308	175		528	420	24
25	429	434	336	689	575	510	337	381	490		312	178		546	426	25
26	435	440	342		554	530	341	385	506		317	180		566	432	26
27	442	447	347		616	554	346	389	524		321	183		590	437	27
28	449	453	351		641	582	350	393	548		324	186		620	443	28
29	456	460	355		674	618	354	397	578		328	189		657	449	29
30	464	467	359		722	665	358	401	619		332	191		709	455	30
31	472	474	363				361	405			335	194			461	31
32	482	482	367				365	410			338	197			467	32
33	492	490	370				368	414			341	200			474	33
34	503	500	374				372	419			345	203			481	34
35	516	510	377				375	424			348	205			488	35
36	530	522	380				378	430			351	208			497	36
37	546	535	383				382	436			353	211			505	37
38	566	550	386				385	443			356	214			514	38
39	593	566	390				389	450			359	217			524	39
40	630	585	393				392	459			362	220			535	40
41		605	396				396	468			364	223			546	41
42		629	399				399	480			367	225			558	42
43		659	402				403	493			369	228			570	43
44		696	405				407	509			372	231			583	44
45		748	408				410	527			374	234			598	45
46			411				414	549			377	237			615	46
47			414				418	574			379	240			635	47
48			417				421	605			382	243			660	48
49			420				425				384	245			693	49
50			423				429				386	248			738	50
51			426				433				389	251				51
52			429				436				391	254				52
53			433				440				393	256				53
54			436				444				396	259				54
55			439				448				398	262				55
56			442				452				400	264				56
57			446				456				402	267				57
58			449				461				404	270				58
59			453				465				407	272				59
60			457				470				409	275				60

Most teachers, however, do not have uniformly high or low achieving students in their classes. How, then, can teachers in such classes tell how appropriate the comparisons they make are? Fortunately, there is an answer.

The teacher knows approximately what his or her class composition is with respect to income and ethnicity. The teacher can then find the composition of the norm group by reading the "Norm Group" description section in the appropriate manual accompanying the standardized test. An example of such a description is presented in Figure 18.4. After studying the description, you can compare your class to the norm group. The closer the correspondence between the class and the norm group, the more confidence you can place in interpreting results using the norms table. The more the discrepancy between the table and the norm group, the less confidence can be placed in interpretations based on the norms table. This is a judgment that one gets better at with time and practice.

But what if you decide there is a large discrepancy between the norm group and your class? Is there any way to interpret the standardized test results? Fortunately, the answer lies in the concept of local norms.

Local Norms.   When a class, school, or district is atypical, that is, unlike the norming sample, or when comparisons among homogeneous local classes or groups are necessary, local norms can be used to make better use of test results. It should be noted, however, that we are not suggesting that local norms be substituted for national norms. We are suggesting that local norms are useful tools that can, in some situations, increase the interpretability of test scores. They do so by enabling more meaningful comparisons to be made among similar students, classes, and schools. Since such norms are established on relatively homogeneous groups, they enable better comparisons within such groups, but fail to allow broader or national comparisons to be made. Table 18.3 compares and contrasts national and local norms.

Establishing Local Norms.   Although establishing norms generally will be the responsibility of the school district's support staff, they are fairly easy to develop. To construct a local norms table, use the following procedures:

1. Collect scores for all individuals in the local group
2. Tally all the obtained scores
3. Construct a simple frequency distribution (refresh your memory by rereading this procedure in Chapter 12)
4. Compute percentile ranks for each score in the table (see Chapter 13)
5. Refer to the table as you would a national norms table

Next, we will turn to the final question addressing test-related factors that influence standardized test interpretation:

Were standardized procedures followed?

FIGURE 18.4 | Norm group description from the SRA Achievement Series

STANDARDIZATION DEMOGRAPHICS

The descriptive data gathered on the norming population enable schools to determine to what extent schools similar to them were represented. Students in 542 schools participated in the 1978 spring and fall standardizations of the Achievement Series; 492 of the schools (91 percent) responded to a School/Community Characteristics Questionnaire. (See Appendix A.) Of the total number of schools, 396 participated in the spring standardization; of these, 358 responded to the questionnaire. Of the total number of schools, 457 participated in the fall standardization; of these, 428 responded to the questionnaire.

Schools were identified by: (1) the geographic region in which they were located, (2) the district-size stratum to which they belonged, (3) their participation in the spring standardization and/or participation in the fall standardization, and (4) whether part of the Large City, Nonpublic, or Title I norms groups. (The sites of districts that participated in the standardizations are presented in Appendix B.)

Responses to the School/Community Characteristics Questionnaire were analyzed and the results are presented in Tables 10 to 13. Table 10 contains the summaries by geographic region, Table 11 contains the summaries by district size, Table 12 contains the summaries for schools participating in the spring standardization and belonging to the national and subgroup norms groups, and Table 13 contains the summaries for schools participating in the fall standardization and belonging to the national and subgroup norms groups.

REGIONAL AND DISTRICT SIZE CHARACTERISTICS

Regional Characteristics

Characteristics of the schools that participated in the standardizations varied in different regions of the country. Schools in the East North Central and South Atlantic states had the fewest Title I students and the Pacific states had the most. All regions had approximately the same percent of Special Education students. In all regions, the majority of students were white. The South Atlantic states had the highest percentage of black students, the Mountain states had the highest percentage of American In-

dian students, and the Pacific states had the highest percentage of Hispanic and Oriental/Asian students. Student turnover was smallest in the New England states and largest in the Mountain states.

In regard to the characteristics of the communities in which these schools were located, the smallest populations were found in the East South Central states. Medium-sized populations were found in the New England and Middle Atlantic states and larger populations were found in the West North Central, South Atlantic, and Mountain states. Population sizes of school communities varied in the East North Central, West South Central, and Pacific states. The predominant community types were urban, suburban, and rural for the East and West North Central and Pacific states; urban and suburban in the South Atlantic and Mountain states; suburban and rural in the Middle Atlantic states; and rural in the East South Central states. The dwelling areas in all regions were within the middle range (between above average and below average). Dwelling areas in the Middle Atlantic states tended to be at the higher end of the range and dwelling areas in the Pacific states tended to be at the lower end of the range. The occupational levels of families were approximately the same in all regions. The majority of families were in skilled, semi-skilled, or service occupations. Median family incomes generally ranged between $5000 and $20,000. Percentages were larger at the lower end of the range in the South Atlantic and the East and West South Central states. In all but the Pacific states, the majority of the heads of families completed high school and a smaller percentage had some college experience. In the Pacific states, the majority of the heads of families had vocational training.

District Size Characteristics

Characteristics of the schools that participated in the standardizations also varied by the size of the school district. Approximately the same percentage of Title I and Special Education students was found in all schools regardless of district size. The majority of the students in the schools were white; the largest and smallest districts had the largest percentage of nonwhite students. The student turnover rate was highest in the large districts and lowest in the small districts.

FIGURE 18.4 ▎ Norm group description from the SRA Achievement Series (continued)

The population characteristics of the communities in which the schools were located matched those of the district populations as a whole. The large districts were in urban areas, middle-sized districts were in suburban or a mixture of suburban and rural areas, and the small districts were in rural areas. The majority of dwelling areas were reported as average in most district size; there were, however, more below-average dwelling areas in the largest and smallest districts. The majority of families had skilled or service occupations and had median family incomes of between $5000 and $20,000. Large districts had more families with median incomes greater than $20,000. The majority of heads of families were high school graduates with either vocational training or some college experience. The large districts had more heads of families who were college graduates and more who had some college experience.

NATIONAL AND SUBGROUP CHARACTERISTICS

A comparison of the national and Large City norms groups (spring and fall samples) revealed the following characteristics:

■ Schools in both spring and fall Large City norms groups had a greater percentage of black and Hispanic students than schools in the national norms groups for spring and fall.

■ Schools in the spring and fall Large City norms groups had a smaller percentage of white students than schools in the national norms groups for spring and fall.

■ Schools in the spring and fall Large City norms groups, had a higher rate of student turnover than schools in the national norms groups for spring and fall.

Here, the teacher needs to think back to the day the test was administered. Were any required procedures or wording altered or omitted? Was extra time or too little time afforded? Was help made available above and beyond what was permissible according to the test manual? If no such violations occurred, no more need be done about this consideration. If one or more violations did occur, then the teacher must realize that the test's reliability has been affected to some unknown extent. Obviously, this reduces the confidence you can place in the test results. Since you will never be sure how reliability has been affected by such violations, or be certain the violations resulted in increased or decreased scores, there is little you can do to correct for such errors—except, of course, to prevent them.

This completes our discussion of test-related factors to be considered in interpreting standardized tests. Now, let's consider several equally important student-related factors.

Student-Related Factors

The variety of student-related factors that can affect test-score interpretation can be divided into several categories: age, sex, and development; motivation; emotional state on the test day; handicaps; and aptitude.

Age, Sex, and Development.   An awareness of individual differences has influenced educational practice for many years. We read and hear about students being visual or auditory learners, high or low IQ, advanced or delayed, and so forth. Yet,

	National Norms	*Local Norms*
TABLE 18.3 — A Comparison and Contrast of National and Local Norms		
Composition	Large numbers of students of various ethnicity and income selected to represent U.S. population.	All students in a specific school or district.
Use	Compare local performance to a national norm.	Compare local performance to a local norm.
Advantage	Allows broad, general comparisons in areas of broad concern (e.g., college entrance, scholarships).	Allows comparisons in areas of local or immediate concern (e.g., academic gain within homogeneous groups, placement in local classes).
Disadvantage	Not useful in comparisons when relatively homogeneous groups are involved.	Not useful for making broad comparisons at a national level

we sometimes fail to consider three of the most obvious of the individual differences among children—age, sex, and stage of development.

Typically, norms tables are broken into three or four sections to correspond to various times of the year. Students are expected to know more, and therefore answer more items correctly in May than in October due to the effects of schooling. This makes sense, of course, but what about the case of a first grader who turns *six* the day *before* school starts, compared to the first grader who turns *seven* the day *after* school starts? Should both students, all other factors except age being equal, be expected to improve their test scores equally? If you are familiar with younger elementary-age children, your answer would likely be a firm *no*. Five-, six-, and seven-year-olds show very different rates of development in different areas. Furthermore, there are differences that correlate with sex. Girls tend to master verbal skills and reading earlier than boys. Norms tables for achievement tests generally do not take such factors into account. The reasons for academic performance are complex and, of course, involve more than just age, sex, and stage of development. Do not treat them as though they alone determine test performance, but do not neglect these factors in interpreting standardized test scores.

Motivation. Ever find it hard to be "up " for a test? If you are like most of us, it happens from time to time. At those times your performance is less likely to reflect your actual level of achievement than if you were up for the test. Most pupils have little trouble getting ready for a teacher-made achievement test—they know that their grades depend on it. With standardized tests, however, motivation can be a problem.

Both pupils and their parents have made more sophisticated use of standardized tests over the last few years. Many realize that such tests do not affect a child's grades in school, but at the same time may not realize that such results are often used for instructional grouping and other instructional decisions that will affect their child later. Believing standardized tests are not important often leads pupils to take a who-cares attitude toward standardized tests. Such an attitude is sometimes unintentionally transmitted by teachers in an effort to minimize the anxiety some pupils experience over tests. The result can be a decline in motivation and a consequent decline in performance.

Emotional State on the Test Day.
Just as teachers get emotionally upset from time to time, so do their students. This does not simply refer to students who are nervous about the test, but also to students who may be undergoing severe stress for personal reasons, such as an argument before the test, a dispute at home, or some destabilizing effect within the family. One cannot function at one's best when depressed, angry, or very nervous. When you find these characteristics exhibited by a student shortly before the test, make a note of it and consider it when you interpret the student's test performance at a later date.

Handicaps.
There is a sizeable percentage of students in the public schools who suffer from physical and/or emotional problems that hinder academic achievement. Naturally, students suffering from such handicaps should not be expected to perform as well on standardized tests as nonhandicapped students. The implications for test interpretation depend on the type and severity of the handicap. Time and space prevent us from considering all of these, and usually the burden of test interpretation in such cases falls on teachers trained in special education. However, Chapter 20 will deal in detail with issues related to testing the handicapped student.

Aptitude.
Aptitude and *potential* can be considered synonymous for our purposes. They refer to the "maximum" we can expect from a student, as indicated by a student's score on a test of academic aptitude or potential. Such tests are often referred to as IQ tests or intelligence tests. IQ tests will be discussed in more depth in Chapter 19. For now, all we need to know is that such tests provide us with a benchmark or standard against which to compare achievement test scores.

The academic aptitude test provides us with an estimated ceiling for a student's academic performance. The academic achievement test, on the other hand, measures actual academic performance. Traditionally, students have been labeled overachievers or underachievers based on the relationship between their academic aptitude and academic achievement. Figure 18.5 illustrates an underachiever, an overachiever, and a student achieving at expectancy.

Student A in Figure 18.5 is a student with considerable potential who is not achieving up to his or her potential. Student B is a student with moderate potential

FIGURE 18.5 | Relative levels of aptitude and achievement for an underachiever, an overachiever, and a student achieving at expectancy

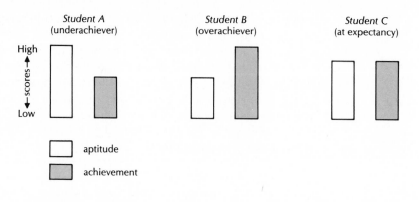

who is achieving above his or her potential. More accurately, this "overachiever" is a student whose obtained aptitude score (not necessarily true score) is lower than his or her obtained achievement score. Student C represents a student achieving at the level we would expect, given his or her aptitude score. The obtained aptitude score is equivalent to the obtained achievement score.

Obviously, it is necessary to have an aptitude score to enable you to determine whether a student is achieving at *expectancy* (the level you would expect, given the student's aptitude). However, school district policies vary in requiring the administration of aptitude tests. Depending on your district, you may have aptitude tests administered to students every few years, or only in the fourth and ninth grades, or not at all.

If you find aptitude test scores in your students' folders, you can use them to enhance your achievement test interpretation. However, be careful not to simply label your students underachievers or overachievers.

Most aptitude tests yield more than one overall IQ score. Many yield a *verbal* and *nonverbal* score, or a *language* and *nonlanguage* score, or a *verbal* and a *quantitative* score. Quantitative scores represent general math or number ability. When the aptitude or IQ test yields a verbal score and a nonverbal score or a quantitative score, more relevant comparisons are possible than when only one overall score is reported. Consider the following example:

Donna, a new fifth grader, obtained the following scores on the Cognitive Abilities Test (an aptitude test) at the beginning of fourth grade. (*Note:* $\overline{X}$ = 100, SD = 15)

Verbal = 100
Quantitative = 130

Donna's scores on the California Achievement Test (CAT) given at the end of fourth grade are as follows:

	Percentile Rank
Reading Vocabulary	66
Reading Comprehension	60
Reading Total	63
Math Concepts	99
Math Computation	99
Math Total	99

Donna's parents have requested a conference with you. They want you to "push" her harder in reading until her reading scores match her math scores, which have been superior.

What would you do? How would you interpret Donna's scores? Would you "push" her in reading? Before you answer these questions, let's make Donna's data interpretable. We can do so by using the bar graph comparisons used earlier to illustrate the concepts of underachievement and overachievement. This time we will add measurement scales to each graph.

We know that an obtained IQ score of 100 is at the fiftieth percentile on an IQ test with a mean of 100 and a standard deviation of 15. We also know that on the same test an IQ score of 130 is at the ninety-eighth percentile, two standard deviations above the mean. In the graphs in Figure 18.6 our percentile scales do

FIGURE 18.6 | A comparison of Donna's aptitude and achievement scores

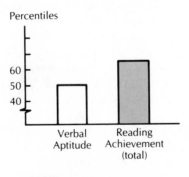
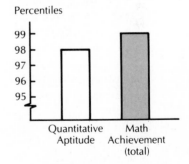

not correspond directly to each other, but this is of little consequence since we are not interested in comparing reading with math. Rather, we are interested in comparing verbal aptitude with reading total, both of which are on the same scale, and quantitative aptitude with math total, which are also on a common scale.

From the graphs, we would conclude that Donna's obtained math achievement score actually *exceeds* the obtained math aptitude score. According to our popular but somewhat misleading terminology she is "overachieving" in math. Unless she is paying a high price socially or emotionally for working so hard at math, we see no problem here. Hence, the qualifier "over" in the word "overachiever" should not imply a negative valuation of what has been accomplished by this student. But Donna's parents are not concerned with her math achievement; they are concerned with her reading achievement. They want her "pushed," which suggests they feel she can do better than she has in the past. That is, Donna's parents feel she is underachieving in reading. Is she?

Based on a comparison of her obtained verbal aptitude score and her obtained reading achievement score, our conclusion would have to be no. In fact, Donna is "overachieving" in reading, too. That is, her obtained reading achievement score exceeds her obtained verbal aptitude score; she is actually performing above expectancy. Would you agree that she needs to be pushed? By now, we should hope not. In fact, you might suggest to Donna's parents that they ease up, using your skills in the interpretation of standardized test results to substantiate your suggestion.

Aptitude-Achievement Discrepancies

What we have been doing is making a general or global decision about whether Donna is achieving at her expected level, as indicated by her aptitude score. In other words, are there any differences between her aptitude and her achievement? When these differences are large enough to indicate substantial variation in the traits being measured, we call them *aptitude-achievement discrepancies.*[*]

But when is a difference a discrepancy? How large must the gap be before we call a difference a discrepancy? Does this begin to sound familiar? We hope so, but if it does not, this next question should help: How large a difference do we need between an aptitude score and an achievement score before we can conclude that the difference is due to a "real" discrepancy, rather than a "chance" difference? In Chapter 17 we learned how to use the standard error of measurement (S_m) and band interpretation to discriminate real from chance differences among subtests in an achievement test battery. This same principle can be applied to discriminate real discrepancies from chance differences when dealing with aptitude and achievement test scores.

We will consider an example in a moment, but first let's review one aspect of band interpretation. Recall that we can use the 68-percent (Score $\pm$ 1 S_m) or 95-

*The procedures described in this section are intended to provide the regular classroom teacher with an easy-to-use standard for identifying students who may be in need of further testing, diagnosis, or classification. These procedures are not intended to classify a student on the basis of an aptitude-achievement discrepancy.

percent (Score $\pm$ 2 S$_m$) methods, depending on how conservative we want to be regarding the educational decisions to be made. If such findings are kept within the classroom and little of consequence is to follow from a band interpretation, or if comparisons are limited to those among subtests on an achievement battery, the 68-percent approach may be appropriate. However, when student achievement is compared to student aptitude, often profound or at least important educational decisions or conclusions are reached. Indeed, aptitude-achievement discrepancies, when based on individual rather than group tests, are in many states one of the main criteria for determining if a child is to receive special educational services. While decisions such as placement in special education do not come about solely on the basis of aptitude-achievement discrepancies, the special education referral process often begins with a teacher recognizing such a discrepancy and becoming aware that a student is not achieving up to potential. Certainly such an important educational step should be approached with caution. Thus, we would strongly encourage you to use the more conservative, 95-percent approach any time you search for aptitude-achievement discrepancies.

Let's turn to an example that illustrates how aptitude-achievement discrepancies are determined. Table 18.4 lists scores obtained by three students on the California Achievement Test and an aptitude test, the Cognitive Abilities Test. Inspect the table. Are there any aptitude-achievement discrepancies? Are you having trouble answering?

Before going any further, let's try to make some sense out of the table. Provided are three types of scores for the California Achievement Test: grade equivalents, percentile ranks, and standard scores. It is more often the case than not that several scores are reported for each student. However, aptitude scores, like those in our table from the Cognitive Abilities Test, are typically reported in standard scores only. The first step in determining aptitude-achievement discrep-

---

TABLE 18.4 | Scores for Max, Betty, and Robert Reported in Standard Scores (SS), Percentile Ranks (%), and Grade Equivalents (GE)

																		Cognitive Abilities Test*	
	Reading Recognition			Reading Comprehension			Reading Total			Math Concepts			Math Computation			Math Total				
Name	GE	%	SS	GE	%	SS	GE	%	SS	GE	%	SS	GE	%	SS	GE	%	SS	Verbal	Quanti-tative
Max	2.2	13	82	2.3	15	83	2.2	14	82	1.9	9	79	2.5	17	85	2.2	13	85	81	89
Betty	2.9	25	89	3.3	34	94	3.1	30	92	3.2	32	93	3.6	42	97	3.4	37	95	112	120
Robert	5.4	84	116	5.8	89	121	5.6	87	118	4.6	68	107	4.8	73	109	4.7	70	108	114	118
	$S_m = 3.5$			$S_m = 3.0$			$S_m = 3.3$			$S_m = 3.5$			$S_m = 2.5$			$S_m = 3.0$			$S_m = 3.5$	$S_m = 3.5$

*$\overline{X} = 100$, SD $= 15$

Note: S_m is in standard score units. The values provided are illustrative estimates only. Actual values will differ somewhat.

ancies is to be sure both sets of scores are on the same scale. If for some reason standard scores are not included on your score report, request a copy of the test manual and convert the scores you do have (for example, either grade or age equivalents or percentiles) to standard scores. Such conversions normally require using only the appropriate table or tables in the manual. Instructions on how to perform the necessary operations will be provided in the manual, and they likely will differ somewhat from test to test.

After you have converted all scores to standard scores, the remaining steps are very similar to those we followed in the band interpretation section of Chapter 17. Once our scores are all on the same scale, determine the S_m for each subtest. This is important because each subtest will have a somewhat different S_m. Do not use the S_m for the whole test, as this would give an inaccurate or misleading interpretation in many cases. In Table 18.4 the S_m is listed under each subtest. While the S_m is usually not included in score reports, you can find the S_m for each subtest in the test manual. You could also compute the S_m for each subtest, using the formula $S_m = SD \sqrt{1 - r}$. To do so, you would need to look up the reliability of each subtest in the manual. However, most manuals will give you S_m for each subtest.

After determining the S_m for each subtest, add and subtract $2S_m$ to each obtained score. This gives us the range of scores for each subtest within which we are 95-percent sure the student's true score lies. Remember, we are advising use of the more conservative 95-percent approach in determining aptitude-achievement discrepancies. Using Table 18.4 here are the data for Betty's reading and verbal IQ scores:

Name	Subtest	Obtained Score	S_m	95% Range
Betty	Verbal IQ	112	3.5	105 −119
	Reading Recognition	89	3.5	82 − 96
	Reading Comprehension	94	3.0	88 −100
	Reading Total	92	3.3	85.4− 98.6

Now we are ready to complete our band interpretation and identify any aptitude-achievement discrepancies. Transfer your data to a table like the one used in Chapter 17 as shown in Table 18.5.

Inspection of the table reveals there are real differences between Betty's verbal aptitude or IQ and her reading achievement. Even though we have used the conservative 95-percent approach, there is no overlap between her verbal aptitude and her reading achievement. We could state with considerable confidence that a difference this large indicates a real discrepancy.

Keep in mind, however, that when an aptitude-achievement discrepancy is found, the teacher's task is only beginning. Why the discrepancy exists must be determined, and then appropriate steps taken to remediate it.

This concludes our discussion of aptitude-achievement discrepancies. Recall why we began this discussion: to consider comparing actual student achievement to individual potentials, not just to each other, or to a local or national norm. Stu-

| TABLE 18.5 | Band interpretation of Betty's verbal IQ and reading scores (95% level) |

SUBTESTS

dents have differing levels of potential and searching for aptitude-achievement discrepancies helps sensitize you to these differences. Grouping and instructional planning, not to mention standardized score interpretation, are facilitated and aided when student achievement is considered in relation to potential, not simply in relation to norms. The benefactors of such an approach to standardized test interpretation are likely to be both you and your students

We have now discussed several test-related and student related factors considered important to standardized test interpretation. It may seem as though these factors are too many and too complex to deal with every time you have to interpret standardized test scores. However, with time and practice they become second nature—if you make yourself consider them in your initial attempts at standardized test interpretation. Let's turn now to individualized score reports, our final topic in this chapter.

INDIVIDUALIZED SCORE REPORTS

Test publishers offer a variety of reports for test users, ranging from small stick-on labels that contain only identification information and test scores, to rather comprehensive reports such as those illustrated in Figures 18.7 and 18.8. The stick-on labels are designed to be affixed to report cards or cumulative folders to provide a concise record of past or current achievement. Individual score reports are designed to provide more information to better enable the teacher to diagnose a student's strengths and weaknesses.

FIGURE 18.7 | An individual score report from the Iowa Tests of Basic Skills

SCHOOL: HILLSIDE ELEM **TEACHER:** MRS MARY SCHEELAND
STUDENT: CARTER, THOMAS **GRADE** 5 **LEVEL** 11 **FORM** 7 **DATE TESTED** 10/81 **I.D. NO**

THE RIVERSIDE PUBLISHING COMPANY — Iowa Tests of Basic Skills — STUDENT CRITERION-REFERENCED SKILLS ANALYSIS

	V VOCA	R READ	L-1 SPEL	L-2 CAP	L-3 PUNT	L-4 USAGE	L TOT LANG	W-1 VIS	W-2 REF	W TOT WK	M-1 STM	M-2 CON	M-3 PRO	M TOT COM	CMPL MATH	SST COMP	SC SOC	SCIEN
GE	35	42	39	35	48	47	42	52	27	40	34	40	38	37	39			
PR	16	28	24	15	42	42	29	50	5	23	7	22	9	8	19			

PAGE 4 PROCESS NO 000-0480-000

SKILLS	NUMBER ATTEMPTED	NUMBER CORRECT	NUMBER OF ITEMS	PERCENT CORRECT FOR THIS STUDENT	CLASS AVERAGE PERCENT CORRECT	NATIONAL AVERAGE PERCENT CORRECT
VOCABULARY (N= 18)	39	10	39	26	53	53
Nouns	9	5	9	56	64	55
Verbs	14	3	14	21	50	53
Modifiers & Connectives	16	2	16	13	50	50
READING (N= 18)	54	17	54	31	47	45
Facts	18	8	18	44	50	47
Inferences	17	4	17	24	44	42
Generalizations	19	5	19	26	47	46
SPELLING (N= 18)	39	14	40	35	55	53
Consonants	16	7	16	44	58	55
Vowels	19	5	19	26	50	48
No Mistakes	4	2	5	40	63	61
CAPITALIZATION (N= 18)	30	9	30	30	52	49
Names and Titles	5	1	5	20	49	49
Dates and Holidays	4	2	4	50	71	66
Place Names	6	2	6	33	43	38
Organizations and Groups	5	3	5	60	50	37
Linguistic Conventions	4	1	4	25	51	46
No Mistakes	4	0	4	0	69	71
→PUNCTUATION (N= 18)	30	12	30	40	52	46
→ Terminal Punctuation	10	1	10	10	51	48
→ Use of Commas	7	5	7	71	60	44
→ Other Punctuation	6	3	6	50	40	37
→ Overpunctuation	4	1	4	25	43	39
→ No Mistakes	3	2	3	67	70	63
→USAGE (N= 18)	29	13	30	43	46	51
→ Use of Verbs	11	4	11	36	49	51
→ Use of Pronouns	4	3	4	75	53	56
→ Use of Modifiers	3	0	4	0	25	41
→ Use of Context	8	5	8	63	41	42
→ No Mistakes	3	1	3	33	67	65

SKILLS	NUMBER ATTEMPTED	NUMBER CORRECT	NUMBER OF ITEMS	PERCENT CORRECT FOR THIS STUDENT	CLASS AVERAGE PERCENT CORRECT	NATIONAL AVERAGE PERCENT CORRECT
→VISUAL MATERIALS (N= 18)	46	21	46	46	50	44
→ Map Reading	29	12	29	41	52	46
→ Reading Graphs & Tables	17	9	17	53	45	40
REFERENCE MATERIALS (N= 18)	45	9	45	20	48	50
Alphabetizing	9	3	9	33	43	44
Using Table of Contents	7	3	7	43	67	67
Using an Index	8	0	8	0	48	57
Using a Dictionary	9	1	9	11	51	48
Using Encyclopedias	5	1	5	20	46	48
Using General Reference Materials	7	1	7	14	35	36
MATH CONCEPTS (N= 18)	37	8	37	22	51	46
Numeration, Number Systems, and Sets	9	2	9	22	47	47
Equations, Inequalities and Number Sentences	5	0	5	0	52	48
Whole Numbers; Integers	7	2	7	29	52	46
Fractions	7	1	7	14	52	41
Geometry and Measurement	9	3	9	33	55	46
MATH PROBLEM SOLVING (N= 18)	27	8	27	30	50	45
Single-Step Problems: Addition – Subtraction	11	4	11	36	51	52
Single-Step Problems: Mutiplication – Division	6	1	6	17	42	39
Multiple-Step Problems: Combined Use of Basic Operations	10	3	10	30	53	45
MATH COMPUTATION (N= 18)	44	11	45	24	52	42
Whole Numbers	37	10	38	26	57	55
Fractions	7	1	7	14	23	18

LEGEND: Areas of Greatest Need are Underlined.
Areas that Represent Strengths are Marked with Arrows.

Although individual score reports differ somewhat from publisher to publisher, they commonly report the following:

identification information (pupil's name, age, teacher's name, school, grade, date)

requested scores (raw scores, grade equivalents, percentile ranks, standard scores, scores developed by the publisher)

percentile bands for each subtest, enabling the user to discriminate real from chance differences in scores

a breakdown of the student's performance by subskill areas

FIGURE 18.8 | An individual score report from the SRA Achievement Series keyed to illustrate data included

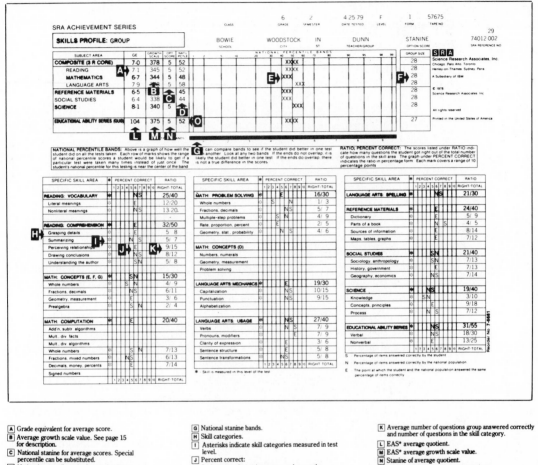

Publishers also provide a variety of other reports, including alphabetical lists and rank-order lists. On request, many publishers will send a representative to schools or districts to describe the variety of scoring services available.

In this chapter we have described various aspects of standardized test construction, administration, and interpretation. In the next chapter we will discuss the various types of standardized tests, describe some of these, and provide a step-by-step approach to follow in planning and implementing a comprehensive standardized testing program in your school district.

SUMMARY

This chapter introduced you to standardized tests, their use, administration and interpretation. Its major points were:

1. Standardized tests are carefully constructed by specialists and they carry specific and uniform, or standardized, administration and scoring procedures.
2. Standardized tests may be achievement, aptitude, interest, or personality tests.
3. Standardized achievement tests facilitate comparisons across districts and regions because of uniformity of content, administration, and scoring and a common basis for comparison—the norms table.
4. Standardized achievement tests are frequently used to make comparisons over time or across students, schools, or districts.
5. Although standardized achievement tests are not as useful as teacher-made tests to the classroom teacher, accountability requirements have made it necessary for teachers to administer and interpret them.
6. When administering standardized tests, all administrators should uniformly follow instructions in order to minimize error in test administration.
7. Although grade-equivalent scores are commonly used, they have several limitations including the following:
   a. They tend to be misinterpreted as indicative of skill levels, rather than relative degrees of performance.
   b. Equal differences in units do not reflect equal changes in achievement.
   c. They have limited applicability except where subjects are taught across all grade levels.
   d. They tend to be seen as standards rather than norms.
   e. Comparability across subjects is difficult.
8. Age equivalents are much less commonly used and suffer from limitations similar to those of grade equivalents.
9. Percentile ranks compare a student's performance with that of his or her peers. Although percentile ranks are superior to grade and age equivalents, they suffer from the following two disadvantages:
   a. They are often confused with percent correct.
   b. Equal differences in units do not reflect equal changes in achievement.
10. Standard scores also compare a student's performance with that of his or her peers. In addition, equal differences in units do reflect equal differences in

achievement. Standard scores are superior to percentile ranks for test interpretation, but tend to be not well understood by many educators and much of the general public.

11. Percentile ranks are recommended for interpreting standardized test results to the public. However, their limitations must be kept in mind.

12. Both test-related and student-related factors should be considered in interpreting standardized test results.

13. Test-related factors require the teacher to assess the test's reliability and validity, the appropriateness of the norm group, and the extent to which standardized procedures were adhered to.

14. When a class is considerably different in composition from the norm group, the appropriateness of comparison to the norm group becomes questionable. In such situations local norms may be established to enable more valid comparisons to be made.

15. Differences in student-related factors require the teacher to consider the child's age, sex and development, motivation, emotional state on the test day, handicaps, and aptitude in interpreting standardized test scores.

16. Students whose obtained achievement scores are lower than their obtained academic aptitude scores are said to be underachievers.

17. Students whose obtained achievement scores are higher than their obtained academic aptitude scores are said to be overachievers.

18. Students whose obtained achievement and academic aptitude scores are equivalent are said to be achieving at expectancy.

19. Students whose obtained achievement scores show "real" discrepancies when compared with their obtained academic aptitude scores have aptitude-achievement discrepancies. Band interpretation using 95-percent levels is recommended for such comparisons.

20. Interpreting standardized test scores by comparing students to their individual potential or aptitude can lead to more effective educational decision making than comparing students to the norms.

21. A variety of scores and score reports are available from publishers.

For Practice

1. "Our principal is so insensitive," said Donna. "He knows Billy Brown has trouble reading, but yet he won't let me help him read the test questions when we give the California Achievement Test next week." Should the principal allow Donna to read the questions to Billy? Support your decision with arguments based on points made in this chapter.

2. "Blanketiblank Public Schools Again Score Below National Average on CTBS—Mayor Calls for Freeze on Teacher Pay Until Scores Reach National Average." As a teacher in the Blanketiblank Public Schools, how would you respond to such a newspaper headline? In your response, critique both the assumption underlying the headline and suggest an alternative way to measure pupil progress.

*3. Consider the following data obtained from the Wechsler Intelligence Scale for Children–Revised (WISC-R) and the Stanford Achievement Test at the end of fourth grade.

Student	Verbal IQ	Reading Vocabulary		Reading Comprehension	
		GE	SS	GE	SS
Bonnie	107	5.9	113	6.5	119
Chris	94	4.5	93	4.0	88
Jack	125	5.8	112	5.6	110
	$S_m = 3.0$	$S_m = 2.5$		$S_m = 3.5$	
		$\overline{X} = 100$, SD = 15			

After inspecting the data above, answer the following questions:

 a. Is each student's achievement about what we would expect? If not, who is not achieving at expectancy?

 b. Are there any aptitude-achievement discrepancies?

4. Check your work in question 3 above by constructing a table like Table 17.5 and subject the scores to a band interpretation. Now answer the same questions again.

5. Mr. Simpson "simply can't understand" why his third-grade son can't skip fourth grade. "After all," he says, "your own test scores show he's reading and doing math at a fifth grade level." Tactfully, explain to Mr. Simpson why his son may not really be ready for fifth grade reading and math.

6. Mr. Gregg, fresh out of college (and a tests and measurements course), is constantly extolling the virtues of standard scores over other types of converted scores. Parent conferences are coming up and he feels confident that the parents he meets with will "finally get a clear and precise interpretation of their childrens' test results," because he will interpret the tests using standard scores, not grade or age equivalents, or percentiles. As a "seasoned veteran," what kind of advice would you give to Mr. Gregg?

*The answer for question 3 appears in Appendix D.

TYPES OF STANDARDIZED TESTS

In the first part of this chapter we will describe various types of standardized tests with which classroom teachers frequently come into contact. First we will consider the achievement test battery, the single-subject achievement test, and the diagnostic test. Next, we will consider individual and group tests of academic aptitude. Finally, various personality tests that sometimes appear in student records will be described. Our intention is *not* to evaluate or recommend any of these tests. Each of the tests we describe is simply an "accepted" test with satisfactory psychometric (mental measurement) properties. At the same time we do not mean to imply that the tests we have selected are the *only* tests with acceptable psychometric properties. The question is how appropriate is a test for you, your school, or your district. The answer to this question depends on a variety of factors. Several of these test-related factors were discussed in Chapter 18. They will be referred to again in this chapter when we describe a step-by-step process that can be used to evaluate standardized tests and to develop a comprehensive school-wide or district-wide testing program.

STANDARDIZED ACHIEVEMENT TESTS

The first standardized tests came into existence around the turn of the century. These tests were tests of a single achievement area, such as spelling. Single-subject achievement tests are still used today, although they are largely confined to the secondary grades.

A variation of the single-subject achievement test is the diagnostic achievement test. However, use of the diagnostic test is normally limited to those elementary and secondary school pupils who are experiencing academic difficulty. These tests are administered to "diagnose" or indicate the specific cause or causes of a problem (for example, faulty letter identification) in some general academic area (for example, reading recognition). Seldom are such tests administered to an entire class or grade. Typically, students are selected for diagnostic testing after a single-subject test or an achievement battery has indicated a problem in some general academic area.

The most frequently used type of achievement test is the achievement test battery, or survey battery. Such batteries are widely used, often beginning in the first grade and administered each year thereafter. There are several reasons survey batteries are more popular than single-subject achievement tests. The major advantages of survey batteries over single-subject achievement tests are identified here:

1. Each subtest is coordinated with every other subtest resulting in common administration and scoring procedures, common format, and minimal redundancy.
2. Batteries are less expensive and less time consuming to administer than several single-subject tests.
3. Each subtest is normed on the same sample, making comparisons across subtests, both within and between individuals, easier and more valid.

This last point is probably the major reason batteries have come into such widespread use. Recall that we often use standardized tests to compare students, classes, or schools. It takes less time to make these comparisons when a single norm group is involved than when several are involved. Furthermore, the likelihood of clerical errors is minimized when single, comprehensive score reports from a battery are used to make comparisons, as opposed to several single-subject score reports.

Of course, batteries have their disadvantages, too, and these are:

1. The correspondence (content validity) of various subtests in the battery may not be uniformly high.
2. The battery, emphasizing breadth of coverage, may not sample achievement areas in as much depth as a single-subject achievement test.

Nonetheless, most districts conclude that these limitations are offset by the advantages of an achievement battery. Next, we will describe briefly some of the more popular achievement test batteries.

Achievement Test Batteries, or Survey Batteries

California Achievement Test (CAT). This battery is published by CTB/ McGraw-Hill and is appropriate for students in grades 1.5–12. It has five levels appropriate for various grades, and two alternate forms of the test are available. Scores are provided for Reading (vocabulary and comprehension), Language (mechanics, usage, structure, and spelling), and Mathematics (computation, concepts, and problems). The CAT has been standardized simultaneously with the Short Form Test of Academic Aptitude, facilitating identification of aptitude-achievement discrepancies.

Comprehensive Tests of Basic Skills (CTBS). Like the Cat, the CTBS is published by CTB/McGraw-Hill. However, it is appropriate for students in grades K–12. Seven levels of the test are available for students in the various grades, and an alternate form can be obtained. Level A is considered a preinstructional or readiness test and provides scores for Letter Forms, Letter Names, Listening for Information, Letter Sounds, Visual Discrimination, Language, Sound Matching, and Mathematics. Level B provides scores for Reading, Language, Mathematics, and Total Battery. Level B is designed to be administered to pupils who have completed their first year of instruction. The remaining levels, C, 1, 2, 3, and 4, yield scores in Reading, Language, Mathematics, Reference Skills (except for Level C), Science, and Social Studies. A Total Battery score is also provided, composed of Reading, Language, and Mathematics scores. Like the CAT, the CTBS has been standardized simultaneously with the Short Form Test of Academic Aptitude.

Iowa Tests of Basic Skills (ITBS). This battery is published by Houghton-Mifflin. It is appropriate for students in grades 3–9 and thus has more limited applicability than either the CAT or the CTBS. The ITBS was normed on the same sample as the Cognitive Abilities Test, an academic aptitude test. Thus, determination of aptitude-achievement discrepancies is facilitated when these two tests are used. Scores are provided for Vocabulary, Reading Comprehension, Language Skills (spelling, capitalization, punctuation, usage), Work-Study Skills (map reading, reading graphs and tables, knowledge and use of reference materials), and Arithmetic Skills (arithmetic concepts, arithmetic problem solving).

Metropolitan Achievement Tests (MAT). Harcourt Brace Jovanovich publishes this battery, which is appropriate for students in grades K–9. Six levels span the various grades, and two alternate forms of the Primer level and three alternate forms of the other five levels are available. The Primer level includes scores for Listening for Sounds, Reading, and Numbers. The next level, Primary I, includes scores for Word Knowledge, Word Analysis, Reading, Mathematics Computation, and Mathematics Concepts. Primary II includes these plus Spelling and Mathematics Problem Solving. The remaining levels all provide scores for Word Knowledge,

Reading, Language, Spelling, Mathematics Computation, Mathematics Concepts, and Mathematics Problem Solving. In addition, Science and Social Studies scores are available for the two highest levels.

Sequential Tests of Educational Progress (STEP).

This battery is published by the Educational Testing Service. It is appropriate for grades 4–14, consists of four levels, and two alternate forms are available. Scores are provided at the lowest three levels for English Expression, Reading, Mechanics of Writing, Mathematics Computation, Mathematics Basic Concepts, Science, and Social Studies. The highest level of the STEP does not include the Mechanics of Writing and Mathematics Basic Concepts Subtests.

SRA Achievement Series (SRA).

Published by Science Research Associates, the battery is appropriate for students in grades 1–9. Five levels cover the grade range, and no alternate forms are available. The two lowest levels include subtests for Reading (word verbal-picture association, sentence-picture association, comprehension, vocabulary), Mathematics (concepts and computation), and Language Arts (alphabetization, capitalization, punctuation, spelling, and usage). The three highest levels include subtests for Reading (comprehension, vocabulary, total), Language Arts (usage, spelling, total), Mathematics (concepts, computation, total), Social Studies, Science, and Uses of Sources.

Stanford Achievement Test Series.

Like the MAT, this battery is published by Harcourt Brace Jovanovich. It is appropriate for grades 1.5–9.5. Six levels are provided for the various grades and two alternate forms are available. Subtests for Reading, Mathematics, and Language Arts are available at all levels. Except for the lowest level, scores are also provided for Science, Social Studies, and, except at the highest level, Listening Comprehension. A unique feature of the Stanford Achievement Test is that the test is available as either a basic battery, including only the Reading, Mathematics, and Language Arts subtests, or as a complete battery, including all the subtests. Practice tests are also available for all but the highest level.

Single Subject Achievement Tests

Gates-MacGinitie Reading Tests.

This test is published by Teachers College Press. It is appropriate for grades 1–12 and uses seven levels to cover these grades. Two alternate forms are available for the lowest three levels, and three alternate forms are available for the four highest levels. The lower three levels include subtests measuring Vocabulary and Comprehension. The fourth level is actually a subtest to measure reading Speed and Accuracy. The upper three levels contain subtests measuring Vocabulary, Comprehension, and Speed and Accuracy. The formats vary across the levels, with stimuli ranging from pictorial at the lower levels to increasingly complex prose at the higher level. Items measure recognition rather than recall.

Modern Math Understanding Test (MMUT). Published by Science Research Associates, this test is designed for grades 1–9. The three areas of mathematics measured at each level are Foundations, Operations and Geometry, and Measurement. Each of these areas is broken down further into the following: knowledge and computation, elementary understanding, problem solving and application, and structure and generalization.

Nelson Reading Test, Forms 3 and 4, and the Nelson-Denny Reading Test, Forms C and D. These tests are published by Houghton-Mifflin. Forms 3 and 4 are appropriate for grades 3–9, and Forms C and D for grade 9 through college/adult. Each form includes a Vocabulary and a Reading Comprehension subtest. An optional Word Parts test for Form 3 yields scores for Sound-Symbol Correspondence, Root Words, and Syllabication. A Reading Rate subtest is included for Form 4 and Forms C and D.

Diagnostic Achievement Tests

Diagnostic Tests and Self-Helps in Arithmetic. This test is published by CTB/ McGraw-Hill and is designed for use in grades 3–12. The test actually consists of three components: Screening Tests, Diagnostic Tests, and Self-Help exercises. Three screening tests cover Whole Numbers, Fractions, and Decimals and help identify which area or areas require further diagnostic testing, while a fourth screening test is more general and also consists of more difficult items. Its use is generally restricted to secondary students. Dependent on a student's errors in the screening tests, one or more of the following twenty-three diagnostic tests would be administered:

Addition Facts	Subtraction of Like Fractions
Subtraction Facts	Addition of Unlike Fractions
Multiplication Facts	Subtraction of Unlike Fractions
Division Facts	Multiplication of Fractions
Uneven Division Facts	Division of Fractions
Addition of Whole Numbers	Addition of Decimals
Subtraction of Whole Numbers	Subtraction of Decimals
Multiplication of Whole Numbers	Multiplication of Decimals
Division of One-Place Numbers	Division of Decimals
Division of Two-Place Numbers	Percent
Regrouping Fractions	Operation of Measures
Addition of Like Fractions	

Each diagnostic test is also cross-referenced to the others to assist in isolating the difficulty. That is, missing an item such as "$414 \times 361 =$" may be due to an error in adding, placing, or multiplying. By cross-referencing with related diagnostic tests, the examiner is able to determine where in the process the breakdown occurred. The Self-Helps are linked to the diagnostic test items. These provide examples of similar problems worked out in detail and indicate the steps involved in arriving at the correct answers. Pupils are advised to study the examples and then attempt the exercise.

Gates-McKillop Reading Diagnostic Test. Published by Teachers College Press, this text is designed for use at all grade levels. Two forms of the test are available. It is administered individually, and the pupil responds orally. Scores are provided for Oral Reading, Word Perception, Phrase Perception, Blending Word Parts, Giving Letter Sounds, Naming Letters, Recognizing Visual Forms of Sounds of Nonsense Words, Initial Letters, Final Letters, Vowels, Auditory Blending, Spelling, Oral Vocabulary, Syllabication, and Auditory Discrimination. Like the Diagnostic Tests and Self-Helps in Arithmetic, cross-referencing of subtests helps pinpoint weaknesses. However, no estimate of reading comprehension is available, and all scores depend on the pupil's *oral* reading level. At times a pupil's oral reading achievement may be significantly different from his or her silent reading achievement.

Stanford Diagnostic Reading Test. Published by Harcourt Brace Jovanovich, this test is designed for grades 2.5–8.5. Unlike the Gates-McKillop, this test can be group administered with pupils responding on paper. Two levels are provided. The lower level provides scores for Reading Comprehension, Vocabulary, Auditory Discrimination, Syllabication, Beginning and Ending Sounds, Blending, and Sound Discrimination. The higher level battery provides scores for Reading Comprehension (literal, inferential, and total), Vocabulary, Syllabication, Sound Discrimination, Blending, and Rate of Reading.

STANDARDIZED ACADEMIC APTITUDE TESTS

Thus far in this chapter we have discussed tests that are used to measure past achievement. The intent of these tests is to identify what students have learned. At times, however, we are also interested in measuring an individual's potential for learning or an individual's academic aptitude. Such information is useful in making selection and placement decisions and to determine whether students are achieving up to their potential, that is, to indicate aptitude-achievement discrepancies. In short, aptitude tests are used to predict *future* learning. Achievement tests are used to measure *past* learning.

The History of Academic Aptitude Testing

The development of tests to predict school achievement began in France at the beginning of the twentieth century. France had embarked on a program of compulsory education, and the minister of public instruction realized that not all

French children had the cognitive or mental potential to be able to benefit from instruction in regular classes. "Special" classes were to be established for the instruction of such children. Admission to these "special" classes was to be dependent on the results of a medical and psychological evaluation. However, no tests were available at the time that could be used to identify children who had the cognitive or mental potential to benefit from instruction in regular classes. In 1905 Alfred Binet and his assistant, Theo Simon, were commissioned to develop such a test. The aim of their test was to measure a trait that would predict school achievement.

They revised their test in 1908 and again in 1911. The concept of mental age (as opposed to chronological age) as an index of mental development was introduced with the first revision and refined with the second. Since Binet was commissioned to develop a test that would predict school achievement, he was concerned with the predictive validity of his scale and repeatedly studied its validity for use in the public schools.

By the time of his death in 1911, Binet's scale was widely used and heralded as an "intelligence" test. English translations of the 1908 and 1911 revisions were made, and in 1916 a Stanford University psychologist, Louis Terman, standardized the Binet test on American children and adults. This version of the test became known as the Stanford-Binet Intelligence Scale or IQ test, and was revised and/or restandardized again in 1937, 1960, and 1972. Hence what had begun as a test designed to predict *school achievement* had evolved into a test of intelligence.

Since Binet's seminal work, several other "intelligence" or IQ tests have been developed. Some, like the Binet, are designed to be administered individually (for example, Wechsler Intelligence Scale for Children–Revised, Wechsler Adult Intelligence Scale–Revised, Slosson Intelligence Test); others are designed for group administration (for example, Cognitive Abilities Test, Otis-Lennon Mental Ability Test, Kuhlmann-Anderson Intelligence Tests). While each of these tests is different from the Binet, each also has similarities and correlates strongly with the Binet. Recall that tests that correlate strongly measure much the same thing. Recalling that Binet's test predicts school achievement, it is no surprise that both individually and group administered "intelligence" tests also predict school achievement. In short, a test developed to predict school achievement has come to be considered as a test of intelligence.

Why all the fuss? There would be no need for such a fuss if we knew that the tests *actually* measured intelligence. We *do* know they predict academic achievement. But do they measure intelligence? To answer this question, we would need first to define intelligence and then determine whether people who score high on intelligence tests possess more of this "stuff" than people who score low on intelligence tests. Unfortunately, we can't agree on what the "stuff" of intelligence is. Theorists have been hypothesizing and arguing for decades about what intelligence is, and the debate will likely go on for decades more. Consequently, since we do not agree on what "intelligence" is, we cannot be sure we are measuring it. Discussions of definitions and theories of intelligence may be found in most graduate-level measurement tests. For our purposes, we will conclude that the tests mentioned here and others like them, do predict school achievement. We are not at all sure, however, that they are measuring intelligence. Since we are not sure they are measuring intelligence, we are reluctant to call them intelligence tests. We can use such tests intelligently though, by restricting their use to what we know they can do—predict school achievement. Before we review some of the more common of these tests, we will consider two important aspects of the scores such tests yield: their stability, and other characteristics they predict.

Stability of IQ Scores

In general, IQ scores tend to increase in stability with increases in age. In other words, IQ scores for younger children are less reliable or more subject to error than IQ scores for older children and adults. Furthermore, test-retest reliabilities tend to decline as the time interval between test and retest increases. Table 19.1 illustrates these relationships.

As Table 19.1 indicates, little is gained in terms of predicting later performance by administering IQ tests to children less than four years of age. Once children reach the age of about six, their IQ scores tend to remain fairly stable. Remember, this is *not* to say that an individual's obtained score is not likely to change at all, only that changes are likely to be small and not affect much the individual's overall percentile rank in the general population.

What Do IQ Tests Predict?

Academic Achievement. We have said that IQ tests, or tests of academic aptitude, predict school achievement. But just how well they do predict school achievement depends on what we use as an outcome measure. Correlations between IQ tests and standardized achievement tests generally range from .70 to .90. However, correlations between school IQ tests and grades generally range from .50 to .60. Standardized achievement tests tend to be carefully constructed

---

TABLE 19.1 | Approximate Correlations Between Individual IQ Tests and Retests

Age at First Test	Age at Second Test	Approximate Correlation
2	14	.20
4	14	.55
6	14	.70
8	14	.85
10	14	.90

and measure outcomes similar to those measured by academic aptitude tests. Keeping this in mind and realizing that grades tend to be considerably more subjective, it is no surprise that the correlation with grades is somewhat lower. As might be expected, IQ scores also correlate highly with the highest level of schooling completed.

Job Success.

In any criterion-related validity study, the size of the obtained correlation will depend on the particular outcome measure or criterion measure employed. Ghiselli (1966) reported that when completion of a training program is considered as a criterion for job success, moderately strong correlations are found (.38 to .53). However, when the criterion was defined as on-the-job performance, considerably lower correlations were found. These ranged from $-.10$ for sales clerks to .33 for salesmen. In short, tests of academic aptitude appear to be far less effective in predicting job success than they are at predicting academic achievement. Part of the reason for this may be the often subjective nature of the criteria used to rate job success (for example, supervisor's ratings). Just as subjectivity in teacher-assigned grades may lead to a lower correlation between IQ and school performance, subjectivity in determining job success may be responsible for the lower correlation between ratings of job success and IQ test scores.

Emotional Adjustment.

No firm conclusion may be drawn about the relationship between IQ and emotional adjustment. At the beginning of the century, it was commonly held that very high IQ individuals tended to have more severe emotional and adjustment problems than individuals with more "normal" IQs. However, a long-term follow-up (over several decades) of high IQ individuals begun by Terman in 1921 did much to dispel this myth. Current thinking suggests that high IQ individuals have emotional difficulties about as frequently as low to moderate IQ individuals.

Happiness.

Perhaps in part because we do not have a suitable definition or measure of happiness, we do not really know the extent to which IQ scores may predict happiness. Since they do predict school achievement and to a lesser extent job success, we might infer there would be a positive correlation between IQ and happiness. However, such a position is not supported by research and assumes that school and job success are themselves correlated with happiness.

In summary, the characteristic that IQ tests predict most strongly is school achievement. Recall that the first IQ test was developed to predict school achievement. Eighty years later, in spite of repeated attempts to modify and improve on the IQ test, we find that it still does best just what it was designed to do. Although it has been used in a variety of ways, the IQ test remains, first and foremost, a good predictor of school achievement. Whatever else it measures or predicts, it does so far less effectively and efficiently. Our recommendation is to recognize IQ tests for what they are—predictors of school achievement and avoid the tendency to make them into something they are not. In the next section we will describe briefly some of the commonly used group and individually administered IQ tests.

Individually Administered Academic Aptitude Tests

Stanford-Binet Tests of Intelligence. This test is published by Houghton-Mifflin and is appropriate for individuals from ages 2 through adult. The test yields a single IQ score and is comprised of a variety of tasks that require the examinee to respond to concrete pictorial stimuli at the lower age levels and abstract verbal stimuli at the higher age levels. These tasks include requiring recall of past learning, relationship thinking, judgment, interpretation, inference, short-term memory, attention, concentration, and other cognitive skills. The Binet, especially at the upper elementary ages, is a highly verbal test. Since a quantitative or nonverbal IQ score is not available, aptitude-achievement comparisons for math are not nearly as easy as they would be with a test that provided a quantitative IQ score.

Wechsler Intelligence Scale for Children–Revised (WISC-R). This test is published by the Psychological Corporation. It is appropriate for students between six and sixteen years of age. Along with its companion tests, the Wechsler Preschool and Primary Scale of Intelligence (WPPSI) and the Wechsler Adult Intelligence Scale–Revised (WAIS-R), the Wechsler scales are the most popular individually administered IQ tests. They yield Verbal IQ scores, Performance (nonverbal) IQ scores, and Full-Scale IQ scores. Twelve WISC-R subtest scores are also provided:

Verbal	*Performance*
Information	Picture Completion
Similarities	Picture Arrangement
Arithmetic	Block Design
Vocabulary	Object Assembly
Comprehension	Coding
Digit Span (optional)	Mazes (optional)

The Verbal IQ score is the average of the first five verbal subtest scores. The Performance IQ score is the average of the first five performance subtest scores. The Full-Scale IQ score results from all ten of the subtest scores.

Group Administered Academic Aptitude Tests

Cognitive Abilities Tests. Published by Houghton-Mifflin, this test is appropriate for children in grades K–13. It includes a nonreading test at the lowest two levels and eight multi-level tests that provide Verbal, Quantitative, and Nonverbal scores. This test was normed simultaneously with the Iowa Tests of Basic Skills, facilitating aptitude-achievement comparisons. The nonreading test has four subtests: oral vocabulary, relational concepts, multimental, and quantitative. The

Verbal test includes vocabulary, sentence completion, verbal classification, and verbal analogies subtests. The Quantitative test measures quantitative comparisons, number series, and equation building. The Nonverbal subtests eliminate reliance on reading ability entirely. It consists of items to measure figure analogies, figure classification, and figure synthesis.

Otis-Lennon Mental Ability Tests. This test is published by Harcourt Brace Jovanovich and is appropriate for grades K–12. An earlier version of this test is called the Otis Quick-Scoring Mental Ability Test. The test requires as little as thirty minutes to administer at the lower levels and up to fifty minutes at the higher levels. Although this test compares favorably with other IQ tests, a disadvantage is that only a Total IQ score is provided.

Short Form Test of Academic Aptitude (SFTAA). Published by CTB/McGraw-Hill, this test is appropriate for grades 1.5–12.0. Five levels of the test cover the grade range. The SFTAA is a revision of an earlier test called the California Test of Mental Maturity. It yields Language, Non-Language, and Total scores and consists of four subtests: Vocabulary, Analogies, Sequences, and Memory. This test was standardized simultaneously with both the California Achievement Test (CAT) and the Comprehensive Test of Basic Skills (CTBS), thus facilitating aptitude-achievement comparisons.

STANDARDIZED PERSONALITY ASSESSMENT INSTRUMENTS

Of the types of standardized tests with which the classroom teacher comes in contact, personality tests are probably the least used and the least understood. Perhaps this is the way it should be, since teachers are mainly concerned with academic development and are not trained in personality development or assessment. Nonetheless, teachers cannot help but have some impact on and ideas about personality development, and results from such tests do show up in pupil folders. Interpretation of such tests is beyond the scope of this text and the training of classroom teachers. Thus, we will limit ourselves to considering briefly what personality is, the two major approaches to personality assessment, and then describe briefly several examples of personality tests.

What is Personality?

Much like intelligence, no one has arrived yet at a definitive, universally accepted definition of personality. We do know that people tend to behave in certain relatively fixed ways across various situations. One such pattern of typical and expected behavior may be considered to be a personality *trait*. For example, individuals who tend to become nervous or anxious when speaking in front of groups tend to become anxious in any public speaking situation—large or small. A personality trait for such individuals would be anxiety. All of an individual's traits or characteristics, taken together, comprise an individual's personality. Thus, perhaps we can define personality as the typical or characteristic ways individuals behave. This is a deceptively simple definition, however. Allport and Odbert (1936) estimated that the number of typical ways individuals behave is in the *thousands*. If we accept this definition, then, we must admit that the task of measuring these traits would be an enormous one. Nevertheless the task has been approached with considerable success over the last sixty years. Essentially, the efforts to measure personality have moved in two directions: objective personality assessment and projective personality assessment. We will describe each of these and then some examples of each type of assessment instrument.

Objective Personality Assessment.

Objective personality assessment usually employs self-report questionnaires. Items are often based on questions used in psychiatric interviews. The first instrument of this type appeared during World War I. Since then, they have gained considerable popularity among psychologists, the military, and industry. This approach provides a lengthy list of statements, adjectives, or questions to which examinees respond. A variety of formats have been employed, including checklists, true-false, and multiple-choice. Some items are obviously indicative of serious psychopathology, others are much more subtle. In most cases *individual* responses are not that meaningful in the interpretation. Instead, patterns of responses or a profile of scores is relied on for interpretation.

Objective personality instruments have the advantage of being economical to administer. They can be group administered and monitored by a clerk rather than requiring the time and training or a psychiatrist or psychologist for valid administration. Major disadvantages include their sometimes questionable validity, a tendency to mark answers in a safe or socially desirable fashion (thereby perhaps masking certain traits), or attempts to fake a normal or pathological response pattern. This latter point has received extensive attention by personality test developers, and validity scales have been built into some instruments to inform the examiner that responses have been faked.

Projective Personality Assessment.

Projective personality assessment involves requiring examinees to respond to unstructured or ambiguous stimuli (for example, incomplete sentences, inkblots, abstract pictures). The basic theory underlying projective personality testing can be summarized as follows:

1. With the passage of time, response tendencies in various situations tend to become resistant to change and tend to reproduce themselves in the presence of various stimuli.
2. When presented with suggestive or ambiguous stimuli, examinees will respond to them in ways that relate to conscious or unconscious motives, beliefs, or experiences.

3. Projective tests, by presenting stimuli that are suggestive of various aspects of the individual's life (for example, mother-father relationships, the need for achievement) or are ambiguous, will make individuals respond in ways that reflect their conscious or unconscious motives, beliefs, or experiences.

A major advantage of projective over objective tests is that the stimuli are often sufficiently abstract to allow scoring criteria to detect a variety of appropriate and inappropriate behavior. Such techniques may uncover a broader range of psychopathology and allow for the use and interpretation of unique responses. Major disadvantages of projective techniques include questionable validity related to their often complex scoring rules and their expense. Projective personality tests always require administration and scoring by an appropriately trained psychologist or psychiatrist.

Objective Personality Tests

Adjective Checklist. Published by the Consulting Psychologists Press, this instrument is appropriate for individuals in grade nine through adults. It consists of an alphabetical list of adjectives and is usually completed in about 15 minutes. The subject checks those adjectives that are applicable. Scores can be obtained in 24 variables, including self-confidence, self-control, counseling readiness, and various needs and aspects of personal adjustment.

Edwards Personal Preference Schedule (EPPS). This instrument is published by the Psychological Corporation and is appropriate for college students and adults. It is normally completed in 45–50 minutes. Subjects respond by choosing one of a pair of statements that apply to them. Each statement represents a need, and each of these needs is assessed by nine pairs of statements.

Minnesota Multiphasic Personality Inventory (MMPI). Published by the Psychological Corporation, this instrument is appropriate for individuals age 14 through adult. It generally takes about one hour to complete. The MMPI is the most widely used of the objective personality tests and has been in use for over forty years. It requires individuals to respond to 399 statements presented in true-false format. Responses are scored on several scales, including concern for bodily functioning, depression, hysteria, psychopathological tendencies, paranoia, anxiety, schizophrenia, level of mental activity, and social comfort. The MMPI is widely used as a screening instrument in psychiatric, educational, military, industrial, and government institutions.

Myers-Briggs Type Indicator (MBTI). This instrument is published by the Educational Testing Service. It is appropriate for grades nine through adult and requires about one hour to complete. The format is forced-choice and scores are yielded for introversion versus extroversion, sensation versus intuition, thinking versus feeling, and judgement versus perception. The MBTI has been in use for over thirty years and enjoys widespread popularity.

Projective Personality Tests

Rorschach Inkblot Technique.

This test is published by Hans Huber Medical Publisher, Berne, Switzerland. It consists of ten cards or plates. Each card contains an inkblot, some black-and-white, some colored. Examinees are asked to describe what they "see" in the ambiguous blot. Responses are scored according to location, content, and a variety of other factors, including whether form or color was used to construct the image, whether movement is suggested, and whether shading or texture was considered. Scoring is complex, and although acceptable validity data are scant, the Rorschach has been one of the most popular projective tests used by clinical psychologists. In the hands of a skilled clinician it can yield a surprising variety of information.

Thematic Apperception Test (TAT).

Published by the Harvard University Press, the TAT is designed for individuals age ten through adults. Adaptations of the test for younger children (Children's Apperception Test) and senior citizens (Senior Apperception Test) are also available. The subject is presented with a series of pictures (usually ten or twelve of the total of thirty) and asked to make up a story to fit each picture. The pictures vary in degree of structure and ambiguity. The record of stories is then examined to determine the projection of the subject's personality, as indicated by recurrent behavioral themes, needs, perceived pressures, and so on. Interpretation is often complex and requires an appropriately trained psychologist or psychiatrist.

This concludes our discussion of the types of standardized tests. By no means all-inclusive, our presentation of various types of tests has focused on those tests with which the average classroom teacher is most likely to come into contact. In the remainder of this chapter we will discuss how these tests, or tests like them, are evaluated in planning and implementing a comprehensive school or district-wide testing program.

PLANNING A SCHOOL- OR DISTRICT-WIDE TESTING PROGRAM

In the past, the average classroom teacher could be expected to have little, if any, input into the development of a district-wide testing program. In many cases administrators design testing programs without considering the needs and limitations of local schools. Unfortunately, when local school personnel do not have input into decisions concerning a district-wide testing program, are not apprised of the reasons for decisions, and yet are forced to abide by these decisions, resistance is usually encountered. Such resistance may take a variety of forms, including decreased motivation for the testing program—an attitude that may easily be transmitted to students. Furthermore, with the passage of time, an adversarial rather than a collegial relationship often develops between test administrators and local school personnel. The effect of this can be an increase in error in testing and a subsequent decline in the reliability and validity of the assessment.

Fortunately, more and more school districts are working to minimize this us-against-them attitude and are soliciting input from local school personnel in developing and implementing district-wide testing programs. In the future it is more likely than in the past that you will be asked to serve on a committee that will decide your district's testing program. Following we provide a brief, logical approach to guide your participation on such a committee. In fact, it may be the case that you are one of the few individuals on the committee who has a logical approach to the selection of a comprehensive and efficient test battery.

Step 1: Ask the Right Question

All too often the first question asked is "What tests should we use?" In reality such a question is quite premature. The first question to ask is "What is the purpose of our testing?" Defining the purpose makes the remaining steps go much more smoothly and efficiently. A good testing program *matches* the purposes of testing—just like a good item matches the objective it is measuring. Asking the right question also decreases the likelihood that you will simply "borrow" another district's program. While this option is tempting and appears to be a timesaver, it can also backfire in the long run. Not all districts have the same needs or are interested in answering the same questions. Therefore, no one testing program can be all things to all districts. First and foremost, then, consider the purpose or purposes of the testing program, using the selections offered in Table 19.2.

Step 2: Decide on the Purposes for Your Testing Program

At this stage the committee decides which of these purposes are to be filled by the testing program. Obviously, standardized tests need not be included for everyday instructional decisions or grading, as these purposes are already being served by tests constructed within the classroom. In your school or district, one of the other purposes or uses listed in Table 19.2 may not be necessary. For example, there is no point in going through the time and expense of administering a reading readiness test at the end of kindergarten for placement purposes if there is no difference in instructional methods or grouping in the first grade. On the other hand, if students are placed into different groups, depending on readiness scores, and instruction is altered accordingly, then your test is useful for placement, grouping, and instructional planning.

Once the uses or purposes of testing have been identified, the focus of the committee begins to shift to considerations about the tests themselves. These con-

TABLE 19.2 | Purposes of Educational Testing and Types of Tests Appropriate for Each Purpose

Purposes	Appropriate Tests	
	Teacher-made tests	Standardized tests
Classroom:	X	
Grading	X	
Achievement Gains	X	X
Diagnostic	X	X
Grouping	X	X
Instructional Planning	X	X
Aptitude/Achievement Discrepancies		X
Academic Potential		X
Guidance		X
Administrative:		
Selection		X
Placement		X
Special Education Placement		X
Program Evaluation		X
Public Relations		X

siderations are general, relating to the integration of the overall testing program, as well as focused, relating to the specific tests.

Step 3: Consider the Program's Integration

Redundancy. Frequently a district finds itself administering more than one test to measure the same thing or for the same purpose. Such overtesting or redundancy is more likely when tests are required by funding agencies at several levels: district, regional, state, and national. Funding for programs often comes from one or some combination of these sources, and each source wants data to support its funding efforts. Usually, these data take the form of test scores which districts are required to provide to ensure continued funding. To be helpful, each of these sources usually recommends a test or variety of tests that are "acceptable." All too often, schools and districts feel they must use a different test for each source. In reality, the results from a single survey battery may meet the requirements of several funding sources, as well as district feedback and accountability needs. For example, a district may administer the California Achievement Test to determine which schools qualify for Title I funding and the Iowa Test of Basic Skills to meet district needs for feedback about achievement levels. The purpose in each case is to obtain data about achievement levels. There is no reason to administer both batteries. Either one would provide the necessary information.

In other cases, districts get overly test-conscious and seem to test regardless of whether they need it. An example would be districts in which achievement batteries are administered at the beginning *and* at the end of the year. In general, if test results are *not* used, only filed away, overtesting is likely. Worksheet A has been developed to help you minimize redundancy and overtesting.

To use Worksheet A, in Figure 19.1, first list the main purposes of testing identified in Step 2. Next, indicate the grade levels for which the purpose is appropriate (e.g., a reading readiness test would be appropriate in late kindergarten or early first grade). Then indicate the test you currently use or plan to use for each purpose. Afterwards compare the various tests to the purposes to determine whether any of them may serve more than one purpose at the appropriate grade level. After doing so, indicate the test you will retain for each purpose. If you succeed in eliminating even one test, you will save your district much time and money, as well as adding to the amount of time that teachers can spend in teaching rather than testing.

Timing.   A test should fit the purpose of testing, but it should also be administered at the right time to allow maximum use of the test results. If information is needed prior to the beginning of the school year, the right test ought to be administered toward the end of the previous school year, not after school has started. This rather obvious fact is not always considered when testing programs are being

FIGURE 19.1   Worksheet A: Minimizing Redundancy

Purpose of testing	Grade levels	Original test used for this purpose	Possible tests for this purpose	Test retained	Com- ments

planned. The following general guidelines may be referred to in planning a program:

Time of School Year	Purpose of Testing
Early	Selection
	Placement/Grouping
	Diagnostic
Late	Program Evaluation
	Achievement Gains
	Guidance

Time considerations also relate to the frequency of testing. Should tests be administered each year or only in selected years? Nowadays, it is common for districts to administer yearly achievement batteries, readiness tests in kindergarten or first grade, academic aptitude tests in third or fourth grade and again in fifth or sixth grade, and a general aptitude test and interest inventory in eleventh grade.

Continuity.   A well-integrated program will also consider testing as a whole from grade K–12. When test data are accumulated over several years on a pupil, these data become increasingly useful for interpretive purposes. This is especially true if these data are collected from the same battery or batteries of tests. While it is possible to convert scores from the California Achievement Test to equivalent scores from the Iowa Tests of Basic Skills, it is certainly less time consuming and costly to use scores from the same battery for a period of years. Comparisons also are facilitated by retaining the same battery since the comparisons are in relation to the same norm group. Naturally, as tests become dated, or district goals and objectives change over the course of time, it may be necessary to switch batteries to maintain relevance and content validity. We are not advocating sticking with the same battery for fifty years, only that careful thought and consideration be paid to issues like content validity, relevance, and the likelihood of revision in the near future. This latter point is a very practical one. If you are seriously considering switching tests, and the test you want to switch to will be revised in the next year or two, it is probably worth postponing the switch until after the revision. This way you will avoid having to adjust old scores to new scores after the revision. You will have a fresh start and not have to be concerned about revision for several years.

Step 4:Evaluate and Select the Specific Tests

At this stage we are *finally* ready to answer the question "Which tests should we use?" Having completed Worksheet A, we have eliminated redundancy in our program, but now we want to evaluate each test remaining in our program to see not just that it fits the relevant purpose(s) of testing, but that our final selection actually has acceptable psychometric and practical characteristics. Worksheet B will guide us in our evaluation. Should we find that our "final selection" from Worksheet A fails to get acceptable ratings on psychometric or practical grounds, do not despair! This simply means that other comparable tests will have to be evaluated until we find one that has acceptable ratings. Once this is determined, this more appropriate test may be substituted for the "final selection" from Worksheet A and should still meet the purpose(s) of testing met by the previous test. Before considering Worksheet B, however, let's consider where the information necessary to complete the worksheet comes from.

There are several sources of information about standardized tests available, including publishers' test catalogs, *Tests in Print, Mental Measurements Year-books,* and specimen sets.

Publishers' Test Catalogs.

Test catalogs include all tests a publisher offers, usually with a variety of descriptive information, such as subtest names, content covered, appropriate age and grade levels, administration time, number of forms and levels, cost, scoring services and reports available, and limited psychometric information. Publishers' catalogs are designed to present tests favorably and are often less than objective in their presentations. Nonetheless, they are one way to familiarize yourself with the variety of tests available and get an idea of whether a test is likely to fit your district's instructional emphasis.

Tests in Print.

Tests in Print is a reference book that lists most of the tests in use today, the names and addresses of the publishers, and somewhat less descriptive information than is available from publishers' catalogs. However, it is unbiased in presenting this information. *Test in Print* is a comprehensive reference. Much of the practical information you may need about tests is available in this single volume, saving you the trouble of having to leaf through many catalogs.

Mental Measurements Yearbooks.

Mental Measurements Yearbooks is a set of eight comprehensive reference books about tests, covering virtually all tests published over the last several decades. The yearbooks contain critical reviews of the tests by knowledgeable and respected reviewers, such as measurement specialists and educational psychologists. They also contain summaries of test reviews published in professional journals and other sources. The reviews give you the benefit of an expert's appraisal of each test's strengths and weaknesses. This probably is the best source for accurate and critical information about both the test's psychometric and practical characteristics.

Specimen Sets.

A specimen set includes a copy of the test booklet, answer sheet, administrator's manual, and technical manual. These enable you to examine first-hand the test format, content validity for your school or district, and other factors. Before ordering hundreds or thousands of tests, it makes sense to order an inexpensive specimen set for any tests under consideration.

Usually, information will be gleaned from several or all these sources in evaluating a standardized test. Let's turn to Worksheet B.

| FIGURE 19.2 | Worksheet B: Test Evaluation/Comparison Form |

Purpose: _____

Test name from Worksheet A	Content validity	Reliability	Norms	Costs	Time and ease of administration	Alternative form	Chance of revision

Worksheet B, in Figure 19.2, is almost self-explanatory. First, jot down the purpose for testing then put down the name of the test under consideration. Completing the remainder of the form involves rating the test for each column. How you rate the tests on each dimension is up to you. You might use a two-point scale (acceptable/not acceptable) or some five-point scale. What is important is that you consider each dimension, especially content validity. To provide the information that will enable you to rate the test, use one or more of the sources already described. Remember, should your "final selection" from Worksheet A be rated unacceptable, substitute another comparable test (the tests we reviewed earlier in this chapter might provide you with some possibilities) and rate it. After reviewing several tests, you may find that none is acceptable in all dimensions—but certainly one will be more acceptable than the others. This should be your final choice for the purpose stated.

Step 5: Develop a Specific and a District-Wide Testing Schedule

Although you have evaluated your tests and selected your final package, you still need to plan the specific testing schedules for each test and a general coordinated testing schedule for the district. Such planning should be completed long *before* the beginning of the school year. This will enable copies of the schedule to be sent out to school personnel for their consideration and input at the beginning of the school year. Remember our initial point—all too often such input and consideration is neglected, resulting in resistance to the testing program. If you've gone through all the time and effort of planning such a program, take a bit more time to check it out with other local school personnel, which should result in better co-operation and a smooth test administration and collection period. While no particular format is perfect for all specific and district-wide schedules, Worksheet C, Figure 19.3, is offered as one example. All you need to do is fill in the tests and dates.

This completes our step-by-step approach to planning a comprehensive and efficient school or district-wide testing program. It also completes our discussion of standardized tests. Next, we will turn to testing and evaluating the handicapped child in the regular classroom.

FIGURE 19.3 | Worksheet C: District-Wide and Specific Testing Schedule

District-Wide Testing Schedule

Grade	Test	Test Materials to Schools	Testing Dates	Answer Sheets Collected
1				
2				
3				
4				
5				
6				
7				
8				
9				
10				
11				
12				

Specific Testing Schedule—Test

Task	Due Date
1. Order tests and materials.	
2. Distribute materials and instructions.	
3. Distribute general testing schedules.	
4. Train testers and proctors.	
5. Arrange for scoring.	
6. Train teachers in interpretation.	
7. Administer tests.	
8. Collect tests and score them.	
9. Distribute results.	
10. Prepare and distribute reports.	

SUMMARY

This chapter has described various types of standardized tests, reviewed briefly examples of each type, and presented you with a step-by-step approach to follow in planning a school or district-wide standardized testing program. Its major points were:

1. The survey battery is the type of achievement test most frequently used today.
2. The main advantages of a survey battery over several single-subject tests are:
   a. Coordinated subtests
   b. Savings in time and expense
   c. A common norm group
3. The disadvantages are that:
   a. Content validity may vary across subtests.
   b. Depth of coverage may be less than that obtained with a single-subject test.
4. Single-subject achievement tests are mainly used in the secondary grades.
5. Diagnostic achievement tests are usually administered only to selected students who have already exhibited difficulties in achievement.
6. Academic aptitude or IQ tests are used to predict future learning; achievement tests measure past learning.
7. Academic aptitude tests were initially developed about eighty years ago to predict school performance, but came to be known as intelligence tests. Today, they still do a good job of predicting school performance.
8. After about age six, IQ scores tend to be fairly stable for the remainder of an individual's life. Prior to age six, and especially during the first few years of life, they tend to be unstable.
9. One definition of *personality* is the typical and characteristic ways people behave.
10. The objective approach to personality assessment relies on self-report questionnaires that are economical but suffer from questionable validity, social desirability, and faking.
11. Projective personality assessment is based on the theory that when individuals are presented with suggestive or ambiguous stimuli, these stimuli will elicit responses that are fairly rigid and reflective of conscious or unconscious motives, beliefs, or wishes.
12. Projective tests are more flexible than objective personality tests but suffer from questionable validity and greater expense.
13. In planning a school or district-wide testing program the following steps are recommended:
    a. Ask the right question (What are the purposes of testing?)
    b. Decide on the purposes of testing
    c. Consider the program's integration (redundancy, timing, and continuity)
    d. Evaluate and select specific tests
    e. Develop a district-wide testing schedule

For Discussion

1. Identify two advantages and two disadvantages of standardized tests.
2. Discuss some of the ways IQ scores should be used and some of the ways they should not be used. Give specific examples.
3. Describe the advantages and disadvantages of objective versus projective personality tests. If your personality were being measured, which would you choose?
4. For two standardized achievement tests of your own choosing, find the information that is required to complete Worksheet B. Which of these two tests would you recommend as the better one for the purpose stated?

20
CHAPTER

TESTING AND MEASURING THE HANDICAPPED CHILD IN THE REGULAR CLASSROOM

The purpose of this chapter is to acquaint you with the field of special education, especially as it relates to the testing and measurement skills of the regular classroom teacher. The field of special education has undergone tremendous change in the past decade, and this change is being felt in almost every sector of the school and the community.

While new developments have stirred innovation and change within the field of special education, they have also presented a challenge to general educators. Specifically, new laws and policies governing the handicapped have made the regular classroom teacher more aware of and more actively involved in the work of the special educator. These new laws and policies also have implications for the testing and measurement skills of the regular classroom teacher. Therefore, we begin this chapter by reviewing some of the recent events in the field of special education that have led up to these new laws and policies and then indicate specifically how the testing and measurement skills of the regular classroom teacher play a role in their implementation.

SPECIAL EDUCATION: RECENT HISTORY

Even before the relatively recent changes in the laws and policies governing the education of the handicapped, the field of special education had experienced tremendous growth in its programs and services. It has been noted that one effect of both world wars was to promote greater social acceptance of the handicapped. As disabled veterans returned home to regain productive and socially respectable roles, federal and state programs grew to facilitate their readjustment and employment. These programs were eventually extended to other, nonveteran handicapped groups, laying the foundation for our modern era of special services for the handicapped.

Along with the relaxation of social stereotypes of the handicapped in the postwar era came the establishment of organizations for parents of the handicapped. Prior to this period in history, parents of handicapped children were beleaguered not only with the psychological problems of adjusting to the presence of the handicapped child, but also with the anxieties and guilt accompanying negative social valuation of the handicapped child. Parents of the handicapped became organized specifically for the purpose of obtaining recognition of and appropriate educational services for their children. Out of these organizations grew strong national movements, such as the National Association of Retarded Citizens and the United Cerebral Palsy Association, which are still recognized today as influential in stimulating the allocation of federal and state resources to research, services, and personnel training for the handicapped. Today, parent associations remain powerful in influencing services to practically every handicapped child subgroup.

Between 1948 and 1958 the number of mentally retarded children alone in public schools more than doubled, as did the number of programs for these pupils. By 1956 all states had laws pertaining to education of handicapped children and were engaged in funding local school programs. During the 1960s, additional federal legislation was enacted and financial support provided for research, demonstration programs, and teacher training. The Council for Exceptional Children, founded in 1922, underwent rapid growth, which supported a greater facilitating role for this organization in the development of programs and services at the national level. This growing federal involvement was highlighted in 1968 with the establishment of the Bureau of Education for the Handicapped, a separate federal agency with its own budget and programs.

Critical Court Cases

In the decades of rapid expansion and change in special education, conflicts inevitably arose among parents, professionals, and governing authorities regarding the most effective and appropriate programs for all handicapped children. These conflicts moved special education into the arenas of litigation and legislation, and several important court cases since 1950 have shaped significantly the present pattern of services. As we will see, these cases also have had considerable influence in shaping the role of general education in providing instruction to the handicapped.

Although specific litigation relating to educational rights of handicapped children did not emerge until the early 1970s, the foundation for interpretation of constitutional principles in special education cases was laid in what may be the landmark civil rights case of this century. *Brown vs. the Topeka, Kansas, Board of Education* represented the Supreme Court response to four similar cases brought on behalf of black children seeking admission to the public schools of their community on a nonsegregated basis. In his delivery of the Court's opinion, Chief Justice Warren stated:

> Today, education is perhaps the most important function of state and local governments. Compulsory school attendance laws and the great expenditure for education both demonstrate our recognition of the importance of education to our democratic society. It is required in the performance of our most basic public responsibilities, even service in the armed forces. It is the very foundation of good citizenship. Today it is a principal instrument in awakening the child to cultural values, in preparing him for later professional training, and in helping him adjust normally to his environment. In these days it is doubtful that any child may reasonably be expected to succeed in life if he is denied the opportunity of an education. Such an opportunity, where the state has undertaken to provide it, is a right which must be made available to all on equal terms. [Futhermore,] we conclude that in the field of public education the doctrine of separate but equal has no place. Separated educational facilities are inherently unequal. Therefore, we hold the plaintiffs . . . are, by reason of the segregation complained of, deprived of the equal protection of the laws guaranteed by the Fourteenth Amendment. (Kirp & Yudof, 1974, pp. 294–95)

The turbulent period of the late 1950s and early 1960s proved that even Supreme Court decisions can be mitigated by other powerful social institutions, including the public schools. Over a decade of social action and litigation were required before relatively stable mechanisms existed to guarantee Fourteenth Amendment rights of minority children in schools across the land, and even more time elapsed before these rights were extended to the handicapped. As activism on behalf of handicapped children grew in the decades of the 1950s and 1960s, schools were beginning to come to grips with Constitutional equal opportunity and due process issues relating to the educational rights of handicapped children.

Prior to the 1970s, most state and local public school programs exercised the option to serve or not to serve handicapped children in their programs. As a result, segregation or outright exclusion of such children was common on the grounds that no services were available that could benefit them in the public schools. A gradual reversal of this trend, on the basis of Fourteenth Amendment principles, was initiated in 1971 in the case of *Pennsylvania Association of Retarded Children vs. the Commonwealth of Pennsylvania.* The decision in this case held, in essence, that the state was obligated to provide mentally retarded children an appropriate program of public school education and training. The decision was based on equal protection and due process provisions, as was the *Brown* case. A section of the opinion foreshadowed some of the reasoning of subsequent legislation:

It is the Commonwealth's obligation to place each mentally retarded child in a free, public program of education and training appropriate to the child's capacity, within the context of a presumption that, among the alternative programs of education and training required by statute to be available, placement in a regular public school class is preferable to placement in any other type of program of education and training. (*Pennsylvania Association for Retarded Children vs. Commonwealth of Pennsylvania*, 334 F. Supp. 1257, E.D. Pa. 1971)

Immediately following the *Pennsylvania* decision in 1972, a similar case was brought from the District of Columbia. *Mills vs. the Board of Education* sought to extend the right of free and appropriate education to all handicapped children, not just the mentally retarded. These included children labeled as behavioral problems, hyperactive, emotionally disturbed, blind, deaf, and speech or learning disabled. The plaintiffs argued that the school district had denied such children not merely an equal education, but in fact any education at all, while providing free education to other children of the District. Of particular concern was the reassignment or expulsion of children without a hearing, as required by due process standards. The court ruled in favor of the plaintiffs, thus including all types of handicapped children in the judicial interpretation of the Fourteenth Amendment.

Other important federal cases in the late 1960s and early 1970s contributed still further to the content of current law. *Hobson vs. Hansen* (1969) represented a challenge to the pupil classification or tracking system in the District of Columbia public schools. Of special concern here was the observed concentration of minority and disadvantaged children in the "special remedial" and "compensatory" tracks. The main thrust of the decision in this case established that the tracking system tended to deprive children of their rights to equal educational opportunity, and equal protection and due process of law in assignment to special groups:

It has been assumed here that [ability] grouping can be reasonably related to the purposes of public education. [However,] the track system—as administered by the District of Columbia public schools—has become a system of discrimination founded on socioeconomic and racial status rather than ability. (Kirp & Yudof, 1974, p. 682)

Issues of particular concern to the court were the physical segregation of students, the disparity of educational opportunity, and the kinds of tests used in assigning students to tracks. The court's remedy was to abolish altogether the tracking system in that school district, thus providing the forerunner of what would become known as *mainstreaming*—or the practice of placing the handicapped child in the regular classroom.

A more specific treatment of student classification and labeling followed soon after *Hobson.* In the case of *Larry P. vs. Riles,* a number of black elementary school children asked the California circuit court to issue an injunction preventing the San Francisco school district from using IQ tests to place any black children in special classes for the "educable mentally retarded." Plaintiffs claimed that, because the IQ tests themselves were biased, use of such tests for placement purposes constituted a violation of their Fourteenth Amendment rights. In rendering its opinion, the court demonstrated concern over several important dimensions of the case. Of most concern was the disproportionate numbers of minority children in educable mentally retarded classes, relative to their numbers in the general population. Also, concern was expressed over probable injury to students incorrectly placed, owing to lower teacher expectations for retarded children, risks of peer group rejection and resulting feelings of inferiority in children so placed, and risks of later damage due to the recording of such placement on school records accessible to colleges, prospective employers, and the military. Since evidence supported the conclusion that the IQ test was the most important consideration in placement of children in special classes, the court ruled in favor of the plaintiffs, stating:

> It is hereby ordered that defendants be restrained from placing black students in classes for the educable mentally retarded on the basis of criteria which place primary reliance on the results of IQ tests . . . if the consequences of use of such criteria is racial imbalance in the composition of such classes. (Kirp & Yudof, 1974, pp. 666–67)

Public Law 94–142

It remained for Congress to put the piecemeal statements of handicapped children's educational rights derived from the courts into a coherent national legislative program. A major issue was the millions of handicapped children in the country who were excluded from public education, receiving educational services in inappropriate settings, or receiving services at the unnecessary expense of their families. Also at issue were the futures of children perhaps destined for institutional care at great taxpayer expense, children who might otherwise become partially self-sustaining with the provision of appropriate education. The result of all these concerns was Public Law (PL) 94-142, the Education for All Handicapped Children Act of 1974.

This new law greatly extended the scope and impact of all previous legislation regarding the handicapped. Specifically, it added new provisions mandating the provision of *free* public education to *all* handicapped children, the expansion of the federal role in financing special education, and the creation of enforcement machinery to assure compliance with the law. For the first time it was made clear that failure to comply with, or to work toward compliance of, the provisions of PL 94-142 would result in the loss of *all* federal funds to a school system. Furthermore, the law placed enforcement responsibility not in the hands of the U.S. Office of Education, but in the hands of the U.S. Office of Civil Rights, which is empowered to investigate complaints and arbitrate compliance issues. Thus, PL 94-142 was vastly strengthened over preceding legislation.

Many professionals and members of the handicapped community have rightly regarded PL 94-142 as a landmark piece of legislation in the history of education for handicapped children. In an important sense, this law has pulled together many vitally important, yet disparate and fragmented social policy initiatives generated by parents and professionals acting in piecemeal fashion through state and federal courts and state legislatures. The intent of this law is highly focused: to guarantee the right of a free, appropriate program of public school education to all handicapped children in the nation. Backing up this intent are federal commitments to evaluate a school district's compliance with the law, enforce its compliance with federal dollars, and discourage noncompliance through well-defined mechanisms of investigation and enforcement.

THE FIELD OF SPECIAL EDUCATION AND THE REGULAR CLASSROOM TEACHER

Since the enactment of PL 94-142, "public education for all" has come to mean the responsibility to provide for every child of school age programs and services that are appropriate to his or her educational needs. PL 94-142 extends to all handicapped children of school age our basic constitutional right to be educated and, beyond this, ensures that the public education that the handicapped child receives will be in the least restrictive environment compatible with his or her educational needs. The special education profession and the public schools have chosen to interpret PL 94-142 as a mandate to provide minimally restrictive educational and supportive services to the handicapped, whenever possible, in the context of the regular school program. Thus, the significance of this law for the regular classroom teacher is profound: for some types of handicaps and for some instructional objectives, the regular classroom will be the least restrictive alternative for meeting the educational needs of the handicapped.

The accumulative effect of the changes of the past decade on the education of the handicapped can be noted in Figure 20.1. All handicapping conditions considered, it can be noted that approximately 67 percent of handicapped children were provided their *primary* educational services in the regular classroom. While separate classes continue to be the predominant placement for mentally retarded children, Figure 20.1 reveals that the proportion whose *primary placement* was in the regular classroom during the 1977–78 school year was approximately 37 percent. This is a substantial increase from the post–World War II era, when mentally retarded children were almost exclusively served in separate classes, if their condition was mild or moderate, or in separate facilities, if their disability was severe.

Over the past few decades handicapped students have been classified and defined in a number of ways. New definitions of handicapping conditions will continue to evolve as more and more becomes known about this subgroup of

FIGURE 20.1 ▌ Environments in Which 3- to 21-year-old Handicapped Students Were Served During the 1977–78 School Year

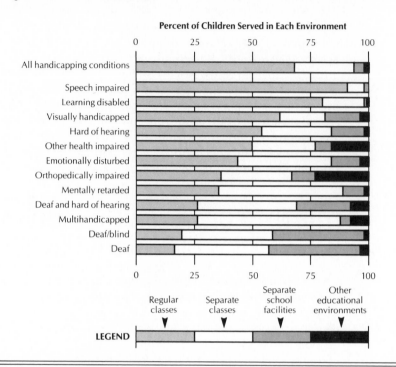

Percent of Children Served in Each Environment

Source: U.S. Office of Education, *Progress toward a free appropriate public education, a report to Congress on the implementation of P.L. 94-142: The Education for All Handicapped Children Act.* O.E. Publication No. 79-05003 H.E. 19.117/2:979 (January 1979).

school children. However, before the significance of a handicapping condition for public school instruction can be discussed, the question that must be asked is "What kind of handicap?" For this question, a number of categories of handicapping conditions have been identified to indicate the types of special services and instruction most appropriate to a handicapped child. These categories usually include the physically handicapped, auditorially handicapped, visually handicapped, mentally retarded, emotionally disturbed, learning disabled, speech handicapped, autistic, and multiply handicapped, which are described in Figure 20.2.

The purpose of these categories, however, is not to label the handicapped child but to identify specific students whose physical, emotional and/or cognitive functions are so impaired from any cause that they cannot be adequately or safely educated without the provision of special services. Although these special services are the direct responsibility of the special education program within a school, the regular classroom teacher is expected to provide a contributory and supportive role in the provision of these services. One of the main features of this contributory and supportive role is the acquisition, reporting, and interpretation

FIGURE 20.2   Categories of Handicapping Conditions

Physically Handicapped
Students whose body functions or members are impaired by congenital anomaly and disease or students with limited strength, vitality, or alertness due to chronic or acute health problems.

Auditorially Handicapped
Students who are hearing impaired (hard of hearing) or deaf.

Visually Handicapped
Students who, after medical treatment and use of optical aids, remain legally blind or otherwise exhibit loss of critical sight functions.

Mentally Retarded
Students with significantly subaverage general intellectual functioning existing concurrent with deficiencies in adaptive behavior. Severity of retardation is sometimes indicated with the terms *profound, trainable,* and *educable.* Generally, only some students who are *educable* are placed in the regular classroom.

Emotionally Disturbed
Students who demonstrate an inability to build or maintain satisfactory interpersonal relationships, who develop physical symptoms or fears associated with personal or school problems, who exhibit a pervasive mood of unhappiness under normal circumstances or who show inappropriate types of behavior under normal circumstances.

Learning Disabled
Students who demonstrate a significant discrepancy between academic achievement and intellectual abilities in one or more of the areas of oral expression, listening comprehension, written expression, basic reading skills, reading comprehension, mathematical calculation, mathematics reasoning, or spelling, which is not the result of some other handicap.

Speech Handicapped
Students whose speech is impaired to the extent that it limits the communicative functions.

Autistic
Students with severe disturbances of speech and language, relatedness, perception, developmental rate, or motion.

Multiply Handicapped
Students who have any two or more of the handicapping conditions described above.

of data pertaining to the performance of the handicapped child in the regular classroom. Judgments from structured observations and anecdotal records of the handicapped child in the regular classroom as well as from formal test scores are typical of the types of data you may be expected to provide special educators. Regular classroom teachers can be expected to contribute individual performance data on the handicapped children in their classrooms for use in implementing any one or combination of the special services required by PL 94-142, which include the services of child identification, individual assessment, Individual Educational Plan (IEP) development, individualized instruction, and review of the Individualized Educational Plan.

Child Identification

Child identification consists of a school or school district's procedures for identifying handicapped children who are in need of special education. Students needing special education services may never have entered school or could be among those students attending school in need of special services but who have not been identified as handicapped. It is in the identification of these students that you may be expected to play an important role.

One stage of this identification is the referral process by which a child comes into contact with and is recommended for special services. While referrals may be made by parents, physicians, community agencies, and school administrators as a result of district-wide testing or screening, students may also be recommended for special services by you. For students who are currently enrolled in regular education, you will be the most likely individual to identify students with needs for special services. In such cases you will become a liaison between the child and the special education staff within a school. In this capacity it will be your responsibility for accumulating and reporting to qualified personnel data that can accurately portray:

1. The student's current educational status, including attendance records, grades, achievement data, and written accounts of classroom observation
2. Previous instructional efforts and strategies provided the student and the result of those efforts
3. Data about the child reported or provided to the teacher by parents.

Referrals are processed through a referral committee which usually includes the professional who recommends the child for special services, the building principal or designated representative, a special educator, a school psychologist and/or educational diagnostician, and the classroom teacher or any other individual who has knowledge of the student's performance and the placement alternatives available. The purpose of the committee is to reach a decision (usually in writing) regarding the educational alternatives appropriate to the child. Obviously, it is important that you not only play a prominent role on this committee when you are recommending a child for special services but that the data provided by you in support of special services be valid, reliable, and accurate. This can only be accomplished by applying sound measurement principles and by selecting the data that most accurately characterize the child's need for particular kinds of services.

An example of one of the many measurement skills you will need in helping identify students who may be in need of special services concerns the distinction between the slow learner and the learning disabled. Slow learners are not included among those considered for special education services under PL 94-142 but instead represent another subpopulation of students who may be recommended for remedial programs, Title I programs, or other supplementary programs that may be available in a school or school district. *Learning disabled,* on the other hand, is a distinction that is included within the population of students for whom PL 94-142 is intended. A student who is learning disabled is one who has been determined by a multidisciplinary team not to be achieving commensurate with his or her age and ability levels. This designation is used when a lack of achievement is found in oral expression, listening comprehension, written comprehension, basic reading skills, reading comprehension, mathematics calculation, mathematic reasoning, and/or spelling, after appropriate learning experiences appropriate to the student's age and ability level have been provided. Generally, the term *learning disabled* does not include students whose severe discrepancy between ability and achievement is primarily the result of some other handicapping condition (for example, hearing impairment or mental retardation) or is solely the result of environmental, cultural, or economic disadvantage.

A discrepancy between intellectual ability and academic achievement that is severe enough to qualify a student as learning disabled is generally considered to be one in which

1. The student's assessed intellectual functioning is above the mentally retarded range, but where the student's assessed educational functioning in one or more of the areas specified is greater than one standard deviation below the mean for the school district, or
2. The student's assessed educational functioning is greater than one standard deviation below the student's intellectual functioning.

Generally, when a student's educational performance is below the mean of the district, but consistent with the student's intellectual functioning, the student is not classified as learning disabled. You may recall from Chapter 18 that this reasoning is consistent with the rationale we have employed to identify significant aptitude-achievement discrepancies.

As can be noted from the previous description, many measurement decisions are required in making such a designation for a particular child. Although this designation is made cooperatively by a multidisciplinary team, comprising regular teachers, special educators, school administrators and special service staff, such as counselors, psychologists, and diagnosticians, you will be expected to be knowledgeable about the validity, reliability, and accuracy of the tests from which the discrepancies between achievement and academic aptitude are derived. Also, as the sole source of a recommendation that a particular child be examined for a potential learning disability, your "preassessment" of a potential handicap must not only be derived from valid, reliable, and accurate classroom data, but also must be consistent with the measurement distinctions made between "slow learners" and those who may be properly designated as having a learning disability. In other words, the classroom teacher who continually refers "slow learners" to the multidisciplinary team or who fails to take note of the learning disabled student among slow learners in his or her classroom will be neither a respected nor knowledgeable member of the multidisciplinary team.

Individual Assessment

A second process to which you may be expected to contribute is individual child assessment. Individual assessment is the collecting and analyzing of information about a student in order to identify an educational need in terms of

1. The presence or absence of a physical, mental, or emotional disability,
2. The presence or absence of a significant educational need, and
3. The identification of specific learning competencies of the student together with specific instructional or related services that could improve and maintain the student's competencies.

Although the individual assessment of a child's capabilities falls within the responsibilities of certified professionals who have been specifically trained in assessing the handicapped, you can and often will be expected to corroborate the findings of these professionals with performance data from the classroom. The corroborative data you can be expected to provide fall into the following categories:

> language
> physical
> emotional/behavioral
> sociological
> intellectual

The data you provide in these categories will be used to complete individual assessment reports of the type shown in Figure 20.3. This one is from the admission, review, and dismissal committee, composed of members of the multidisciplinary team. First and foremost among these data are formal and informal indications taken from workbooks, homework assignments, weekly and unit tests, and classroom observation as to the student's language dominance and proficiency in both the expressive and receptive domains. Often, your observation and recording of these data will suggest to special educators the validity of the standardized tests that may have been given to the student and whether they may have been given in a language other than that in which the child is dominant.

Corroborative data pertaining to the physical attributes of the student can also be recorded. Only you may be in a position to observe on a daily basis the ability of the child to manipulate objects necessary for learning, to remain alert and attentive during instruction, and to control bodily functions in a manner conducive to instruction. In some instances you may provide the only data available as to the physical ability of the child to benefit from regular class instruction.

You can also provide useful data about the emotional behavior of the handicapped child. These data may be derived from standardized behavior checklists,

FIGURE 20.3 | Individual Assessment Data from the Admission, Review and Dismissal Committee Report

Admission, Review, and Dismissal (ARD) Committee Report
Page 3

Student _Miller, Jeremy_

ID# _072431_

II. INDIVIDUAL EDUCATIONAL PLAN
(as noted on page 1 of this report)

A. Present Levels of Competencies:
(Complete AREAS as appropriate)

*Specify name as appropriate; may include Norm-Referenced Tests, Curriculum/Performance-Based and Criterion-Referenced Tests, and Teacher Observation(s).

	Eval. Date	Eval. Method Data Source*	Grade/Age Level	Severe Discrep.	Information on Current Functioning (include information on strengths/weaknesses as appropriate)
MATHEMATICS CALCULATION					Jeremy is functioning on grade level in math. He is currently learning subtraction of 2-digit numbers with borrowing. This is an area of strength for him.
REASONING					
READING BASIC SKILLS	10/15/85	Woodcock/Johnson Teacher Informal Inventory	1.0	✓	Reading is an area of weakness for Jeremy. He is currently functioning below grade level in both comprehension and skills in reading.
COMPREHENSION	10/15/85	Woodcock/Johnson Teacher Informal Inventory	1.0	✓	
SPELLING/WRITTEN EXPRESSION	10/15/85	T.O.W.L. Brigance	P	✓	Jeremy has difficulty both orally and manually producing correct spelling. He is unable to write a complete sentence with correct capitalization and punctuation.
OTHER: _____					
PRE-VOC/ VOCATIONAL					Indicate skills which may be prerequisite to participation in vocational education.
PHYSICAL	10/18/85	Health History Inventory O.T. Assessment	Below Age Level		Indicate physical abilities/disabilities which would affect participation in instructional settings or in P.E. Jeremy's fine motor coordination is not adequately developed for his age. It hinders his ability to learn writing skills.
SPEECH/LANGUAGE	10/18/85	Language Sample - Speech Therapy Assessment	Below Age Level		Jeremy's language development is below average. He has a significant need for articulation instruction. This weakness currently impedes his performance in oral expression.
INTELLECTUAL/ DEVELOPMENTAL	10/15/85	WISC-R	Average Range		Jeremy's performance on the WISC-R indicates that he is of average intelligence for his age.
SOCIAL/ BEHAVIORAL	10/15/85	Informal Assessment Parent + Teacher Reports			Indicate behaviors which would affect educational placement, programming or discipline. Jeremy is a cooperative student. He gets along well with both peers and adults. This is an area of strength for him.

FOR EMOTIONALLY DISTURBED STUDENTS ONLY -- AS NOTED IN THE ASSESSMENT REPORT (Date:_____) one or more of the following characteristics have been exhibited over a long period of time, have occurred to a marked degree, and have adversely affected his/her educational performance:

___ an inability to learn which cannot be explained by intellectual, sensory or health factors;
___ an inability to build or maintain satisfactory interpersonal relationships with peers/teachers;
___ inappropriate types of behavior or feelings under normal circumstances;
___ a general pervasive mood of unhappiness or depression; or
___ a tendency to develop physical symptoms or fears associated with personal or school problems.

Date of Meeting: _10-24-85_

in-class structured observations, anecdotal records, adaptive behavior scales, sociograms, and student-teacher interactions that have been designed either to corroborate the need for special services or to monitor the progress of the child in the regular classroom. Several of these sources of data were discussed in Chapters 10 and 11.

A fourth area in which you may be expected to provide data pertains to the sociological and environmental influences on the child which may, in part, influence the child's classroom behavior. Sociological data about a child are often obtained through communications with the family and knowledge of the circumstances leading up to and/or contributing to the student's intellectual and emotional behavior. The extent to which the child's home life and out-of-school support and services contribute to the educative function can provide an important adjunct to in-school data.

Finally, there is the student's intellectual functioning as demonstrated by verbal and nonverbal performance and by the child's behavior. Although verbal and nonverbal behavior is usually assessed by professionals certified in special education, you may be asked to provide corroborating data pertaining to the child's adaptive behavior. Adaptive behavior is the degree to which the student meets standards of personal independence and social responsibility expected of his or her age and cultural group. Within the context of the classroom, you will have many opportunities to observe the social functioning of the child and gain insights into the appropriateness of this functioning, given the age range and cultural milieu in which the child operates. In fact, you may be the only individual in a position to provide trustworthy data about this side of the handicapped child's social and interactive behavior.

All of the data discussed here are the responsibility of certified teaching and support personnel within a school or school district. These personnel may include educational diagnosticians, school psychologists, counselors, special educators, and, of course, the regular classroom teacher. Although each of these individuals has responsibility for only those parts of the overall assessment to which he or she is assigned and qualified, it would not be an overstatement to say that with PL 94-142 and the widespread concern for the educational needs of the handicapped, contributions of the regular classroom teacher to the overall assessment of the child will not be taken lightly. As can be noted from the previous list of data, the regular classroom teacher will be expected to make a considerable contribution to determining the educational needs of children whose constitutionally guaranteed right to education may require special services. This contribution may be in the form of either corroborating the findings of other professionals or as a source of data whose unique day-to-day contact with the child allows for observation and assessment unequaled by other school personnel.

Individual Educational Plan Development

A third stage in which you may become involved in the implementation of PL 94-142 is in helping develop the Individual Educational Plan (IEP) for each handicapped student in your classroom. A student receives special education services only after a multidisciplinary team, usually comprising a special educator, regular classroom teacher, school psychologist, school administrator, and, when possible, a parent, has reviewed data from the comprehensive assessment. As noted, data from this assessment are expected to address the language, physical, emotional/behavioral, sociological, and intellectual functioning of the child. If from this assessment it is determined that the student has a physical, mental, or emotional disability that establishes his or her eligibility to receive special education services, an IEP is written to state short- and long-term objectives for the instructional and related services to be delivered to the child and to specify the least restrictive environment in which the instruction is to take place. A portion of an Individual Educational Plan is shown in Figure 20.4.

The IEP developed for each student by the multidisciplinary team generally includes:

1. A statement of the student's present competencies taken from the overall assessment data, which generally includes:
   a. The competencies of the student in academic content areas or his or her developmental skills level.
   b. The physical abilities and disabilities exhibited by the student, which could affect his or her participation in instructional settings, including, for example, physical education and vocational education.
   c. Social, emotional, and psychological behaviors demonstrated by the student and which affect his or her educational program.
2. A statement of long-term (annual) and short-term (weekly, monthly) instructional objectives. Short-term instructional objectives represent intermediate steps designed to lead the student to the achievement of end-of-year objectives. The statement of these objectives generally is accompanied by a designation of the person or persons responsible for implementing the activities designed to help the student achieve the objective and may include a statement of special materials, resources, or methods used in achieving the objective.
3. A statement of the specific educational services to be provided the student within the least restrictive environment designated. These services should relate directly to the long- and short-term objectives for the student.
4. A statement of the dates for the initiation of the services, the approximate amount of time to be spent providing each service, and a justification for the services and settings in which they will be provided.
5. A statement of the criterion for and time of evaluating each long- and short-term objective.

As should now be obvious, writing the IEP is a complex and comprehensive process. When the least restrictive environment designated for a student is the regular classroom, the IEP cannot be written without the assistance and cooperation of the regular classroom teacher. It should be obvious as well that you will have to play a significant role in monitoring and reporting the progress the student is making toward fulfilling the objectives of the IEP. As progress data must be re-

FIGURE 20.4 | Portion of an Individual Education Plan

Individual Educational Plan: Educational Priorities Stated as Annual Goals and Short-term Objectives

Page _4_ of _4_

Goal: *Jeremy will demonstrate reading comprehension and word attack skills at the 2.0 grade level.*

Objectives	Criteria	Evaluation Procedure	Date of Review	Code
Complete all reading skills assignments in the 1st grade text and workbook	85% accuracy average of assignments	Record of completion and grades for text and workbook assignments.	6/2/85	
Answer detail recall, sequence and conclusion questions at a 2.0 grade level selection.	95% accuracy	Informal reading inventory. Brigance Criterion-referenced Inventory		

Goal: *Jeremy will write complete sentences of at least 5 words with correct capitalization and punctuation*

Objectives	Criteria	Evaluation Procedure	Date of Review	Code
Capitalize the beginning word of each sentence. Capitalize proper nouns. Use period, question mark, or exclamation mark as end punctuation correctly	Write 5 sample sentences without any punctuation or capitalization errors.	Written Sample: Informal test of written expression.	6/2/85	

Goal: *Jeremy will spell words orally and in written form correctly at the 1.5 grade level.*

Objectives	Criteria	Evaluation Procedure	Date of Review	Code
Complete all spelling units with weekly spelling tests.	80% accuracy average of test scores. 1.5 grade level on inventories	Informal spelling inventory based on the spelling text word list. Brigance Criterion-referenced Inventory Test of written spelling	6/3/85	

Related Service Goal: *Jeremy will correctly articulate "l" and "r" sounds and express himself in complete, descriptive sentences of at least 6 words in length.*

Objectives	Criteria	Evaluation Procedure	Date of Review	Code
Read orally a passage containing 10 words with beginning, medial, and final "r" and "l" sounds. Describe a current activity in complete, descriptive sentences, orally of at least 6 words in length	100% accurate pronunciation Can perform this task upon request.	Language Sample Informal assessment by the Speech Therapist	6/2/85	

Related Service Goal: *Jeremy will write legible capital and lower-case letters in word and sentence form upon request in manuscript.*

Objectives	Criteria	Evaluation Procedure	Date of Review	Code
Write all alphabet letters in upper-case form correctly in manuscript Write all alphabet letters in lower-case form correctly in manuscript	Legibility of writing of all manuscript letters, both upper and lower case	Written Sample. Informal assessment by Occupational Therapist.	6/2/85	

ported back to the multidisciplinary team at regularly scheduled intervals for decision-making purposes, its reliability, validity, and accuracy is of utmost importance. Since you may be the sole link between the child and the team for relatively long periods of time, your measurement skills to systematically observe, record, and monitor the performance of the handicapped child become of paramount importance with respect to the effective implementation of the IEP of the handicapped student.

Individualized Instruction

A fourth stage in which you may become involved in the implementation of PL 94-142 is in providing individualized instruction to the handicapped student. Individualized special education instruction is the day-to-day instruction provided to a handicapped student based on the objectives set forth in the student's IEP. This program of individualized instruction should be consistent with the needs of the handicapped student and your curriculum. Your activities may include providing any or all of the following:

> Specific instructional objectives based on student needs as stated in the IEP
>
> Learning activities appropriate to each student's learning style and presented as specifically and sequentially as needed for the student to progress toward attainment of each instructional objective
>
> Instructional media and materials used for each learning activity selected on the basis of the student's learning style
>
> An instructional setting that provides multiple arrangements for learning
>
> A schedule of teaching time assuring the provision of instruction to each handicapped student in individual or group arrangements
>
> Procedures by which the teacher measures, records, and reports each handicapped student's progress

You may be responsible for documenting the provision of an individualized instructional program for each handicapped child in your classroom as well as for monitoring and recording the success of the individualized program. The writing of specific instructional objectives in accord with the student's IEP and the preparation and administration of teacher-made tests to record student progress toward these objectives are tasks for which you may also be responsible.

Reviewing the IEP

In general, school districts will have an established set of procedures or a system for reviewing each handicapped student's progress based on the objectives stated in the student's IEP. The purpose of this review is not only to determine the student's progress toward the objectives of the plan but also to determine the need for modifying the plan and for further special services. A critical aspect of this review is documenting the movement of a student to either a more or less restrictive environment or release from all special educational services.

Recommendations for major changes in the IEP, including changes in the student's placement (for example, to a more or less restrictive environment), is the responsibility of the multidisciplinary team. However, all persons involved in implementing the student's IEP are likely to be involved in this review. For example, among the many pieces of information that must be gathered prior to a major change in a student's placement are:

The number of instructional options that have been attempted, including those within the regular classroom

The appropriateness of the long- and short-range educational objectives, including those written by the regular classroom teacher

The reliability, validity, and accuracy of the testing that led or contributed to a review of the student's current placement, including testing completed within the regular classroom

A student may only be moved to a more restrictive environment, even temporarily, if sufficient data exist documenting that the student's behavior warrants such action. These data generally attempt to establish that

The student's behavior being examined was not solely caused by the handicapping condition.

Adjustments in the student's IEP, including alternative educational programs, were tried in an attempt to prevent the recurrence of the undesirable behavior leading to reconsideration of the child's placement.

In each of these areas, data provided by the classroom teacher are often critical, since you may be in the most advantageous position to make these assessments about the everyday performance of the student. Here, as elsewhere with the implementation of PL 94-142, the reliability, validity, and accuracy of the data you provide will be a direct reflection of the testing and measurement skills you have acquired.

⎮SUMMARY

This chapter has acquainted you with the field of special education and its relationship to the regular classroom teacher. Its major points were:

1. The field of special education has undergone tremendous growth with respect to its programs and services as well as significant change with respect to the laws and policies governing the education of the handicapped.

2. The most recent and significant of these laws and policies has been PL 94-142 and the policies that have followed from it. PL 94-142 guarantees the right of every handicapped child of school age to receive free public education appropriate to his or her needs.

3. The special education profession and the public schools have chosen to interpret "education that is appropriate to the needs of a handicapped child" as that which not only matches and builds upon the child's current level of intellectual and/or emotional functioning, but also that is provided in the least restrictive environment conducive to meeting the intellectual and emotional needs of the child.

4. For some handicapped students and for some instructional objectives, the regular classroom will be the least restrictive environment.

5. The role of the regular classroom teacher in implementing PL 94-142 includes responsibilities in
   a. child identification
   b. individual assessment
   c. Individual Educational Plan (IEP) development
   d. individualized instruction
   e. review of the IEP

6. An example of the measurement skills needed by the regular classroom teacher for child identification is initially distinguishing students who are potentially learning disabled from those who are "slow learners."

7. An example of the measurement skills needed by the regular classroom teacher for individual assessment is collecting and analyzing information pertaining to the learning competencies of the student and the effects of specific instructional activities on these competencies.

8. An example of the measurement skills needed by the regular classroom teacher for IEP development is writing short- and long-term instructional objectives for the student, specifying both the outcome to be reached and the instructional activities to be implemented.

9. An example of the measurement skills needed by the regular classroom teacher for individualized instruction is documenting the implementation of an individualized instructional program for each handicapped child and monitoring and recording the success of this program.

10. An example of the measurement skills needed by the regular classroom teacher to review the IEP is determining the reliability, validity, and accuracy of the measurement procedures used to indicate the need to change the child's placement to either a more or a less restrictive environment.

For Discussion

1. List four implications of Public Law 94-142 for how you will construct tests for use in your classroom.

2. Describe at least two methods for distinguishing a slow learner from a child with a learning disability.

3. Assume you are asked by a multidisciplinary team to monitor and collect data on one of your students who may be mildly retarded. What types of information would you collect and in what form would you report these data to the multidisciplinary team?

21

CHAPTER

THE MICROCOMPUTER IN TESTING AND MEASUREMENT

Within the past few years a trendy new gadget has entered the educational scene: the microcomputer. Until recently, microcomputers in education have typically been used for instruction; use of the microcomputer for classroom measurement has been much more limited. As a result, the classroom teacher may not be aware of how the microcomputer can be an asset in classroom testing and measurement. As more and more teacher time gets devoted to paperwork, the time-thrifty teacher will need the microcomputer to generate test items and tests, to perform item and test analyses, to create, update, and maintain test and instructional objective files, and to store, compute, and analyze grades.

It is a fact of life that the entry of microcomputers into education has been met with acceptance and advocacy but also with skepticism and resistance. Any innovation as far-reaching in impact as the microcomputer must develop cautiously and be based on research evidence of its effectiveness. Too often advocates overzealously "sell" educators on the microcomputer's benefits, only to see them gather dust due to their tendency to frustrate users unfamiliar with computer jargon and procedures. Worse yet, until recently the computer programs that "direct" microcomputers in performing educational tasks have been, generally, unimaginative and poorly written. As a result of these badly designed applications as well as unmet expectations of what the microcomputer can do, some educators have come to dismiss the potential of the microcomputer.

Consequently, today we see microcomputers both touted as a boon and criticized as a bane to education. Do these positions sound familiar to you? Do you remember our discussion of the opposing views of pro-test and anti-test advocates in Chapter 1? Our position here is somewhat similar. We see microcomputers as an aid to educators. They are neither wonderful nor terrible. The wise classroom teacher can use this aid to speed and improve the classroom measurement process. In order to be able to use the microcomputer effectively, it is necessary that you learn something about the microcomputer. In the first part of this chapter we will familiarize you with microcomputers in general. We will discuss what a microcomputer is, describe the components of a microcomputer system, and explain how a microcomputer works. Next, we will describe how many of the measurement activities described in this text actually can be facilitated or improved through the use of a microcomputer and describe briefly some available software. Finally, we will provide you with a step-by-step guide that can be used to ensure that you or your school does not purchase the "wrong" computer and thereby join the ranks of those who may disregard this promising innovation.

WHAT IS A COMPUTER?

The computer is a tool that is used to manage or process information more effectively and efficiently than can any human being. It is an information processor. The kinds of processing it can perform include filing information (much like a manual system in a filing cabinet), subjecting information to statistical procedures (much like a statistician with a hand calculator), and, perhaps of more relevance to us, they also can be used to generate and analyze tests and test items, create test data files, and store scores and other relevant information on one or many pupils. Other uses of computers include writing music, creating art, creating graphics (pictorial representations), and a variety of other applications. For our purpose, we will primarily consider the role of computers in test and test-item construction, analysis, and storage.

TYPES OF COMPUTERS

There are three major types of computers: the mainframe computer, minicomputer, and microcomputer.

Mainframe Computer

Remember when you went through registration and the computer made a mistake in your registration? This was not the work of a microcomputer but the work of a *mainframe computer*. These are the computers that are housed in the computation center at your university or college. In the past this is what we typically associated with the term *computer*. These are huge pieces of machinery which are very much subject to variations in temperature and humidity. This is why they are often housed in separate buildings where temperature and humidity can be maintained at precise levels. Because they are extremely expensive, they are primarily owned or shared by large institutions.

Minicomputer

Another type of computer is the *minicomputer*. These computers are often used by large businesses. They are smaller and less complex than a mainframe computer. These computers are found most often in offices and are often used by computer programmers or operators to manage the large amounts of information and clerical tasks generated by a company or business. These computers are also quite expensive but are less costly than mainframe computers.

Microcomputer

The third type of computer is the *microcomputer*. Microcomputers are the computers you see advertised in newspapers, magazines, and on television. They are the Ataris, Apples, Commodores, TRS-80s, and a variety of other small and relatively inexpensive computers. These computers sell for anywhere from $50 to as much as $3,000. They are the computers that seem to have the most potential for the classroom, since they are affordable and can easily perform the tasks that educators most often need done. Now, let's turn to a description of the various components involved in a microcomputer system.

MICROCOMPUTER SYSTEM COMPONENTS

Components of a microcomputer system can be divided into two major categories: hardware and software. Within each of these categories are a great variety of components. It is an unfortunate fact of microcomputing that almost every manufacturer creates its own hardware (the actual machine itself) and its own software (instructions that allow the hardware to be used in a given situation). This means that there is very little interchangeability among the many different parts that different manufacturers produce and sell. It would be impossible in the space we have available here to do justice to all the various firms currently in the educational microcomputing arena. Therefore, we will only provide general descriptions of the various components of a computer system to help introduce you to the computer jargon, enable you to understand better how a microcomputer works, and allow you to intelligently engage in the computer-selection process.

Hardware

The basic hardware components of a microcomputer system consist of a keyboard, a central processing unit (called CPU), and a video-display terminal. Additional hardware units, called *peripherals,* often include some combination of the following: an audiocassette recorder, a disk-drive unit, a modem, and a printer. Figure 21.1 shows what each of these components typically looks like.

    To complicate the issue further, many microcomputers have the capability to be upgraded by the addition of plug-in cartridges or circuit boards. Extra mem-

FIGURE 21.1 | Hardware Components of a Microcomputer System

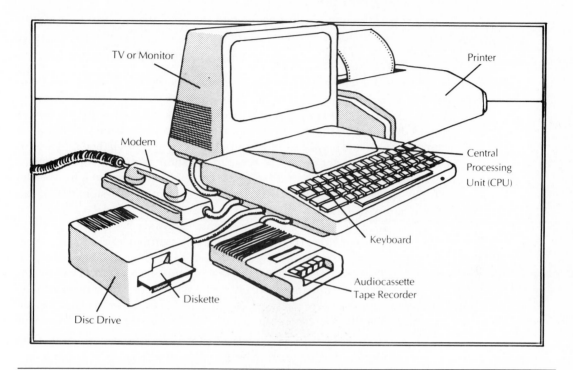

ory (the capacity to store information) is a common add-on. For example, you may purchase a microcomputer with 16K of memory, which means the computer's memory can hold 16,000 characters of information—each letter, number, punctuation, or space in a sentence, for example, is a character. However, many educational computer programs require 32K (32,000) to 48K (48,000) characters of memory to operate. Rather than buying a new computer with larger than 16K memory to operate a new program, it may be possible simply to purchase additional memory boards or cartridges to add to your 16K memory computer in order to upgrade it to the necessary 32K or 48K levels. Generally such add-ons are also classified as hardware. Next, let's find out what the word *software* means.

Software

Software refers to the computer programs, or list of step-by-step instructions, that tell a computer what to do. If you have ever played with a home videogame in which you had to plug a cartridge into the videogame unit, you were actually plugging a computer program into the videogame unit. This program or software tells the computer how to play the videogame with you. The cartridge you plugged in is one example of software. In educational settings software may appear on cartridges such as these, but, more typically, it is stored on either audiocassettes or what are known as disks.

Audio cassettes, just like the ones that music is recorded on, can serve as storage devices for computer programs. Disks also are storage devices but are significantly more efficient and can hold many more times the information than can cassettes. This means that more lengthy or elaborate computer programs can be stored on disks. The most commonly found diskette is the *floppy disk* (so called because it easily bends), but *hard disks* that have an even greater capacity to store information are gaining popularity. The disk containing the computer program is inserted into the disk drive to run the computer program. Alternatively, a computer program may be stored on an audiocassette, which then is placed in the audiocassette recorder to run the program. In short, a microcomputer needs both hardware and software in order to perform the functions for which it was designed. The hardware and software taken together complete a system which can perform a variety of functions.

A tremendous amount of education-oriented software has recently become available. *Software packages* (computer programs) useful to teachers range from programs designed to teach students how to read more critically or how to add, subtract, multiply, and divide, to programs that provide simulations of various situations, which require students to actively problem-solve or plan solutions to the problems presented. Software packages also have been developed that help teachers construct objective tests, score these tests, and analyze the test data as well as help the teacher manage such clerical functions within the classroom as keeping grades and recording homework, attendance, and tardiness.

The kinds of software and hardware available to you will be largely dependent on the insight and expertise of the individual or committee that selects the hardware and software for your particular school. In too many cases, individuals in schools have purchased hardware without first evaluating their software or program needs. This can be a costly mistake, since software from one manufacturer created for a particular type of computer (for example, for the Apple II computer) will not operate on another computer (for example, TRS-80). Thus, you may find yourself in a position where, although your school has microcomputers available, the software programs that are available are either inappropriate or inadequate for your needs. Purchasing a microcomputer hardware package without first evaluating school, classroom, or district instructional software needs is like purchasing a textbook without knowing what subject you will teach. We turn now to how a microcomputer processes information.

HOW A MICROCOMPUTER SYSTEM WORKS

A microcomputer stores, alters, combines, and compares information. That is, it *processes* information. Just what is this process? Let's look at the three stages involved: input, processing, and output.

Input: The Program and the Measurement Data

The program is the how-to-do-it manual for a microcomputer. It is a step-by-step set of specific directions that tells the central processing unit (CPU) of the computer what it is to do with the information you give it. In order for the computer to be able to "listen" to the program, the program must be entered into the computer's memory. This can be done by plugging in a cartridge, cassette, or diskette on which the program is written, or by actually writing a program into the computer's memory by typing in the instructions at the computer's keyboard. Although writing a computer program yourself may never be necessary, should you need to write one, it will require knowledge of one of several computer languages. These languages comprise special words that have specific meanings that the computer understands. You may have learned (or will learn) one of more of these languages in a computer literacy course. If you did, you probably learned a computer language called BASIC (Beginner's All-Purpose Symbolic Instruction Code). BASIC is a widely used interactive programming language that can be used for testing and measurement tasks and most school-related instruction. It is simple and fun to learn and it is flexible enough to be used for almost any testing and measurement problem (computing reliability, validity, test scoring and recording, etc.) and any instructional problem (teaching vocabulary, arithmetic, solving social studies problems, conducting simulated chemistry and physics experiments, etc.). If you were to write a simple program in BASIC, telling the computer to find the mean of four student scores, the program would look like the following:

```
 5   REM CALCULATE THE MEAN OF 4 NUMBERS
10   PRINT "ENTER THE 4 NUMBERS FOR WHICH
15   PRINT  YOU WISH TO CALCULATE THE MEAN"
20   INPUT A, B, C, D
25   LET X = (A + B + C + D)/4
30   PRINT "THE MEAN IS; X"
40   END
```

Here is a translation of some of the words that appear in the program:

REM   allows you to add REMarks within a program for your information

PRINT   allows you to print a variable or expression (to help whoever uses your program)

INPUT   allows you to input data from the keyboard

LET   allows you to assign a new value to a specified variable

END   is the last statement in every BASIC Program

When you use the program written here, only the second, third, and sixth lines would appear on the video screen. The mean you requested would appear in place of the "X" in line six. Of course, BASIC can be used to solve far more complicated problems than this, including word problems, such as the teaching of reading or vocabulary. This short example should give you a feel for the simple procedures that need be learned in order for you to write your own programs.

Since you are likely to hear of them, here are some other computer languages often used with microcomputers:

COBOL.   COmmon Business Oriented Language. A computer language designed mainly for programming business applications.

PASCAL.   A high-level, general purpose programming language, similar to BASIC but allowing more sophistication.

FORTRAN.   FORmula TRANslater. A computer language designed primarily for programming scientific applications.

APL.   A Programming Language. A computer language designed primarily for programming mathematical applications.

LOGO.   A simple-to-learn computer language which emphasizes graphic applications.

PILOT.   A simplified computer language, PILOT is one type of "authoring program" that enables an individual without training in BASIC or any other formal computer language to develop instructional and measurement programs.

Unless you have had training in one of these computer programming languages, you will likely be using already-written programs on cartridge, cassette, or diskette. Whether you use already packaged software or program the computer yourself, you will need to input the data, or the information, you want the computer to process. For classroom measurement purposes, these data may be in the form of text (for example, instructional objectives, test items, or complete tests) or numbers (test scores, item analysis data). Fortunately, the inputing of data to the microcomputer is straightforward and knowledge of a programming language is not necessary. The software you are using will tell you what to input and when. In short, if you can type, you can operate a microcomputer software package. Loading a program into a microcomputer's memory and the feeding of data into memory in accord with the directions the program gives you constitute the input.

Processing: The Central Processing Unit (CPU)

Once the data have been entered via the keyboard, the CPU begins processing the data according to the instructions it gets from the program. The CPU is often referred to as the "brain" of the microcomputer. This is an unfortunate choice of words, since the CPU is really not very "brainy." It cannot think, it cannot feel, it cannot be creative. However, it is an extremely obedient and fast machine. The

CPU does exactly and only what it is told to do by the program, that is by the human programmer—no more and no less. Thus, a "smart" program will make the computer appear smart, and a "dumb" program will make it appear dumb.

After the CPU completes processing the data according to the program's directions, it sends the results of its processing to the video monitor, printer, or to a memory storage center for future access. This may be either on a cassette or a diskette. The result of the CPU's processing is called *output*.

Output (Video, Printed Copy, Storage)

Output is the end result of the CPU's processing. Output is the product we want the computer to produce. Most often this will be processed information. Output for measurement purposes may be in a variety of forms including item analysis and statistical data, test items, tests, student names, grades, objectives, and even the identification of student strengths and weaknesses.

Typically, output is first viewed on the video monitor. Afterward, decisions are made whether to eliminate, save, or print all or parts of the output. If it is to be printed, a special command is used to activate the printer. This will provide what is called *hard copy* of the output. If you decide to save the information on cassette or diskette, another command is used to accomplish this. The output may then be obtained as needed at any time from the cassette or tape. If the output (tests, items, test scores) will be used more than once, it is saved to avoid having to input it at a later time. Figure 21.2 summarizes how a computer operates. Now that you have a better understanding of what microcomputers are and how they operate, let's consider how they can facilitate classroom measurement.

FIGURE 21.2 | How a Microcomputer Works

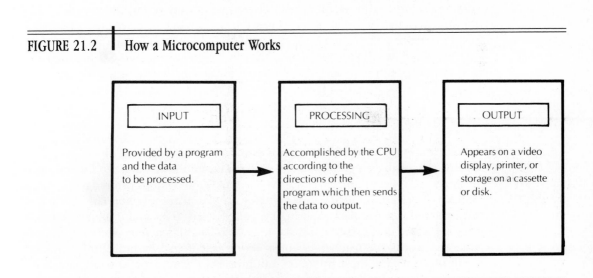

INPUT	PROCESSING	OUTPUT
Provided by a program and the data to be processed.	Accomplished by the CPU according to the directions of the program which then sends the data to output.	Appears on a video display, printer, or storage on a cassette or disk.

MICROCOMPUTER APPLICATIONS IN CLASSROOM MEASUREMENT

In this section we will describe how microcomputers can facilitate and improve various aspects of measurement practice. We will first consider the various ways in which a microcomputer can assist the classroom teacher with instructional objectives; test items; test development and analysis; scoring or grading and recording of in-class and homework assignments, projects, and tests; assignment of final marks; and various statistical analyses. Next, we will describe briefly some commercial software that is available currently for such applications. Our brief review of these products neither is intended to be exhaustive, since new software is being developed rapidly, nor is intended to be an endorsement of the products mentioned. As will be discussed in the last section, "Selecting a Microcomputer," of this chapter, the reader is encouraged to "test drive" *any* software package prior to purchase, regardless of how appropriate it may appear from our brief review, or anyone else's.

Instructional Objectives

One of the measurement tasks teachers find tedious is the writing of instructional objectives. Educational software will not minimize the necessary skills and time initially needed to construct good instructional objectives, but a word processing program (a program that allows you to add, delete, shift, or revise written information quickly and efficiently) would enable teachers to modify their objectives from year to year to reflect changing educational trends and goals. This would minimize clerical time and increase the amount of time you would have available for instructional or other measurement tasks. Saving instructional objectives on a cassette or diskette would facilitate analysis of objectives and sharing of well-written objectives among teachers at the same grade level, saving still more time and leading to better-written objectives, thereby improving measurement practice.

Test Items

Similar reasoning applies to test items as applies to instructional objectives. With a word-processing program, you can easily make minor or major modifications to test items or even complete tests as well as have new versions printed much more quickly by the printer than you or a typist would with a typewriter. This could be a major time saver. Similarly, sharing of well-written items could be facilitated if they are stored on a cassette or diskette available to all teachers. Software is available that assists the teacher in constructing test items. By indicating common faults of a test item, these programs minimize the chances that you will construct and use poor items. Programs will also likely soon be available that will generate alternate forms of tests according to instructional objectives and difficulty levels.

Given a pool of test items the computer could be instructed to make a number of smaller tests based on common objectives and at prespecified difficulty levels, thereby ensuring that different tests would be comparable.

Tests

There likely will soon be software available that will guide the classroom teacher through the entire test construction process, from writing instructional objectives, through matching items to objectives, to assembling and analyzing the test. It is in this last area, test and item analysis, that the microcomputer's power and convenience may prove most beneficial. Programs to compute item difficulty levels and discrimination indices are available, and quantitative item analyses of objective test items are now a reality for the busy classroom teacher. Also available are programs that enable the teacher to determine the reliability of classroom tests. Statistical packages and data management programs make it possible for classroom teachers to keep accurate and comprehensive records of student performances over the course of the year, and over several years. This enables the teacher to compare classes, tests, and curricula, to identify aptitude-achievement discrepancies, and to evaluate the effects of new instructional techniques on test performance. For the first time, the classroom teacher is able to objectively and scientifically analyze data from classroom tests without all the hand calculation that otherwise would be necessary. When these data are considered along with standardized test data, they enhance instruction, and the satisfaction of pupils, parents, and administrators with the measurement process.

Grades

Just as microcomputers enable teachers to collect and analyze test scores, other computer programs enable teachers to do the same with grades. Trends like grade inflation or declines in basic skills would be made easier to identify and correct if these data are stored for ready reference. Software already is available that can automatically keep track of student performance for an entire class of students as they work their way through an instructional program. When used as an adjunct to more traditional educational methods, such an approach can go far toward providing an extra dose of drill and practice or tutorial assistance to students in need, without adding to the teacher's already heavy instructional and record-keeping burden.

Statistical Analysis

While we have already mentioned several ways in which the statistical power of the microcomputer can be used in measurement applications, a variety of other applications also exist. These include computing summary statistics for grade level, school or PTA meetings and the preparation of reports for parent conferences.

We do not believe the previous list of applications of the microcomputer to testing and measurement is exhaustive. At the same time, we hope we have not overwhelmed you or presented too unrealistic a picture of what we believe can be the potential impact of microcomputers on testing and measurement in the classroom. We believe these applications will save teachers time, lead to better measurement practice, and provide the teacher with important data regarding instructional methods that ordinarily would not be available at the time they are needed.

Measurement-Related Software

Following is a sample of some available software packages that can accomplish some of the previous tasks. Yearly updated lists of similar software can be obtained from Data Pro Research Corporation, Delray, NJ 08075, as well as from popular computing magazines.

AEN Grading System.
The AEN Grading System alphabetizes, calculates, and grades reports of any number of students, categories of students, or combination of students. The program uses number grades or any of three types of letter grades. Available from Avant-Garde, 1907 Garden Avenue, P.O. Box 3570, Eugene, OR 97403. Telephone (503) 345-3043. Hardware: Apple II and II Plus; minimum memory 48K.

Cactus Grade Book.
The Cactus Grade Book program features student data maintained on separate disks; data back-up prompted and accomplished from within the program; grade files accessible by other programs for more specialized analysis; extra-credit assignments; and printouts of student, class and statistical data. Available from Cactusplot Company, 1442 North McAllister, Tempe, AZ 85281. Telephone (602) 945-1667. Hardware: Apple II and II Plus; Apple IIe; IBM Personal Computer; IBM Personal Computer XT; IBM PCjr; minimum memory 48K.

Classroom Grade Management System.
This is a grade-management and reporting system for the classroom teacher. The package provides a full set of grade reports for each student, including current grade; all test, quiz, and homework scores; grade weighting; and class standing. The package also contains a graphic capability for charting plus data security features. Available from Hayden Software Company, 600 Suffolk Street, Lowell, MA 01853. Telephone (617) 937-0200. Hardware: Apple II and II Plus; minimum memory 48K.

Compu-Mark.
Compu-Mark is designed for educators with little or no computer experience. Simple data entry provides a method of keeping neat, organized records of marks and attendance. Compu-Mark will weight marks, monitor incomplete assignments, alphabetize student names, and record comments. Printed formats include report cards, mark summaries, class averages, and percentiles.

Available from Peters Software Products, 6715 8th Street NE., Suite 221, Calgary, Alberta, Canada T2E 7H7. Telephone (403) 275-9124. Hardware: Apple II and II Plus; Apple IIe; minimum memory 48K.

CompuGrade.
CompuGrade can be used from first grade through college. The program allows the user to average an entire semester's grades; give various weights to specific tests or assignments; use curves to raise class average; pull a class summary, with or without averages, at any point in the term; and allow for students picking up or dropping classes. The program will also save and reload class files from disk. Available from Right on Programs, P.O. Box 977, Huntington, NY 11743. Telephone (516) 271-3177. Hardware: Apple II and II Plus; Apple IIe; Commodore PET; Commodore-64; minimum memory 48K.

Grade Reporter.
The Grade Reporter contains two packages. The large class program prints reports that can be posted on a bulletin board and makes histograms of test scores. The small program prepares detailed grade reports that can be given to each student. Available from Cross Educational Software, Inc., 1802 North Trenton, P.O. Box 1536, Ruston, LA 71270. Telephone (318) 255-8921. Hardware: Apple II and II Plus; Apple IIe; minimum memory 48K.

Grade Reporting.
Grade Reporting is designed to calculate and maintain data on students, courses, instructors, and enrollment. Some of the data calculated and maintained are course weights, honor points, pass/fail grades, cumulative credits, half and quarter year courses, incompletes, transfers, etc. It will print report cards and honor rolls. It calculates each GPA, earned credits, and class ranks. It stores and retrieves information alphabetically, numerically, and by a user-defined key. Available from Unicom, Division of United Camera, 297 Elmwood Avenue, Providence, RI 02907. Telephone (401) 467-5600. Hardware: Apple II and II Plus; Apple IIe; minimum memory 48K.

Gradebook.
This program aids teachers in recording student grades by a variety of methods and then reporting grades as total points received, percent grade, and letter grade. The report may be just the summary results or include a listing of all assignments. The program features: enter new students at any time; names alphabetized within the class period; enter assignments at any time; review student scores on the monitor, receive a printout of individual students or the entire class; print an alphabetical roster; and instructor security with an access code. Available from Apple Country Computers, 626 North Jerome Lane, East Wenatchee, WA 98801. Telephone (509) 884-3767. Hardware: Apple II and II Plus, Apple IIe.

Gradebook.
This package is designed to store the records for up to 9 classes of 30 students each or use blank data disks in a 2-drive system for unlimited storage. Enter the class list and let the computer handle the rest. The Apple will alphabetize the class list, compute statistics for an entire class, and reproduce all records

with the help of a printer. In addition, this program allows the teacher the option of changing scores or class rosters at any time. Available from Scholastic Software, 129 Wall Street, West, Lyndhurst, NJ 07071. Telephone (201) 939-8050. Hardware: Apple II and II Plus; minimum memory 32K.

GradeCalc.

GradeCalc is a grade and attendance management package designed to emulate the functions of a gradebook. The teacher has on file all the raw grades and assignment information. This file can then average grades using a variety of methods from percentage scores to symbolic grades. Reports for cumulative listing of missing assignments and reports on grade totals, average gradebook listings, and assignment summaries are generated. Available from Tamarack Software, Inc., P.O. Box 247, Darby, MT 59829. Telephone (406) 821-4596. Hardware: Commodore-64; Atari 800; Apple II and II Plus; Apple IIe; minimum memory 32K.

Grading System.

The Grading System is designed to help school administrators and teaching professionals keep track of grades, cumulative averages, and school credits. Student registration and class scheduling features are included along with the input of reporting period grades) and the automatic preparation of report cards and honor roll lists. Human engineering features include keyboard entry routines for grade input and the use of a lightpen as a fast-entry tool. The system handles both numerical and "letter" grading systems and provides a set of customizing programs which remodel the system to fit user-defined needs. It prepares class rosters, student class schedules, and student grade summaries and is capable of handling up to 600 students per disk. Any school using this system can define its own grading system, report card comments, honor roll definitions, and credit requirements. Available from CMA Micro Computer, 55722 Santa Fe Trail, Yucca Valley, CA 92284. Telephone (619) 365-9718. Hardware: Apple II and II Plus, Apple III; minimum memory 48K.

Grading System Programs PC.

This system provides a set-up routine allowing administrators to tell the system the various grade values they wish to use, the number of reporting periods they will use, and how to weight the various grading periods to compute the semester and yearly grade-point averages. The system can be custom tailored to accommodate up to 25 courses per student, with up to 1,800 students per school Other system features include a special midterm reporting element which allows the preparation of student progress reports or "downslips." This element provides for up to 99 user-definable comments which may be optionally printed to the student's actual report card. The package also contains an element which automatically transfers information from CMA's Class Scheduling program (see separate write-up) to the Grading System. Available from CMA Micro Computer, 55722 Santa Fe Trail, Yucca Valley, CA 92284. Telephone (619) 365-9718. Hardware: IBM Personal Computer; minimum memory 128K.

Multi Program Recordkeeper.

Multi Program Recordkeeper stores individual and class records for Random House programs on a central student data disk. The system is capable of holding records of up to 300 students and scores for up to 3,000 lessons. The system will monitor individual and class performance in multiple programs in several subject areas. The user inputs a record for each student and then set up class files. The system reports scores by individual, class, or lesson. It provides most recent scores and class ranking. Available from Random House, Inc., 400 Hahn Road, Westminister, MD 21157. Telephone (800) 638-6460. Hardware: Apple II and II Plus; Apple IIe; Radio Shack TRS-80 Model III; minimum memory 48K.

Report Card.

This grading system calculates student and class averages. The system allows various sorting and printing options that may be used to rank students within their class and then posts the results. The program keeps a permanent record of scores from all tests, quizzes, lab assignments, and homework assignments. Each student activity can have any maximum score and can be individually weighted for its effect on the student's final grade. A custom editor provides fixing of incorrect entries and replacing of incomplete grades and actual test scores. Available from Sensible Software, 24011 Seneca Drive, Oak Park, MI 48237. Telephone (313) 399-8877. Hardware: Apple II and II Plus; minimum memory 48K.

School Information Management System.

The main module of this package allows the creation of a data file of up to 99 variables per file. The user may selectively print, list, edit, or delete information and merge and sort variables. The statistics module calculates means, standard deviation, cross tabulation, frequency distributions, multiple regression. It also has a function for performing arithmetic calculations among variables to create new data (gain scores, composite scores). The school administration module creates, labels, and plots student score profiles and Chapter 1 evaluation models. It also converts percentiles to normal curve equivalent scores. The test scoring module allows agencies to score their own tests and develop tests from an item bank. It accesses the Scantron Model 1200 ½-page reader and computes and prints domain and objective scores, mastery/nonmastery indicators, and counts for individuals or groups. The package is compatible with mark sense readers for test scoring and/or data entry. Software development to read custom designed forms is available. Available from Powell Systems, Inc. (PSI), 3355 Bee Cave Road, Suite 304, Austin, Tx 78746. Telephone (512) 327-4425. Hardware: IBM Personal Computer; Apple IIe, Kaypro II and Kaypro 4; CP/M Operating System; minimum memory 64K.

SRA Micro Test Administration System (MTAS).

MTAS helps users develop, administer, and score tests, as well as analyze test results, for a single classroom or an entire school. Users can create and augment their own test-item banks, print custom-designed tests using items from one or more of these banks, score the tests, print test results, and summarize those results. The system can generate reports for an entire test or break down results by topic. Summaries can be for one class or for several. One disk contains all the programs needed to create test files and print tests. A second disk contains all the programs needed to score tests and print reports. Available from Science Research Associates, Inc., 155 North Wacker Drive, Chicago, IL 60606. Telephone (312) 984-7000. Hardware: Apple II and II Plus; minimum memory 48K.

Teacher's Gradebook.
Teacher's Gradebook allows the user to summarize, retrieve, update or manipulate and report data dealing with class administration, student grades, rosters, and absences. The features include password protection, data entry and retrieval, and versatile record structure. Available from Dynacomp, Inc., 1427 Monroe Avenue, Rochester, NY 14618. Telephone (800) 828-6772. Hardware: Apple II and II Plus; Atari 800; Atari 400; minimum memory 48K.

Test Analysis.
Test Analysis provides grading and analysis of multiple-choice test items when coupled with a Scantron optical reader. Provides grade distributions, student and class averages, standard deviation, student-choice distribution, identification of confusing questions. Grades can be adjusted and curved also. Available from Classroom Consortia Media, Inc., 57 Bay Street, Staten Island, NY 10301. Hardware: IBM PC, IBM PC JR, IBM PC XT, Monroe OC 8820; minimum memory 128K.

Test Analysis Program.
Test Analysis Program scores multiple-choice tests and furnishes an item analysis of the test. Data are input from card readers or scoring machine (Scantron), using mark-sense cards or sheets. Tests of up to 100 items can be scored. Reports include student protocols, response summaries, distribution and standard statistics and item analysis. Available from Bertamax, Inc., 3646 Stoneway North, Seattle, WA 98103. Hardware: IBM PC; TRS-80 III; minimum memory 48K.

ZES Authoring System.
The ZES System contains a series of programs that allow the instructor to create or amend lessons, cartesian graphs, data frames, and student records. It is also capable of keeping elaborate student records, including general status, a summary of the student's performance, detailed report of student answers, as well as a class report. Programming knowledge is not required with ZES System. Available from Avant-Garde, 1907 Garden Avenue, P.O. Box 3570, Eugene, OR 97403. Telephone (503) 345-3043. Hardware: Apple II and II Plus; minimum memory 48K.

The final section of this chapter concerns the process of selecting a microcomputer. We believe this section to be one the most important, since purchasing the wrong computer will likely do little more to improve educational measurement than would selection of the wrong standardized test.

SELECTING A MICROCOMPUTER

In Chapter 19 we presented a step-by-step approach to the design and implementation of a schoolwide testing program. In this section we will present a similar step-by-step approach to the selection of a microcomputer. As a classroom teacher, you may not have much to say about the kinds of software and hardware your school selects. As with standardized test selection, too often it is the case that such decisions tend to be made at administrative levels without soliciting input from classroom teachers. However, you may be asked for input, and if you are, the decision-making steps presented in this chapter should help organize your thinking and perhaps the thinking of the selection committee. Furthermore, there is no reason you could not use this same process to select a microcomputer for yourself.

As we mentioned before, the exploding popularity of microcomputers has brought with it some resistance. Part of this negative reaction stems from the underutilization of microcomputers once they are brought into a school setting. Unfortunately, all too often they are relegated to the category of typewriters or game machines. Even more disconcerting, the authors have seen many simply gather dust. By following these guidelines, you will minimize the likelihood that these valuable resources will be wasted in your school.

STEPS IN THE MICROCOMPUTER SELECTION PROCESS

Step 1: Identify Objectives

Identify specific objectives for the use of the microcomputer. This is probably self-evident, but too frequently overlooked. Sometimes the only objective seems to be "get a microcomputer," or to "get as many microcomputers as we can." When such objectives dominate thinking, the end result is all too often a microcomputer that fails to run the software needed to achieve your educational goals. Indeed, the authors are aware of situations wherein naive school personnel have fallen prey to beeps, blinking lights, high-technology jargon, and a high-pressure salespitch, ending up with a microcomputer but no software that is suitable to their purposes.

Our first recommendation, then, is that specific objectives be identified. "To aid in testing" is not specific enough. "To generate alternate forms of multiple-choice tests" or "to maintain records of student achievement in resource rooms without requiring teacher assistance" are specific objectives. In formulating objectives, consider the following:

What are the Uses to Which the Computer Will Be Put?
Computer programs are available to assist in test construction, administration, scoring, analysis, and storing of records. Other education-related uses for microcomputers include ad-

ministrative (accounting, attendance, grading, word-processing, recordkeeping, planning, and projecting), instructional (drill and practice in basic skills, tutorial, and simulations), programming (teachers and students learning computer languages), instructional management (classroom recordkeeping), guidance and research applications.

What Future Uses Can Be Anticipated?

Plan hardware and software applications for your school and school district as it will be five years from now. If enrollment is increasing, project what it is likely to be in five years and use these data in helping determine how many computers may be needed. Most important, try to determine how specific subject-matter specialists in math, chemistry, English, social studies, and so on see the future role of the computer in their disciplines. Will science instructors be turning to more specialized applications of the computer for graphic simulations of lab experiments? Will language arts teachers be using the computer almost exclusively for word processing and tutorial training in composition writing? These trends and requirements should play an important role in the types of hardware and software that are purchased. They also speak for the need for any specific recommendations to be the result of an interdisciplinary team of teachers.

What Grade Levels Are Being Considered for Microcomputer Use?

Since the tasks required of the computer differ considerably by grade level, so should the type and complexity of the computer. Computer literacy and the learning of BASIC can be accomplished adequately on a computer that costs no more than $200. Sophisticated problem-solving simulations that might be standard fare in high-school social studies and science classes require a somewhat larger and more expensive computer. Most schools or school districts need a mix of computers, but that mix can be very different depending on whether the school is lower elementary, upper elementary, or secondary; whether computers must serve both students and teachers; and whether the computers must serve all subject-matter areas or only certain ones.

Step 2: Identify Software

Identify the software necessary to meet your specific objectives. If Step 1 looked complicated and time-consuming, wait until you get to Step 2! There are literally thousands of educational programs on the market. For measurement purposes, the supply of educational software is not so large. However, you still must evaluate each software program individually to determine whether it meets your needs. Unfortunately, there is a great deal of variability in the quality of software. How does one go about reviewing such software? Fortunately, many reputable software distributors will make available to school personnel examination copies of their programs. In some cases representatives will be sent to the school upon request.

These requests should be written on school or district letterhead to elicit their co-operation. If a manufacturer or distributor refuses to cooperate, avoid purchasing their wares. Reputable firms will not shy away from making their programs available to schools on an examination basis. Once you have screened the software that is available for your purposes and made your selection, then you are ready for the next step.

Step 3: Identify Special Features

Using your objectives and the software you have selected, identify the features you will need in your microcomputer and related components. This is important if the software and hardware is to be compatible, that is, if the microcomputer is to have sufficient memory to run the software or the color or graphics capability called for by the software. Some of the features to consider include memory, peripherals, keyboard, video monitor, video display, graphics, color, sound and music, language, and cost and service.

Memory.   In general the more memory, the better. Be sure you know how much your software requires. Your microcomputer must have at least that amount. An 8K memory is small, 64K is about average, 128K is large.

Peripherals.   What kind and how many peripherals will you need to meet your objectives? Printers, cassette recorders, disk drives, light pens to provide input by pointing to a place on the video display, voice synthesizers to hear programs that "speak," and modems to connect your microcomputer to other computers via telephone lines all ought to be considered.

Keyboard.   If your microcomputer is to be used by young children, a membrane keyboard (a one-piece, pressure-sensitive plate) will be superior to a typewriter-like keyboard and vice versa if your objectives include teaching programming or word processing. Also, consider whether a separate number pad, which would be desirable for heavy math use, is necessary.

Video monitor.   While you can use a television set as a monitor, it will not produce the character or image quality that monitors designed for computers do. Consider color versus black-and-white versus a green phosphorous screen. Also consider size. Color is usually best (but most expensive), green phosphorous being adequate for most applications. Black and white will be the least expensive but sometimes the most difficult to read.

Video Display.   The video display is what is shown on the monitor—the length and width of text presented on the monitor. Microcomputers vary in display width from as little as 20 characters to 80 characters (the width of a typewritten page), and, in length from 16 to 32 lines. For test construction this can be a critical feature, especially if you include graphs, since a screen less than 80 characters wide will present a misleading idea of what your actual printed output will look like. Another aspect of the display to be considered is whether upper- and lower-case letters are needed or included. It should be noted that certain software programs can alter aspects of the video display. Although your computer may be only a 40-character display, it may be upgraded to an 80-character display with appropriate software. Also, add-on circuit boards can upgrade a display to 80-character width.

Graphics.   Will you use graphics in your test construction process or will other users need graphics? If so, get a computer with as high resolution graphics as you can, since this will provide better quality of detail.

Color.   This can often enhance a rather dull test or other program. From four to sixteen colors are available on various microcomputers.

Sound or Music.   This capability enables you to provide an auditory cue or signal to students at various points in a testing program. Others may use it for entertainment or creative purposes. Not all microcomputers include sound as a standard feature.

Languages.   Determine which languages are best suited to your needs. For most testing and instructional uses BASIC is adequate. Other languages may be needed to meet special needs.

Cost and Service.   Don't forget your budget, and don't forget someone will have to set up and maintain your system. Shopping for the best price can be a false economy if you cannot get quick and reliable service after the usual 90-day warranty runs out.

Step 4: Compare

Once you've identified the features you need, compare the different machines and rate them. To facilitate this step, use the rating chart in Table 21.1. Once you have identified the units that best meet your needs, get hands-on experience with each unit before making your final selection. Too often individuals fail to put in the necessary hands-on time and purchase on impulse or recommendation from someone who may have different needs. In such cases dissatisfaction or disgust may be the outcome. Now perhaps you can see why so many microcomputers sit unused or are underused in schools. No tool, no matter how good, is helpful if it's not used. When the opportunity presents itself, use the microcomputer to make your teaching easier and more effective.

TABLE 21.1	Rating Microcomputers by Features

Features			*Microcomputers Considered*		
	1	*2*	*3*	*4*	*5*
Available software (list for your objectives)					
Memory (16K, 24K, 48K, 64K, 128K, 512K)					
Peripherals (disk drive, cassette, printer, voice synthesizer, light pen)					
Keyboard (membrane, typewriter)					
Video monitor (size, black/white, green phosphorous, color)					
Video display (width in characters, length in lines)					
Graphics (high resolution, yes/no)					
Sound/Music (yes/no)					
Languages (BASIC, COBOL, PASCAL, LOGO, FORTRAN, APL, others)					
Cost ($)					
Service (Warranty service availability)					

SUMMARY

In this chapter we have introduced you to issues related to testing and the micro-computer. Its major points are:

1. The microcomputer is a tool that manages and processes information. As such it can be used by the classroom teacher to generate test items and tests, perform item and test analyses; create, update, and maintain instructional objectives; and store, compute, and analyze grades.

2. A mainframe computer is a large and expensive machine housed in a specially prepared facility where temperature and humidity can be maintained at precise levels.

3. A minicomputer is a smaller and less expensive machine than a mainframe, used primarily by businesses to manage large amounts of information and to perform clerical tasks.

4. A microcomputer is the smallest and least expensive computer that is applicable to the instructional, measurement, and other data-processing needs of schools.

5. Components of a microcomputer system can be divided into hardware and software.
   a. Hardware components consist of a keyboard, a central processing unit (called a CPU), and a video-display terminal. Additional hardware components (called peripherals) consist of audiocassette recorders, disk drives, modems, and printers.
   b. Software consists of the computer programs that give step-by-step directions to the computer. Computer programs can be stored on plug-in cartridges, audiocassettes, or disks.

6. Generally, computer software is not interchangeable from one brand of microcomputer to another. This necessitates the careful matching of software and computer before making a purchase.

7. The work of a microcomputer can be divided into three stages: input, processing, and output.
   a. The input stage consists of giving the computer the instructions and data with which it will work. This is ordinarily accomplished with a computer program and by typing data into the computer from a keyboard. Instructions may also be given directly to the computer through the use of a computer language. BASIC (Beginner's All-Purpose Symbolic Instructional Code) is a popular and easy-to-learn computer language.
   b. The process step consists of converting the input to a form specified by the computer program.
   c. Output is the final product produced by the computer which appears on the video-display or printer. Output may be in a variety of forms, including item analyses, descriptive data, test items, tests, student names, grades, objectives, and even the identification of student strengths and weakness.

8. The microcomputer can be used for:
   a. Storing, updating, and printing instructional objectives
   b. Randomly selecting test items from a large pool of items according to objective, difficulty level, or some other criteria
   c. Calculating quantitative item analyses, indicating test item faults
   d. Keeping records of student performance over different tests
   e. Calculating, averaging, and storing grades
   f. Tracking changes in pupil test performance as a result of new teaching methods, instructional materials, or curricula
   g. Summarizing large amounts of data by grade level and school
9. Steps in selecting a microcomputer consist of the following:
   a. Identifying your specific objectives for the use of a microcomputer
   b. Identifying the software available to meet your specific objectives
   c. Identifying the features you will need in your computer and related software to meet your objectives
   d. Comparing the different computers and rating them according to the features listed in Table 21.1

For Discussion

1. The terms *hardware* and *software* come up repeatedly when educators discuss microcomputers. Imagine you are talking with a teacher who is totally unfamiliar with such jargon. How would you explain the difference between these terms? What examples could you give of each?
2. Having helped the teacher become familiar with hardware and software, the teacher asks, "How does a computer work?" Assume you can't run and hide. How would you respond to this question? (*Hint*: Try to organize your answer around the terms *input, processing,* and *output.)*
3. Imagine that you have access to a microcomputer at your school. To what measurement-related uses could you put the computer? (*Note*: Respond in terms of your own area of specialization—reading, math, science, special education, and so on.)
4. Because of your recent completion of a course in Tests and Measurements that included microcomputer selection and use, your principal designates you to be his representative at the district's Committee for Computer Acquisitions. At the first meeting the chairperson asks whether anybody has any objections to "simply getting as many ABC Computers as our budget allows, and then building our computer training around them." How would you respond? What would your alternative recommendation(s) be?

22

CHAPTER

IN THE CLASSROOM:
A SUMMARY DIALOGUE

|T| he following is a dialogue between Ms. Wilson, a sixth-grade teacher, and some of the school staff with whom she works. Ms. Wilson is three months into her first teaching assignment at a middle school in a medium-sized metropolitan school district. We begin our dialogue with Ms. Wilson on a Friday afternoon as she wraps up the final class session before a quarterly testing period is to begin.

MS. WILSON: I know you all feel we've covered a tremendous amount this year. Well, you're right. We have. And now it's time to find out how much you've learned. It's important for you to know how well you're doing in each subject so you can work harder in the areas where you might need improvement. It's also nice to know in what areas you might be smarter than almost everyone else. So, next week, I want you to be ready to take tests over all the material we have covered so far. (*A few students groan in unison.*) Remember, this will be your chance to show me how smart you are. I want you to get plenty of sleep Sunday night so you'll be fresh and alert Monday. (*As the bell rings, Ms. Wilson shouts over the commotion of students leaving the classroom.*) Don't forget, I'll be collecting homework on Monday!

(*As Ms. Wilson collapses into her chair, Mr. Palmer, an experienced teacher, walks in.*)

MR. PALMER: Glad this grading period is just about over. Next week will be a nice break, don't you think? Just reviewing and giving tests. It'll sure be nice to have this weekend free without any preparations to worry about.

MS. WILSON: You mean you won't be making up tests this weekend!

MR. PALMER: No. I have tests from the last three years which I've been refining and improving. With only a few modifications, they'll do fine.

MS. WILSON: You're awfully lucky. I'm afraid I haven't had a chance to even think about how I'm going to test these kids. All these subjects to make tests for, and then all the scoring and grading to do by next Friday. I think I'm going to have an awful weekend.

MR. PALMER: Will you be giving criterion-referenced or norm-referenced tests?

MS. WILSON: Umm . . . well . . . I don't know. I remember hearing those terms in a tests and measurement class I once took, but I guess I just haven't had time to worry about those things until now. I suppose I'm going to have to get my old textbook out tonight and do some reviewing. Gosh! I hope I can find it.

MR. PALMER: Well, if you use norm-referenced tests, there are some available in Ms. Cartwright's office. You know, she's the counselor who is always so helpful with discipline problems. In fact, she has a whole file full of tests.

MS. WILSON: Will *you* be using norm-referenced tests next week?

MR. PALMER: Not really. For these mid-semester grades, I like to make my tests very specific to what I've been teaching. At this point in the year it seems to provide better feedback to the kids and parents—especially the parents. Anyway, the parents aren't really interested in where their kid scores in relation to other students until later in the semester, when I've covered more content and the kids have had a chance to get their feet on the ground.

MS. WILSON: You mean these norm-referenced tests don't cover specifically what you've taught?

MR. PALMER: (*trying to be tactful*) Well, no. Not exactly. I guess you *have* forgotten a few things since you've taken that tests and measurement course.

MS. WILSON: I guess so.

MR. PALMER: Why don't you make a test blueprint and compare it to some of the items in Ms. Cartwright's test file.

MS. WILSON: A test *what* print?

MR. PALMER: A test *blue*print. You know, where you take the objectives from your lesson plans and construct a table that shows the content you've been teaching and the level of complexity—knowledge, comprehension, application—that you're shooting for. Then, see how Ms. Cartwright's tests match the test blueprint.

MS. WILSON: But, what if I didn't write down all my objectives. I had objectives of course, but I just didn't write them down all the time, or when I did, I usually didn't keep them for long. You know what I mean? (*No comment from Mr. Palmer.*) And I don't think I wrote them so they included levels of complexity according to that taxonomy-of-objectives thing I think you're referring to.

MR. PALMER: But, I'm afraid without objectives you won't know if the items on Ms. Cartwright's tests match what you've taught. Would you believe that last year a teacher in this school flunked half his class using a test that didn't match what he taught. Boy, what a stir that caused!

MS. WILSON: (*looking worried*) I guess I'll have to start from scratch then. It looks like a *very long weekend.*

MR. PALMER: Of course, you might consider giving some essay items.

MS. WILSON: You mean long-answer, not multiple-choice questions?

MR. PALMER: Yes, but you'll have to consider the time it will take to develop a scoring guide for each question and in grading all of those answers. And, then, of course, only some of your objectives may be suited to an essay format.

MS. WILSON: (*trying to sort out all of what Mr. Palmer just said without sounding too stupid*) By scoring guide, do you mean the right answer?

MR. PALMER: Well, not quite. As you know, essay items can have more than one right answer. So, first you will have to identify all the different elements that make an answer right and then decide how to weigh or assign points to each of these elements, depending on what percentage of the right answer they represent.

MS. WILSON: How do you decide that?

MR. PALMER: (*trying to be polite and being evasive for the sake of politeness*) Well . . . very carefully.

MS. WILSON: I see. (*long pause*). Well, maybe my old tests and measurement book will have something on that.

MR. PALMER: I'm sure it will.

MS. WILSON: Sounds as though I have my work cut out for me. I guess I'll just have to organize my time and start to work as soon as I get home.

(*Mr. Palmer and Ms. Wilson leave the classroom and meet Mr. Smith, another teacher.*)

MR. SMITH: You won't believe the meeting I just had with Johnny Haringer's parents!

MR. PALMER AND MS. WILSON: What happened?

MR. SMITH: Well, they came to see me after Johnny missed an A by two points on one of my weekly math tests. It was the first time that he had missed an A the entire semester.

MS. WILSON: Were they mad?

MR. SMITH: They were at first. But, I stayed calm and explained very carefully why two points on the test really should make a difference between an A and a B.

MS. WILSON: What kinds of things did you tell them?

MR. SMITH: Well, luckily I keep student data from past years for all my tests. This allows me to calculate reliability and validity coefficients for my tests using one of the microcomputers in the math lab. I simply explained to Johnny's parents, in everyday, commonsense language, what reliability and validity of a test meant, and then gave them some statistical data to support my case. I also explained the care and deliberation I put into the construction of my tests—you know, all the steps you go through in writing test items and then checking their content validity and doing qualitative and quantitative item analyses. I think they got the idea of just how much work it takes to construct a good test.

MS. WILSON: And?

MR. SMITH: And after that they calmed down and were very responsive to my explanation. They even commented that they hadn't realized the science of statistics could be so helpful in determining the reliability and validity of a test. They even commended me for being so systematic and careful. Can you believe that?

MS. WILSON: Umm . . . reliability and validity? Do you mean we have to know the reliability and validity for every test we use?

MR. SMITH: Ever since that lawsuit by the parents of some kid over at Central for unfair testing, the school board has made every teacher individually responsible for using reliable and valid tests.

(*Looking surprised, Ms. Wilson turns to Mr. Palmer and Mr. Palmer slowly and painfully nods to indicate his agreement with what Mr. Smith has been saying.*)

MS. WILSON: Boy! I don't think I could explain reliability and validity that well—at least not to parents—and I know I wouldn't have the slightest idea of how to compute them.

MR. SMITH: Well, I guess we won't have any preparations to worry about this weekend . . . nothing but review and testing next week. You kids have a nice weekend.

MR. PALMER: Well, it may not be all that bad. You've got that tests and measurement text at home and next quarter. Who knows? You may have time to plan for all this ahead of time.

MS. WILSON: (*being purposely negative*) That's if I don't have to explain reliability and validity to some irate kid's parents, construct a test blueprint, learn the difference between norm-referenced and criterion-referenced tests, make a scoring key for an essay test, and, of course, compute some test item statistics I probably can't even pronounce!

MR. PALMER: Let's get to your car before the roof falls in.

MR. PALMER: (*to Ms. Wilson under his breath*) Speaking of the roof!

(*The principal approaches them.*)

PRINCIPAL: Ah, Ms. Wilson. I'm glad I ran into you. How'd things go for you this quarter?

MS. WILSON: Very well, thank you. I really like my classroom and the parents I've met have been very nice. All my students—well almost all—have made me feel at home.

PRINCIPAL: Good. I've had good reports about your teaching, and your classroom discipline and management seems to be improving. I suppose you're all set for the end of this grading period. It's only a week away you know. (*The principal looks at Ms. Wilson for some kind of response.*)

MS. WILSON: (*after a brief pause she responds almost inaudibly*) Yes.

PRINCIPAL: Well, that's excellent because you know how much emphasis our parents place on grades. All of our teachers spend a lot of time on grading. We've never had a serious incident in this regard like they've had over at Central. I'd like to think it was because of my policy that every teacher be responsible for using reliable and valid tests *and* for interpreting test scores to parents. I only wish that all teachers in the state would have to prove themselves competent in tests and measurement to be certified, like they do in some other states. I'm sure there would be a lot fewer angry students and parents, if this were the case. Well, Ms. Wilson, glad things are going so well. Have a nice weekend now. You, too, Mr. Palmer.

MS. WILSON: Thank you.

MR. PALMER: You too.

MS. WILSON: I don't think I've had a more miserable Friday afternoon. I can only guess what the weekend will be like.

MR. PALMER: Maybe I can help. (*Ms. Wilson looks directly at him.*) I have this tests and measurement book called *Educational Testing and Measurement: Classroom Application and Practice,* which covers the kinds of things that might be helpful in preparing your tests for next week. If you're not busy, why don't I bring it over and help you with those tests.

MS. WILSON (*straining to be reserved and matter-of-fact*) I guess that would be . . . OK. (*then, with a sigh of relief*) Yes, I think that would be fine.

You might think this scenario is a bit farfetched. It may come as a surprise, but we are willing to bet that something like this will happen to you long before the end of your first grading period. The incidents we have described repeat themselves thousands of times each school day in schools across the country. Unlike the preceding story some have less happy endings. Let's examine the testing issues that confronted Ms. Wilson.

CRITERION-REFERENCED VERSUS NORM-REFERENCED TESTS

One of the first issues that Ms. Wilson had to deal with was whether to use criterion-referenced or norm-referenced tests. Of course, she hardly knows the difference between them, so it should be no surprise later if there are misunderstandings between her, her pupils, and their parents over the meaning of her grades. Recall that criterion-referenced tests report test scores in relation to the test. That is, they are graded in terms of the number or percent of items a student gets correct. Grades—such as A, B, C, etc.—are usually assigned indicating the level of knowledge or skill that was attained. These grades should reflect estimates of the level of performance necessary to do well according to certain criteria, for example, to divide and multiply four-digit numbers with decimals, to divide and multiply fractions, or to square whole numbers. It is these types of criteria that Mr. Smith is likely to have related to Johnny Haringer's parents in order to explain why the two-point difference in Johnny's test score should make a difference. In other words, Mr. Smith's grades were based on real performance skills that Johnny's parents could understand and appreciate. For most interim grades from which teachers are expected to diagnose learning difficulties and prepare remedial instruction, criterion-referenced tests are, generally, the most useful. Unfortunately, Ms. Wilson forgot or never knew that one of the first steps in preparing a test is to determine the *purpose* of the test.

If Ms. Wilson's purpose (and the school's) for this grading period was to determine where each student stood in reference to other students, an existing norm-referenced test might have been perfectly adequate. Needless to say, this testing purpose might have saved Ms. Wilson's weekend. Generally, however, interim grading periods are used for the purpose of providing feedback to students, their parents, and the teacher as to how well students have learned and teachers have taught specific skills. This objective usually calls for the use of a criterion-referenced test.

Even if Ms. Wilson had decided beforehand to use criterion-referenced tests, Mr. Palmer's suggestion of looking at Ms. Cartwright's norm-referenced tests was a good one. This is especially true in light of Mr. Palmer's suggestion that a test blueprint be used to determine which, if any, items from these tests matched the specific content that Ms. Wilson taught. As long as these norm referenced tests were not to be given to these students at a later time, items from them might be effectively used in a criterion-referenced test, saving Ms. Wilson from preparing every item from scratch.

INSTRUCTIONAL OBJECTIVES

Another issue raised in the course of this dialogue concerned the proper use of instructional objectives. One implication should be clear. Instructional objectives not only help teachers organize their teaching—they help them write tests, too. However, Ms. Wilson took a careless approach to writing instructional objectives, so they could not very well be used to help construct her tests. It's likely that some failed to specify the level of behavior or the conditions under which the behavior could be expected to be performed. This would prevent her from matching her instruction to the items in Ms. Cartwright's test files. It also means that Ms. Wilson must rely only on her memory as to what was and was not covered during the thirteen-week grading period. Let's hope Ms. Wilson's tests don't ask her students questions that were never formally taught or taught at a level different than that represented by her test items.

Lawsuits involving unfair testing stem from situations similar to that in which Ms. Wilson now finds herself. Settlements against teachers and districts can occur if it can be shown that some harm has come to the student as a result of the neglect of proper testing procedures. Ms. Wilson seems to be in such a precarious position on this issue that we can only hope her weekend makes up for the effort that was missing earlier in the semester. Given that this is an interim grading period in which formal decisions about a student's progress are not likely to be made, Ms. Wilson will probably avoid any serious problems—this time.

THE TEST BLUEPRINT

We've already discussed the use of the test blueprint, but a few more points about this important tool can be made. Recall from Chapter 5 that a test blueprint is simply a table that lists the important objectives to be taught and the levels of student behavior that can be expected from these objectives. In the cells of the table are placed the number or percent of items that cover each topic at a particular level of behavior. The test blueprint can be an important device for planning a test when it is used to decide the number of items that should be written for each major objective as well as for evaluating an existing test when it is used to determine how well a test compares in types and numbers of items with what has been taught.

Ms. Wilson had the opportunity of using a test blueprint in both of these ways. Had a test blueprint been prepared, Ms. Wilson could have quickly sorted through Ms. Cartwright's test file to determine if the content of any test items matched the content of any of the cells in the test blueprint. This might have precluded the need for Ms. Wilson to personally write every test item needed. The key to preparing a test blueprint is the preparation of behavioral objectives that include the level of behavior that is being taught. Unfortunately, Ms. Wilson now must pay for failing to properly prepare behavioral objectives with the more arduous task of constructing all new test items and the uncertainty of whether these test items accurately and fairly reflect the content she has taught.

ESSAY ITEMS AND THE ESSAY SCORING GUIDES

Recall that another suggestion given by Mr. Palmer was that some of the items Ms. Wilson needed could be essay items. Mr. Palmer's suggestion was probably based upon the notion that a large block of content could be tested with one or a few essay items. While the implication here is that some time could be saved in the test preparation process for some content areas by writing essay items, Mr. Palmer was correct in suggesting that essay items will only be appropriate for some content areas and some teaching objectives (for example, where rote recall and memorization of facts were not the primary objectives). Also, it should be recognized that the time needed to prepare scoring guides and to grade essay items might outweigh the fact that the initial essay question might be easy to write. Ms. Wilson seemed to be unaware of the need for scoring guides, presumably thinking that essay items are simply scored right or wrong as multiple-choice items are. But, as was seen in Chapter 7, this is not the case. Points are assigned to essay items in relation to the extent to which the student includes in his or her answer the elements of a good response. The scoring of essay items requires specifying these elements before the grading begins and identifying examples of the different alternatives that might adequately represent the elements of a good response. All this takes considerable time and effort, which Ms. Wilson did not expect.

Like many new teachers, Ms. Wilson probably saw the essay item as an easy way out of having to write many different test items. As Mr. Palmer pointed out, though, scoring essays reliably is time-consuming. Nevertheless, Ms. Wilson should have considered essay items. We say this because it is entirely likely, even probable, that some of the content Ms. Wilson has taught during the semester *should* be tested with essay items. Since Ms. Wilson will have to cram all of her test construction into a single weekend, it is unlikely that time can be spent in identifying which content is best tested with an essay format and in preparing scoring guides. Here again, an earlier start on a test blueprint might have paid rich dividends in time saved later.

RELIABILITY, VALIDITY, AND TEST STATISTICS

Mr. Smith raised the important issues of reliability and validity. Nothing could be more fundamental to a good test than its reliability and validity—that is, its capacity to consistently give the same or similar score over repeated testings and to measure what it is supposed to measure. These two terms have technical meanings, which were presented in Chapters 15 and 16, but they also have practical, commonsense meanings, and these should be second-nature to any beginning teacher.

The practical or commonsense notions that lie behind the concepts of reliability and validity are far more present in our everyday lives than is frequently believed. These two words, *reliability* and *validity*, appear in all types of writing—from newspapers and weekly news magazines to popular books as well as in the language of businessmen and women, engineers, nurses, social workers, and people from all walks of life. The significance of this fact for the teacher is that parents and even some of your students will be aware of these concepts and will not hesitate to confront you with them (albeit sometimes inaccurately) when they feel they may be used to their advantage. It is unfortunate that many parents have only a partial or limited knowledge of these concepts as they apply to testing. But, it is even more unfortunate that some teachers are unable to correct the misunderstandings that parents sometimes have about these concepts. It is not that most teachers lack textbook definitions for these terms, but that they are unable to convert these definitions to the practical language that students and their parents are likely to understand. Of course, the main advantage for the teacher knowing practical ways to discuss the concepts of reliability and validity is that they can be invaluable tools in communicating the meaning of test scores to parents and in justifying and defending decisions based upon these test scores.

Mr. Smith's interaction with Johnny Haringer's parents provided some evidence of a practical as well as technical knowledge of reliability and validity. Mr. Smith was able to defuse a potentially difficult meeting with Johnny's parents essentially because he could talk *their* language. He described reliability and validity with words that *they* could relate to. This is how Mr. Smith was able to strike a responsive chord, to get beneath the emotional issue that brought him together with Johnny's parents, and to communicate a commonsense understanding of the characteristics of a good test. This commonsense understanding went a long way toward turning a potentially nasty confrontation into a useful and productive meeting about Johnny's progress.

Recall also that Mr. Smith went beyond the simple commonsense notions of reliability and validity to actually show Johnny's parents some statistics indicating his test's reliability and validity. While most standardized tests will have these statistics already calculated and displayed for the teacher in the test's manual, the teacher will have to understand the test manual and give parents a faithful interpretation of what all the statistics mean, if the situation requires. Most of what was covered in Chapters 12 through 18 was intended to prepare the teacher for this task. On the other hand, Mr. Smith's test probably was not standardized and, therefore, Mr. Smith needed to calculate these statistics. Here, the availability of a computer program for calculating test statistics and his knowledge of the uses of a microcomputer made this easy. Any first-year teacher, particularly one in his or her first quarter of teaching, could not be expected to be prepared as well as Mr. Smith. But note that Mr. Smith made a point of saying that he always kept his test scores on file, probably in the microcomputer's memory. When time permitted, he used the microcomputer to calculate the necessary statistics to show a test's reliability and validity. This foresight paid off handsomely in his meeting with Johnny's parents. It would have been impossible for Mr. Smith to have calculated these statistics on the spot and probably even unlikely that they could have been calculated between the time Johnny's parents called for an appointment and the actual time the meeting took place. Instead, Mr. Smith used the microcomputer to calculate reliability. The computer program he used might have computed reliability using the Odd-Even or Kuder-Richardson method and validity by correlating a test's scores with end-of-semester or end-of-year test scores as was described in Chapters 15 and 16.

Even though Mr. Smith's reliability and validity statistics were not determined with student data from Johnny's test, they were calculated with student data from past semesters in which students similar to Johnny took the same test. As long as Mr. Smith's data were not too dated, they are acceptable evidence of the test's reliability and validity. Mr. Smith's foresight is within the reach of every teacher, and, if we are to take seriously the principal's admonition that parents and teachers place a great deal of emphasis on testing in this school, we suspect Ms. Wilson should plan on having some of this same foresight.

| GRADES AND MARKS

There is no better way in which to end this chapter, and indeed this book, than by reinforcing the critical role that grades and marks play in the testing process. As the most visible sign of the testing and measurement process, grades and marks stand as the end products that can make or break a test. Since Ms. Wilson had not thought about whether a criterion-referenced or norm-referenced strategy was appropriate, it is unlikely that she had given much thought about what marks or grades would be used in reporting the results of her tests to parents and students. Would she simply have used the school's formal reporting system to convey all the pertinent facts about a student's performance or would there be other marks that might make finer distinctions and interpretations of a student's strengths and weaknesses? Would Ms. Wilson even know the strengths and weaknesses of her students at the end of this testing? And, if so, how would they be communicated to students and parents?

It was apparent from Mr. Smith's discussion with Johnny's parents that information was available from his tests that separated students into more than simply A's, B's, C's, and so on. Specific differences between an A and a B presumably were recorded or at least could be retrieved from the test score data for the parent-teacher conference. Perhaps Mr. Smith's test was divided into a certain number of competencies, each of which could be marked "pass" or "fail." Then, maybe an A was based upon a student achieving "passes" on all competencies, a B based upon a student achieving "passes" on 9 out of 10 competencies, and so on. By making further differentiations across letter grades, Mr. Smith armed himself with some powerful ammunition as to why Johnny deserved a B, even though he missed an A by only two points. Mr. Smith learned the important point that grades are meaningless to students and parents unless some criterion can be attached to them that is seen as being of value to parents and teachers. Telling Johnny's parents that Johnny does not know how to divide and multiply two-digit numbers that have decimals—such as those that occur on end-of-year examinations, balancing a checkbook, in homework assignments in the next grade, and in finding the best buy per ounce among competing products in a grocery store—goes a lot further to convince his parents that Johnny has a weakness that must be remedied than simply telling them that Johnny deserves a B, not an A.

These are only a hint of the many problems involved in choosing grades and marks, which were covered in Chapter 9. Even if a test is meticulously constructed, has high reliability and validity, and has been carefully administered and graded, it still can be considered a poor test, unless the grades that are based upon it can be communicated meaningfully to parents and students. While Mr. Smith has obviously given some thought to this aspect of testing, Ms. Wilson still has this lesson to learn.

SOME FINAL THOUGHTS

In the previous discussion of issues related to our dialogue, we admittedly have been pretty hard on Ms. Wilson. Even in this seemingly small slice of classroom life, Ms. Wilson has been confronted with more problems than she can possibly deal with in the time available to her for constructing the following week's tests. But if you think this brief dialogue has been hard on Ms. Wilson, you will be surprised to learn that these are not all the problems that she would need to confront in the real world. We believe we have been kind to Ms. Wilson by limiting her distress and discomfort to one Friday afternoon and to only the few measurement concepts we chose to discuss in our dialogue. The real world of the classroom is not so accommodating. It presents testing and measurement problems every day of the week and each week of the school year. Also, the cast of characters will be larger in the real world than the few who were included here. And we haven't even begun to characterize the different responses of students and parents, each of whom produce a unique challenge to the teacher who must explain and justify testing decisions.

After reading this book, you should have a better understanding of the practical side of testing and maybe even some insights into how to handle yourself should similar situations arise. But real life is not easily portrayed on the pages of a book. For you, the reader, and for us, the authors, it occurs only in classrooms, and this of course is why we have chosen to spend the better part of our lives in those classrooms. Our advice is to use this book to prepare for that real world. Review its contents often and keep this book close at hand for future reference. Combine the skills you have learned with your good judgment and experience and you will be sure to continue to learn as you teach.

A

APPENDIX

MATH SKILLS REVIEW

This review of math skills covers all operations necessary to complete the calculations in this text. The Self-Check Test and answer key that appear at the end of the appendix can help you determine which skills you may need to review.

Order of Terms

The order of terms in addition is irrelevant.

$$2 + 3 = 3 + 2 = 5$$

The order of terms in subtraction is important.

$$3 - 2 \neq 2 - 3$$

The order of terms in multiplication is also irrelevant.

$$3(2) = 2(3) = 6$$

There are several ways to write "multiplied by."

$$3 \times 2 = 3(2) = 3 \cdot 2 = 6$$

The order of terms in division is important.

$$6/2 \neq 2/6$$

There are several ways to write "divided by."

$$4 \div 2 = 4/2 = 2\overline{)4} = 2$$

Order of Operations

When multiplying (or dividing) the sum (or difference) of several numbers by another number, you may either multiply (divide) or add (subtract) first.

$$2(3 + 4) = 2(7) = 14 \text{ or } 2(3 + 4) = 6 + 8 = 14$$
$$3(5 - 1) = 3(4) = 12 \text{ or } 3(5 - 1) = 15 - 3 = 12$$

$$\frac{6 + 4}{2} = \frac{10}{2} = 5 \text{ or } \frac{6 + 4}{2} = \frac{6}{2} + \frac{4}{2} = 3 + 2 = 5$$

$$\frac{9 - 6}{3} = \frac{3}{3} = 1 \text{ or } \frac{9 - 6}{3} = \frac{9}{3} - \frac{6}{3} = 3 - 2 = 1$$

The operations within parentheses are done first. Within the parentheses, multiplication and division are done before addition and subtraction. After math in the parentheses is finished, other multiplications and divisions are done before additions and subtractions.

$$(3 - 2) - 4(6 + 1) + 8 = \qquad (4/2) + 3(2 + 6) - 3 =$$
$$1 - 4(7) + 8 = \qquad\qquad 2 + 3(8) - 3 =$$
$$1 - 28 + 8 = -19 \qquad\qquad 2 + 24 - 3 = 23$$

$$(6 + 4) - 6(3 - 2) + 11 =$$
$$10 - 6(1) + 11 =$$
$$10 - 6 + 11 = 15$$

Fractions

Addition and subtraction require the fractions to have the same denominator. If a common denominator is not obvious, this may be accomplished by multiplying the two denominators. In order to keep the value of the new fractions equal to that of the original fractions, the numerators are multiplied by the denominator of the other fraction (cross-multiplying).

$$\frac{1}{2} + \frac{1}{4} = \frac{4}{8} + \frac{2}{8} = \frac{6}{8} = \frac{3}{4}$$

$$\frac{2}{3} - \frac{2}{5} = \frac{10}{15} - \frac{6}{15} = \frac{4}{15}$$

$$\frac{1}{5} + \frac{1}{2} = \frac{2}{10} + \frac{5}{10} = \frac{7}{10}$$

This could also be accomplished by multiplying both the numerator and the denominator of each fraction by the denominator of the other fraction.

$$\frac{1}{2} + \frac{1}{4}$$

$$\frac{1}{2} \times \frac{4}{4} = \frac{4}{8} \text{ and } \frac{1}{4} \times \frac{2}{2} = \frac{2}{8} \text{ so } \cdot \frac{4}{8} + \frac{2}{8} = \frac{6}{8} = \frac{3}{4}$$

$$\frac{2}{3} - \frac{2}{5}$$

$$\frac{2}{3} \times \frac{5}{5} = \frac{10}{15} \text{ and } \frac{2}{5} \times \frac{3}{3} = \frac{6}{15} \text{ so } \frac{10}{15} - \frac{6}{15} = \frac{4}{15}$$

$$\frac{1}{5} + \frac{1}{2}$$

$$\frac{1}{5} \times \frac{2}{2} = \frac{2}{10} \text{ and } \frac{1}{2} \times \frac{5}{5} = \frac{5}{10} \text{ so } \frac{2}{10} + \frac{5}{10} = \frac{7}{10}$$

To multiply two fractions, simply multiply across the numerators and across the denominators.

$$\frac{3}{4} \times \frac{1}{2} = \frac{3}{8} \qquad \frac{2}{7} \times \frac{1}{3} = \frac{2}{21} \qquad \frac{3}{6} \times \frac{1}{3} = \frac{3}{18}$$

To divide two fractions, invert the divisor and then multiply.

$$\frac{3}{8} \div \frac{1}{2} = \frac{3}{8} \cdot \frac{2}{1} = \frac{3}{4} \qquad \frac{2}{3} \div \frac{3}{4} = \frac{2}{3} \cdot \frac{4}{3} = \frac{8}{9}$$

$$\frac{1}{2} \div \frac{3}{5} = \frac{1}{2} \cdot \frac{5}{3} = \frac{5}{6} \qquad \frac{3}{4} \div \frac{4}{5} = \frac{3}{4} \cdot \frac{5}{4} = \frac{15}{16}$$

To simplify multiplication and division of fractions you may cancel out equal amounts in the numerators and denominators.

$$\frac{1}{2} \cdot \frac{2}{3} \div \frac{1}{9} = \frac{1}{2} \cdot \frac{2}{3} \cdot \frac{9}{1} = \frac{1}{\cancel{2}_1} \cdot \frac{\cancel{2}^1}{\cancel{3}_1} \cdot \frac{\cancel{9}^3}{1} = \frac{3}{1} = 3$$

$$\frac{3}{24} \cdot \frac{8}{9} \div \frac{1}{2} = \frac{3}{24} \cdot \frac{8}{9} \cdot \frac{2}{1} = \frac{\cancel{3}^1}{\cancel{24}_3} \cdot \frac{\cancel{8}^1}{\cancel{9}_3} \cdot \frac{2}{1} = \frac{2}{9}$$

$$\frac{1}{32} \div \frac{1}{16} \cdot \frac{3}{4} = \frac{1}{32} \cdot \frac{16}{1} \cdot \frac{3}{4} = \frac{1}{\cancel{32}_2} \cdot \frac{\cancel{16}^1}{1} \cdot \frac{3}{4} = \frac{3}{8}$$

Mixed Numbers

In addition and subtraction, it is only necessary to have the denominators of the fractions the same.

$$2\frac{1}{4} + 3\frac{1}{3} = 2\frac{3}{12} + 3\frac{4}{12} = 5\frac{7}{12}$$

$$8\frac{2}{3} - 3\frac{2}{7} = 8\frac{14}{21} - 3\frac{6}{21} = 5\frac{8}{21}$$

$$6\frac{2}{3} + 4\frac{1}{4} = 6\frac{8}{12} + 4\frac{3}{12} = 10\frac{11}{12}$$

In subtraction it is sometimes necessary to "borrow" from the whole number in order to subtract the fractional part.

$$4\frac{1}{2} - 2\frac{2}{3} = 4\frac{3}{6} - 2\frac{4}{6}$$

You cannot subtract the fractions, but since $1 = \frac{6}{6}$ you can convert $4\frac{3}{6}$ to $3\frac{9}{6}$, so

$$3\frac{9}{6} - 2\frac{4}{6} = 1\frac{5}{6}$$

An easier way to convert mixed numbers is to multiply the whole number by the denominator of the fraction, then add the numerator.

$$3\frac{1}{2} = \frac{(3\cdot2)+1}{2} = \frac{6+1}{2} = \frac{7}{2}$$

$$2\frac{3}{4} = \frac{(2\cdot4)+3}{4} = \frac{8+3}{4} = \frac{11}{4}$$

$$8\frac{1}{3} = \frac{(8\cdot3)+1}{3} = \frac{24+1}{3} = \frac{25}{3}$$

Decimals

To convert a fraction to a decimal fraction, perform simple division.

$$\frac{3}{8} = 8\overline{)3.000}^{.375} \qquad \frac{1}{2} = 2\overline{)1.0}^{.5} \qquad \frac{3}{4} = 4\overline{)3.00}^{.75}$$

The number of decimal places is not changed by addition or subtraction.

$$
\begin{array}{r} .2 \\ + .5 \\ \hline .7 \end{array}
\qquad
\begin{array}{r} .68 \\ - .32 \\ \hline .36 \end{array}
\qquad
\begin{array}{r} .374 \\ - .234 \\ \hline .140 \end{array}
\qquad
\begin{array}{r} .949 \\ + .055 \\ \hline 1.004 \end{array}
$$

In multiplication, the number of decimal places in the answer is equal to the total of the number of places in the numbers you are multiplying.

$$
\begin{array}{r} .42 \\ \times .003 \\ \hline .00126 \end{array}
\qquad
\begin{array}{r} .81 \\ \times .2 \\ \hline .162 \end{array}
\qquad
\begin{array}{r} .5 \\ \times .5 \\ \hline .25 \end{array}
\qquad
\begin{array}{r} .24 \\ \times .02 \\ \hline .0048 \end{array}
$$

In division, the divisor is converted to a whole number by moving the decimal point to the right as many places as necessary. The decimal point in the number you are dividing into must be moved the same number of places to the right.

$$.25\overline{)1.000} \text{ becomes } 25\overline{)100.0}^{\,4.0}$$

$$.32\overline{)6.4} \quad \text{becomes } 32\overline{)640.}^{\,20.}$$

$$.482\overline{)14.46} \text{ becomes } 482\overline{)14460.}^{\,30.}$$

Squares and Square Roots

Squaring a number is multiplying it by itself.

$$3^2 = 3(3) = 9 \qquad 4^2 = 4(4) = 16$$

Taking a square root is finding a number which, when multiplied by itself, equals the number of which you are taking the square root.

$$\sqrt{4} = +2 \text{ or } -2 \text{ since } 2(2) = 4 \text{ and } -2(-2) = 4$$

$$\sqrt{16} = 4 \text{ or } -4 \text{ since } 4(4) = 16 \text{ and } -4(-4) = 16$$

$$\sqrt{9} = 3 \text{ or } -3 \text{ since } 3(3) = 9 \text{ or } -3(-3) = 9$$

Algebra

To solve equations, you must get the unknown (usually symbolized by x) on one side of the equation, and all other numbers on the other side. This is done by adding, subtracting, multiplying, or dividing *both* sides of the equation by the same number.

$$2x = 4$$

Divide both sides by 2 $\qquad \dfrac{2x}{2} = \dfrac{4}{2}$

$$x = 2$$

$$\dfrac{x}{6} = 3$$

Multiply both sides by 6 $\qquad \dfrac{6x}{6} = 3(6)$

$$x = 18$$

$$x + 3 = 9$$

Substract 3 from both sides $\quad (x + 3) - 3 = 9 - 3$

$$x = 6$$

$$x - 4 = 6$$

Add 4 to both sides $\qquad (x - 4) + 4 = 6 + 4$

$$x = 10$$

This procedure can also be done in combinations of the above.

$$2x + 4 = 10$$

Substract 4 from both sides $\qquad (2x + 4) - 4 = 10 - 4$

$$2x = 6$$

Divide both sides by 2 $\qquad \dfrac{2x}{2} = \dfrac{6}{2}$

$$x = 3$$

$$3x + 15 = 75$$

Subtract 15 from both sides $\qquad (3x + 15) - 15 = 75 - 15$

$$3x = 60$$

Divide both sides by 3
$$\frac{3x}{3} = \frac{60}{3}$$
$$x = 20$$

$$4x + 10 = 110$$

Subtract 10 from both sides
$$(4x + 10) - 10 = 110 - 10$$
$$4x = 100$$

Divide both sides by 4
$$\frac{4x}{4} = \frac{100}{4}$$
$$x = 25$$

Self-Check Test

DIRECTIONS: Solve the following problems:

_____ 1. $13^2 =$ _____

_____ 2. Convert $\frac{1}{4}$ to a decimal _____

_____ 3. $\sqrt{144} =$ _____

_____ 4. $24(380 + 20) =$ _____

_____ 5. $\frac{2}{5} + \frac{3}{15} =$ _____

_____ 6. $144 \div .048 =$ _____

_____ 7. $16x + 10 = 330$ _____

_____ 8. $\frac{2}{3} \div \frac{7}{10} =$ _____

_____ 9. $1.32 \cdot .07 =$ _____

_____ 10. $2\frac{2}{3} + 6\frac{1}{12} =$ _____

_____ 11. Convert $\frac{1}{5}$ to a decimal _____

_____ 12. $\frac{2}{3} \div \frac{14}{15} \cdot \frac{2}{5} =$ _____

_____ 13. $(24 - 15) - 2(17 + 4) + 32 =$ _____

_____ 14. $1.375 + .139 =$ _____

_____ 15. $9x + 72 = 342$ $x =$ _____

Answers: **1.** $13 \times 13 = 169$;   **2.** .25;   **3.** 12 or −12;   **4.** 9,600;
5. $\frac{3}{5}$;   **6.** 3000;   **7.** 20;   **8.** $\frac{20}{21}$ **9.** .0924;   **10.** $8\frac{3}{4}$;
11. .2;   **12.** $\frac{2}{7}$;   **13.** −1;   **14.** 1.514;   **15.** 30

APPENDIX

PEARSON PRODUCT MOMENT CORRELATION

The following example illustrates the raw score method for computing the Pearson Product Moment Correlation Coefficient (r). Listed in the X and Y columns are pairs of raw scores for each student. The X^2 column lists the square of each X score. The Y^2 column lists the square of each Y score. The XY column lists the cross products of the X and Y columns (X multiplied by Y).

Name	X	Y	Step 1 X^2	Step 2 Y^2	XY	
Art	10	14	100	196	140	
Ben	7	12	49	144	84	
Cathy	5	7	25	49	35	
Debbie	9	12	81	144	108	
Eugene	6	9	36	81	54	
Fred	11	15	121	225	165	
Glenda	2	5	4	25	10	
Henry	2	4	4	16	8	
Mary	5	14	25	196	70	
Sharon	4	7	16	49	28	
	61	99	461	1125	702	**Step 3**

To compute a Pearson Product Moment Correlation Coefficient for the above data, follow these steps:

1. Square each X score, and each Y score.
2. Multiply each person's X score (not the squared X score) times the same person's Y score (again, not the squared Y score).
3. Sum the X, Y, X², Y², and XY columns.
4. Plug the values into the following formula:

$$r = \frac{\Sigma XY - \dfrac{(\Sigma X)\ (\Sigma Y)}{N}}{\sqrt{\Sigma X^2 - \dfrac{(\Sigma X)^2}{N}}\ \sqrt{\Sigma Y^2 - \dfrac{(\Sigma U)^2}{N}}}$$

where ΣXY is the sum of the XY column,
ΣX is the sum of all X scores,
ΣY is the sum of all Y scores,
N is the number of persons observed,
ΣX^2 is the sum of the X² column, and
ΣY^2 is the sum of the Y² column.

$$r = \frac{702 - \dfrac{(61)\ (99)}{10}}{\sqrt{461 - \dfrac{(61)^2}{10}}\ \sqrt{1125 - \dfrac{(99)^2}{10}}}$$

$$= \frac{702 - \dfrac{6039}{10}}{\sqrt{461 - \dfrac{3721}{10}}\ \sqrt{1125 - \dfrac{9801}{10}}}$$

$$= \frac{702 - 603.9}{\sqrt{461 - 372.1}\ \sqrt{1125 - 980.1}}$$

$$= \frac{98.1}{\sqrt{88.9}\ \sqrt{144.9}}$$

$$= \frac{98.1}{(9.43)\ (12.04)}$$

$$= \frac{98.1}{113.54}$$

$$= .86$$

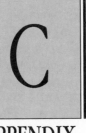

APPENDIX

STATISTICS AND MEASUREMENT TEXTS

Anastasi, A. *Psychological Testing,* 5th ed. New York: Macmillan, 1982.

Bartz, A. E. *Basic Statistical Concepts,* 2nd ed. Minneapolis: Burgess, 1981.

Cronbach, L. J. *Essentials of Psychological Testing,* 3d ed. New York: Harper & Row, 1970.

Downie, N. M., & Heath, R. W. *Basic Statistical Methods.* New York: Harper & Row, 1983.

Lyman, H. B. *Test Scores and What They Mean,* 3d ed. Englewood Cliffs, New Jersey: Prentice-Hall, 1978.

Phillips, J. L. *Statistical Thinking.* San Francisco: Freeman, 1982.

Stahl, S. M., & Hennes, J. D. *Reading and Understanding Applied Statistics: A Self-Learning Approach,* 2d ed. St. Louis: Mosby, 1980.

Young, R. K., & Veldman, D. J. *Introductory Statistics for the Behavioral Sciences,* 4th ed. New York: Holt, Rinehart, & Winston, 1981.

D

APPENDIX

ANSWERS FOR PRACTICE QUESTIONS

Chapter 4

3. (a) B, (b) E, (c) B, (d) E, (e) B, (f) B, (g) E, (h) B
5. (1) c, (2) d, (3) e, (4) a, (5) f, (6) b

Chapter 5

4. (1) D, (2) A, (3) B, (4) E, (5) F
5. (a) $2 + 1 + 0 = 3$; (b) $30 + 30 = 60$

Chapter 6

3. (a) The "a" should be "a/an."
   (b) National origin of the names in the stem provides a clue to the answer.
   (c) Contains an absolute, opinionated.
   (d) Multiple defensible answers, lacks specificity.
   (e) Begins with a blank, lacks specificity.
   (f) Lists should be titled and arranged in some logical order. Too wide a variety of concepts being measured, making some answers obvious (i.e., nonhomogeneous lists).

Chapter 8

1. .22, .64
2. .40, −.33
3. (a) ambiguity, (b) miskeyed, (c) ambiguity, (d) guessing, (e) miskeyed
4. p = .25, D = .10. The key discriminates positively, but not all distractors discriminate negatively. Probably some guessing and/or ambiguity.

Chapter 10

6. 2.0
7. (a) AV; (b) AP; (c) AV; (d) AV; (e) AP; (f) AP; (g) AP; (h) AP; (i) AV
8. (a) Too many thoughts (double-barreled)
   (b) Uses a negative, factual
   (c) References the past
   (d) Uses an absolute
   (e) Not direct or clearly written

Chapter 12

1. Grade 1, positively skewed; grade 3, normal; grade 5, negatively skewed
2. Group 1: N = 10, R = 13 (inclusive R = 14), $\overline{X}$ = 93.3, MDN = 94.0, Mode = 90, 94, and 97
   Group 2: N = 10, R = 36 (inclusive R = 37), $\overline{X}$ = 89.6, MDN = 92.5, Mode = 97
   The difference in means is caused by the score of 61 in Group 2. For Group 1 the mean would be the best measure of central tendency. For Group 2 the median would be the best measure of central tendency.
3. Use from 8 to 10 intervals. Choose the number that best demonstrates variations in the frequency of scores.
4. (1) c, (2) c, (3) a, (4) b, (5) b
5. P_{25} = 93.5; P_{50} = 99
6. (a) normal; (b) negatively skewed; (c) positively skewed
7. (a) simple frequency distribution, small number and range of scores
   (b) list, small number but large range
   (c) grouped frequency distribution, large number and range of scores

Chapter 13

1. N = 10, Mode = 5, Median = 4.5, Mean = 4.0, standard deviation = 1.61, Variance = 2.6, Range = 5 (inclusive R = 6)
2. (a) 2.0, 3.2, 4.0, 4.5

      (b) 75, 106, 112.5, 121.5

      (c) 125, 88, 85, 78

      (d) about 15%, 82%, 34.13%, about 11%

3. (a) 1.33, (b) 74.5, (c) about 16%
4. 35
5. John, −1.0, 40; Mary, +2.0, 70; Jim, +.5, 55; Claire, −1.5, 35
6. (a) 42.5, 121 (b) 700

Chapter 14

2. Curvilinear. Income goes up until age 60, then income decreases with age.
3. .844, positive and strong
4. .713
5. (a) 4, (b) 7, (c) 1, (d) 2
6. Disagree. A third variable, yet unmeasured, could cause both big feet and large vocabularies in the same individuals making the relationship only appear causal. More likely, however, since such a variable probably could not be identified, it would be appropriate to regard the high correlation as erroneously caused by insufficient N or sampling.
7. It restricts the variability of scores and, hence, cannot reveal the covariation of X and Y scores in the larger distribution of scores.

Chapter 15

1. The concurrent validity coefficient is −.97. The test has no concurrent validity when compared with the old test.
2. Predictive validity: correlate the test scores with scores on a subsequent test in social studies, or with end of quarter grades in social studies. Construct validity: correlate the test scores with ratings on citizenship, scores on a test of social awareness or any test which measures a part of what the new test measures. Conversely, it would also be correlated with the exact opposite of what the test measures.
3. Both Test A and Test C would be acceptable. Test C is unusual because predictive validity is higher than concurrent. Normally the opposite is true.
4. Test C is most acceptable, followed by Test A and Test B.
5. (a) content   (d) predictive

   (b) predictive   (e) concurrent

   (c) concurrent   (f) content
6. A lower correlation is expected since your gifted group is homogeneous. Therefore, the strength of the correlation is limited due to the truncated range of scores involved.

Chapter 16

1. Test C
2. r = .75
3. a. internal consistency; b. internal consistency; c. test-retest
4. Test C
5. (a) test-retest   (d) alternate-forms
   (b) alternate-forms (long interval)   (e) test-retest
   (c) split-half
6. Test B
7. Use neither test, unless acceptable validity can be established.

Chapter 17

In the problem at the end of Chapter 17, there is a real difference between John's reading and math scores, but not between his writing and science scores.

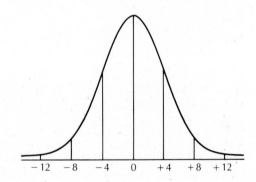

1. S_m = 4.00
2. 95% = 8 − 24; 99% = 4 − 28; 68% = 12 − 20
3. Within-student (illness), within-test (poor items), within-administration (timing), within-scoring (miskeys)
4. (a) Most subject to administrative and scoring; least subject to within-test.
   (b) Most subject to within-student; least subject to within-test.
   (c) Most subject to within-test; least subject to within-student.
   (d) Most subject to all sources.
   (e) Least subject to all sources.

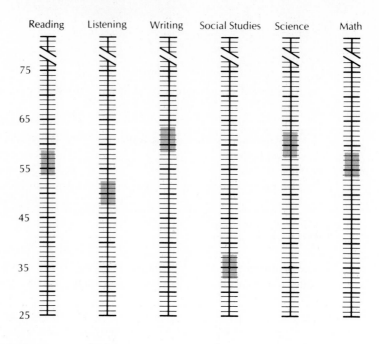

Subtest	Band
Reading	53.6–58.4
Listening	47.6–52.4
Writing	58.6–63.4
Social Studies	32.6–37.4
Science	57.6–62.4
Math	53.6–58.4

$$S_m = SD\sqrt{1-r}$$
$$= 8\sqrt{1-.91}$$
$$= 8\sqrt{.09}$$
$$= 8(.3)$$
$$= 2.4$$

Social studies is significantly lower than all. Listening is significantly lower than all but social studies. Writing is significantly higher than all. Other differences are due to chance.

6. None shows real differences.

7. Differences of this size and direction are expected since each method is affected by different sources of error.

8. S_m for A = 6
S_m for B = 5, scores from A would fluctuate most.

Chapter 18

3. (a) Jack is achieving below expectancy, Bonnie is above, and Chris is at expectancy.

(b) There is an aptitude-achievement discrepancy between Jack's Verbal IQ and his Vocabulary and Comprehension achievement.

Suggested Readings

Chapter 1

American Psychological Association. *Standards for Educational and Psychological Tests*. Washington, D.C.: APA, 1974.

Bloom, B. S., J., Hastings, T., & Madaus, G. F. *Handbook on Formative and Summative Evaluation of Student Learning*. New York: McGraw-Hill. 1971.

DuBois, P. H. *The History of Psychological Testing*. Boston: Allyn and Bacon, 1970.

Dyer, H. S. Is Testing a Menace to Education? *New York State Education,* 49 (1961): 16–19.

Ebel, Robert. The Social Consequences of Educational Testing. *School and Society,* 92 (1964):331–334.

Goslin, D. A. *Teachers and Testing*. New York: The Russell Sage Foundation, 1967.

Gronlund, N. E. *Determining Accountability for Classroom Instruction*. New York: Macmillan Publishing Co., Inc., 1974. Chapter 5.

Kirkland, M. C. The Effects of Tests on Students and Schools. *Review of Educational Research* 41, no. 4 (October 1971):303–50.

Linn, R. L. "Demands, cautions, and suggestions for setting standards." *Journal of Educational Measurement,* 15 (1978):301–308.

Sandman, P. M. *Students and the Law*. New York: Collier, 1971, 109.

Sharp, E. W. How Teachers See Testing. *Educational Leadership,* 24 (1966):141–43.

Tyler, R. W., & Wolf, R. M. (eds.). *Crucial Issues in Testing*. Berkeley, Calif.: McCutchan (for National Society for the Study of Education), 1974.

Valente, W. D. *Law in the Schools*. Columbus: Charles E. Merrill, 1980.

Wellingham, W. W. (ed.). Invasion of Privacy in Research and Testing. Proceedings of a symposium sponsored by the National Council on Measurement in Education and published as a supplement to *Journal of Educational Measurement* 4, no. 1 (Spring 1967):1–31.

Wrightstone, J. W., Hogan, T. P., & Abbott, M. M. Accountability in Education and Associated Measurement Problems. *Test Service Notebook* 33, New York: Harcourt Brace Jovanovich, 1972.

Chapter 2

Cronbach, L. J. *Essentials of Psychological Testing,* 3rd ed. New York: Harper and Row, Publishers, 1970. Chapter 2.

Glaser, R., & Nitko, A. J. Measurement in Learning and Instruction. In Robert L. Thorndike, ed., *Educational Measurement,* 2d ed., 625–70. Washington, D.C.: American Council on Education, 1971.

Hills, J. R. Use of Measurement in Selection and Placement. In Thorndike, ed., *Educational Measurement,* 2d ed., 680–732.

Jones, L. V. The Nature of Measurement. In Thorndike, ed., *Educational Measurement,* 2d ed., 335–55.

Schultz, R. E. The Role of Measurement in Education: Servant, Soulmate, Stoolpigeon, Statesman, Scapegoat, All of the Above, and/or None of the Above. *Journal of Educational Measurement,* 8, no. 3 (Fall 1971):141–46.

Thorndike, R. L. Educational Measurement for the Seventies. In Thorndike (ed.), *Educational Measurement,* 2d ed., 3–14.

Chapter 3

Airasian, P. W., & Madaus, G. F. Criterion-Referenced Testing in the Classroom. *National Council on Measurement in Education,* 3 (1972):1–8.

Block, J. H., & Anderson, L. W. *Mastery Learning in Classroom Instruction.* New York: Macmillan Publishing Co., Inc., 1975.

Ebel, R. L. Criterion-Referenced Measurement: Limitations. *School Review,* 79 (1971): 282–88.

Ebel, R. L. Evaluation and Education Objectives. *Journal of Educational Measurement,* 10 (1973):273–79.

Gronlund, N. E. *Preparing Criterion-Referenced Tests for Classroom Instruction.* New York: Macmillan Publishing Co., 1973. Chapter 6.

Hambleton, R. K., & Eignor, D. R. Guidelines for Evaluating Criterion-Referenced Tests and Test Manuals. *Journal of Educational Measurement,* (1978):321–27.

Mehrens, W. A., & Lehmann, I. J. *Measurement and Evaluation in Education and Psychology.* New York: Holt, Rinehart & Winston, 1973. Chapter 7.

Novick, M. R., & Lewis, C. Prescribing Test Length for Criterion-Referenced Measurement. In C. W. Harris, M. C. Alkin, & W. J. Popham (Eds.), *Problems in Criterion-Referenced Measurement.* Los Angeles: Center for the Study of Evaluation, University of California, 1974.

Popham, W. J. *Educational Evaluation.* Englewood Cliffs: Prentice-Hall, 1975.

Chapter 4

Krathwohl, D. R., & Payne, D. A. The Nature and Definition of Educational Objectives, and Strategies for Their Assessment, Chapter 2 in R. L. Thorndike (ed.), *Educational Measurement.* Washington, D.C.: American Council on Education, 1971.

Mager, Robert F. *Measuring Instructional Intent.* Belmont, Calif.: Fearon Publishers, 1973.

Payne D. A. (ed.). *Curriculum Evaluation.* Lexington, Mass.: D. C. Heath & Company, 1974. Section 2.

Chapter 5

Bloom, B. S., Hastings, J. T., & Madaus, G. F. *Handbook on Formative and Summative Evaluation of Student Learning.* New York: McGraw-Hill Book Company, 1971.

Educational Testing Service. *Making the Classroom Test: A Guide for Teachers.* Princeton, N.J.: ETS, 1973.

Gronlund, N. E. *Stating Behavioral Objectives for Classroom Instruction.* New York: MacMillan Publishing Co., 1970.

Harrow, A. J. *A Taxonomy of the Psychomotor Domain.* New York: David McKay, 1972.

Kratwohl, D. R., Bloom, B. S. & Masia, B. B. Defining and Assessing Educational Objectives. Chapter 2 in R. L. Thorndike (ed.), *Educational Measurement.* Washington, D.C.: American Council on Education, 1971.

Mager, R. *Preparing Instructional Objectives.* Palo Alto, Calif.: Fearon, 1962.

Mager, R. *Preparing Objectives for Programmed Instruction.* San Francisco: Fearon Publishers, 1962.

Noll, V. H., & Scannell, D. P. *Introduction to Educational Measurement,* 3d ed. Boston: Houghton Mifflin Company, 1972. Chapter 6.

Synd, R. B., & Picard, A. J. *Behavioral Objectives and Evaluation Measures: Science and Mathematics.* Columbus, Ohio: Charles E. Merrill Publishers, 1972. Chapter 10.

Vargas, J. *Writing Worthwhile Behavioral Objectives.* New York: Harper & Row, 1972.

Chapter 6

Bloom, B. S., Hastings, J. T., & Madaus, G. F. *Handbook on Formative and Summative Evaluation of Student Learning.* New York: McGraw-Hill Book Company, 1971.

Chase, C. Relative Length of Option and Response Set in Multiple-Choice Items. *Educational and Psychological Measurement,* 24 (1964):861–66.

Ebel, R. How to Write True-False Items. *Educational and Psychological Measurement,* 31 (1971):417–26.

Ebel, R. L. *Essentials of Educational Measurement.* Englewood Cliffs, N.J.: Prentice-Hall, 1972. Chapter 7.

Educational Testing Service. *Making the Classroom Test: A Guide for Teachers.* Princeton, N.J.: Educational Testing Service, 1961.

Educational Testing Service. *Multiple-Choice Questions: A Close Look.* Princeton, N.J.: Educational Testing Service, 1963.

Gronlund, N. E. *Constructing Achievement Tests.* Englewood Cliffs, N.J.: Prentice-Hall, 1968. Chapter 4.

Jones, P. D., & Kaufman, G. G. *The Existence and Effects of Specific Determiners in Tests.* Paper presented at the 82d annual convention of the American Psychological Association, New Orleans, August 1974.

Lord, F. M. Optimal Number of Choices per Item—A Comparison of Four Approaches. *Journal of Educational Measurement,* 14 (1977):33–38.

McMorris, R., Brown, J., Snyder, G., & Pruzek, R. Effects of Violating Item Construction Principles. *Journal of Educational Measurement,* 9 (1972):287–95.

Mehrens, W. A., & Lehmann, I. J. *Measurement and Evaluation in Education and Psychology.* New York: Holt, Rinehart & Winston, 1973. Chapter 10.

Sanders, N. M. *Classroom Questions: What kinds?* New York: Harper & Row, 1966.

Stanley, J. C., & Hopkins, K. D. *Educational and Psychological Measurement and Evaluation.* Englewood Cliffs, N.J.: Prentice-Hall, 1972. Chapter 10.

Storey, A. G. *The Measurement of Classroom Learning.* Chicago: Science Research Associates, Inc., 1970. Chapter 5.

Wesman, A. G. Writing the Test Item. Chapter 4 in R. L. Thorndike (ed.), *Educational Measurement.* Washington, D.C.: American Council on Education, 1971.

Williamson, M., & Hopkins, K. The Use of "None-of-These" versus Homogeneous Alternatives on Multiple-Choice Tests: Experimental Reliability and Validity Comparisons. *Journal of Educational Measurement,* 4 (1967):53–58.

Chapter 7

Chase, C. I. The Impact of Some Obvious Variables on Essay Test Scores. *Journal of Educational Measurement,* 5 (1968):315–18.

Coffman, W. E. Essay Examinations. Chapter 10 in R. L. Thorndike (ed.), *Educational Measurement.* Washington, D.C.: American Council on Education, 1971.

Ebel, R. L. *Essentials of Educational Measurement.* Englewood Cliffs, N.J.: Prentice-Hall, 1972. Chapter 6.

Harari, H., & McDavid, J. W. Names, Stereotypes and Teachers' expectations. *Journal of Educational Psychology.* 65 (1973):222–25.

Huck, S., & Bounds, W. Essay Grades: An Interaction Between Graders' Handwriting Clarity and the Neatness of Examination Papers. *American Educational Research Journal.* 9 (1972):279–84.

Huff, D. *Score: The Strategy of Taking Tests.* New York: Appleton-Century-Crofts, 1961. Chapter 12.

Klein, S. P., & Hart, F. M. Chance and Systematic Factors Affecting Essay Grades. *Journal of Educational Measurement* 5, no. 3 (Fall 1968):197–206.

Marshall, J. C. Composition Errors and Essay Examination Grades Re-Examined. *American Educational Research Journal,* 4 (1967):375–85.

Marshall, J. C., & Powers, J. Writing Neatness, Composition Errors and Essay Grades. *Journal of Educational Measurement,* 6 (1969):97–101.

Mehrens, W. A., & Lehmann, I. J. *Measurement and Evaluation in Education and Psychology.* New York: Holt, Rinehart & Winston, 1973. Chapter 8.

Chapter 8

Anastasi, A. *Psychological Testing,* 5th ed. New York: Macmillan Publishing Co., 1982. Chapter 8.

Cureton, Edward E. Simplified Formulas for Item Analysis *Journal of Educational Measurement,* 3, no. 2 (Summer 1966):187–89.

Diederich, P. *Shortcut Statistics for Teacher Made Tests.* Princeton, N.J.: Educational Testing Service, 1960.

Dizney, Henry. Characteristics of Classroom Test Items Identified by Students as 'Unfair.' *Journal of Educational Measurement,* 2, no. 1 (June 1965):119–21.

Huck, S., & Bowers, N. D. Item Difficulty Level and Sequence Effects in Multiple-Choice Achievement Tests. *Journal of Educational Measurement,* 9 (1972):105–11.

Klosner, N. C., & Gellman, E. K. The Effect of Item Arrangement on Classroom Test Performance: Implications for Content Validity. *Educational and Psychological Measurement,* 33 (1973):413–18.

Lange, A., Lehmann, I., & Mehrens, W. Using Item Analysis to Improve Tests. *Journal of Educational Measurement,* 4 (1967):65–68.

Lueptow, L. B., Early, K., & Garland, T. N. The Validity of Student Evaluations of Objective Test Items. *Educational and Psychological Measurement,* 36 (1976):939–44.

Mehrens, W. A., & Lehmann, I. J. *Measurement and Evaluation in Education and Psychology.* New York: Holt, Rinehart & Winston, 1973. Chapter 11.

Pack, E. C. The Effects of Testing Upon Attitude Towards the Method and Content of Instruction. *Journal of Educational Measurement,* 9 (1972):141–44.

Pyrczak, F. Validity of the Discrimination Index as a Measure of Item Quality. *Journal of Educational Measurement,* 10 (1973):227–31.

Thorndike, R. L. (ed.). *Educational Measurement.* Washington, D.C.: American Council on Education, 1971. See Chapter 5, Chapter 6, Chapter 7, and Chapter 8.

Chapter 9

Blair, G. M., Jones, R. S., & Simpson, R. H. *Educational Psychology,* 4th ed. New York: Macmillan Publishing Co., 1975. Chapter 19.

Breland, H. Conversions of High School Grade Averages Reported in Different Systems. *Research Bulletin* 73–30. Princeton, N.J.: Educational Testing Service, 1973.

Gatta, L. A. An Analysis of the Pass-Fail Grading System as Compared to the Conventional Grading System in High School Chemistry. *Journal of Research in Science Teaching,* 10 (1973):3–12.

Goldberg, Lewis. Grades as Motivants. *Psychology in the Schools,* 2 (1965):17–24.

Gronlund, N. E. *Improving Marking and Reporting in Classroom Instruction.* New York: Macmillan Publishing Co., 1974.

Gronlund, N. E. *Measurement and Evaluation in Teaching.* New York: Macmillan, 1976. Chapter 19.

Hills, J. R. *Measurement and Evaluation in the Classroom.* Columbus, Ohio: Charles E. Merrill, 1981. Chapters 14–19.

Karlins, Marvin. Academic Attitudes and Performances as a Function of Differential Grading Systems: An Evaluation of Princeton's Pass-Fail System. *Journal of Experimental Education,* 37 (1969):38–50.

Musgrave, G. Ray. *The Grading Game: A Public School Fiasco.* New York: Vintage Press, 1970, 156.

Palmer, O. Seven Classic Ways of Grading Dishonestly. *The English Journal,* 51 (1962): 464–67.

Stallings, W. M., & Smock, H. R. The Pass-Fail Grading Option at a State University: A Five Semester Evaluation. *Journal of Educational Measurement,* 8 (1971):153–60.

Syan, M. R. Letter Grade Achievement in Pass-Fail Courses." *Journal of Higher Education,* 41 (1970):638–44.

Terwillinger, James S. Individual Differences in the Marking Practices of Secondary School Teachers. *Journal of Educational Measurement,* 5, no. 1 (Spring 1968): 9–15.

Terwilliger, J. S. *Assigning Grades to Students.* Glenview, Ill.: Scott, Foresman and Company, 1971.

Thorndike, R. L. Marks and Marking Systems, in *Encyclopedia of Educational Research,* 4th ed. New York: Macmillan Publishing Co., 1969, 759–66.

Tomasson, R. F. Acronymic Grading. *American Sociologist,* 1972, 7,8.

Trow, William C. On marks, norms, and proficiency scores. *Phi Delta Kappan,* 47 (1966): 171–73.

Chapter 10

Anastasi, A. *Psychological Testing,* 5th ed. New York: Macmillan Publishing Co., 1982. Chapter 17.

Brandt, R. M. *Studying Behavior in Natural Settings.* New York: Holt, Rinehart & Winston, 1972.

Cronbach, L. J. *Essentials of Psychological Testing,* 3d ed. New York: Harper & Row Publishers, 1970. Chapter 17.

Edwards, A. *Techniques of Attitude Scale Construction.* New York: Appleton-Century-Crofts, 1957.

Feldman, M. J., & Cerah, N. L. Social Desirability and the Forced-Choice Method, *Journal of Consulting Psychology,* 24 (1960):480–482.

Gronlund, N. E. *Sociometry in the Classroom.* New York: Harper & Brothers, 1959.

Lindzey, G., & Borgatta, E. F. Sociometric Measurement. In Lindzey (ed.), *Handbook of Social Psychology,* vol. 1, *Theory and Method,* pp. 405–48. Cambridge, Mass.: Addison-Wesley Publishing Co., 1954.

Lindzey, G., & Byrne, D. Measurement of Social Choice and Interpersonal Attractiveness. In G. Lindzey and E. Aronson (eds.), *Handbook of Social Psychology,* vol. 2. Reading, Mass.: Addison-Wesley Publishing Co., 1968.

Oppenheim, A. N. *Questionnaire Design and Attitude Measurement.* New York: Basic Books, 1966.

Shaw, M. E., & Wright, J. M. *Scales for the Measurement of Attitudes.* New York: McGraw-Hill Book Company, 1967.

Stanley, J. C., & Hopkins, K. D. *Educational and Psychological Measurement and Evaluation.* Englewood Cliffs, N.J.: Prentice-Hall, 1972, Chapter 12.

TenBrink, T. D. *Evaluation: A Practical Guide for Teachers.* New York: McGraw-Hill Book Company, 1974. Chapter 11.

Walker, D. K. *Socioemotional Measures for Preschool and Kindergarten children.* San Francisco: Jossey-Bass, 1973.

Webb, E. J., Campbell, D. T., Schwartz, R. D., & Sechrest, L. *Unobtrusive Measures: Nonreactive Research in the Social Sciences.* Chicago: Rand McNally, 1966.

Chapter 11

Borich, G. *The Appraisal of Teaching: Concepts and Process.* Reading, Mass.: Addison-Wesley, 1977.

Borich, G., & Madden, S. *Evaluating Classroom Instruction: A Sourcebook of Instruments.* Reading, Mass.: Addison-Wesley, 1977.

Edmunds, A. *Techniques of Attitude Scale Construction.* New York: Appleton, 1957.

Gronlund, N. *Sociometry in the Classroom.* New York: Harper and Row, 1959.

Heyas, R., & Lippitt, R. Systematic Observational Techniques. In G. Lindzey (ed.), *Handbook of Social Psychology,* vol. 1. Cambridge, Mass.: Addison-Wesley, 1954. Chapter 10.

Johnson, D., & Bommarito, J. *Tests and Measurement in Child Development.* San Francisco, Calif.: Jossey-Bass, 1971.

Kerlinger, F. *Foundations of Behavioral Research.* New York: Holt, 1969, 467–581.

Lake, D., Miles, M., & Earle, R. (eds.) *Measuring Human Behavior.* New York: Columbia University, Teachers College Press, 1973.

Osgood, C., Suci, G., & Tannenbaum, P. *The Measurement of Meaning.* Urbana, Ill.: University of Illinois Press, 1957.

Shaw, M., & Wright, J. *Scales for the Measurement of Attitudes.* New York: McGraw-Hill, 1967.

Simon, A., & Boyer, E. (eds.) *Mirrors for Behavior: An Anthology of Observation Instruments.* Philadelphia, Penn.: Research for Better Schools, 1970.

Walker, D. *Socioemotional Measures for Preschool and Kindergarten Children.* San Francisco, Calif.: Jossey-Bass, 1973.

Chapters 12–14

See Appendix C.

Chapter 15

American Psychological Association. *Standards for Educational and Psychological Tests.* Washington, D.C.: APA, 1974.

Anastasi, A. *Psychological Testing,* 5th ed. New York: Macmillan Publishing Co., 1982. Chapter 6.

Astin, A. W. Criterion-Centered Research. *Educational and Psychological Measurement,* 24, no. 4 (Winter 1964):807–22.

Costin, F. Three-Choice versus Four-Choice Items: Implications for Reliability and Validity of Objective Achievement Tests. *Educational and Psychological Measurement,* 32 (1972):1035–38.

Cronbach, L. J. Validity. Chapter 14 in R. L. Thorndike (ed.), *Educational Measurement.* Washington, D.C.: American Council on Education, 1971.

Ebel, Robert. Obtaining and Reporting Evidence of Content Validity. *Educational and Psychological Measurement,* 16 (1956):269–82.

Ebel, Robert. Must All Tests Be Valid? *American Psychologist,* 16 (1961):640–47.

Frisbie, D. A. Multiple Choice versus True-False: A Comparison of Reliabilities and Concurrent Validities. *Journal of Educational Measurement,* 10 (1973):297–304.

Lord, F. M. The Effect of Random Guessing on Test Validity. *Educational and Psychological Measurement,* 24 (1964): 745–48.

Popham, W. J., & Husek, T. R. Implications of Criterion-Referenced Measurement. In W. J. Popham (ed.), *Criterion-Referenced Measurement.* Englewood Cliffs, N.J.: Educational Technology Publications, 1971.

Wesman, A. G. *Double-Entry Expectancy Tables.* Test Service Bulletin, no. 45. New York: The Psychological Corporation, 1966.

Chapter 16

American Psychological Association. *Standards for Educational and Psychological Tests*. Washington, D.C.: APA, 1974.

Anastasi, A. *Psychological Testing,* 5th ed. New York: Macmillan Publishing Co., 1982. Chapter 5.

Bauernfeind, R. H. *Building a School Testing Program,* 2d ed. Boston: Houghton Mifflin Company, 1969. Chapter 6.

Board, C., & Whitney, D. R. The Effect of Selected Poor Item-Writing Practices on Test Difficulty, Reliability, and Validity. *Journal of Educational Measurement,* 9 (1972):225–33.

Costin, F. Three-Choice versus Four-Choice Items: Implications for Reliability and Validity of Objective Achievement Tests. *Educational and Psychological Measurement,* 32 (1972):1035–38.

Diederich, P. *Short-Cut Statistics for Teacher-Made Tests*. Princeton, N.J.: Educational Testing Service, 1973.

Frisbie, D. A. Multiple Choice versus True-False: A Comparison of Reliabilities and Concurrent Validities. *Journal of Educational Measurement,* 10 (1973):297–304.

Lord, F. M. The Relation of the Reliability of Multiple-Choice Tests to the Distribution of Item Difficulties. *Psychometrika,* 17 (1952):181–94.

Oosterhof, A. C., & Glasnapp, D. R. Comparative Reliability and Difficulties of the Multiple-Choice and True-False Formats. *Journal of Experimental Education,* 42 (1974):62–64.

Popham, W. J., & Husek, T. R. Implications of Criterion-Referenced Measurement. In W. J. Popham (ed.), *Criterion-Referenced Measurement*. Englewood Cliffs, N.J.: Educational Technology Publications, 1971.

Wesman, Alexander G. Reliability and Confidence. *Test Service Bulletin of the Psychological Corporation,* no. 44 (May 1952):2–7.

Chapter 17

American Psychological Association. *Standards for Educational and Psychological Tests*. Washington, D.C.: APA, 1974.

Anastasi, A. *Psychological Testing,* 5th ed. New York: Macmillan Publishing Co., 1982. Chapter 5.

Diederich, P. *Short-Cut Statistics for Teacher-Made Tests*. Princeton, N.J.: Educational Testing Service, 1973.

Doppelt, J. E. *How Accurate Is a Test Score?* Test Service Bulletin, no. 50. New York: The Psychological Corporation, 1956.

Lord, F. M. Tests of the Same Length Do Have the Same Standard Error of Measurement. *Educational and Psychological Measurement,* 19 (1959):233–39.

Wesman, Alexander G. Reliability and Confidence. *Test Service Bulletin of the Psychological Corporation,* no. 44 (May 1952):2–7.

Chapter 18

American Psychological Association. *Standards for Educational and Psychological Tests*. Washington, D.C.: APA, 1974.

Anastasi, A. *Psychological Testing,* 5th ed. New York: Macmillan Publishing Co., 1982. Chapter 4.

Bauernfeind, R. *Building a School Testing Program,* 2d ed. Boston: Houghton Mifflin, 1969.

Carroll, J. B. The Aptitude-Achievement Distinction: The Case of Foreign Language Aptitude and Proficiency. In D. R. Green (Ed.), *The Aptitude Achievement Distinction.* Monterey, Calif.: CTB/McGraw-Hill, 1974.

Cronbach, L. J. *Essentials of Psychological Testing,* 3d ed. New York: Harper and Row, Publishers, 1970. Chapter 3.

Green D. R. (Ed.). *The Aptitude Achievement Distinction.* Monterey: CTB/McGraw-Hill, 1974.

Hambleton, R. K., & Eignor, D. R. Guidelines for Evaluating Criterion-Referenced Tests and Test Manuals. *Journal of Educational Measurement,* 15 (1978):321–27.

Humphreys, L. G., Levy, J., & Taber, T. Predictability of Academic Grades for Students of High and Low Academic Promise. *Educational and Psychological Measurement,* 33 (1973):385–92.

Ingle, R. B., & De Amico, G. The Effect of Physical Conditions of the Test Room on Standardized Achievement Test Scores. *Journal of Educational Measurement* 6, no. 4 (Winter 1969):237–40.

Katz, M. *Selecting an Achievement Test: Principles and Procedures.* Princeton, N.J.: Educational Testing Service, 1973.

Lennon, R. T. Scores and Norms, in *Encyclopedia of Educational Research,* 4th ed. New York: Macmillan Publishing Co., 1969, 1206–11.

Lyman, H. B. *Test Scores and What They Mean.* Englewood Cliffs, N.J.: Prentice-Hall, Inc., 1971.

Ricks, J. H. *Local Norms— When and Why,* Test Service Bulletin, no. 58. New York: The Psychological Corporation, 1971.

Seashore, H. G. *Methods of Expressing Test Scores,* Test Service Bulletin, no. 48. New York: The Psychological Corporation, 1955.

Thorndike, Robert L. *The Concepts of Over- and Underachievement.* New York: Bureau of Publications, Teachers College, Columbia University, 1963.

Trentham, L. L. The Effect of Distractions on Sixth-Grade Students in a Testing Situation. *Journal of Educational Measurement,* 12 (1975):13–17.

Chapter 19

Allport, G. W. *Personality: A Psychological Interpretation.* New York: Holt, 1937.

Anastasi, A. *Psychological Testing,* 5th ed. New York: Macmillan Publishing Co., 1982. Chapter 14.

Bauernfeind, R. H. *Building a School Testing Program,* 2d ed. Boston: Houghton Mifflin Company, 1969. Chapter 14.

Blanton, W. E., Farr, R., & Tuinman, J. J. (eds.). *Reading Tests for the Secondary Grades: A Review and Evaluation.* Newark, Delaware; International Reading Association, 1972.

Cronbach, L. J. *Essentials of Psychological Testing,* 3d ed. New York: Harper and Row, Publishers, 1970. Chapter 7.

Edwards, A. J. *Individual Mental Testing, Part II: Measurement.* Scranton, Penn.: Intext, 1972.

Edwards, A. L. *The Measurement of Personality Traits by Scales and Inventories.* New York: Holt, Rinehart and Winston, 1970.

Getzels, J., & Madaus, G. F. Creativity, in *Encyclopedia of Educational Research,* 4th ed. New York: Macmillan Publishing Co., 1969, 267–75.

Guilford, J.P. *The Nature of Human Intelligence.* New York: McGraw-Hill, 1967.

Holt, R. R. *Assessing Personality.* New York: Harcourt Brace Jovanovich, 1971.

Karmel, L. J. *Measurement and Evaluation in the Schools.* New York: Macmillan Publishing Co., 1970. Chapter 2.

Katz, M. *Selecting an Achievement Test: Principles and Procedures.* Princeton, N.J.: Educational Testing Service, 1973.

Kelly, E. L. Consistency of Adult Personality. *American Psychologist,* 10 (1955): 659–81.

Kleinmuntz, Benjamin. *Personality Measurement: An Introduction.* Homewood, Ill.: Dorsey Press, 1967.

Lanyon, R., & Goodstein, L. D. *Personality Assessment.* New York: John Wiley & Sons, 1971.

Mehrens, W. A., & Lehmann, I. J. *Standardized Tests in Education,* 2d ed. New York: Holt, Rinehart & Winston, 1975. Chapter 3.

Noll, V. H., & Scannell, D. P. *Introduction to Educational Measurement,* 3d ed. Boston: Houghton Mifflin Company, 1972. Chapter 9.

Samuda, R. J. *Psychological Testing of American Minorities: Issues and Consequences.* New York: Dodd, Mead & Co., 1975.

Chapter 20

Carroll, J. B. The Aptitude-Achievement Distinction: The Case of Foreign Language Aptitude and Proficiency. In D. R. Green (Ed.), *The Aptitude Achievement Distinction.* Monterey, Calif.: CTB/McGraw-Hill, 1974.

Cleary, T. A., Humphreys, L. G., Kendrick, S. A., & Wesman, A. Educational Use of Tests with Disadvantaged Students. *American Psychologist,* 30 (1975):15–41.

Gronlund, N. E. *Individualizing Classroom Instruction.* New York: Macmillan Publishing Co., 1974.

Howell, K. W., Kaplan, J. S., & O'Connell, C. Y. *Evaluating Exceptional Children: A Task Analysis Approach.* Columbus, Ohio: Charles E. Merrill, 1979.

Smith, R. M. (ed.). *Teacher Diagnosis of Educational Difficulties.* Columbus, Ohio: Charles E. Merrill, 1969.

Valente, W. D. *Law in the Schools.* Columbus, Ohio: Charles E. Merrill, 1980.

Yoshida, R. K. Out-of-Level Testing of Special Education Students with a Standardized Achievement Battery. *Journal of Educational Measurement,* 13 (1976):215–21.

Chapter 21

Bates, W. *The Computer Cookbook.* Englewood Cliffs, N.J., Prentice-Hall, 1983.

Coburn, P. *Practical Guide to Computers in Education.* Reading, Mass.: Addison-Wesley, 1982.

Dunn, S., & Morgan, V. *The Apple Personal Computer for Beginners.* Englewood Cliffs, N.J., Prentice-Hall, 1982.

Hollerbach, L. *A 60-Minute Guide to Microcomputers.* Englewood Cliffs, N.J., Prentice-Hall, 1982.

Lieff, J. *How to Buy a Personal Computer Without Anxiety.* Cambridge, Mass.: Bollinger, 1982.

Poole, L., McNiff, M., & Cook, S. *Your Atari Computer—A Guide to Atari 400/800 Personal Computers.* Berkeley, Calif.: Osborne/McGraw-Hill, 1982.

Smith, C. (ed.). *Microcomputers in Education.* New York: John Wiley & Sons, 1982.

References

Allport, G. W., & Odbert, H. S. 1936. Trait-Names: A Psycho-Lexical Study. *Psychological Monographs,* 47: 1–171.

Bloom, B., Englehart, M., Hill, W., Furst, E., & Krathwohl, D. 1956. *Taxonomy of Educational Objectives: The Classification of Educational Goals, Handbook 1: Cognitive Domain.* New York: Longmans, Green.

Coffman, W. E. 1971. Essay Examinations. In R. J. Thorndike (Ed.), *Educational Measurement,* 2d ed. Washington, D.C.: American Council on Education.

Ghiselli, E. E. 1966. *The Study of Occupational Aptitude Tests.* New York: Wiley.

Honzik, M. P., McFarlane, J. W., & Allen, L. 1948. The Stability of Mental Test Performance between Two and Eighteen Years. *Journal of Experimental Education,* 17:209–324.

Kirp, D. L., & Yudof, M. G. 1974. *Educational Policy and the Law: Cases and Materials.* Berkeley: McCutchan.

Likert, R. 1932. A Technique for the Measurement of Attitudes. *Archives of Psychology,* 140.

Lord, F., & Novick, M. 1968. *Statistical Theories of Mental Test Scores.* Reading, Mass.: Addison-Wesley.

Miller, G. A. 1956. The Magic Number Seven, Plus or Minus Two: Some Limits on Our Capacity for Processing Information. *Psychological Review,* 63:81–97.

Osgood, C. E., Suci, G. J., & Tannenbaum, P. H. 1957. *The Measurement of Meaning.* Urbana, Illinois: University of Illinois Press.

Pennsylvania Association for Retarded Children v. Commonwealth of Pennsylvania. 334 F. Supp. 1257 (E.D. Pa. 1971).

Pinchach, B. M., & Breland, H. M. 1973. Grading Practices in American High Schools. *Research Bulletin.* Princeton, New Jersey: Educational Testing Services.

Thorndike, R., & Hagen, E. *Measurement and Evaluation in Psychology and Education.* New York: Wiley, 1977.

Tuckman, B. W., 1975. *Measuring Educational Outcomes.* New York: Harcourt Brace Jovanovich.

INDEX

Ability. *See* Academic aptitude
Absolutes, avoiding
  in attitude statements, 166
  in true-false items, 70–71
Academic achievement. *See also* Standardized
    achievement tests
  comparison of aptitude with, 143–44
  comparison of effort with, 144
  comparison of improvement with, 144
  discrepancies between aptitude and, 348–51,
    362, 389
  IQ scores as predictors of, 364, 365
  marking based on, 138-41
  process of evaluating, 133
Academic aptitude. *See also* Standardized
    academic aptitude tests
  concept of, 345
  discrepancies between achievement and,
    348–51, 362, 389
  marks based on comparisons with, 143–44
Accountability, 3, 11–12, 133, 207, 328–30
Accuracy. *See also* Error
  of Individual Educational Program data,
    393–96
  meaning of, 277, 303
  of standardized tests, 337–38
Achievement. *See* Academic achievement
Adaptive behavior, 392
Adjective Checklist, 369
Administering the test. *See* Test administration
Administrative policy decisions, 15
Affective domain taxonomy, 57–59
AFN Grading System, 408
Age
  and IQ score stability, 364
  and standardized achievement test scores,
    343–44
Age-equivalent scores, 333–34, 336
Algebra, 437–38
Allport, G. W., 368
Alpha, coefficient, 295–96
Alternate-forms reliability
  effect of error on, 316, 317, 318

internal consistency reliability versus, 294, 295
  meaning of, 292–94
Ambiguity, in test items, 75, 128–29
Analogies, in multiple-choice items, 86
Analysis level
  definition of, 56
  essay items at, 100, 102, 108
  multiple-choice items at, 84
Analyzing the test. *See* Item analysis
Anecdotal records
  advantages/disadvantages of, in evaluating
    products, procedures, and performances,
    202
  for handicapped students, 390–92
  method of, 172–74
  in oral performance evaluation, 197, 199–201
Answer keys
  checking, 117, 121
  definition of, 123
  miskeying, 128, 315
  preparing, 121
APL, 404
Application level
  definition of, 55–56
  essay items at, 100, 108
  multiple-choice items at, 84
Approach behaviors, 157, 159, 160, 167–68
Aptitude. *See* Academic aptitude
Assembling the test, 115–18
Asymmetrical distributions, 220–21
Attitudes
  definition of, 155–56
  methods of measuring, 158–71, 296
  positive/negative, 156–57
  purpose of measuring, 157–58
  test administrator, 315
  test-taking, 119
Audiocassette recorders, as computer
    peripherals, 400, 402. *See also*
    Microcomputers
Auditorially handicapped, 383, 387
Autism, 387
Avoidance behaviors, 157, 159, 160, 167–68

Also Available from
Scott, Foresman and Company
Good Year Books

Good Year Books are reproducible resource and activity books for teachers and parents of students in preschool through grade 12. Written by experienced educators, Good Year Books are filled with class-tested ideas, teaching strategies and methods, and fun-to-do activities for every basic curriculum area. They also contain enrichment materials and activities that help extend a child's learning experiences beyond the classroom.

Good Year Books address many educational needs in both formal and informal settings. They have been used widely in preservice teacher training courses, as a resource for practicing teachers to enhance their own professional growth, and by interested adults as a source of sound, valuable activities for home, summer camp, Scout meetings, and the like.

Good Year Books are available through your local college or university bookstore, independent or chain booksellers, and school supply and educational dealers. For a complete catalog of Good Year Books, write:

Good Year Books
Department PPG-T
1900 East Lake Avenue
Glenview, Illinois 60025